THE CREATION OF PATRIARCHY

WOMEN AND HISTORY

Volume One: The Creation of Patriarchy

The Creation of Patriarchy

GERDA LERNER

New York   Oxford

OXFORD UNIVERSITY PRESS

1986

Oxford University Press

Oxford New York Toronto
Delhi Bombay Calcutta Madras Karachi
Kuala Lumpur Singapore Hong Kong Tokyo
Nairobi Dar es Salaam Cape Town
Melbourne Auckland

and associated companies in
Beirut Berlin Ibadan Nicosia

Published by Oxford University Press, Inc.
200 Madison Avenue, New York, New York 10016

Library of Congress Cataloging-in-Publication Data

Lerner, Gerda, 1920–
Women and history.
Bibliography: v. 1, p.   Includes index.
Contents: v. 1. The creation of patriarchy—
1. Women—History. I. Title.
HQ1121.L47 1986   305.4'09   85-21578
ISBN 0-19-503996-3 (v. 1)

Printing (last digit): 9 8 7 6 5 4 3 2 1
Printed in the United States of America
on acid-free paper

For

Virginia Warner Brodine and Elizabeth Kamarck Minnich

*whose thought has challenged and confirmed mine
and whose friendship and love
have strengthened and supported me*

Acknowledgments

This book has been eight years in the making. It began in 1977 with a few questions which had occupied my attention, off and on, for over fifteen years. They led me to the hypothesis that it is the relationship of women to history which explains the nature of female subordination, the causes for women's cooperation in the process of their subordination, the conditions for their opposition to it, the rise of feminist consciousness. I had then in mind the formulation of a "general theory" on women in history, and it took nearly five years of work to show me that such a goal was premature. The sources in Ancient Near Eastern culture were so rich, and yielded so many insights, that I realized I would need an entire volume to explore this material. Thus the project expanded into two volumes.

I presented the theoretical outline of my projected work in a workshop at the conference "The Second Sex—Thirty Years Later: A Commemorative Conference on Feminist Theory" at New York University, Sept. 27–29, 1979. In this workshop I had the benefit of the stimulating comments made by the writer Elizabeth Janeway and the philosopher Elizabeth Minnich. A revised version of this paper was presented at the 1980 meeting of the Organization of American Historians, San Francisco, April 9–12, 1980. The session was presided over by Mary Benson. The helpful critical comments by Sara Evans and George M. Frederickson furthered my understanding.

In the initial stages of my research, I was greatly aided by a Guggenheim Foundation grant in 1980–81, which gave me a year in which to read in anthropology and feminist theory and to study the problem of the origin of slavery. One result of that year's work was the chapter "The Slave Woman," which I presented at the Berkshire Conference of Women Historians at Vassar College in June 1981. I greatly benefitted from the insightful critique of Elise Boulding and Linda Kerber and from the comments of Robin Morgan, who examined the material from the vantage point of a feminist theoretician. My paper, in a revised form was published as "Women and Slavery" in *Slavery and Abolition: A Journal of Comparative Studies*, Vol. 4, no. 3 (December 1983), pp. 173–198.

A chapter of this book was published as "The Origin of Prostitution in Ancient Mesopotamia" in *SIGNS: Journal of Women in Culture*, Vol. XI, no. 2 (Winter 1985).

The Graduate School of the University of Wisconsin-Madison has supported my research on this book with a summer research grant in 1981 and with grants for project assistants. My appointment as Wisconsin Alumni Research Foundation Senior Distinguished Research Professor in 1984 gave me a semester free from teaching obligations, which enabled me to do final revisions and complete the book. I am deeply grateful not only for the tangible support, but for the encouragement of my work implicit in it. The Women's Studies department of the University of Wisconsin-Madison twice offered me an opportunity to share my work in progress with faculty and students, whose keen and lively criticism was of considerable help to me. I am also greatly appreciative of the hospitality offered to me as a visiting scholar by the department of History, University of California at Berkeley in the Spring term 1985.

My work on this book presented me with unusual challenges. To step outside one's own discipline and training is in itself a difficult undertaking. To do so asking large questions and attempting to remain critical of the answers provided in the major conceptual frameworks of the thought of Western civilization is daunting, at the least. I represented in my own person all the internalized obstacles that have stood in the way of women's thinking on a grand scale, as men have done. I could not have persisted in the effort without the encouragement provided by the community of feminist thinkers in general and the very specific and personal encouragement provided for me by friends and colleagues within that community. Virginia Brodine, Elizabeth Minnich, Eve Merriam, Alice Kessler-Harris, Amy Swerdlow, the late Joan Kelly, Linda Gordon, Florencia Mallon, Steve Stern, and Stephen Feierman gave me friendship and support and were endlessly patient listeners and critics. In addition to their help along the way Brodine, Minnich, Gordon, and Kessler-Harris read a late draft of the manuscript. Their sympathetic response and detailed criticism sent me off on a final revision which dramatically changed the book. They confirmed and sharpened my thought and helped me to stay with the process until I found the form which expresses my meaning. That is constructive criticism at its best and I am thankful for it. I hope they will like the outcome.

Other colleagues at the University of Wisconsin-Madison, whose criticism of one or several chapters enriched my understanding are: Judy Leavitt (History of Medicine), Jane Shoulenburg (Women's History), Susan Friedman and Nellie McKay (Literature), Virginia Sapiro (Political Science), Anne Stoller (Anthropology), and Michael Clover (History and Classics). Colleagues from other institutions— Ann Lane (Women's History, Colgate University), Rayna Rapp (Anthropology, The New School for Social Research), Joyce Riegelhaupt (Anthropology, Sarah Lawrence College), Jonathan Goldstein (Classics, University of Iowa), and Evelyn Keller (Mathematics and Humanities, Northeastern University)—provided criticism from the vantage point of their particular disciplines and were helpful with bibliographical suggestions.

Very special thanks are due to those specialists in Assyriology, who, despite my being an outsider to their field, offered me advice, criticism, and many helpful leads. I am grateful for their generosity, interest, and collegiality. The help they provided does not necessarily imply their support of my conclusions; although I have been guided by their suggestions, any errors of fact or interpretation are my responsibility. I would like to thank Jack Sasson (Religion, University of North Carolina, Chapel Hill), Jerrold Cooper (Near Eastern Studies, The Johns Hopkins University), Carole Justus (Linguistics, University of Texas at Austin), Denise Schmandt-Besserat (Middle Eastern Studies, University of Texas at Austin), and especially Anne Draffkorn Kilmer (Near Eastern Studies, University of California at Berkeley) for their reading of the entire manuscript, their criticism and the many suggestions for references and sources they offered me. Over and above this, Denise Schmandt-Besserat shared bibliographies in her specialty, made suggestions for further contacts among experts in Assyriology, and raised a number of searching questions that caused me to rethink some of my conclusions. Ann Kilmer did more than anyone else to orient me in her field, to help me with difficult passages and with translations, to direct me to references in recent specialized journals, and to open the library resources of her department to me. My gratitude for her generosity and kindness goes beyond words. The Assyriologist Rivkah Harris and Michael

Fox (Hebrew Studies, University of Wisconsin-Madison), who read several chapters, disagreed with my thesis and some of my conclusions, but generously helped with criticism and references.

From the inception of this work to its conclusion, Sheldon Meyer of Oxford University Press has given support, encouragement, and trust. He has read the manuscript in its various versions and has patiently endured the many delays and detours necessary to bring it to its final form. Above all, he has brought a sympathetic sensitivity to bear on his readings and has always encouraged me to express my meaning without regard to any external considerations. I am deeply grateful for his supportive understanding.

The fine skills of Leona Capeless have made the technical work of copyediting a pleasure for the author and have greatly helped the book. My sincerest thanks to her.

My project assistants Nancy Isenberg and Nancy MacLean have earned my gratitude for the many ways in which they have made research and technical work easier for me. They may possibly be rewarded for their years of effort in having learned more about the Ancient Near East than they ever thought they needed to know. I am grateful also for the work Leslie Schwalm did in copying the photos and to my project assistant Renee DeSantis for her care in helping me read proofs. The typing of the manuscript and bibliography was done with meticulous care by Anita Olsen, who has earned my gratitude and appreciation for her skill and patience.

I am indebted for their knowledge, courtesy, and help to the librarians and staff at the Wisconsin State Historical Society and Wisconsin University Memorial Libraries, both in Madison, Wisconsin; the University of California Library at Berkeley and The British Library, London, England. My thanks also to the archivists at the Schlesinger Library, Radcliffe College, Cambridge, Massachusetts, and The Fawcett Library, London, England.

To the feminist scholars who have wrestled with questions similar to mine and have found other answers; to the students and audiences who helped me test out my ideas over these years and to the anonymous and voiceless women who for millennia have asked questions of origin and of justice—my thanks. This work could not have been done without you nor can it live unless it speaks to and for you.

Madison, Wisconsin   G.L.
October 1985

Contents

A Note on Definitions   xiii

A Note on Chronology and Methodology   xv

Introduction   3

One. Origins   15

Two. A Working Hypothesis   36

Three. The Stand-in Wife and the Pawn   54

Four. The Woman Slave   76

Five. The Wife and the Concubine   101

Six. Veiling the Woman   123

Seven. The Goddesses   141

Eight. The Patriarchs   161

Nine. The Covenant   180

Ten. Symbols   199

Eleven. The Creation of Patriarchy   212

Appendix: Definitions   231

Notes   245

Bibliography   283

Index   305

Illustrations appear between pages 160 and 161.

A Note
on Definitions

The need for re-definition and the inadequacy of terms for describing the female experience, the status of women in society, and the various levels of women's consciousness present a problem to all feminist thinkers. Readers particularly interested in questions of feminist theory may therefore wish to turn to the Appendix after reading the Introduction and read the chapter "Definitions" before proceeding. The reader with a more general interest may prefer to look up certain terms and their definitions when they occur in the text. The section "Definitions" is an attempt to redefine and accurately describe what is unique to women and what distinguishes their experience and consciousness from that of other groups of subordinate people. It is therefore both a linguistic and a theoretical discussion of terminology.

A Note on Chronology and Methodology

Since events in Ancient Mesopotamia were recorded by scribes in reference to the names of various rulers and officials, there is a problem of chronology when dealing with Ancient Mesopotamian records. By cross-referencing the dates of rulers with significant astronomical events, which ancient scribes have recorded, scholars have arrived at an absolute chronology in calendar years for the first millennium B.C. If one deals with events in the second and third millennium B.C., one has only a relative sequence of events to work with. For the second millennium B.C. scholars have constructed three chronologies (high, middle, and low) by comparing recorded dates of kings with astronomical data and with data from radiocarbon-dated artifacts. Thus all dates in this period are approximations. I have generally used middle chronology dating. Some discrepancies in the text have occurred where authorities I have cited have used a different method of dating and my quotes from their text have reflected their dating. These discrepancies are particularly apparent in the dating of the pictures, where I have uniformly followed the dates listed by the respective museums, even when those dates disagreed with dates in the text.*

I have followed the same policy in regard to the spelling of Mesopotamian names: unless otherwise noted, I have used the latest

---

*Jonathan Glass, "The Problem of Chronology in Ancient Mesopotamia," *Biblical Archeologist*, vol. 47, no. 2 (June 1984), p. 92.

spellings, but I have retained the author's spelling in citations, even if it differs from the spelling I have used.

When quoting passages translated from cuneiform texts I have followed the practice of letting square brackets stand for restorations in the text and round brackets for the translators' interpolations. Otherwise, in the text written by me, square brackets indicate the author's comments or interpolations.

Another methodological problem common to all who work with ancient Mesopotamian sources is that the sources, while plentiful for certain periods and locations, are uneven as to time and place. Due to the vagaries of archaeological discoveries we have a great deal of information about certain places and periods, little about others. This gives us an inevitably distorted picture of the past. Since there are far fewer sources concerning women than men, the problem is compounded for those dealing with the history of women. It is well to keep these constraints in mind when evaluating the generalizations offered.

THE CREATION OF PATRIARCHY

Introduction

WOMEN'S HISTORY is indispensable and essential to the emancipation of women. After twenty-five years of researching, writing, and teaching Women's History, I have come to this conviction on theoretical and practical grounds. The theoretical argument will be more fully developed in this book; the practical argument rests on my observation of the profound changes in consciousness which students of Women's History experience. Women's History changes their lives. Even short-term exposure to the past experience of women, such as in two-week institutes and seminars, has the most profound psychological effect on women participants.

And yet, most of the theoretical work of modern feminism, beginning with Simone de Beauvoir and continuing to the present, has been ahistorical and negligent of feminist historical scholarship. This was understandable in the early days of the new wave of feminism, when scholarship on the past of women was scant, but in the 1980s, when excellent scholarly work in Women's History is abundantly available, the distance between historical scholarship and feminist criticism in other fields persists. Anthropologists, literary critics, sociologists, political scientists, and poets have offered theoretical work based on "history," but the work of Women's History specialists has not become part of the common discourse. I believe the reasons for this go beyond the sociology of the women doing feminist criticism and beyond the constraints of their academic background and training. The reasons lie in the conflict-ridden and highly problematic relationship of women to history.

What is history? We must distinguish between the unrecorded past—all the events of the past as recollected by human beings—and History—the recorded and interpreted past.* Like men, women are and always have been actors and agents in history. Since women are half and sometimes more than half of humankind, they always have shared the world and its work equally with men. Women are and have been central, not marginal, to the making of society and to the building of civilization. Women have also shared with men in preserving collective memory, which shapes the past into cultural tradition, provides the link between generations, and connects past and future. This oral tradition was kept alive in poem and myth, which both men and women created and preserved in folklore, art, and ritual.

History-making, on the other hand, is a historical creation which dates from the invention of writing in ancient Mesopotamia. From the time of the king lists of ancient Sumer on, historians, whether priests, royal servants, clerks, clerics, or a professional class of university-trained intellectuals, have selected the events to be recorded and have interpreted them so as to give them meaning and significance. Until the most recent past, these historians have been men, and what they have recorded is what men have done and experienced and found significant. They have called this History and claimed universality for it. What women have done and experienced has been left unrecorded, neglected, and ignored in interpretation. Historical scholarship, up to the most recent past, has seen women as marginal to the making of civilization and as unessential to those pursuits defined as having historic significance.

Thus, the recorded and interpreted record of the past of the human race is only a partial record, in that it omits the past of half of humankind, and it is distorted, in that it tells the story from the viewpoint of the male half of humanity only. To counter this argument, as has often been done, by showing that large groups of men, possibly the majority of men, have also for a long time been eliminated from the historical record through the prejudiced interpretations of intellectuals representing the concerns of small ruling elites, is to beg the question. One error does not cancel out another; both conceptual errors need correction. As formerly subordinate groups, such as peasants, slaves, proletarians, have risen into positions of

---

*In order to emphasize the difference I will spell "history," the unrecorded past, with a lower-case h, and "History," the recorded and interpreted past, with an upper-case H.

power or at least inclusion in the polity, their experiences have become part of the historical record. That is, the experiences of the males of their group; females were, as usual, excluded. The point is that men and women have suffered exclusion and discrimination because of their class. No man has been excluded from the historical record because of his sex, yet all women were.

Women have been kept from contributing to History-making, that is, the ordering and interpretation of the past of humankind. Since this process of meaning-giving is essential to the creation and perpetuation of civilization, we can see at once that women's marginality in this endeavor places us in a unique and segregate position. Women are the majority, yet we are structured into social institutions as though we were a minority.

While women have been victimized by this and many other aspects of their long subordination to men, it is a fundamental error to try to conceptualize women primarily as victims. To do so at once obscures what must be assumed as a given of women's historical situation: Women are essential and central to creating society; they are and always have been actors and agents in history. Women have "made history," yet they have been kept from knowing their History and from interpreting history, either their own or that of men. Women have been systematically excluded from the enterprise of creating symbol systems, philosophies, science, and law. Women have not only been educationally deprived throughout historical time in every known society, they have been excluded from theory-formation. The tension between women's actual historical experience and their exclusion from interpreting that experience I have called "the dialectic of women's history." This dialectic has moved women forward in the historical process.

The contradiction between women's centrality and active role in creating society and their marginality in the meaning-giving process of interpretation and explanation has been a dynamic force, causing women to struggle against their condition. When, in that process of struggle, at certain historic moments, the contradictions in their relationship to society and to historical process are brought into the consciousness of women, they are then correctly perceived and named as deprivations that women share as a group. This coming-into-consciousness of women becomes the dialectical force moving them into action to change their condition and to enter a new relationship to male-dominated society.

Because of these conditions unique to themselves, women have had a historical experience significantly different from that of men.

I began by asking the question: what are the definitions and concepts we need in order to explain the unique and segregate relationship of women to historical process, to the making of history and to the interpretation of their own past?

Another question which I hoped my study would address concerned the long delay (over 3500 years) in women's coming to consciousness of their own subordinate position in society. What could explain it? What could explain women's historical "complicity" in upholding the patriarchal system that subordinated them and in transmitting that system that subordinated them and in transmitting that system, generation after generation, to their children of both sexes?

Both of these are big and unpleasant questions because they appear to lead to answers indicating women's victimization and essential inferiority. I believe that is the reason these questions have not earlier been addressed by feminist thinkers, although traditional male scholarship has offered us the patriarchal answer: women have not produced important advances in thought because of their biologically determined preoccupation with nurturance and emotion, which led to their essential "inferiority" in regard to abstract thought. I begin instead with the assumption that men and women are biologically different, but that the values and implications based on that difference are the result of culture. Whatever differences are discernible in the present in regard to men-as-a-group and women-as-a-group are the result of the particular history of women, which is essentially different from the history of men. This is due to the subordination of women to men, which is older than civilization, and to the denial of women's history. The existence of women's history has been obscured and neglected by patriarchal thought, a fact which has significantly affected the psychology of men and women.

I began with the conviction, shared by most feminist thinkers, that patriarchy as a system is historical: it has a beginning in history. If that is so, it can be ended by historical process. If patriarchy were "natural," that is, based on biological determinism, then to change it would mean to change nature. One might argue that changing nature is precisely what civilization has done, but that so far most of the benefits of that domination over nature which men call "progress" has accrued to the male of the species. Why and how this happened are historical questions, regardless of how one explains the causes of female subordination. My own hypothesis on the causes and origins of women's subordination will be more fully discussed in Chapters One and Two. What is important to my analysis is the insight that the relation of men and women to the knowledge of their past is in itself a shaping force in the making of history.

If it were the case that the subordination of women antedated Western civilization, assuming that civilization to have begun with the written historical record, my inquiry had to begin in the fourth millennium B.C. This is what led me, an American historian specializing in the nineteenth century, to spend the last eight years working in the history of ancient Mesopotamia in order to answer the questions I consider essential to creating a feminist theory of history. Although questions of "origin" initially interested me, I soon realized that they were far less significant than questions about the historical process by which patriarchy becomes established and institutionalized.

This process was manifested in changes in kinship organization and economic relations, in the establishment of religious and state bureaucracies, and in the shift in cosmogonies expressing the ascendancy of male god figures. Basing myself on existing theoretical work, I assumed these changes occurred as "an event" in a relatively short period, which might have coincided with the establishment of archaic states or which might have occurred perhaps somewhat earlier, at the time of the establishment of private property, which brought class society into being. Under the influence of Marxist theories of origin, which will be more fully discussed in Chapter One, I envisioned a kind of revolutionary "overthrow" which would have visibly altered existing power relations in society. I expected to find economic changes leading to changes in ideas and religious explanatory systems. Specifically, I was looking for visible changes in the economic, political, and juridical status of women. But as I entered into the study of the rich sources in the history of the Ancient Near East and began to look at them in historical sequence, it became clear to me that my assumption had been too simplistic.

The problem is not one of sources, for these are certainly ample for the reconstruction of a social history of ancient Mesopotamian society. The problem of interpretation is similar to the problem faced by a historian in any field approaching traditional history with questions pertaining to women. There is little substantive work on women available, and what there is, is purely descriptive. No interpretations or generalizations concerning women have as yet been offered by specialists trained in the field.

Thus, the history of women and the history of the changing relations of the sexes in Mesopotamian societies still need to be written. I have the greatest respect for the scholarship and technical and linguistic knowledge of scholars working in Ancient Near Eastern Studies and am certain that from among their ranks will eventually come a work, which will synthesize and put into proper perspective the largely untold story of women's changing social, political, and economic status in the third and second millennia B.C. Not being a trained Assyriologist and being unable to read the cuneiform texts in their original languages, I did not attempt to write such a history.

I did, however, observe that the sequence of events seemed to be rather different from what I had anticipated. While the formation of archaic states, which followed upon or coincided with major economic, technological, and military changes, brought with it distinct shifts in power relations among men, and among men and women, there was nowhere evidence of an "overthrow." The period of the "establishment of patriarchy" was not one "event" but a process developing over a period of nearly 2500 years, from app. 3100 to 600 B.C. It occurred, even within the Ancient Near East, at a different pace and at different times in several distinct societies.

Further, women seemed to have greatly different status in different aspects of their lives, so that, for example, in Babylon in the second millennium B.C. women's sexuality was totally controlled by men, while some women enjoyed great economic independence, many legal rights and privileges and held many important high status positions in society. I was puzzled to find that the historical evidence pertaining to women made little sense, when judged by traditional criteria. After a while I began to see that I needed to focus more on the control of women's sexuality and procreativity than on the usual economic questions, so I began to look for the causes and effects of such sexual control. As I did this, the pieces of the puzzle began to fall into place. I had been unable to comprehend the meaning of the historical evidence before me because I looked at class formation, as it applied to men and women, with the traditional assumption that what was true for men was true for women. When I began to ask how class definition was different for women than for men at the very inception of class society, the evidence before me made sense.

I will, in this book, develop the following propositions:

a) The appropriation by men of women's sexual and reproductive capacity occurred *prior* to the formation of private property and class society. Its commodification lies, in fact, at the foundation of private property. (Chapters One and Two)

b) The archaic states were organized in the form of patriarchy; thus from its inception the state had an essential interest in the maintenance of the patriarchal family. (Chapter Three)

c) Men learned to institute dominance and hierarchy over other people by their earlier practice of dominance over the women of their own group. This found expression in the institutionalization of slavery, which began with the enslavement of women of conquered groups. (Chapter Four)

d) Women's sexual subordination was institutionalized in the earliest law codes and enforced by the full power of the state. Women's cooperation in the system was secured by various means: force, economic dependency on the male head of the family, class privileges bestowed upon conforming and dependent women of the upper classes, and the artificially created division of women into respectable and not-respectable women. (Chapter Five)

e) Class for men was and is based on their relationship to the means of production: those who owned the means of production could dominate those who did not. For women, class is mediated through their sexual ties to a man, who then gives them access to material resources. The division of women into "respectable" (that is, attached to one man) and "not-respectable" (that is, not attached to one man or free of all men) is institutionalized in laws pertaining to the veiling of women. (Chapter Six)

f) Long after women are sexually and economically subordinated to men, they still play active and respected roles in mediating between humans and gods as priestesses, seers, diviners, and healers. Metaphysical female power, especially the power to give life, is worshiped by men and women in the form of powerful goddesses long after women are subordinated to men in most aspects of their lives on earth. (Chapter Seven)

g) The dethroning of the powerful goddesses and their replacement by a dominant male god occur in most Near Eastern societies following the establishment of a strong and imperialistic kingship. Gradually the function of controlling fertility, formerly entirely held by the goddesses, is symbolized through the symbolic or actual mating of the male god or God-King with the Goddess or her priestess. Finally, sexuality (eroticism) and procreativity are split in the emergence of separate goddesses for each function, and the Mother-Goddess is transformed into the wife/consort of the chief male God. (Chapter Seven)

h) The emergence of Hebrew monotheism takes the form of an attack on the widespread cults of the various fertility goddesses. In the writing of the Book of Genesis, creativity and procreativity are ascribed to all-powerful God, whose epitaphs of "Lord" and "King" establish him as a male god, and female sexuality other than for procreative purposes becomes associated with sin and evil. (Chapter Eight)

i) In the establishment of the convenant community the basic symbolism and the actual contract between God and humanity assumes as a given the subordinate position of women and their exclusion from the metaphysical covenant and the earthly covenant community. Their only access to God and to the holy community is in their function as mothers. (Chapter Nine)

j) This symbolic devaluing of women in relation to the divine becomes one of the founding metaphors of Western civilization. The other founding metaphor is supplied by Aristotelian philosophy, which assumes as a given that women are incomplete and damaged human beings of an entirely different order than men (Chapter Ten). It is with the creation of these two metaphorical constructs, which are built into the very foundations of the symbol systems of Western civilization, that the subordination of women comes to be seen as "natural," hence it becomes invisible. It is this which finally establishes patriarchy firmly as an actuality and as an ideology.

WHAT IS THE RELATIONSHIP OF IDEAS, and specifically of ideas about gender,* to the social and economic forces that shape history? The matrix of any idea is reality—people cannot conceive of something they have not themselves experienced or at least that others have before them experienced. Thus, images, metaphors, myths all find expression in forms which are "prefigured" through past experience. In periods of change, people reinterpret these symbols in new ways, which then lead to new combinations and new insights.

What I am attempting to do in my book is to trace, by means of historical evidence, the development of the leading ideas, symbols, and metaphors by which patriarchal gender relations were incorporated into Western civilization. Each chapter is built around one of these metaphors for gender, as indicated by the chapter title. In this book I have endeavored to isolate and identify the forms in which Western civilization constructed gender and to study them at moments or in periods of change. These forms consist of social norms

---

Sex is the biological given for men and women. *Gender* is the cultural definition of behavior defined as appropriate to the sexes in a given society at a given time. Gender is a set of cultural roles; therefore it is a cultural product which changes over time. (The reader is urged to consult the sections sex and gender in Definitions, pp. 231–43.

embodied in social roles, in laws, and in metaphors. In a way, these forms represent historical artifacts, from which it is possible to deduce the social reality which gave rise to the idea or to the metaphor. By tracing the changes in metaphor or image, it should be possible to trace the underlying historical developments in society, even in the absence of other historical evidence. In the case of Mesopotamian society, the abundance of historical evidence makes it possible, in most cases, to confirm one's analysis of symbols by comparison with such hard evidence.

The major gender symbols and metaphors of Western civilization were largely derived from Mesopotamian and, later, from Hebrew sources. It would of course be desirable to extend this study so as to include Arabic, Egyptian, and European influences, but such an enterprise would demand more years of scholarly work than I can, at my age, expect to undertake. I can only hope that my effort at reinterpretation of the available historical evidence will inspire others to continue to pursue the same questions with their specific expertise and the more refined scholarly tools available to them.

When I began this work, I conceived it as a study of the relationship of women to the making of the world's symbol-system, their exclusion from it, their efforts at breaking out of the systematic educational disadvantaging to which they were subjected, and, finally, their coming into feminist consciousness. But as my work in ancient Mesopotamian sources progressed, the richness of the evidence compelled me to enlarge my book to two volumes, the first volume ending in approximately 400 B.C.. The second volume will deal with the rise of feminist consciousness and cover the Christian era.

Although I believe that my hypotheses have wide applicability, I am not, on the basis of the study of one region, attempting to offer "a general theory" on the rise of patriarchy and sexism. The theoretical hypotheses I offer for Western civilization will need to be tested in and compared with other cultures for their general applicability.

AS WE UNDERTAKE THIS EXPLORATION, how are we, then, to think of women-as-a-group? Three metaphors may help us see from our new angle of vision:

In her brilliant 1979 article, Joan Kelly spoke of the new "doubled vision" of feminist scholarship:

> . . . *woman's place is not a separate sphere or domain of existence but a position within social existence generally.* . . . [F]eminist thought

is moving beyond the split vision of social reality it inherited from the recent past. Our actual vantage point has shifted, giving rise to a new consciousness of woman's "place" in family and society. . . . [W]hat we see are not two spheres of social reality (home and work, private and public), but two (or three) sets of social relations.[1]

We are adding the female vision to the male and that process is transforming. But Joan Kelly's metaphor needs to be developed one step further: when we see with one eye, our vision is limited in range and devoid of depth. When we add to it the single vision of the other eye, our range of vision becomes wider, but we still lack depth. It is only when both eyes see together that we accomplish full range of vision and accurate depth perception.

The computer provides us with another metaphor. The computer shows us a picture of a triangle (two-dimensional). Still holding that image, the triangle moves in space and is transformed into a pyramid (three-dimensional). Now the pyramid moves in space creating a curve (the fourth dimension), while still holding the image of the pyramid and the triangle. We see all four dimensions at once, losing none of them, but seeing them also in their true relation to one another.

Seeing as we have seen, in patriarchal terms, is two-dimensional. "Adding women" to the patriarchal framework makes it three-dimensional. But only when the third dimension is fully integrated and moves with the whole, only when women's vision is equal with men's vision, do we perceive the true relations of the whole and the inner connectedness of the parts.

Finally, another image. Men and women live on a stage, on which they act out their assigned roles, equal in importance. The play cannot go on without both kinds of performers. Neither of them "contributes" more or less to the whole; neither is marginal or dispensable. But the stage set is conceived, painted, defined by men. Men have written the play, have directed the show, interpreted the meanings of the action. They have assigned themselves the most interesting, most heroic parts, giving women the supporting roles.

As the women become aware of the difference in the way they fit into the play, they ask for more equality in the role assignments. They upstage the men at times, at other times they pinch-hit for a missing male performer. The women finally, after considerable struggle, win the right of access to equal role assignment, but first they must "qualify." The terms of their "qualifications" are again set by the men; men are the judges of how women measure up; men grant or deny admission. They give preference to docile women and to those who fit their job-description accurately. Men punish, by ridicule, exclusion, or ostracism, any woman who assumes the right to interpret her own role or—worst of all sins—the right to rewrite the script.

It takes considerable time for the women to understand that getting "equal" parts will not make them equal, as long as the script, the props, the stage setting, and the direction are firmly held by men. When the women begin to realize that and cluster together between the acts, or even during the performance, to discuss what to do about it, this play comes to an end.

Looking at the recorded History of society as though it were such a play, we realize that the story of the performances over thousands of years has been recorded only by men and told in their words. Their attention has been mostly on men. Not surprisingly, they have not noticed all the actions women have taken. Finally, in the past fifty years, some women have acquired the training necessary for writing the company's scripts. As they wrote, they began to pay more attention to what women were doing. Still, they had been well trained by their male mentors. So they too found what men were doing on the whole more significant and, in their desire to upgrade the part of women in the past, they looked hard for women who had done what men did. Thus, compensatory history was born.

What women must do, what feminists are now doing is to point to that stage, its sets, its props, its director, and its scriptwriter, as did the child in the fairy tale who discovered that the emperor was naked, and say, the basic inequality between us lies within this framework. And then they must tear it down.

What will the writing of history be like, when that umbrella of dominance is removed and definition is shared equally by men and women? Will we devalue the past, overthrow the categories, supplant order with chaos?

No—we will simply step out under the free sky. We will observe how it changes, how the stars rise and the moon circles, and we will describe the earth and its workings in male and female voices. We may, after all, see with greater enrichment. We now know that man is not the measure of that which is human, but men and women are. Men are not the center of the world, but men and women are. This insight will transform consciousness as decisively as did Copernicus's discovery that the earth is not the center of the universe.

We may play our separate parts on the stage, sometimes exchanging them or deciding to keep them, as it works out. We may discover new talent among those who have always been living under the umbrella of another's making. We may find that those who had previously taken upon themselves the burden of both action and definition may now have more freedom for playing and experiencing the pure joy of existence. We are no more under an obligation to describe what we will find than were the explorers sailing to the distant edge of the world, only to find that the world was round.

We will never know unless we begin. The process itself is the way, is the goal.

ONE

Origins

THE SHREDS OF HARD EVIDENCE—tools, graves, pottery shards, the remains of dwellings and shrines, the ambiguous artifacts on cave walls, skeletal remains and the story they tell—all these lie before us in bewildering diversity. We tie them together with myths and speculation; we match them against what we know of "primitive" people surviving into the present; we use science, philosophy, religion to construct a model of that distant past before civilization began.

The approach we use in interpretation—our conceptual framework—determines the outcome. Such a framework is never value-free. We ask the questions of the past we want answered in the present. For long periods of historical time the conceptual framework which formed our questions was assumed as a given, undiscussed and unchallengeable. As long as the Christian teleological view dominated historical thought, pre-Christian history was seen merely as a preparatory stage for the true history, which began with the birth of Christ and would end with the Second Coming. When Darwinian theory dominated historical thought, pre-history was seen as a "barbaric" stage in the evolutionary progress of humankind from the simpler to the more complex. That which succeeded and survived was by the very fact of its survival considered superior to that which vanished and had thus "failed." As long as androcentric assumptions dominated our interpretations, we read the sex/gender arrangements prevailing in the present backward into the past. We assumed the existence of male dominance as a given and considered any evidence to the contrary merely an exception to the rule or a failed alternative.

Traditionalists, whether working within a religious or a "scientific" framework, have regarded women's subordination as universal, God-given, or natural, hence immutable. Thus, it need not be questioned. What has survived, survived because it was best; it follows that it should stay that way.

Scholars critical of androcentric assumptions and those seeing the need for social change in the present have challenged the concept of the universality of female subordination. They reason that if the system of patriarchal dominance had a historic origin, it could be ended under altered historical conditions. Therefore, the question of the universality of female subordination has, for over 150 years, been central to the debate between traditionalists and feminist thinkers.

For those critical of patriarchal explanations, the next important question is: if female subordination was not universal, then was there ever an alternative model of society? This question has most often taken the form of the search for a matriarchal society in the past. Since much of the evidence in this search derives from myth, religion, and symbol, there has been little attention given to historical evidence.

For the historian, the more important and significant question is this: how, when, and why did female subordination come into existence?

Therefore, before we can undertake a discussion of the historical development of patriarchy, we need to review the major positions in the debate on these three questions.

The traditionalist answer to the first question is, of course, that male dominance is universal and natural. The argument may be offered in religious terms: woman is subordinate to man because she was so created by God.[1] Traditionalists accept the phenomenon of "sexual asymmetry," the assignment of different tasks and roles to men and women, which has been observed in all known human societies, as proof of their position and as evidence of its "naturalness."[2] Since woman was, by divine design, assigned a different biological function than man was, they argue, she should also be assigned different social tasks. If God or nature created sex differences, which in turn determined the sexual division of labor, no one is to blame for sexual inequality and male dominance.

The traditionalist explanation focuses on woman's reproductive capacity and sees in motherhood woman's chief goal in life, by implication defining as deviant women who do not become mothers. Woman's maternal function is seen as a species necessity, since societies could not have survived into modernity without the majority of women devoting most of their adult lives to child-bearing and child-rearing. Thus the sexual division of labor based on biological differences is seen as functional and just.

A corollary explanation of sexual asymmetry locates the causes of female subordination in biological factors affecting males. Men's greater physical strength, their ability to run faster and lift heavier weights, and their greater aggressiveness cause them to become hunters. As such they become the providers of food for their tribes and are more highly valued and honored than women. The skills deriving from their hunting experience in turn equip them to become warriors. Man-the-hunter, superior in strength, ability, and the experience derived from using tools and weapons, "naturally" protects and defends the more vulnerable female, whose biological equipment destines her for motherhood and nurturance.[3] Finally, this biological deterministic explanation is extended from the Stone Age into the present by the assertion that the sexual division of labor based on man's natural "superiority" is a given and therefore as valid today as it was in the primitive beginnings of human society.

This theory, in various forms, is currently by far the most popular version of the traditionalist argument and has had a powerful explanatory and reinforcing effect on contemporary ideas of male supremacy. This is probably due to its "scientific" trappings based on selected ethnographic evidence and on the fact that it seems to account for male dominance in such a way as to relieve contemporary men of all responsibility for it. The profound way in which this explanation has affected even feminist theoreticians is evident in its partial acceptance by Simone de Beauvoir, who takes as a given that man's "transcendence" derives from hunting and warfare and the use of the tools necessary for these pursuits.[4]

Quite apart from its dubious biological claims of male physical superiority, the man-the-hunter explanation has been disproven by anthropological evidence concerning hunting and gathering societies. In most of these societies, big-game hunting is an auxiliary pursuit, while the main food supply is provided by gathering activities and small-game hunting, which women and children do.[5] Also, as we will see below, it is precisely in hunting and gathering societies that we find many examples of complementarity between the sexes and societies in which women have relatively high status, which is in direct contradiction to the claims of the man-the-hunter school of thought.

Feminist anthropologists have recently challenged many of the earlier generalizations, which found male dominance virtually universal in all known societies, as being patriarchal assumptions on the part of ethnographers and investigators of those cultures. When feminist anthropologists have reviewed the data or done their own field work, they have found male dominance to be far from universal. They have found societies in which sexual asymmetry carries no connotation of dominance or subordination. Rather, the tasks performed by both sexes are indispensable to group survival, and both sexes are regarded as equal in status in most aspects. In such societies the sexes are considered "complementary"; their roles and status are different, but equal.[6]

Another way in which man-the-hunter theories have been disproven is by showing the essential, culturally innovative contributions women made to the creation of civilization by their invention of basketry and pottery and their knowledge and development of horticulture.[7] Elise Boulding, in particular, has shown that the man-the-hunter myth and its perpetuation are social-cultural creations which serve the interest of maintaining male supremacy and hegemony.[8]

Traditionalist defenses of male supremacy based on biological-deterministic reasoning have changed over time and proven remarkably adaptive and resilient. When the force of the religious argument was weakened in the nineteenth century the traditionalist explanation of women's inferiority became "scientific." Darwinian theories reinforced beliefs that species survival was more important than individual self-fulfillment. Much as the Social Gospel used the Darwinian idea of the survival of the fittest to justify the unequal distribution of wealth and privilege in American society, scientific defenders of patriarchy justified the definition of women through their maternal role and their exclusion from economic and educational opportunities as serving the best interests of species survival. It was because of their biological constitution and their maternal function that women were considered unsuited for higher education and for many vocational pursuits. Menstruation and menopause, even pregnancy, were regarded as debilitating, as diseased or abnormal

states which incapacitated women and rendered them actually inferior.[9] ·

Similarly, modern psychology observed existing sex differences
with the unquestioned assumption that they were natural, and constructed a psychological female who was as biologically determined
as had been her forebears. Viewing sex roles ahistorically, psychol-
ogists had to arrive at conclusions from observed clinical data which
reinforced predominant gender roles.[10]

Sigmund Freud's theories further reinforced the traditionalist explanation. Freud's normal human was male; the female was by his
definition a deviant human being lacking a penis, whose entire psychological structure supposedly centered on the struggle to compensate for this deficiency. Even though many aspects of Freudian theory would prove helpful in constructing feminist theory, it was Freud's
dictum that for the female "anatomy is destiny" which gave new
life and strength to the male supremacist argument.[11]

The often vulgarized applications of Freudian theory to child-
rearing and to popular advice literature lent new prestige to the old
argument that woman's primary role is as child-bearer and child-
rearer. It was popularized Freudian doctrine which became the prescriptive text for educators, social workers, and the general audiences
of the mass media.[12]

Recently, E. O. Wilson's sociobiology has offered the traditionalist view on gender in an argument which applies Darwinian ideas
of natural selection to human behavior. Wilson and his followers
reason that human behaviors which are "adaptive" for group survival become encoded in the genes, and they include in these behaviors such complex traits as altruism, loyalty, and maternalism. They
not only reason that groups practicing a sex-based division of labor
in which women function as child-rearers and nurturers have an
evolutionary advantage, but they claim such behavior somehow becomes part of our genetic heritage, in that the necessary psychological and physical propensities for such societal arrangements are se-
lectively developed and genetically selected. Mothering is not only a
socially assigned role but one fitting women's physical and psychological needs. Here, once again, biological determinism becomes prescriptive, in fact a political defense of the status quo in scientific
language.[13]

Feminist critics have revealed the circular reasoning, absence of
evidence and unscientific assumptions of Wilsonian sociobiology.[14]
From the point of view of the nonscientist, the most obvious fallacy

of sociobiologists is their ahistoricity in disregarding the fact that modern men and women do not live in a state of nature. The history of civilization describes the process by which humans have distanced themselves from nature by inventing and perfecting culture. Traditionalists ignore technological changes, which have made it possible to bottle-feed infants safely and raise them to adulthood with caretakers other than their own mothers. They ignore the implications of changing life spans and changing life cycles. Until communal hygiene and modern medical knowledge cut infant mortality to a level where parents could reasonably expect each child born to them to live to adulthood, women did indeed have to bear many children in order for a few of them to survive. Similarly, longer life expectancy and lower infant mortality altered the life cycles of both men and women. These developments were connected with industrialization and occurred in Western civilization (for whites) toward the end of the nineteenth century, occurring later for the poor and for minorities due to the uneven distribution of health and social services. Whereas up to 1870 child-rearing and marriage were co-terminus—that is, one or both parents could expect to die before the youngest child reached adulthood—in modern American society husbands and wives can expect to live together for twelve years after their youngest child has reached adulthood, and women can expect to outlive their husbands by seven years.[15]

Nevertheless, traditionalists expect women to follow the same roles and occupations that were functional and species-essential in the Neolithic. They accept cultural changes by which men have freed themselves from biological necessity. The supplanting of hard physical labor by the labor of machines is considered progress; only women, in their view, are doomed forever to species-service through their biology. To claim that of all human activities only female nurturance is unchanging and eternal is indeed to consign half the human race to a lower state of existence, to nature rather than to culture.

The qualities which may have fostered human survival in the Neolithic are no longer required of modern people. Regardless of whether qualities such as aggressiveness or nurturance are genetically or culturally transmitted, it should be obvious that the aggressiveness of males, which may have been highly functional in the Stone Age, is threatening human survival in the nuclear age. At a time when overpopulation and exhaustion of natural resources represent a real danger for human survival, to curb women's procreative capacities may be more "adaptive" than to foster them.

Further, in opposition to any argument based on biological determinism, feminists challenge the hidden androcentric assumptions
in the sciences dealing with humans. They have charged that in biology, anthropology, zoology, and psychology such assumptions have
led to a reading of scientific evidence that distorts its meaning. Thus,
for example, animal behavior is invested with anthropomorphic significance, which makes patriarchs of male chimpanzees.[16] Many
feminists argue that the limited number of proven biological differences among the sexes has been vastly exaggerated by cultural interpretations and that the value put on sex differences is in itself a
cultural product. Sexual attributes are a biological given, but gender
is a product of historical process. The fact that women bear children
is due to sex; that women nurture children is due to gender, a cultural construct. It is gender which has been chiefly responsible for
fixing women's place in society.[17]

Let us now look briefly at the theories which deny the universality of female subordination and which postulate an earlier stage
of either female dominance (matriarchy) or female equality with men.
The main explanations are Marxist-economic and maternalist.

Marxist analysis has been very influential in determining the
questions asked by feminist scholars. The basic work of reference is
Frederick Engels's *Origin of the Family, Private Property and the
State*, which describes "the world historic defeat of the female sex"
as an event deriving from the development of private property.[18]
Engels, basing his generalizations on the work of nineteenth-century
ethnographers and theoreticians such as J. J. Bachofen and L. H.
Morgan, postulated the existence of classless communist societies prior
to the formation of private property.[19] Such societies may or may
not have been matriarchal, but they were egalitarian. Engels assumed a "primitive" division of labor between the sexes.

> The man fights in the wars, goes hunting and fishing, procures the
> raw materials of food and the tools necessary for doing so. The woman
> looks after the house and the preparation of the food and clothing,
> cooks, weaves, sews. They are each master in their own sphere: the
> man in the forest, the woman in the house. Each is owner of the
> instruments which he or she makes and uses. . . . What is made and
> used in common is common property—the house, the garden, the
> long boat.[20]

Engels's description of the primitive sexual division of labor reads
curiously like a description of European peasant households read back

into pre-history. The ethnographic information on which he based these generalizations has been disproven. In most primitive societies of the past and in all hunting/gathering societies still existent today, women provide on the average 60 percent or more of the food. To do so they often range far from home, carrying their babies and children with them. Further, the assumption that there is one formula and one pattern for the sexual division of labor is erroneous. The particular work done by men and women has differed greatly in different cultures, largely depending on the ecological situation in which the people find themselves.[21] Engels theorized that in tribal societies the development of animal husbandry led to commerce and to ownership of herds by individual heads of families, presumably male, but he was unable to explain how this took place.[22] Surpluses from herding were appropriated by men and became private property. Once having acquired such private property, men sought to secure it to themselves and their heirs; they did so by instituting the monogamous family. By controlling women's sexuality through the requirement of prenuptial chastity and by the establishment of the sexual double standard in marriage, men assured themselves of the legitimacy of their offspring and thus secured their property interest. Engels stressed the connection between the breakdown of older kinship relations based on communal property ownership and the emergence of the individual family as the economic unit.

With the development of the state, the monogamous family changed into the patriarchal family, in which the wife's household labor "became a *private service;* the wife became the head servant, excluded from all participation in social production." Engels concluded:

> The overthrow of the mother right was the *world historical defeat of the female sex.* The man took command in the home also; the woman was degraded and reduced to servitude; she became the slave of his lust and a mere instrument for the production of children.[23]

Engels used the term "Mutterrecht," hereafter referred to as "Mother Right," derived from Bachofen, to describe matrilineal kinship relations, in which the property of men did not pass to their children but to their sisters' children. He also accepted Bachofen's model of the "historic" progression in family structure from group marriage to monogamous marriage. He reasoned that monogamous marriage was viewed by woman as an improvement in her condition, since with it she acquired "the right to give herself to *one* man only." Engels also called attention to the institutionalization of prostitution, which he described as an indispensable prop for monogamous marriage.

Engels's speculations on the nature of female sexuality have been criticized as reflecting his own sexist Victorian values in their unexamined assumption that nineteenth-century standards of female prudery could explain the actions and attitudes of women at the dawn of civilization.[24] Yet, Engels made major contributions to our understanding of women's position in society and history: (1) He pointed to the connection between structural changes in kinship relations and changes in the division of labor on the one hand and women's position in society on the other. (2) He showed a connection between the establishment of private property, monogamous marriage, and prostitution. (3) He showed the connection between economic and political dominance by men and their control over female sexuality. (4) By locating "the world historical defeat of the female sex" in the period of the formation of archaic states, based on the dominance of propertied elites, he gave the event historicity. Although he was unable to prove any of these propositions, he defined the major theoretical questions for the next hundred years. He also limited the discussion of "the woman question" by offering a persuasive, single-cause explanation and directing attention to a single event, which he likened to a revolutionary "overthrow." If the cause of women's "enslavement" was the development of private property and the institutions that evolved from it, then it followed logically that the abolition of private property would liberate women. In any case, most of the theoretical work done on the question of the origin of women's subordination has been directed toward proving, improving, or disproving Engels's work.

Engels's basic assumptions about the nature of the sexes were based on an acceptance of evolutionary theories of biology, but his great merit was to point up the impact of societal and cultural forces in structuring and defining sexual relations. Parallel to his model of social relations, he developed an evolutionary theory of sex relations, in which monogamous marriage among the working classes in a socialist society stood at the apex of development. In thus linking sexual relations to changing social relations he broke with the biological determinism of the traditionalists. In his calling attention to the sexual conflict built into the institution as it emerged within private property relations, he reinforced the linkage between economic-social change and what we today would call gender relations. He defined monogamous marriage as formed in early state society as "the subjection of one sex by the other, as the proclamation of a conflict between the sexes entirely unknown hitherto in prehistoric times." He continued significantly:

> The first class opposition that appears in history coincides with the development of the antagonism between man and woman in monogamous marriage, and the first class oppression with that of the female sex by the male.[25]

These statements offered many promising avenues for theory-building, about which more will be said below. But Engels's identification of the relation of the sexes as "class antagonism" has been a dead end which for a long time kept theorists from properly understanding the differences between class relations and relations between the sexes. This was compounded by the insistence of Marxists that questions of sex relations must be subordinated to questions of class relations, expressed not only theoretically but in practical politics, wherever they had the power to do so. New feminist scholarship has only recently begun to forge the theoretical tools with which to correct these errors.

The structuralist anthropologist Claude Lévi-Strauss also offers a theoretical explanation in which women's subordination is crucial to the formation of culture. But unlike Engels, Lévi-Strauss postulates a single building block out of which men constructed culture. Lévi-Strauss sees in the incest taboo a universal human mechanism, which lies at the root of all social organization.

> The prohibition of incest is less a rule prohibiting marriage with the mother, sister or daughter, than a rule obliging the mother, sister, or daughter to be given to others. It is the supreme rule of the gift.[26]

The "exchange of women" is the first form of trade, in which women are turned into a commodity and are "reified," that is, they are thought of more as things than as human beings. The exchange of women, according to Lévi-Strauss, marks the beginning of women's subordination. It in turn reinforces a sexual division of labor which institutes male dominance. Lévi-Strauss nevertheless sees the incest taboo as a positive and necessary step forward in creating human culture. Small self-sufficient tribes had to relate to neighboring tribes either in constant warfare or find a way toward peaceful coexistence. Taboos on endogamy and incest structured peaceful interaction and led to alliances among tribes.

The anthropologist Gayle Rubin accurately defines this exchange system as it impinges on women:

> Exchange of women is a shorthand for expressing that the social relations of kinship system specify that men have certain rights in female kin, and that women do not have the same rights in their male kin . . . [It is] a system, in which women do not have full rights to themselves.[27]

We should note that in Lévi-Strauss's theory men are the actors who impose a set of structures and relations on women. Such an explanation cannot be considered adequate. How did this happen? Why was it women who were exchanged, why not men or small children of both sexes? Even granting the functional usefulness of the arrangement, why would women have agreed to it?[28] We will explore these questions further in the next chapter in our effort to construct a workable hypothesis.

Lévi-Strauss's considerable impact on feminist theorists has resulted in a shift in attention from the search for economic origins to the study of the symbolic and meaning systems of societies. The most influential work was Sherry Ortner's 1974 essay, in which she persuasively argued that in every known society women are identified as being closer to nature than to culture.[29] Since every culture devalues nature as it strives to rise above it through mastery, women become symbolic of an inferior, intermediate order of being. Ortner showed that women were so identified because:

> 1. woman's body and its function . . . seem to place her closer to nature; 2. woman's body and its functions place her in *social* roles that in turn are considered to be at a lower order of the cultural process than man's; and 3. woman's traditional social roles, imposed because of her body and its functions, in turn give her a different psychic structure . . . which . . . is seen as being closer to nature.[30]

This brief essay provoked a long and highly informative debate among feminist anthropologists and theorists, which still continues. Ortner and those who agree with her argue strongly for the universality of female subordination, if not in actual social conditions, then in the meaning systems of society. Opponents of this viewpoint object to the claim of universality, criticize its ahistoricity, and reject the placing of women in the position of passive victims. Finally, they challenge the implicit acceptance in the feminist structuralist position of the existence of an unchanging and immutable dichotomy between male and female.[31]

This is not the place to do justice to the richness and sophistication of this ongoing feminist debate, but the discussion of the universality of female subordination has already yielded so many alternative explanations that even those who answer it positively are aware of the shortcomings of that question-setting. More and more, as the debate deepens, it becomes clear that single-cause explanations and claims of universality will not adequately answer the question of causes. The great merit of the functionalist position is to reveal the narrowness of merely economic explanations, while those inclined to emphasize biology and economics are now forced to deal with the power of belief systems, symbols, and mental constructs. Above all, the commonly held belief of most feminists in the societal construction of gender poses a most serious intellectual challenge to traditionalist explanations.

There is another theoretical position which deserves our serious consideration, first, because it is feminist in focus and intent and, second, because it represents a historic tradition in thought about women. Maternalist theory is built upon the acceptance of biological sex differences as a given. Most feminist-maternalists also consider the sexual division of labor built upon these biological differences as inevitable, although some recent thinkers have revised that position. Maternalists sharply differ from the traditionalists in reasoning from this for women's equality and even for the superiority of women.

The first major explanatory theory built on maternalist principles was developed by J. J. Bachofen in his highly influential book, *Das Mutterrecht*.[32] Bachofen's work influenced Engels and Charlotte Perkins Gilman and is paralleled in the thought of Elizabeth Cady Stanton. A wide array of twentieth-century feminists accepted his ethnographic data and his analysis of literary sources and used them to construct a wide range of differing theories.[33] Bachofen's ideas also strongly influenced Robert Briffault as well as a school of Jungian analysts and theorists whose work has had wide popular appeal and currency in twentieth-century America.[34]

Bachofen's basic framework was evolutionist and Darwinian; he described various stages in the evolution of society, leading steadily upward from barbarism to modern patriarchy. Bachofen's original contribution was to claim that women in primitive society developed culture and that there was a stage of "matriarchy" which led society out of barbarism. Bachofen speaks eloquently and poetically of this stage:

At the lowest, darkest stage of human existence [mother-child love was] the only light in the moral darkness. . . . Raising her young, the woman learns earlier than the man to extend her loving care beyond the limits of the ego to another creature. . . . Woman at this stage is the repository of all culture, of all benevolence, of all devotion, of all concern for the living and grief for the dead.[35]

Despite his high valuation of women's role in the dim past, Bachofen regarded the ascendancy of patriarchy in Western civilization as the triumph of superior religious and political thought and organization, which he contrasted negatively with historic development in Asia and Africa. But he advocated, as did his followers, the incorporation of the "feminine principle" of nurturance and altruism in modern society.

Nineteenth-century American feminists developed a full-blown maternalist theory based not so much on Bachofen as on their own redefinition of the patriarchal doctrine of "woman's separate sphere." Yet, there are close parallels in their thinking to Bachofen's ideas of innate, positive "feminine" characteristics. Nineteenth-century feminists, both in America and in England, considered women more altruistic than men because of their maternal instincts and lifelong practice, and more virtuous because of their allegedly weaker sex drives. They believed that these characteristics, which unlike Bachofen they frequently ascribed to women's *historic* role as nurturers, gave women a special mission: to rescue society from the destructiveness, competition, and violence created by men holding unchallenged dominance. Elizabeth Cady Stanton, in particular, developed an argument which blended natural rights philosophy and American nationalism with maternalism.[36]

Stanton wrote at a time when traditionalist ideas about gender were being redefined in the young American republic. In colonial America, as in eighteenth-century Europe, women had been regarded as subordinate to and dependent on their male relatives within the family, even as they were considered, especially in the colonies and under frontier conditions, partners in economic life. They had been excluded from equal access to education and from participation and power in public life. Now, as men created a new nation, they assigned to woman the new role of "mother of the republic," responsible for the raising of male citizens who would lead society. Republican women were now to be sovereign in the domestic sphere, even as men more firmly claimed the public sphere, including economic life, as their exclusive domain. Sex-determined separate spheres, as defined in the "cult of true womanhood," became the prevalent ideology. As men institutionalized their dominance in the economy, in education, and in politics, women were encouraged to adjust to their subordinate status by an ideology which gave their maternal function higher significance.[37]

In the early decades of the nineteenth century, American women in practice and thought redefined on their own the position they should hold in society. While early feminists accepted the existence of separate spheres as a given, they transformed the meaning of this concept by arguing for woman's right and duty to enter the public sphere, because of the superiority of her values and the strength embodied in her maternal role. Stanton transformed the "separate sphere" doctrine into a feminist argument by reasoning that women were entitled to equality because they were citizens and thus enjoyed the same natural rights as men and because as *mothers* they were better equipped than men to improve society.

A similar maternalist-feminist argument was manifest in the ideology of the later suffrage movement and of those reformers who argued, with Jane Addams, that women's work properly extended to "municipal housekeeping." Interestingly, modern feminist-maternalists have reasoned similarly, basing their argument on psychological data and on the evidence of women's historical experience as outsiders to political power. Dorothy Dinnerstein, Mary O'Brien, and Adrienne Rich are the latest in a long line of maternalists.[38]

Because of their acceptance of biological sex differences as determinant, nineteenth-century maternalists were not as concerned with the question of origins as were their twentieth-century followers. But from the beginning with Bachofen, the denial of the universality of female subordination was implicit in the maternalist evolutionary position. There had been an alternative model of human social organization before patriarchy, maternalists asserted. Thus, the quest for matriarchy was central to their thought. If evidence for the existence of matriarchal societies anywhere and at any time could be found, then women's claim to equality and a share in power would have greater prestige and sanction. Until very recently, such evidence as could be found consisted of a combination of archaeology, myth, religion, and artifacts of dubious meaning, held together by speculation. Central to the argument for matriarchy was the ubiquitous evidence of Mother-Goddess figures in many ancient religions, from which maternalists argued for the reality and actuality of female power in the past. We will discuss the evolution of the Mother Goddesses in Chapter Seven in greater detail; here we need to stress only the difficulty of reasoning from such evidence toward the construction of social organizations in which women were dominant. In view of the historical evidence for the coexistence of symbolic idolatry of women and the actual *low* status of women, such as the cult of the Virgin Mary in the Middle Ages, the cult of the lady of the plantation in antebellum America, or that of the Hollywood star in contemporary society, one hesitates to elevate such evidence to historical proof.

The ethnographic evidence on which Bachofen and Engels based their arguments has been largely disproven by modern anthropologists. Such evidence as held up turned out to be evidence not for "matriarchy" but for matrilocality and matriliny. Contrary to earlier-held belief, it is not possible to show a connection between kinship structure and the social position of women. In most matrilineal societies, it is a male relative, usually the woman's brother or uncle, who controls economic and family decisions.[39]

There is now a rich body of modern anthropological evidence available which describes relatively egalitarian societal arrangements and complex and varied solutions by societies to the problem of the division of labor.[40] The literature is based largely on modern tribal societies, with a few examples from the nineteenth century. This raises the problem, especially for the historian, as to the validity of such information for generalizations about prehistoric peoples. At any rate, from the available data it appears that the most egalitarian societies are to be found among hunting/gathering tribes, which are characterized by economic interdependency. A woman must secure the services of a hunter in order to be assured of a meat supply for herself and her children. A hunter must be assured of a woman who will supply him with subsistence food for the hunt and in the event the hunt is unsuccessful. As we have earlier observed, in such societies women supply the major share of the food consumed, yet the product of the hunt is everywhere considered the most valued food and is used for gift exchanges. Such hunting/gathering tribes stress economic cooperation and tend to live peacefully with other tribes. Competition is ritualized in contests of singing or athletics but is not encouraged in daily living. As usual, scholars in the field disagree in their interpretations of the evidence, but the most thorough survey of the evidence yields the generalization that in such societies the relative status of men and women is "separate but equal."[41]

There is considerable controversy among anthropologists over how to categorize any given society. A number of feminist anthropologists and writers have interpreted complementarity or even the absence of clear-cut male dominance as evidence of egalitarianism or even female dominance. Thus, Eleanor Leacock describes the high status of Iroquois women, especially before the European invasion: their powerful public role in controlling food distribution and their participation in the Council of Elders. Leacock interprets these facts as evidence of "matriarchy," defining the term to mean that "women held public authority in major areas of group life."[42] Other anthropologists, viewing the same data and recognizing the relatively high status and powerful position of Iroquois women, focus on the fact that Iroquois women were never the political leaders of the tribe and were not the chiefs. They also point to the uniqueness of the Iroquois situation, which is based on the abundant natural resources available in their environment.[43] One must also note that in all hunting/gathering societies, no matter what women's economic and social status is, women are always subordinate to men in some respects. There is not a single society known where women-as-a-group have decision-making power *over* men or where they define the rules of sexual conduct or control marriage exchanges.

It is in horticultural societies that we most frequently find women dominant or highly influential in the economic sphere. In a sample survey of 515 horticultural societies, women dominate cultivation activities in 41 percent of the cases, yet historically such societies move in the direction of sedentary settlement and plow agriculture, in which men dominate economic and political life.[44] In the horticultural societies studied, most are patrilineal, despite women's decisive economic role. Matrilineal horticultural societies seem to appear mainly under certain ecological conditions—near forest borders, where domesticated animal herds are absent. Because such habitats are disappearing, matrilineal societies are nearly extinct.

Summarizing the research findings concerning female dominance these points can be made: (1) Most of the evidence for female equality in societies derives from matrilineal, matrilocal societies, which are historically transitional and currently vanishing. (2) While matriliny and matrilocality confer certain rights and privileges on women, decision-making power within the kinship group nevertheless rests with elder males. (3) Patrilineal descent does not imply subjugation of women nor does matrilineal descent indicate matriarchy. (4) Seen over time, matrilineal societies have been unable to adapt to competitive, exploitative, techno-economic systems and have given way to patrilineal societies.

The case against the universality of prehistoric matriarchy seems quite clearly proven by the anthropological evidence. Yet the debate over matriarchy rages on, largely because advocates of the matriarchy theory have been vague enough in their definition of the term to include in it various other categories. Those who define matriarchy as a society where women dominate over men, a sort of inversion of patriarchy, cannot cite anthropological, ethnological, or historic evidence. They rest their case on evidence from myth and religion.[45] Others call matriarchy any kind of societal arrangement in which women hold power over any aspect of public life. Still others include any society in which women have relatively high status.[46] The last definition is so vague as to be meaningless as a category. I think one can truly speak of matriarchy only when women hold power *over* men, not alongside them, when that power includes the public domain and foreign relations and when women make essential decisions not only for their kinfolk but for the community. In line with my earlier discussion, such power would have to include the power to define the values and explanatory systems of the society and the power to define and control the sexual behavior of men. It may be noted that I am defining matriarchy as the mirror image of patriarchy. Using that definition, I would conclude that no matriarchal society has ever existed.

There have been and still are societies in which women share power with men in many or several aspects of life and societies in which women in groups have considerable power to influence or check the power of men. There also exist and have historically existed individual women who have all or almost all the powers of men they represent or for whom they act as stand-ins, such as queens and rulers. As this book will show, the possibility of sharing economic and political power with men of their class or in their stead has been precisely a privilege of some upper-class women, which has confined them more closely to patriarchy.

There is some archaeological evidence for the existence of societies in the Neolithic and in the Bronze Age in which women were held in high esteem, which may also indicate that they held some power. Most of this evidence consists of female figures, which have been interpreted as fertility-goddesses; and, for the Bronze Age, of artistic artifacts depicting women with dignity and signs of high status. We will be evaluating the evidence of the goddesses in Chapter

Seven and will discuss Mesopotamian societies in the Bronze Age throughout this book. Let us now briefly review the evidence in one particular case, which is frequently cited by advocates of the existence of matriarchy, that of Čatal Hüyük, in Anatolia (present-day Turkey).

James Mellaart's excavations, in particular in Hacilar and Čatal Hüyük, shed important light on early town development in the region. Čatal Hüyük, a Neolithic urban settlement of 6000 to 8000 persons, was built in successive layers over a period of 1500 years (6250–5720 B.C.), new towns upon the remnants of older settlements. Comparison of the various layers of town settlement at Čatal Hüyük and those of an even older, smaller village, Hacilar (built between 7040–7000 B.C.), offers us insight into an early society undergoing historic change.[47]

Čatal Hüyük was a town built like a beehive of individual abodes which showed little variation in size and furnishing. The houses were entered from the roof, by a ladder; each was equipped with a mud-brick hearth and an oven. Every house had a large sleeping platform, under which the buried skeletons of women and sometimes children were found. Smaller platforms were found in varying positions in the different rooms, with sometimes men and sometimes children buried under them, but never men and children together. Women were buried with mirrors, jewelry, and bone and stone tools; men with their weapons, rings, beads, and tools. The wooden vessels and textiles found on the site indicate a high level of skill and specialization as well as extensive trade. Mellaart found rush rugs, woven baskets, and many objects made of obsidian, which indicates that the town was engaged in long-distance trade and enjoyed considerable wealth. Evidence of a wide variety of food and grains and of domesticated sheep, goats, and dogs was found in the later layers.

Mellaart thinks that only privileged persons were buried in the houses. Out of 400 persons buried there, only eleven had "ochre" burials—that is, their skeletons were painted with red ochre, which Mellaart interprets as a sign of high status. Since most of these were women, Mellaart reasons that women had high status in the society, and he speculates that they may have been priestesses. This piece of evidence is somewhat weakened by the fact that of the 222 adult skeletons found at Čatal Hüyük 136 of them were female, which is an unusually large proportion.[48] If Mellaart then found a majority of the "ochre" burials to be female, that might simply fit the general population sex ratio. It does, however, indicate that females were among high-ranking persons, that is, provided Mellaart's speculation concerning the meaning of the "ochre" burial is correct.

The absence of streets, a large plaza, or a palace and the uniform size and furnishing of the houses led Mellaart to speculate that there was neither hierarchy nor a central political authority at Čatal Hüyük, and that authority was shared among the inhabitants. The first speculation seems appropriate and can be sustained by comparative evidence, but from this it cannot be proven that authority was shared. Authority, even in the absence of a palace structure or formal governing body, might have rested in heads of kin groups or in a group of elders. Nothing in Mellaart's evidence proves shared authority.

The various layers of Čatal Hüyük reveal an extraordinarily large number of shrines, which were extensively decorated with wall paintings, plaster reliefs, and statues. In the lower layers of the excavation there are no figurative representations of humans, only bulls and rams, animal paintings and bull horns. Mellaart interprets these as symbolic representations of male gods. In the 6200 B.C. layer the first representations of female figures appear, with grossly exaggerated breasts, buttocks, and hips. Some are shown seated, one in the act of giving birth; they are surrounded by plaster breasts on the walls, some of which are shaped over animal skulls and jaws. There is also one remarkable statue of a male and female figure embracing and next to it another one of a woman holding a child. Mellaart calls these figures goddesses and notices their association with both life and death (vulture teeth and jaws in the breasts); he also notices their association with flower, grain, and vegetable patterns in the wall decorations and with leopards (symbol of the hunt) and vultures (symbol of death). In the later layers there are no representations of male gods.

Mellaart argues that the male at Čatal Hüyük was an object of pride, valued for his virility, and that his role in procreation was understood. He believes that men and women shared power and community control in the earliest period and that both participated in hunting. The latter is based on the evidence of wall paintings, which show women participating in either a ritual or a hunting scene involving a deer and a boar. That seems a greatly exaggerated conclusion, considering that both paintings show large numbers of men engaged in hunting and surrounding the animal, while there are only two female figures visible, both with legs spread wide apart, which may indicate some sexual symbolism but seems quite incompatible with women participating in hunting.[49] From the structure of the

buildings and the platforms Mellaart deducts that community organization was matrilineal and matrilocal. The latter certainly seems
likely from the evidence. He believes that women developed agriculture and controlled its products. He reasons from the absence of
evidence of blood sacrifice in the shrines that there was no central
authority and no military caste and says that in all of Čatal Hüyük
there is no evidence of warfare over a period of 1000 years. Mellaart
also argues for the fact that women created Neolithic religion and
that they chiefly were the artists.

These findings and the evidence have been subject to differing
interpretations. In a scholarly survey P. Singh details all of Mellaart's evidence and puts it in the context of other such Neolithic
settlements but omits Mellaart's conclusions, other than about the
economy of the town.[50] Ian Todd, a participant in some of the Čatal
Hüyük excavations, in a 1976 study, cautions that the limited nature
of the excavations at Čatal Hüyük makes conclusions about stratification in the society premature. He agrees that the archaeological
findings show a society with a complex social structure, but concludes, "whether the society was indeed matriarchal as has been suggested is unknown."[51] Anne Barstow, in a careful evaluation, agrees
with most of Mellaart's findings. She stresses the significance of his
observations regarding the celebration of the fecundity and strength
of women and of their role in creating religion but finds no evidence
for matriarchy.[52] Ruby Rohrlich takes the same evidence and from
it reasons for the existence of matriarchy. She accepts Mellaart's
generalizations uncritically and argues that his evidence disproves
the universality of male supremacy in human societies. Rohrlich's
essay is important in focusing attention on various bits of evidence
of societal change in regard to the relations of the sexes in the period
of the formation of archaic states, but her blurring of the distinction
between male-female egalitarian relationships and matriarchy obscures our vision.[53]

Mellaart's findings are important, but his generalizations about
the role of women should be used with care. There seems to be clear
evidence of matrilocality and of female goddess worship. The period-
ization of the onset of that worship is equivocal: Mellaart links it to
the onset of agriculture, which he thinks brings higher status to
women. As we will see throughout, the opposite seems to be the
case in many societies. Mellaart might have strengthened his argument by using the findings of one of his coworkers, Lawrence Angel,
who found, by an analysis of skeletal remnants, a significant increase

in the average life-span of Neolithic females over the Paleolithic, from 28.2 to 29.8 years. This gain in female longevity of almost two years must be considered against the average life span of 34.3 years at Čatal Hüyük. In other words, while men lived four years longer than women, there was a considerable gain in longevity for women compared with an earlier period. This gain may have been due to the change from hunting/gathering to agriculture, and it may have given women a relatively more dominant role in that culture.[54] Mellaart's observations about the absence of warfare at Čatal Hüyük must be measured against the abundant evidence of the existence of warfaring and militant communities in neighboring regions. And, finally, we cannot omit from consideration the sudden and unexplained abandonment of the settlement by its inhabitants ca. 5700 B.C., which seems to indicate either military defeat or the inability of the community to adapt to changing ecological conditions. In either case, it would bear out the observation that communities with relatively egalitarian relations between the sexes did not survive.[55]

Still, Čatal Hüyük offers us hard evidence of the existence of some sort of alternate model to that of patriarchy. Adding this to the other evidence we have cited, we can assert that female subordination is not universal, even though we have no proof for the existence of a matriarchal society. But women, like men, have a deep need for a coherent system of explanation that not only tells us what is and why it got to be as it is but allows for an alternate vision of the future.[56] Before proceeding to the discussion of the historical evidence for the establishment of patriarchy, we will, therefore, present such an hypothetical model—to free our minds and souls, to play with possibilities, to consider alternatives.

TWO

A Working Hypothesis

THE BASIC ASSUMPTION with which we must start any theorizing about the past is that men and women built civilization jointly.[1] Starting as we do from the end result and reasoning back, we thus ask a different question than that of a single-cause "origin." We ask: how did men and women in their society-building and in the construction of what we call Western civilization arrive at the present state? Once we abandon the concept of women as historical victims, acted upon by violent men, inexplicable "forces," and societal institutions, we must explain the central puzzle—woman's participation in the construction of the system that subordinates her. I suggest that abandoning the search for an empowering past—the search for matriarchy—is the first step in the right direction. The creation of compensatory myths of the distant past of women will not emancipate women in the present and the future.[2] The patriarchal mode of thought is so built into our mental processes that we cannot exclude it unless we first make ourselves consciously aware of it, which always means a special effort. Thus, in thinking about the prehistoric past of women, we are so much locked into the explanatory androcentric system that the only alternate model that readily comes to mind is that of reversal. If not patriarchy, then there must have been matriarchy. Undoubtedly there were many different modes in which men and women organized society and allocated power and resources. None of the archaeological evidence we have is conclusive and sufficient to allow us to construct a scientifically sound model of that important period of the transition from Neolithic hunting/gathering to sedentary agricultural societies. The way of the anthropologists, who offer us examples of contemporary hunting/gathering societies and draw from them inferences about societies in the fifth millennium B.C., is no less speculative than is that of the philosopher and the specialist in religious studies who reason from literature and myths. The point is that most of the speculative models have been androcentric and have assumed the naturalness of patriarchy, and the few feminist models have been ahistorical and therefore, to my mind, unsatisfactory.

A correct analysis of our situation and how it came to be what it is will help us to create an empowering theory. We must think about gender historically and specifically as it occurs in varied and changeable societies. The anthropologist Michelle Rosaldo arrived at similar conclusions, although starting from a different vantage point. She wrote:

> To look for origins is, in the end, to think that what we are today is something other than the product of our history and our present social world, and, more particularly, that our gender systems are primordial, transhistorical and essentially unchanging in their roots.[3]

Our search, then, becomes a search for the history of the patriarchal system. To give the system of male dominance historicity and to assert that its functions and manifestations change over time is to break sharply with the handed-down tradition. This tradition has mystified patriarchy by making it ahistoric, eternal, invisible, and unchanging. But it is precisely due to changes in the social and educational opportunities available to women that in the nineteenth and twentieth centuries large numbers of women finally became capable of critically evaluating the process by which we have helped to create the system and maintain it. We are only now able to conceptualize women's role in history and thereby to create a consciousness which can emancipate women. This consciousness can also liberate men from the unwanted and undesired consequences of the system of male dominance.

Approaching this quest as historians, we must abandon single-factor explanations. We must assume that if and when events occur simultaneously their relationship to each other is not necessarily causal. We must assume that changes as complex as a basic alteration in kinship structures most likely occurred as the result of a variety of interacting forces. We must test whatever hypothesis we have developed for one model comparatively and cross-culturally. Women's position in society must be viewed always also in comparison with that of the men of their social group and of their time.

We must prove our case not only by material evidence but by evidence from written sources. While we will look for the occurrence of "patterns" and similarities, we must be open to the possibility that similar outcomes, deriving from a variety of factors, might occur as the result of very different processes. Above all, we must view the position of women in society as subject to change over time, not only in its form but also in its meaning. For example, the social role of "concubine" cannot be evaluated by twentieth- or even nineteenth-century standards when we are studying it in the first millennium B.C. This is so obvious an example that to cite it may seem unnecessary, and yet just such errors occur frequently in the discussion of women's past. In particular, gender has, in most societies, such a strong symbolic as well as ideological and legal significance that we cannot truly understand it unless we pay attention to all aspects of its meaning.

The hypothetical construct I will offer is intended only as one of a number of possible models. Even on the limited geographic terrain of the Ancient Near East there must have been many different ways in which the transition to patriarchy took place. Since we will most likely never know just what happened, we are constrained to speculate on what might have been possible. Such utopian projections into the past serve an important function for those who wish to create theory—to know what might have been possible opens us up to new interpretations. It allows us to speculate about what might be possible in the future, free of the confines of a limited and entirely outdated conceptual framework.

Let us begin with the transitional period when hominids evolved from primates, some three million years ago, and let us consider the most basic dyad, mother and child. The first characteristic distinguishing humans from other primates is the prolonged and helpless infancy of the human child. This is the direct result of bipedalism, which led to the narrowing of the female pelvis and birth canal due to upright posture. One result of this was that human babies were born at a greater stage of immaturity than other primates, with relatively smaller heads in order to ease passage through the birth canal. Further, in contrast to the most highly developed apes, human babies are born naked and therefore must experience a greater need for warmth. They cannot grasp their mothers for steady support, lacking the apes' movable toe, so mothers must use their hands or, later, mechanical substitutes for hands to cradle their infants against them.[4] Bipedalism and upright posture led also to the finer development of the hand, the grasping thumb, and greater sensory–hand coordination. One consequence of this is that the human brain develops for many years during the child's period of infancy and complete dependency, and that it is therefore subject to modification through learning and intense cultural molding in a way that is decisively different from animal development. The neurophysiologist Ruth Bleier uses these facts in a telling argument against any theories claiming "innate" human characteristics.[5]

The step from foraging to gathering food for later consumption, possibly by more than one individual, was crucial in advancing human development. It must have fostered social interaction, the invention and development of containers, and the slow evolutionary increase in brain size. Nancy Tanner suggests that females caring for their helpless infants had the most incentive to develop these skills, while males may have, for a long period, continued to forage alone. She speculates that it was these activities which led to the first use of tools for opening and dividing plant food with children and for digging for roots. At any rate, the infant's survival depended on the quality of maternal care. "Similarly, a mother's gathering effectiveness improved her own nutrition and thereby increased her life expectancy and fertility."[6]

We postulate, as Tanner and Bleier do, that in the slow advance from upright hominids to the fully developed humans of the Neanderthal period (100,000 B.C.) the role of females was crucial. Sometime after that period large-scale hunting by groups of men developed in Africa, Europe, and Northern Asia; the earliest evidence for the existence of bows and arrows can be dated only to 15,000 years ago. Since most of the explanations for the existence of a sexual division of labor postulate the existence of hunting/gathering societies, we need to look more closely at such societies in the Paleolithic and early Neolithic periods.

It is from the Neolithic that we derive surviving evidence of cave paintings and sculptures suggesting the pervasive veneration of the Mother-Goddess. We can understand why men and women might have chosen this as their first form of religious expression by considering the psychological bond between mother and child. We owe our insights into the complexities and importance of that bond largely to modern psychoanalytic accounts.[7] As Freud has shown us, the child's first experience of the world is one in which the total environment and the self are barely separated. The environment, which consists mostly of the mother as the source of food, warmth, and pleasure, only gradually becomes differentiated from the self, as the infant smiles or cries to secure gratification of its needs. When the infant's needs are not met and it experiences anxiety and pain associated with cold and hunger, it learns to acknowledge the overwhelming power of "the other out there," the mother. Modern psychological studies have given us detailed accounts of the complex interaction between mother and child and of the ways in which the mother's body response, her smile, her speech help to form the child's concept of world and self. It is in this humanizing interaction that the infant begins to derive pleasure in its ability to impose its will on the environment. The striving for autonomy and the recognition of selfhood are produced in the infant's struggle against the overwhelming presence of the mother.

The psychoanalytic accounts on which these generalizations are based derive from the study of motherhood in modern Western societies. Even so, they stress the crucial importance of the infant's experience of utter dependency and of the mother's overwhelming power for the character formation and identity of the individual. At a time when laws against infanticide as well as the availability of bottle feeding, heated rooms, and blankets provide infants with societal protection, regardless of the mother's inclinations, this "overwhelming power of the mother" seems more symbolic than real. For over two hundred years or more, other caretakers, male and female, could, if the need arose, provide maternal services to an infant without endangering that infant's chances of survival. Civilized society has interposed itself between mother and child and has altered motherhood. But under primitive conditions, before the institutions of civilized society were created, the actual power of the mother over the infant must have been awesome. Only the mother's arms and care sheltered the infant from cold; only her breast milk could provide the nourishment needed for survival. Her indifference or neglect meant certain death. The life-giving mother truly had power over life and death. No wonder that men and women, observing this dramatic and mysterious power of the female, turned to the veneration of Mother-Goddesses.[8]

My point here is to stress the *necessity*, which created the initial division of labor by which women do the mothering. For millennia group survival depended upon it, and no alternative was available.

Under the extreme and dangerous conditions under which primitive humans lived, the survival into adulthood of at least two children for each coupling pair necessitated many pregnancies for each woman. Accurate data on prehistoric life span are hard to come by, but estimates based on skeletal studies place the average Paleolithic and Neolithic life-span between thirty and forty years. In the detailed study of 222 adult skeletons from Çatal Hüyük earlier cited, Lawrence Angel arrives at an average adult male life length of 34.3 years, with a female life length of 29.8 years. (This excludes from consideration those who died in childhood.)[9]

Women would need to have had more pregnancies than live births, as continued to be the case also in historic times in agricultural societies. Infancy was much prolonged, since mothers nursed their infants for two to three years. Thus, we may assume that it was absolutely essential for group survival that most nubile women devote most of their adulthood to pregnancy, child-bearing, and nursing. One would expect that men and women would accept such necessity and construct beliefs, mores, and values within their cultures to sustain such necessary practices.

It would follow that women would choose or prefer those economic activities which could be combined easily with their mothering duties. Although it is reasonable to assume that some women in every tribe or band were physically able to hunt, it would follow that women would not want to hunt regularly for big game, because of their being physically encumbered by children carried in the womb, on the hip, or on the back. Further, while a baby slung on the back might not prevent a mother from participating in hunting, a crying baby might. Examples cited by anthropologists of hunting/gathering tribes in the contemporary world, in which alternate arrangements are made for child care and in which women occasionally do take part in hunting, do not contradict the above argument.[10] They merely show what it is possible for societies to arrange and to try; they do not show what was the likely historically predominant mode which enabled societies to survive. Obviously, given the precarious and short life spans I have cited above for the Neolithic period, tribes which put the lives of their nubile women at risk by hunting or by participating in warfare, thereby also increasing the likelihood of their injury in accidents, would not tend to survive as well as tribes in which these women were otherwise employed. Thus, the first sexual division of labor, by which men did the big-game hunting and children and women the small-game hunting and food gathering, seems to derive from biological sex differences.[11] These biological sex differences are not differences in the strength and endurance of men and women but solely reproductive differences, specifically women's ability to nurse babies. Having said this, I want to stress that my acceptance of a "biological explanation" holds only for the earliest stages of human development and does not mean that a later sexual division of labor based on women's mothering is "natural." On the contrary, I will show that male dominance is a *historic* phenomenon in that it arose out of a biologically determined given situation and became a culturally created and enforced structure over time.

My synthesis does not mean to imply that all primitive societies are so organized as to prevent mothers from economic activity. We know from the study of past and present primitive societies that groups find various ways of structuring the division of labor for child-rearing so as to free mothers for a great variety of economic activities. Some mothers take their children with them over long distances; in other cases older children and old people act as child-tenders.[12] Clearly, the link between child-bearing and child-rearing for women is culturally determined and subject to societal manipulation. My point is to stress that the earliest sexual division of labor by which women *chose* occupations compatible with their mothering and child-raising activities were *functional*, hence acceptable to men and women alike.

Prolonged and helpless human infancy creates the strong mother-child bond. This socially necessary relationship is fortified by evolution during the earliest stages of humankind's development. Faced with new situations and changing environments, tribes and groups in which women did not mother well or which did not guard the health and survival of their nubile women, probably could not and did not survive. Or, seen another way, groups that accepted and institutionalized a functional sexual division of labor were more likely to survive.

We can only speculate on the personalities and self-perceptions of people living under such conditions as prevailed in the Neolithic. Necessity must have imposed restraints on men as well as on women. It took courage to leave the shelter of cave or hut to confront wild animals with primitive weapons, to roam far from home and risk encounters with potentially hostile neighboring tribes. Men and women must have developed the courage necessary for self-defense and the defense of the young. Because of their culture-bound tendency to focus on the activities of men, ethnographers have given us much information about the consequences for the development of self-confidence and competence in man the hunter. Basing herself on ethnographic evidence, Simone de Beauvoir has speculated that it was this early division of labor from which the inequality between the sexes springs and which has doomed woman to "immanence"—to the pursuit of daily, never-ending repetitious toil—as against the daring exploits of man, which lead him to "transcendence." Tool-making, inventions, the development of weapons are all described as deriving from man's activities in pursuit of subsistence.[13] But the psychological growth of women has received far less attention and has usually been described in terms befitting a modern housewife more than a member of a Stone Age tribe. Elise Boulding, in her overview of women's past, has synthesized anthropological scholar-ship to present a considerably different interpretation. Boulding sees in the Neolithic societies an egalitarian sharing of work, in which each sex developed appropriate skills and knowledge essential for group survival. She tells us that food gathering demanded elaborate knowl-edge of the ecology, of plants and trees and roots, their properties as food and as medicine. She describes primitive woman as guardian of the domestic fire, as the inventor of clay and woven vessels, by means of which the tribe's surpluses could be saved for lean times. She describes woman as having elicited from plants and trees and fruits the secrets of transforming their products into healing substances, into dyes and hemp and yarn and clothing. Woman knew how to transform the raw materials and dead animals into nurturing prod-ucts. Her skills must have been as manifold as those of man and certainly as essential. Her knowledge was perhaps greater or at least as great as his; it is easy to imagine that it would have seemed to her quite sufficient. In the development of ritual and rites, of music and dance and poetry, she had as much of a part as he did. And yet she must have known herself responsible for life-giving and nurtur-ance. Woman, in precivilized society, must have been man's equal and may well have felt herself to be his superior.[14]

Psychoanalytic literature and most recently Nancy Chodorow's feminist reinterpretation provide us with useful descriptions of the process by which gender is created out of the fact that women do the mothering of children. Let us see if these theories have validity for describing a process of historical development. Chodorow argues that "the relationship to the mother differs in systematic ways for boys and girls, beginning in the earliest periods."[15] Boys and girls learn to expect from women the infinite, accepting love of a mother, but they also associate with women their fears of powerlessness. In order to find their identity, boys develop themselves as other-than-the-mother; they identify with the father and turn away from emotional expression toward action in the world. Because it is women who do the mothering of children, Chodorow says:

> . . . growing girls come to define and experience themselves as continuous with others; their experience of self contains more flexible or permeable ego boundaries. Boys come to define themselves as more separate and distinct, with a greater sense of rigid ego boundaries and differentiation. The basic feminine sense of self is connected to the world, the basic masculine sense of self is separate.[16]

By the way in which their selfhood is defined against the nurturant mother, boys are prepared for participation in the public sphere. Girls, identifying with the mother and always keeping their close primary relationship with her, even as they transfer their love interest to men, are prepared for greater participation in "relational spheres." Gender-defined boys and girls are prepared "to assume the adult gender roles which situate women primarily within the sphere of reproduction in a sexually unequal society."[17]

Chodorow's sophisticated feminist reinterpretation of the Freudian explanation for the creation of gendered personalities is grounded in industrial Western society and its kinship and familial relations. It is doubtful that it is even applicable to people of color living within such societies, which should make us cautious about generalizing from it. Still, she makes a strong argument for the psychological undergirding upon which social relations and institutions rest. She and others argue convincingly that we must look to "motherhood" in patriarchal society, its structure and the relationships it engenders, if we wish to alter the relations of the sexes and end the subordination of women.[18]

I would speculate that the kind of personality formation Chodorow describes as the result of women mothering children in present-day industrialized societies did not occur in primitive societies of the Neolithic. Rather, women's mothering and nurturing activities, associated with their self-sufficiency in food gathering and their sense of competence in many, varied life-essential skills, must have been experienced by men and women as a source of strength and, probably, magic power. In some societies women jealously guarded their group "secrets," their magic, their knowledge of healing herbs. The anthropologist Lois Paul, reporting on a twentieth-century Guatemalan Indian village, says that the mystery and awe surrounding menstruation contributes in women "to a sense of participation in the mystic powers of the universe." Women manipulate men's fear that menstrual blood will threaten their virility by making of menstruation a symbolic weapon.[19]

In civilized society it is girls who have the greatest difficulty in ego formation. I would speculate that in primitive society that burden must have been on boys, whose fear and awe of the mother had to be transformed by collective action into identification with the male group. Whether mothers and their young children bonded with other such mother-child groups for their gathering and food-processing activities or whether men took the initiative in bringing young boys within their group must remain a matter of conjecture. The evidence from surviving primitive societies shows many different ways in which the sexual division of labor is structured into societal institutions, which bond young boys to males: sex-segregated preparation for initiation rites; membership in same-sex lodges and participation in same-sex rituals are just some of the examples. Inevitably, big-game hunting bands would have led to male bonding, which must have been greatly strengthened by warfare and the preparation necessary to turn boys into warriors. Just as effective mothering skills of women were essential to ensuring tribal survival and must have therefore been greatly appreciated, so were the hunting and warfare skills of men. One can easily postulate that those tribes which did not develop men skilled in warfare and defense eventually succumbed to those tribes that fostered these skills in their men. These evolutionary arguments have frequently been made, but I am here arguing also in favor of a psychological argument based on changing historical conditions. The ego formation of the individual male, which must have taken place within a context of fear, awe, and possibly dread of the female, must have led men to create social institutions to bolster their egos, strengthen their self-confidence, and validate their sense of worth.

Theorists have offered a variety of hypotheses to explain the rise of man, the warrior, and the propensity of men to create militaristic structures. These have ranged from biological explanations (men's higher testosterone levels and greater strength make them more aggressive) to psychological ones (men compensate for their inability to bear children by sexual dominance over women and by aggression toward other men). Freud saw the origin of male aggressiveness in the Oedipal rivalry of father and son for the love of the mother and postulated that men built civilization to compensate for the frustration of their sexual instincts in early childhood. Feminists, beginning with Simone de Beauvoir, have been greatly influenced by such ideas, which made it possible to explain patriarchy as caused either by male biology or by male psychology. Thus, Susan Brownmiller sees man's *ability* to rape women leading to their *propensity* to rape women and shows how this has led to male dominance over women and to male supremacy. Elizabeth Fisher ingeniously argued that the domestication of animals taught men their role in procreation and that the practice of the forced mating of animals led men to the idea of raping women. She claimed that the brutalization and violence connected with animal domestication led to men's sexual dominance and institutionalized aggression. More recently, Mary O'Brien built an elaborate explanation of the origin of male dominance on men's psychological need to compensate for their inability to bear children through the construction of institutions of dominance and, like Fisher, dated this "discovery" in the period of the discovery of animal domestication.[20]

These hypotheses, while they lead us in interesting directions, all suffer from the tendency to seek single-cause explanations, and those basing their arguments on the discoveries connected with animal husbandry are factually wrong. Animal husbandry was introduced, at least in the Near East, around 8000 B.C., and we have evidence of relatively egalitarian societies, such as in Čatal Hüyük, which practiced animal husbandry 2000 to 4000 years later. There cannot therefore be a causal connection. It seems to me far more likely that the development of intertribal warfare during periods of economic scarcity fostered the rise to power of men of military achievement. As we will discuss later, their greater prestige and standing may have increased their propensity to exercise authority over women and later over men of their own tribe. But these factors alone could not have been sufficient to explain the vast societal changes which occurred with the advent of sedentarism and agriculture. To understand these in all their complexity our theoretical model must now take into consideration the practice of the exchange of women.[21]

The "exchange of women," a phenomenon observed in tribal societies in many different areas of the world, has been identified by the anthropologist Claude Lévi-Strauss as the leading cause of female subordination. It may take many different forms, such as the forceful removal of women from their home tribe (bride stealing); ritual defloration or rape; negotiated marriages. It is always preceded by taboos on endogamy and by the indoctrination of women, from earliest childhood on, to an acceptance of their obligation to their kin to consent to such enforced marriages. Lévi Strauss says:

> The total relationship of exchange which constitutes marriage is not established between a man and a woman . . . but between two groups of men, and the woman figures only as one of the objects in the exchange, not as one of the partners. . . . This remains true even when the girl's feelings are taken into consideration, as, moreover, is usually the case. In acquiescing to the proposed union, she precipitates or allows the exchange to take place; she cannot alter its nature.[22]

Lévi-Strauss reasons that in this process women are "reified"; they become dehumanized and are thought of more as things than as humans.

A number of feminist anthropologists have accepted this position and have elaborated on this theme. Matrilocality structures kinship in such a way that a man leaves his family of origin to reside with his wife or his wife's family. Patrilocality structures kinship in such a way that a woman must leave her family of birth and reside with her husband or her husband's family. This observed fact has led to the assumption that the kinship shift from matriliny to patriliny must be a significant turning point in the relation of the sexes, and must be coincident with the subordination of women. But how and why did such arrangements develop? We have already discussed the scenario by which men, possibly recently risen to power due to their warfare skills, coerced unwilling women. But why were women exchanged and not men? C. D. Darlington offers one explanation. He sees exogamy as a cultural innovation, which becomes accepted because it offers an evolutionary advantage. He postulates an instinctive desire in humans to control population to "optimum density" for a given environment. Tribes achieve this by sexual control, by rituals structuring males and females into appropriate sex roles, and by resorting to abortion, infanticide, and homosexuality when necessary. According to this essentially evolutionist reasoning, population control made control over female sexuality mandatory.[23]

There are other possible explanations: supposing grown men were exchanged among tribes, what would ensure their loyalty to the tribe to which they were traded? Men's bond to their offspring was not, then, strong enough to ensure their submission for the sake of their children. Men would be capable of violence against members of the strange tribe; with their experience in hunting and long distance travel they might easily escape and then return as warriors to seek vengeance. Women, on the other hand, would be more easily coerced, most likely by rape. Once married or mothers of children, they would give loyalty to their children and to their children's relatives and would thus make a potentially strong bond with the tribe of affiliation. This was, in fact, the way slavery developed historically, as we will see later. Once again, woman's biological function made her more readily adaptable for this new, culturally created role of pawn.

One might also postulate that not women but children of both sexes might have been used as pawns for the purpose of assuring intertribal peace, as they were frequently used in historical time among ruling elites. Possibly, the practice of the exchange of women got started that way. Children of both sexes were exchanged and on maturity married into the new tribe.

Boulding, always stressing women's "agency," assumes that it was women—in their function of keepers of the homeplace—who engaged in the necessary negotiations which led to intertribal coupling. Women develop cultural flexibility and sophistication by their intertribal linkage role. Women, removed from their own culture, straddle two cultures and learn the ways of both. The knowledge they derive from this may give them access to power and certainly to influence.[24]

I find Boulding's observations useful for reconstructing the gradual process by which women may have initiated or participated in establishing the exchange of women. In anthropological literature we have some examples of queens, in their role of head of state, acquiring many "wives" for whom they then arranged marriages which serve to increase the queen's wealth and influence.[25]

If boys and girls were exchanged as pawns and their offspring were incorporated into the tribe to which they had been given, clearly the tribe holding more girls than boys would increase in population more rapidly than the tribe accepting more boys. As long as children were a threat to the survival of the tribe or, at best, a liability, such distinctions would not be noticed or would not matter. But if, due to changes in the environment or in the tribal economy, children became an asset as potential labor power, one would expect the exchange of children of both sexes to give way to the exchange of women. The factors leading to this development are well explained, I believe, by Marxist structuralist anthropologists.

The process we are now discussing occurs at different times in different parts of the world; yet it shows regularity of causes and outcome. Approximately at the time when hunting/gathering or horticulture gives way to agriculture, kinship arrangements tend to shift from matriliny to patriliny, and private property develops. There is, as we have seen, disagreement about the sequence of events. Engels and those who follow him think that private property developed first, *causing* "the world historic overthrow of the female sex." Lévi-Strauss and Claude Meillassoux believe that it is the exchange of women through which private property is eventually created. Meillassoux offers a detailed description of the transition stage.

In hunting/gathering societies men, women, and children engage in production and consume what they produce. The social relations among them are unstable, unstructured, voluntary. There is no need for kinship structures or for structured exchanges among tribes. This conceptual model (for which it is somewhat difficult to find actual examples) gives way to a transition model, an intermediate state—horticultural society. The harvest, based on roots and cuttings, is unstable and subject to climatic variations. Their inability to preserve crops over several years makes people dependent on hunting, fishing, and gathering as food supplements. In this period, when matrilineal, matrilocal systems abound, group survival demands the demographic equalization of men and women. Meillassoux argues that women's biological vulnerability in childbirth led tribes to procure more women from other groups, and that this tendency toward the theft of women led to constant intertribal warfare. In the process, a warrior culture emerged. Another consequence of this theft of women is that the conquered women were protected by the men who had conquered them or by the entire conquering tribe. In the process, women were thought of as possessions, as things—they became reified—while men became the reifiers because they conquered and protected. Women's reproductive capacity is first recognized as a tribal resource, then, as ruling elites develop, it is acquired as the property of a particular kin group.

This occurs with the development of agriculture. The material conditions of grain agriculture demand group cohesiveness and continuity over time, thus strengthening household structure. In order to produce a harvest, workers of one production cycle are indebted for food and seeds to workers of a previous production cycle. Since the amount of food depends on the availability of labor, production becomes the chief concern. This has two consequences: it strengthens the influence of older males and it increases the tribes' incentive for acquiring more women. In the fully developed society based on

plow agriculture, women and children are indispensable to the production process, which is cyclical and labor intensive. Children have
now become an economic asset. At this stage tribes seek to acquire
the reproductive potential of women, rather than women themselves. Men do not produce babies directly; thus it is women, not
men, who are exchanged. This practice becomes institutionalized in
incest taboos and patrilocal marriage patterns. Elder males, who provide continuity in the knowledge pertaining to production, now
mystify these "secrets" and wield power over the young men by
controlling food, knowledge, and women. They control the exchange
of women, enforce restrictions on their sexual behavior, and acquire
private property in women. The young men must offer labor services to the old men for the privilege of gaining access to women.
Under such circumstances women also become the spoil for the warriors, which encourages and reinforces the dominance of older men
over the community. Finally, "women's world historic defeat" through
the overthrow of matriliny and matrilocality is made possible, and it
proves advantageous to the tribes who achieve it.

It should be noted that in Meillassoux's scheme the control over
reproduction (women's sexuality) *precedes* the acquisition of private
property. Thus, Meillassoux stands Engels on his head, a feat Marx
performed for Hegel.

Meillassoux's work opens new vistas in the debate over origins,
although feminist critics must object to his androcentric model, in
which women figure only as passive victims.[26] We should also note
that Meillassoux's model makes it clear that it is not women who
are being reified, but women's reproductive capacity, yet he and other
structuralist anthropologist continue to speak of the reification of
women. The distinction is important, and we will be discussing it
further. There are other questions his theory does not answer. How
did elder men acquire control over agriculture? If our earlier speculations about social relations of the sexes in hunting/gathering tribes
are correct, and if the generally accepted fact that it was women who
developed horticulture is accurate, then one would expect it to be
women who controlled the product of agricultural labor. But here
other factors must enter our consideration.

Not all societies went through a horticultural stage. In many
societies herding and animal husbandry alone or in conjuction with
gathering activities preceded the development of agriculture. Animal
husbandry was most likely developed by men. It was an occupation
which led to the accumulation of surpluses in livestock, meat, or

pelts. One would expect these to be accumulated by the men who generated them. Further, plow agriculture initially demanded the strength of men, and certainly was not an occupation pregnant women or lactating mothers would have chosen, except in an auxiliary fashion. Thus, agricultural economic practice reinforced men's control over surpluses, which may also have been acquired by conquest in intertribal warfare. Another possible factor contributing to the development of private property in the hands of males may be the asymmetrical allocation of leisure time. Horticultural activities are more productive than subsistence gathering and produce leisure time. But the allocation of leisure time is uneven: men benefit more from it than women, due to the fact that the food-preparation and child-rearing activities of women continue unrelieved. Thus, men presumably could employ their new leisure time to develop craft skills, initiate rituals to enhance their power and influence and manage surpluses. I do not wish to suggest either determinism or conscious manipulation here—quite the contrary. Things developed in certain ways, which then had certain consequences which neither men nor women intended. Nor could they have had an awareness of them, any more than modern men launching the brave new world of industrialization could have had an awareness of its consequences in regard to pollution and its impact on the ecology. By the time consciousness of the process and of its consequences could develop, it was too late, at least for women, to halt the process.

The Danish anthropologist Peter Aaby points out that Meillassoux's evidence was largely based on the European model, involving the interaction of horticultural activity and animal husbandry, and on examples taken from South American lowlands Indians. Aaby cites cases, such as those of Australian hunting tribes, where the control of women exists in the absence of horticultural activity. He next cites the case of the Iroquois, a society in which women were neither reified nor dominated, as an example of horticulturists who do not turn to male dominance. He argues that under ecologically favorable conditions it would be possible to maintain demographic balance within a tribe without resorting to the importation of women. It is not only production relations but also "ecology and social-biological reproduction which are the determining or critical factors. . . ."[27] Nevertheless, since all agricultural societies have reified women's and not men's reproductive capacity, one must conclude that such systems have an advantage in regard to the expansion and appropriation of surpluses over systems based on complementarity between the sexes. In the latter systems there are no means available for forcing producers to increase production.

Neolithic tools were relatively simple, so that anyone could make them. Land was not a scarce resource. Thus, neither tools nor land offered any opportunity for appropriation. But in a situation in which ecological conditions and irregularities in biological reproduction threatened the survival of the group, people would search for more reproducers—that is, women. The appropriation of men, such as captives (which occurs only at a later stage), would simply not fill the needs of group survival. Thus, the first appropriation of private property consists of the appropriation of the labor of women as *reproducers.*[28]

Aaby concludes:

> The connection between the reification of women on the one hand and the state and private property on the other is exactly the opposite of that posed by Engels and his followers. Without the reification of women as a historically given socio-structural feature, the origin of private property and the state will remain inexplicable.[29]

If we follow Aaby's argument, which I find persuasive, we must conclude that in the course of the agricultural revolution the exploitation of human labor and the sexual exploitation of women become inextricably linked.

The story of civilization is the story of men and women struggling up from necessity, from their helpless dependence on nature, to freedom and their partial mastery over nature. In this struggle women were longer confined to species-essential activities than men and were therefore more vulnerable to being disadvantaged. My argument sharply distinguishes between biological necessity, to which both men and women submitted and adapted, and culturally constructed customs and institutions, which forced women into subordinate roles. I have tried to show how it might have come to pass that women agreed to a sexual division of labor, which would eventually disadvantage them, without having been able to foresee the later consequences.

Freud's statement, which I discussed in a different context, that for women "anatomy is destiny" is wrong because it is ahistorical and reads the distant past into the present without making allowances for changes over time. Worse, this statement has been read as a prescription for present and future: not only is anatomy destiny for women, but it *should* be. What Freud should have said is that for women anatomy *once was* destiny. That statement is accurate and historical. What once was, no longer is so, and no longer must be nor should it be so.

WITH MEILLASSOUX AND AABY we have moved from the realm of purely theoretical speculation into the consideration of evidence based on anthropological data from primitive societies in historical time. We have taken material evidence, such as ecology, climate, and demographic factors, into consideration and stressed the complex interplay of various factors which must have affected the developments we are trying to understand. There is no way we can bring hard evidence to bear on these prehistoric transitions other than by inference and comparison with what we know. As we will see, the explanatory hypothesis we have proposed can be checked against later historical evidence at various points.

There are a few facts of which we can be certain on the basis of archaeological evidence. Sometime during the agricultural revolution relatively egalitarian societies with a sexual division of labor based on biological necessity gave way to more highly structured societies in which both private property and the exchange of women based on incest taboos and exogamy were common. The earlier societies were often matrilineal and matrilocal, while the latter surviving societies were predominantly patrilineal and patrilocal. Nowhere is there any evidence of a reverse process, going from patriliny to matriliny. The more complex societies featured a division of labor no longer based only on biological distinctions, but also on hierarchy and the power of some men over other men and all women. A number of scholars have concluded that the shift here described coincides with the formation of archaic states.[30] It is with this period then that theoretical speculation must end, and historical inquiry begin.

THREE

The Stand-In Wife and the Pawn

THE PROCESS BY WHICH scattered Neolithic villages became agricultural communities, then urban centers, and finally states has been called "the urban revolution" or "the rise of civilization." It is a process which occurs at different times in different places throughout the world: first, in the great river and coastal valleys of China, Mesopotamia, Egypt, India, and Mesoamerica; later in Africa, Northern Europe, and Malaysia. Archaic states are everywhere characterized by the emergence of property classes and hierarchies; commodity production with a high degree of specialization and organized trade over distant regions; urbanism; the emergence and consolidation of military elites; kingship; the institutionalization of slavery; a transition from kin dominance to patriarchal families as the chief mode of distributing goods and power. In Mesopotamia, there also occur important changes in the position of women: female subordination within the family becomes institutionalized and codified in law; prostitution becomes established and regulated; with increasing specialization of work, women are gradually excluded from certain occupations and professions. After the invention of writing and the establishment of formal learning, women are excluded from equal access to such education. The cosmogonies, which provide the religious underpinning for the archaic state, subordinate female deities to chief male gods, and feature myths of origin which legitimate male ascendancy.[1]

Most theories of the origin of the archaic state have been single-cause, prime-mover theories, stressing in turn the following as causes: capital accumulation due to new technologies, which results in class stratification and class struggle (Marx, Engels, Childe); the rise of strong bureaucracies due to the need for the development of large-scale irrigation projects (Wittfogel); population increase and population pressure (Fried); population pressure in a circumscribed environment leading to militarism, which in turn leads to state formation (Carneiro). Each of these explanations has been criticized and replaced by more complex, system-oriented explanations, which stress the interactions of a variety of factors. Robert McC. Adams, while recognizing the importance of environmental and technological factors in the growth of civilizations, stressed that the core of the urban revolution lay in changes in social organization. Intensification of agricultural production due to specialization led to a stable food base, which allowed the population to increase. Food redistribution was managed by the temple community, which gave this group the power to coerce farmers and herders to produce surplus. This could best be done by increasing irrigation, which in turn increased the power of the temple elite and led to sharper distinctions of wealth between those who owned land closer to a steady water supply and those who did not. This early class formation led to the next important shift in societal structure—that from kin-based to class-based society.[2]

It is this change from kin-based to class-based social structures which has particular significance for the history of women. Several feminist writers have recently called attention to this aspect of the urban revolution which will be further explored in this chapter. The anthropologist Rayna Rapp points to the conflict between kinship groups and rising elites and concludes that ''kinship structures were the great losers in the civilization process.''

> In prestate societies, total social production was organized through kinship. As states gradually arose, kinship structures got stripped and transformed to underwrite the existence and legitimacy of more powerful politicized domains. In this process . . . women were subordinated with (and in relation to) kinship.[3]

We will need to examine in the case of Mesopotamian societies just how this process of transformation took place and why it took the form it did. We must not imagine this as a linear process, which uniformly developed in different regions, but rather as a slow accretion of incremental changes, which occurred at different speeds in different regions and with varying outcomes. In the words of Charles

Redman, it "should be conceptualized as a series of interacting in-cremental processes that were triggered by favorable ecological and cultural conditions and that continued to develop through mutually reinforcing interactions."[4] There were, overall, three stages in the urban revolution in Mesopotamia: the emergence of temple-towns, the growth of city-states, and the development of national states.

We have earlier discussed Neolithic towns of considerable size, such as Čatal Hüyük and Hacilar in Anatolia, in the sixth and eighth millennia B.C. Even in these early settlements burial customs reveal differences in wealth and status among the town dwellers, as well as the existence of craft specialization and distant trade. One can as-sume that similar village and town communities existed in the Mes-copotamian region. While Čatal Hüyük and Hacilar disappeared as settlements before 5000 B.C., village farming communities in Mes-opotamia gradually spread into the southern lowlands. Growing populations in a constricted space on land, which was fertile only if water was available, inevitably led to the development of irrigation. This would lead to distinctions in wealth, depending on the location of a farmer's land and to tension between communal and private property rights and interests.

In an ecologically constricted space, growing populations can be supplied only by increasing agricultural production or by expansion. The former leads to the development of elites, the latter to the de-velopment of militarism, first on a voluntary, then on a professional basis. In Mesopotamia, these social formations took the form of temple-towns, which developed in the fourth and third millennia B.C.[5] Under conditions of intertribal warfare, the existence of towns acts as a magnet for the populations of surrounding villages, who migrate to the city to find work or to seek protection in times of war or famine. Such populations then became the laborers in the large enterprises which made possible the construction of huge temple complexes and of centralized irrigation projects. The temple engaged in complex religious, political, and economic activities. Archaeologi-cal evidence shows that from 3000 B.C. on temple hierarchies coor-dinated the construction and maintenance of a system of canals that were many miles long and demanded the cooperation of a number of communities. The financing of such vast enterprises, the mainte-nance of labor squads paid in rations, and the investment of sur-pluses in the mass production of certain craft products for export, all led to the consolidation of power and the specialization of function in the hands of a temple bureaucracy. The temple fostered the development of crafts, which implies the strengthening of craft specialization, including metallurgy and the large-scale production of textiles for export. The temple controlled raw materials and monopolized trade. In turn, the management and administration of such large projects fostered the rise of skilled administrative elites and eventually led to the development of standardized information systems.

The first symbol systems, or tokens, developed in connection with trading activities and the keeping of accounts. Out of these tokens developed systems of counting and writing.[6] The earliest clay tablets in Sumer were ration lists; records of tribute and donations and lists of divine names. The invention of fully developed writing which incorporated grammatical elements occurred shortly after 3000 B.C. in Sumer. It marked a watershed in the development of Mesopotamian civilization. It is generally believed that it originated in the temples and palaces and was a knowledge that greatly strengthened the leadership role of the elites. Schools systematically trained scribes to meet all the needs of governance, including sacred knowledge. Later, the establishment of archives further institutionalized the administration of economic and political activities in temple and palace. It is, of course, with the invention of writing and the keeping of written records that history begins.

The protohistoric period (ca.3500-2800 B.C.) coincides with the archaeological Uruk V—Early Dynastic period. It can be assumed that during this period military elites developed next to temple elites and soon became an independent and rival force in society. Military strong men would first become chieftains over villages and later establish their dominance over previously communally held temple lands and herds, gradually pushing the priests into the background. We will examine the process in detail below in the case of Urukagina of Lagash.[7] Later the strongest of these chieftains would set themselves up as kings, usurping power over the temples and treating temple property as their own. In the ensuing centuries of intercity warfare, the strongest of these rulers would unite a number of such city-states into a kingdom or a national state.[8]

The development of militarism combined with the need for a large labor force for the construction of public projects led to the practice of turning captives into slaves and to the eventual institutionalization of slavery, and with it of structured classes. We will discuss this development and its impact on women in detail in the next chapter. What concerns us here is that all these various, interacting, and mutually reinforcing processes went in the direction of strengthening male dominance in public life and in external relations, while weakening the power of communal and kin-based structures. In the protohistoric period kinship groups continued to be important, some holding land titles, others recruiting guilds of craftsmen or organizing recruits for military service. In his comparison of the urban revolution in Mesopotamia (3900-2300 B.C.) and in Central Mexico (100 B.C.–1500 A.D.) Robert McC. Adams finds a similar function performed by Mexican kinship units, the "calpyllis," which are used to distribute wealth and power in the new state. They form guilds, provide men for army service, and are allocated slaves by the state. As the state becomes consolidated, changes in kinship structure become solidified.[9]

In the Inca empire the conquerors extended their rule by forcing conquered villages to provide virgins for state service and as potential wives for Inca noblemen. This interference in the sexual and marriage patterns of the conquered served the dual function of undermining kinship structures and of singling out particular kin groups for alliances with the conquerors.[10] We will see a similar process at work in Mesopotamia in the practice of destroying conquered towns, killing the men, and deporting the women and children to slavery in the land of the conquerors, and in the network of marriage alliances among rulers to cement interstate cooperation.

Modern archaeological work in Mesopotamia has uncovered tens of thousands of clay tablets that document the social order in Sumer in the third millennium and in Babylon in the second millennium B.C., which we will use to highlight changes in the position of women. Such sources can be compared and brought into reference with seals, statues, and other artifacts, as well as with the usual archaeological evidence from graves and town sites. Since many of the clay tablets contain poems, hymns, and laws, in addition to more mundane remnants of commercial and domestic transactions, we can reconstruct this Bronze Age civilization with more evidence than is true for other early civilizations. As will be the case for much of the historical period to follow that age, evidence for upper-class women is easier to come by than for lower-class women. Since we are not attempting to write a social history of women in the Ancient Near East, but rather to trace the evolution of concepts of gender, our account will select significant models and moments rather than attempt a full historic reconstruction.

One of the earliest-known portraits of a woman in Sumer is a carefully sculpted head from Uruk, portraying a woman of great dignity and beauty, who might have been a priestess, a queen, or a goddess. This unique sculpture, dating from between 3100 and 2900 B.C., personifies the major roles played by aristocratic women who were active in temple, palace, and economic management. (See illustration section, number 5.)

It is characteristic of leadership in this early period that there is a merging of divine and secular power personified by the ruler. The king list, a document written down in about 1800 B.C., traces the successive dynasties for the major cities in Mesopotamia back into the third millennium. While the chronologies are somewhat inflated, archaeologists have verified some of the data with other evidence. The earliest Sumerian dynasties were based in the cities of Kish, Warka, and Ur. According to the king list, the founder of the dynasty of Kish was Queen Ku-Baba, who is listed as having reigned a hundred years. She is identified as having formerly been a tavern-keeper, an occupation which puts her at the margins of society. She was later identified with the goddess Kubaba, who was worshiped in Northern Mesopotamia.[11] She is the only woman listed in the king list as reigning in her own right, but the merging of her historic personality with that of a divinity is not unlike that of the mythical demigod Gilgamesh, ruler of Warka, who supposedly reigned in the Early Dynastic period, but for whose historical existence there is no hard evidence, and whose exploits are immortalized in the epic of Gilgamesh.

The excavations at Ur made in 1922–34 by Sir Leonard Woolley in behalf of the British Museum offer us a startling insight into the social structure of Sumerian society in the Early Dynastic period, around 2500 B.C. The discovery of 1850 graves, among them sixteen royal graves, yielded important information about burial customs in a society characterized by class stratification, wealth, and artistic development as well as by a fairly advanced technology.

In one of the graves a lapis lazuli seal inscribed to "Ninbanda, the queen, wife of Mesanepada" identifies a woman, who may have been the wife of a king of the first dynasty of Ur. The evidence of her husband's existence is important in that it confirmed the historical accuracy of the Sumerian king list.[12]

Of particular interest to us are the findings in royal grave 789, that of a king whose identity has not been clearly established, and in grave 800, that of Queen Pu-abi, who probably lived around 2500 B.C.[13] Her identity was established by a cylinder-seal of lapis lazuli inscribed with her name, which was found near her body. In each case the royal body was found in a stone chamber, together with several others, presumably servants. This evidence of human sacrifice illuminates a set of religious beliefs and values associated only with this early period. It is significant that the hundreds of other graves in the cemeteries of Ur show no sign of human sacrifice; only the royal graves do. It is also noteworthy that two queens are buried with their servants, just as the kings are, which would indicate that what was being honored by human sacrifice was kingship and that at this early period this divine quality could reside in a woman as well as in a man.[14]

In graves 789 and 800 the burial chamber was located at the end of a deep pit, which formed the mass grave for the deceased person's retinue. The queen's body was found on a bier; she had been buried with her fancy head-dress of gold, lapis lazuli, and carnelian, an exquisite gold cup in her hand. Two female attendants were crouched against her bier, which was surrounded by burial offerings of splendid metal and stone work. Woolley surmised that during the burial ceremony the queen and her personal servants were buried first in the lowermost tomb chamber, which then was sealed. The second phase of the funeral ceremony took place in the pit surrounding the chamber, where fires were lit, a funeral feast held, and offerings made to the gods. Then the chief domestic servants and courtiers were arrayed in the pit. Some kind of ceremony must have taken place, for musicians in the pit were buried with their fingers still resting on their instruments. The human sacrifices were probably first drugged or poisoned, as evidenced by the presence of a drinking cup near each body, then the pit was immured and covered with earth.[15]

In grave 789, the king's grave, the skeletons of six soldiers were found. They, presumably, were guardians of the pit who had led in oxen drawing four-wheeled carts. In each cart the driver's body remained in the position appropriate to his task. Against the wall there were nine bodies of women adorned in fine jewelry; in all there were sixty-three men and women buried with the king. At a later date part of the entrance shaft to this grave was reused for grave 800, the queen's grave. In this entrance there were an ox-drawn sledge, a lyre and other valuable domestic utensils, and the skeletons of ten men and ten women. The women wore elaborate head-dresses and jewelry and may have been court musicians.

Another grave, named the Great Death Pit, contained the bodies of six men and sixty-eight richly adorned women. Again, six guards were lined up at the entrance; the women consisted of four harpists and sixty-four ladies-in-waiting wearing gold and silver hair ribbons. The arrangement of the graves and the decorations and accompanying objects make it clear that, in the case of the mass graves, not only were there personal servants, presumably slaves, buried with the royal dead but most of the other victims were high-ranking courtiers and persons of distinction. According to Woolley:

> Clearly these people were not wretched slaves killed as oxen might be killed, but persons held in honour, wearing their robes of office, and coming, one hopes, voluntarily to a rite which would in their belief be but a passing from one world to another, from the service of a god on earth to that of the same god in another sphere.[16]

The last point is crucial in interpreting the findings in the cemeteries of Ur. We know that in a later period Sumerian kings were deified after their deaths and even in their lifetime. This evidence of human sacrifice seems to indicate that the practice originated earlier, in the protohistoric period. If the living king or queen had divine attributes and incorporated the divinity, then serving them in another world, the world of the gods, must have meant not supreme sacrifice but supreme honor. The skeletons in the grave pits showed no signs of violence or struggle, so they testify mutely to a belief in the divinity of kings and queens.[17] Another interesting implication from the findings at Ur concerns the conspicuous waste of expensive and finely crafted burial goods. Since these were present mainly in the royal graves, their burial may have served a function for the royal successor. The wasting of resources in the service of the gods is a ritual establishing the legitimacy of the successor, who could assume authority by renouncing the wealth of his predecessor. This would speak to the interpretation that "rituals were still needed to maintain the authority of the king during periods of succession," a fact which other historic evidence tends to support.[18] The burial of the king's chief servants and retainers would also assure that the new king would make a fresh start with his own group of loyal followers.

The royal tombs at Ur tell us that ruling queens shared in the status, power, wealth, and ascription of divinity with kings. They tell us of the wealth and high status of some women at the Sumerian courts, of their varied craft skills, their obvious economic privilege.

But the overwhelming preponderance of female skeletons over male among the buried retainers also speaks to their greater vulnerability and dependency as servants.

The willingness of royal servants to follow their lords into death reflected some of the basic beliefs of Sumerian religion. The world and human beings had been created for the service of the gods. People had no free will but were governed by the decision of the gods. The gods were lords, owning the cities and the temples, which they governed through their human representatives. These might be high-priests or secular rulers who at first governed as representatives of a council of elders. In times of crisis, such rulers might expand their personal power and come into conflict with temple authority. Secular rulers emerged in different cities under different circumstances, but they soon established their own power base.[19]

Thus, in Lagash, ca. 2350 B.C., the ruler Lugalanda seized power over the most important temples, those of the gods Ningirsu and Shulshag and the goddess Bau, by placing them under the administration of an official he had appointed and who was not, as formerly, a priest, and by appointing himself, his wife Baranamtarra, and other members of his family as temple administrators. He also referred to these temples as the private property of the *ensi* (ruler), no longer mentioned the name of the deities in temple documents, and levied taxes on the priesthood. Lugalanda and his wife became the largest landholders. The wife, Baranamtarra, shared in the *ensi's* power, managing her own private estates and those of the temple Bau. She sent diplomatic missions to neighboring states and bought and sold slaves.[20]

It is fortunate that extensive economic records of the temple of the goddess Bau have been preserved. These cover the years of Lugalanda and of his successor Urukagina, a period in which tensions between king and community are visible and the authority of the king is increased. Urukagina's short reign was marked by his "reforms," which he recorded as inscriptions on buildings. Urukagina seized power from Lugalanda, claiming that he acted in behalf of "boatmen, shepherds, fishermen and farmers," and implying that he was helped by the priesthood.[21] In the second year of his reign, Urukagina proclaimed himself king, assuming the title of *lugal*.

The reforms Urukagina proclaimed in his edict are the earliest documented effort to establish basic legal rights for citizens. Urukagina accused his predecessor of having taken over the gods' properties in the temples and claimed he had a covenant with the city-god of Lagash to protect the weak and the widowed from the powerful. He charged that under Lugalanda the "men of the *ensi*" had begun to assert control over the land owned by private owners, invading orchards and appropriating fruit by force. At the same time there had been priestly abuse of power in the form of excessive fees being charged for funerals and religious rituals. Urukagina enacted tax reforms, curbed the power of corrupt officials, and ruled the temples in the names of the gods. But scholars are divided in their evaluation of the effect of his reforms. One school regards his reign as a sort of popular revolution in which free men struggled against wealthier slaveowners; another sees it as indicating a transition from "temple economy" to secular power and kingship.[22] In a more recent analysis, K. Maekawa views Urukagina's "reforms" as an expansion of royal power, in that he developed the concept of the kingship endowed with divine sanction and extended this kingship concept to the domain of his wife, namely, the temple of the goddess Bau. The personnel of this temple greatly expanded in the year Urukagina made himself *lugal*. The concept of divinely endowed kingship had already begun to take hold in the reign of Urukagina's predecessors, but he concretized it in establishing the temple Bau as the second main temple in Lagash.[23] Although Urukagina claimed to have enacted his reforms under divine guidance to stop the abuses of power under his predecessor, they may have simply resulted in strengthening his position. There are no records of other temple-cities available, which would enable one to judge how typical this development was, and Maekawa seems to think it was not typical, but the documents offer us a significant insight in the way the transition to kingship with a new level of authority may have taken place.

The documents from the reign of Urukagina offer us some tantalizing glimpses of the lives of women. One of Urukagina's edicts reads: "Women of former times each married two men, but women of today have been made to give up this crime."[24] The edict continues to state that women committing this "crime" in Urukagina's time were stoned with stones inscribed with their evil intent. Elsewhere, the edict states that "if a woman speaks . . . disrespect- fully(?) to a man, that woman's mouth is crushed with a fired brick."[25] Recent feminist commentators have interpreted these "edicts" as evidence of the former practice of polyandry and of its end during Urukagina's regime.[26] This interpretation seems without substance, since there is no other piece of evidence available from anywhere in Mesopotamia of the practice of polyandry in the third millennium B.C.

The interpretation of cuneiform texts is a highly complex, technical matter and usually depends on corroborating evidence from other texts or from archaeological artifacts. Assyriologists have been justifiably cautious in interpreting this edict in the absence of such evidence. There are, however, at least two possible alternate interpretations of the text: one, that it refers to a tax reform, whereby a tax on divorces was eliminated, thus ending the abuse that a married woman who had not secured a divorce due to its high cost took a second husband. The other possible interpretation is that the edict refers to widows and forbids their remarriage. This seems to me the most likely interpretation, since restrictions on the remarriage of widows appear in various Mesopotamian law codes, and improvements in their situation are enacted in the Hammurabic laws considerably later.[27]

The second edict, concerning a woman's remarks addressed to a man, is even harder to interpret. If it refers to a sexual solicitation or a slanderous statement by a woman to a man, the penalty is relatively mild in terms of Mesopotamian standards of justice. The most we can say about it is that it seems an early instance of the regulation of female behavior by secular authority, although we must remember that Urukagina's edicts did not have the force of laws. The interpretation that Urukagina's edicts denote a sharp and decisive deterioration in the status of women seems unwarranted, especially in view of the additional evidence of women in positions of power, which we will discuss below.

In another of his "reforms" Urukagina decreed that the pay and compensation in food for three male funerary officials be sharply reduced and that a high-priestess be added to the list of funeral officials receiving pay. This tells us nothing about changes in the status of women, but it does tell us about the presence of women in high cultic office, a fact for which there is much corroborating evidence.

The economic records of the temple Bau offer a vivid picture of the various roles and functions women performed in the early parts of the third millennium, at least in Lagash. The temple of the goddess Bau, while its area extended over only approximately one square mile, employed between 1000 and 1200 persons year round. The entire administration of this temple and of its personnel was in the hands of Queen Shagshag, Urukagina's wife, who also managed the temple devoted to the children of the goddess Bau, which was nominally under the administration of the children of the royal couple.

As administrator of these two temples the queen exercised legal and economic authority over her domain. She also functioned as chief priestess in the temple.[28]

In the first year of Urukagina's reign the domestic staff of the queen consisted of 150 slave women employed as spinners and wool-workers, brewers, millers, and kitchen workers. The wage list also mentions one female slave singer and several musicians. Other laborers were free men, who drew weekly supplies of food and were also furnished seed-corn and plow animals. One hundred fishermen provided fish. The male swineherd employed six slave women to grind the grain for feeding the swine. In the kitchen there were fifteen cooks and twenty-seven female slaves doing menial work. The brewery employed forty male workers, who were free men, and six female slaves. Approximately ninety workers took care of animals, among them five cowherds, the chief of whom was the brother of the queen. This latter interesting bit of information from the wage lists tells us, incidentally, that the queen was, as her husband probably was, a commoner by birth.[29]

The record shows that under Urukagina's predecessor each of the royal children had had a complement of servants and had independently held properties. Each child had a wet nurse, a nursemaid, several maids, one cook, one smith, several slave women milling grain, a gardener, and several assistant gardeners. This lavishness was somewhat restricted under Urukagina's regime. There are no wet nurses listed, possibly because the children had outgrown the need of them, nor were there nursemaids. Each child had one or two personal servants, and a hairdresser served them all. Each child also had landholdings of his/her own and the slaves and artisans necessary for the maintenance of these holdings. The fact that King Urukagina consolidated his personal and family power and holdings, despite his assertions to the contrary, can be seen by comparing the personnel lists of the temple Bau for each year of Urukagina's regime: Year I - 434; Year II—the year of his *lugal*ship— 699; Year III - 678. A separately kept list of slave women and their children showed a similarly dramatic increase for Year II: Year I - 135; Year II - 229; Year III - 206; Year IV - 285; Year V - 188; Year VI - 221.[30]

Urukagina was violently overthrown by another usurper-king, Lugalzaggisi, from the city of Umma. Although the latter expanded his holdings and made himself supreme ruler of all of Sumer, he was not able to consolidate his conquests and administer them as a unified state. This feat was accomplished by the man who overthrew him and ended the independence of Lagash, King Sargon of Akkad (ca.2350-2230 B.C.). In the period of Urukagina we can, then, observe the earliest stage of the formation of kingship and city-states, which precedes the formation of nation-states. We notice that militarism and the employment of slave women in the temple estates are already well established. We notice also tensions and conflicts between various groups of property holders: the king and his men, private land- and slaveholders; the priestly rulers of temple estates and free communities of small landholders. In these conflicts, usurpers of the kingship, who by definition were military men, made use of their families, especially their wives, to consolidate and secure their power. Thus women of that class had positions of significant economic, legal, and judicial power and could quite frequently represent their husbands in every respect. At the same time, lower-class women were filling a great variety of economic roles as both artisans and domestic industry workers, while foreign slave women provided a large part of the labor force of the temples. We should also notice that, in the very first effort by a king to establish law and order by proclaiming an edict, one of the aspects of regulation concerns the gender role of women: that is, their right of remarriage and their speech toward men. That fact, while it is inconclusive in isolation, will assume greater significance, as we later analyze the various law codes. In this respect Urukagina's "edict" stands near the beginning of a slow and wavering process of transition in the status of women and the definition of gender, which took almost 2500 years. It is this process this book seeks to document and interpret.

KING SARGON OF AKKAD, a Semitic ruler, founded a dynasty which extended over sections of Sumer, Ashur (Assyria), Elam, and the Euphrates valley (ca. 2371-2316 B.C.). To govern this vast and unruly domain Sargon established garrison cities and made alliances. He also strengthened his rule by installing trusted persons as governors over the formerly independent city-states, which had now become part of his domain. He installed his daughter Enkheduanna as high-priestess of the Moon-God temple in the city of Ur and of the temple of An, the supreme God of Heaven, at Uruk. Since Enkheduanna was also a lifelong cultic devotee of the Sumerian goddess Inanna, her appointment symbolized the fusion of Inanna with the Akkadian goddess Ishtar. It appears that Enkheduanna was highly gifted and politically astute. Sargon spoke Akkadian and elevated this language to the official administrative language, but his daughter was a distinguished poet (the first known woman poet in history), and she wrote in Sumerian. One scholar states that she "used these gifts to propagandize . . . the union of Sumerians and Akkadians into one state capable of carrying Mesopotamian rule . . . to the farthest reaches of the Asiatic Near East."[31]

Enkheduanna's poetry and hymns to the goddess Inanna long survived her. After Sargon's death, the new ruler of Ur removed her from her position as high-priestess. She wrote of this injustice in a long hymn, appealing to the goddess Inanna to redress her injuries and return her to office. Enkheduanna was often quoted and commented upon as a poet in later Sumerian writing.[32]

Similarly, Sargon's grandson, Naram-Shin the Great, appointed his daughter Enmenanna high-priestess at Ur. This practice was then followed by Sumerian and Akkadian rulers for 500 years. The written record shows that "thirteen princely priestesses held office for an average of 35 to 40 years (ca.2280-1800 B.C.)."[33]

After the collapse of the Sargonic empire and the long and complex struggle for dominance among the city-states of Mesopotamia, various rulers developed dynastic and diplomatic marriages as a means of consolidating their military gains or preventing warfare. For example in the period of the Ur III dynasty, the rulers of Ur contracted such marriages of their daughters with the sons of the rulers of Mari and other cities. Some poems and love songs written by "ladies of the Ur III empire" have been preserved.[34] The tradition of dynastic marriages continued in the Near East and in other times and places, wherever dynastic rulers needed to legitimize or fortify their rule over conquered or neighboring territories. It is a higher and more elaborate form of the "exchange of women" practiced much earlier in most societies, and it marked off the daughters of upper-class ruling families for a special and highly ambiguous role. In one sense, they were merely pawns of their families' diplomatic designs and imperialistic ambitions; not unlike their brothers who were sometimes forced to enter such diplomatic marriages and had no more personal choice in the matter than did the women. Yet, as any close study of particular cases must show, these princesses were frequently influential, politically active, and powerful.[35] Their role as future wives in diplomatic marriages demanded that they be given the best available education. Most likely, this trend of educating princesses so they might function as informants and diplomatic representatives of their families' interests once married accounts for the occasional evidence of "equal" educational opportunities for women, even in the face of the general educational disadvantaging of women throughout historical time. What should be remembered is that this tiny group of ruling class daughters never was representative of all women of their time and society.

From the third dynasty of Ur several legal texts known as the Codex Ur-Nammu and from the dynasties of Isin and Lara the Codex Lipit-Ishtar have survived to offer us a glimpse of social and economic life. During this period the practice of the appointment of princesses as high-priestesses continued. The dignified and highly individualized portrait statue of the priestess Enannatumma of Isin, who supposedly also represents the goddess Ningal, gives testimony to the continued prestige and honor accruing to women in the priestly role.[36]

In the period 2000-1800 B.C. continuous warfare and political fragmentation mark the shifting power struggle of various towns and city-states. In ca. 1965 B.C., Shin-kashid of Isin conquered Uruk and founded a dynasty, building a temple in the city of Durum and establishing his daughter Nin-shatapad as high-priestess there. When the king of Lara defeated her father and ended his reign, Nin-shatapad was forced into exile. She wrote an eloquent letter to her conqueror appealing to his generosity to spare the city of Durum and her temple and to restore her to her priestly duties. This letter became a model of its kind and was included in the curriculum of the school of scribes of which she herself had been a graduate.[37] This incident is important not only in showing us the initiative of a woman in public affairs, but because it gives evidence that women of this period were still being trained as scribes.

As we trace the development of the role of the royal wife and daughter as "stand-in" for her husband and father, we can draw on evidence from another culture and place, the city of Mari, which was located far to the north of Sumer in what today is the Iraq-Syrian border. A collection of royal documents, dating from 1790 to 1745 B.C., describe a society which allowed elite women great scope in economic and political activities. Women, just like men, owned and managed property, could contract in their own name, could sue in court and serve as witnesses. They took part in business and legal transactions such as adoptions, sales of property, the giving and taking of loans. A few women appear on the lists of those offering gifts to the king; such gifts were either a tax or a vassal's tribute, which indicates that such women had political standing and rights. Women were also scribes, musicians, and singers. They carried out important religious functions as priestesses, diviners, and prophetesses. Since kings regularly consulted prophets and diviners before undertaking any important decision or before going to war, such persons were actually advisers to the king. The fact that the documents from Mari make no distinction as to the worth of male or female prophets speaks for the relatively equal status of elite women in Mari society.[38] The Assyriologist Bernard Frank Batto explains the position of women at Mari compared with other Mesopotamian cultures as a cultural remnant from an earlier stage of development:

> Only recently emerged from the tribal stage, these Amorite rulers retained many of the features of their tribal heritage in their nascent political economies. In contrast to the developed city-states with their more clearly demarcated and institutionalized offices and chains of command, the Northern Amorite kings seemed to have retained a "patriarchal" style of rule. All authority was retained in the hands of the king, who personally oversaw all operations or a least personally delegated that authority as needed.[39]

The suggestion that the women's "stand-in" role is an aspect of an earlier concept of kingly rule is intriguing and supports my analysis that women's status and roles become more circumscribed as the state apparatus becomes more complex.

Some of the Mari documents offer a vivid picture of the lives and activities of these royal ladies in their role as their male relatives' deputies. The queen, the king's first wife, held independent power in palace, temple, and workshops and served as a stand-in for the king when he was absent on warfare or diplomatic missions. In her own right she managed her property and supervised the female palace personnel. The king's secondary wives, in ranking order, were installed in distant palaces, which the king apparently visited at regular intervals, and where these secondary wives performed similar administrative duties. One such was Kunshimatum, the secondary wife of King Yasmah-Addu of Mari. A letter written by her reveals the extent and the limits of her powers. She had established and managed the king's "house" (palace), and she regularly prayed for the king before the god Dagan. Now, for some unexplained reason, she had fallen into disfavor and had been falsely accused of mismanagement. "Is the household which I have established to be given away (to another)?" Kunshimatum appealed to the king:

> Why then have they so completely alienated me from your affections? What have I taken from your house? Instruct your controllers that they should inspect your house. . . . Save my life. Do you know

that (!) these are (the words) which I constantly pray before Dagan
for you: "Let all be well with Yasmah-Addu that I for my part may
prosper under his protection."[40]

The wife's power, like that of the male vassal, depended on the
will and whim of the king. Like the feudal vassal of a later age,
Kunshimatum understood that only in her lord's protection was there
any safety for her. In her case this protection availed little. Yasmah-
Addu, himself an Assyrian usurper, was overthrown by Zimri-Lim,
who thereby regained the throne of his fathers. At that time Kunshimatum, together with all the other royal ladies, would become
part of the victor's spoils. As later in Israel, the victor acquired the
harem of the former king as part of legitimizing his claim to the
throne.[41] Such a fate had befallen the many daughters of another
Mari king, who reigned before Zimri-Lim. When their father was
deposed by an Assyrian conqueror, these genteelly raised daughters,
who had been trained in the art of singing, were given as slaves to
a minor official in the new government. They were not sent to the
textile factories, but became domestic slaves.[42]

The correspondence of Queen Shibtu with her husband King
Zimri-Lim is of particular importance. B. F. Batto comments about
her: "Shibtu's role is exceptional both in its scope and in the sheer
multiplicity of activities in which she was engaged . . . Her influence was felt everywhere. It is no wonder that so many curried favor
with her."[43]

Queen Shibtu served as her husband's deputy during his frequent absences. She received reports from the administrators of the
city of Mari. The governor of Terqa, a neighboring city, reported to
the queen, "his mistress," on business matters and executed her orders. Governors and vassal kings paid homage to her in terms usually reserved for the ruler himself.[44] Shibtu offered sacrifices, supervised oracles and omen-taking, events of great significance, of which
she regularly advised the king. She also carried out the king's instructions. In one case her husband ordered her to dispose of some
female captives he was sending home:

> In among them are some *ugbabatum* priestesses. Pick out the *ugba-
> batum* priestesses and assign them (i.e. the rest) to the house of the
> female-weavers. . . . Choose from the 30 female-weavers—or how-
> ever many who are choice (and) attractive, who from the toenail(s) to
> the hair of their head(s) have no blemish(?)—and assign them to Wara-
> ilisu. And Wara-ilisu is to give them the Subarean veil(?). Also their

status document is to be changed. Give instructions about their rations, so that their appearance does not worsen. And when you select the female-weavers, let Wara-ilisu guard(?) them . . . .[45]

Here, obviously, the king instructed his wife to select women from among the captives for his harem. His concern for their beauty and his instruction that they be given food adequate to maintain their appearance testify to that. But in a subsequent letter the king countermanded this order. He wrote to his wife:

There will be more (booty) available for my disposition. . . . I will myself select from this booty which I will get, the girls for the veil and will dispatch them to you.[46]

The wife's cooperation in the matter is taken for granted, and her husband's sexual use of the captive women, which served not only to gratify his pleasure but to enhance his property and status, is assumed as a routine matter. Still, as we have seen from the case of Kunshimatum, any new sexual liaison of the husband was a potential threat to the standing of the first wife, even though the latter was legally in a more secure position than secondary wives.

King Zimri-Lim arranged political marriages for his daughters. When he married his daughter Kirum to Khaya-Sumu, the ruler of Ilansura, he also appointed her mayor of Khaya-Sumu's city. Kirum, who seems to have been a quite spirited woman, exercised her authority as mayor. She also corresponded with her father concerning political matters and freely offered him advice. Her activities displeased her husband, who became more and more bitter toward her. The marital conflict was aggravated by the fact that Khaya-Sumu had also married a sister or half-sister of Kirum, a woman named Shibatum. The relationship between the two sisters and which of them is the first and which the secondary wife is not clearly established in the documents available to us.[47] The marriage of two sisters to one husband occurs in a number of instances in Mesopotamian society. In this particular case it worked out badly for Kirum. The husband clearly preferred Shibatum, and the marriage got so bad that Kirum asked her father for permission to return home, which would be tantamount to divorce. In a letter to her father she vividly described one in a long line of domestic quarrels:

(K)Haya-Sumu arose and (spoke) thus to my face. "You exercise the mayorship here. (But) since I will (surely) kill you, let him come— your star—and take you back."[48]

"Your star" is her form of address to her father. The letter continues:

> She arose, Shimatum, before me (saying) as follows: "as for me, let my star do with me whatever he likes, (but) I will do whatever I like!" If he (the king) does not bring me back, I shall die; I will not live.[49]

Despite this desperate plea by Kirum, her father apparently did nothing. In her next letter Kirum threatened more dramatic action: "If my lord does not bring me back, I will head toward Mari (and there) jump (fall) from the roof." This had the desired effect. The father, once again absent on some business, instructed his wife to arrange to bring Kirum back to Mari. There is no formal record of a divorce, but the effect was the same.[50]

King Zimri-Lim had a score of daughters. Eight of them were given in marriage to vassals of their father in hope that this would tie the husbands closer to the king. These women often acted as intermediaries between father and husband. Thus one of the daughters, Tizpatum, appealed to her father to send one hundred troops to help her husband in some local warfare. "Otherwise," she stated,

> the enemy will seize the city. Now, precisely on my account are people concerned about him, saying, "How can he be married to the daughter of Zimri-Lim and be loyal to Zimri-Lim!" Let my father and lord take note of this.[51]

Clearly, the point of such diplomatic marriages was to make secure alliances between local rulers and they implied mutual obligations. One cannot help but be struck by the competent and assertive tone of the daughter's letter.

Another of the daughters married in a diplomatic marriage did not fare so well. Her letters are long and detailed complaints of her husband's ill treatment of her. She, too, appealed to her father to let her return home. In her case the king advised: "Go and manage your household. But if it is not possible, then cover your head and come away to me." This advice did not have the desired result. The daughter fled to a neighboring ruler, where her husband was content to leave her a virtual prisoner. The outcome of her marital troubles is unknown.[52]

Two of the king's daughters were *naditum* priestesses, one dedicated to the god Shamash and his consort Aya at Sippur. Like all such priestesses, she had brought a dowry to the temple and contin-

ued to be provisioned by her family. Some *naditum* were very active
in business enterprises, buying and selling property and slaves and
giving out loans at the usual usurious interest rates. Most of them
kept slaves to do the menial work. In the case of Erishti-Aya, she
did live in a cloister and was not content with that. She performed
an important service by continually praying for the king. She informed him of that fact to bolster her claim for adequate rations.
Her letters are plaintive:

> Now the daughter(s) of your house . . . are receiving their rations of
> grain, clothing, and good beer. But even though I alone am the woman
> who prays for you, I am not provisioned.[53]

This theme recurs in several of her letters. In one of them, written to her mother, she says:

> I am a king's daughter! You are a king's wife! Even disregarding the
> tablets with which your husband and you made me enter the clois-
> ter—they treat well soldiers taken as booty! You, then, treat me well![54]

It is not quite clear whether her complaints are due to the fact
that her parents did neglect her or whether the neglect was on the
part of the temple officials. One of her statements seems to indicate
the latter: "My rations of grain and clothing, with which (my) father
keeps me alive, they (once) gave me, so let them give me (them
now) lest I starve."[55] B. F. Batto notes that similar complaints occur
in the letters of several *naditum* at Sippur. This may reflect, he
thinks, "certain stylization which detracts somewhat from our sense
of immediacy."[56] It may also reflect corruption or negligence on the
part of the temple officials.

Erishti-Aya may have been victimized by her family or by her
superiors at the temple, but her own attitude toward those who served
her was less than charitable. She wrote to her father: "Last year
you sent me two female slaves and one (of those) slaves had to go
and die! Now you have brought me two (more) female slaves (and
of these) one slave had to go and die!" The princess, herself, as she
claimed, threatened with "starvation," was moved to nothing more
than annoyance and irritation by the death of two slaves.[57]

This is some of the information we have about the daughters of
King Zimri-Lim. Their letters offer us intimate glimpses of family
life some 3500 years ago and show a group of articulate and spirited
women engaged in public and private affairs and asserting their rights
in a self-confident manner. Were they an exceptional group of women?

We know that Zimri-Lim delegated more authority and power to the women in his family than was customary. For example, a woman named Addu-duri, who may have been his mother or elder sister, acted as his deputy in supervising religious offerings and oracles at Mari; she purchased supplies and, at other times, made legal decisions.[58] We cannot say with certainty whether other princesses were given similar authority. On the other hand, one might conclude from the violent and successful reaction of Kirum's husband that the granting of independent authority to the wife by her father was an unusual and unacceptable practice.

The rich pictorial remnants of Mesopotamian civilization support the assumption that elite women were respected and accorded dignity in a culture which could see wisdom and authority in the female face and figure. (See illustrations 5, 14, and 15.)

HAVING BRIEFLY SURVEYED the fragments of evidence concerning Mesopotamian women in different cultures over a 1400-year span, what have we learned? We have seen ample evidence of societies in which the active participation of women in economic, religious, and political life was taken for granted. Equally taken for granted was their dependence on and obligation to male kin and/or husbands.

For the ruling elite, their self-interest as usurpers to the kingship demanded that the form in which they establish power become what one observer has aptly called "patrimonial bureaucracy."[59] The security of their power depended on installing family members in important subordinate positions of power. Such family members were, in this early period, quite often women—wives, concubines, or daughters—who, so to speak, become the first liege-lords of their husband/father/king. Thus emerged the role of the "wife-as-deputy," a role in which we will find women from that period forward. We have seen the extent and the limits of her power represented by Queen Shibtu carrying out her husband's orders in ruling the realm and in selecting women for his harem from among the captives. Her image can serve as an apt metaphor for what it means, what it meant then, and what it has meant for nearly 3000 years, for a woman to be upper class. Queen Shibtu's role of "wife-as-deputy" is the highest to which such women can aspire. Their power derives entirely from the male on whom they depend. Their influence and actual role in shaping events are real, as is their power over the men and women of lower rank whom they own or control. But in matters of sexuality, they are utterly subordinate to men. In fact, as we have seen in the cases of several royal wives, their power in economic and political life depends on the adequacy of the sexual services they perform for their men. If they no longer please, as in the case of Kirum or Kunshimatum, they are out of power at the whim of their lord.

Thus, women came to perceive themselves, quite realistically, as dependents of men. This is beautifully expressed in the prayer of Kunshimatum. Like the feudal vassal of a later age, she understood that her only safety was in her lord's protection. It is striking and chilling to contemplate that she prayed not for her own protection, as self-interest might dictate, but for her lord "that I for my part may prosper under his protection." What we see here is the emergence of a set of power relationships in which some men acquired power over other men and over all women. Thus, elite men thought of themselves as those who might acquire power over others, wealth in goods and wealth in sexual services, that is, the acquisition of slaves and concubines for a harem. Women, even the most secure, high-born, and self-confident, thought of themselves as persons depending on the protection of a man. This is the female world of the social contract: women denied autonomy depend on protection and struggle to make the best deal possible for themselves and their children.

If we remember that we are here describing a historical period in which even formal law codes have not yet been written, we can begin to appreciate how deeply rooted patriarchal gender definitions are in Western civilization. The matrix of patriarchal relations between the sexes was already firmly in place before economic and political developments fully institutionalized the state and long before the ideology of patriarchy was developed. At this early stage the transition from one class to another was still fairly fluid and upward mobility was a distinct possibility, even for the lowest classes. Gradually, membership in a particular class became inherited. The decisive transition to the new social organization was the institutionalization of slavery.

In order to understand more about the connection between family structure, the development of slavery as a class system, and the institutionalization of state power, we must look more closely at these aspects of historical development and attempt to reconstruct the texture of the lives of non-elite women.

FOUR

The Woman Slave

Historical sources on the origin of slavery are sparse, speculative and difficult to evaluate. Slavery seldom, if ever, occurs in hunting/gathering societies but appears in widely separated regions and periods with the advent of pastoralism, and later agriculture, urbanization, and state formation. Most authorities have concluded that slavery derives from war and conquest. The sources of slavery commonly cited are: capture in warfare; punishment for a crime; sale by family members; self-sale for debt and debt bondage.[1] Slavery is the first *institutionalized* form of hierarchical dominance in human history; it is connected to the establishment of a market economy, hierarchies, and the state. However oppressive and brutal it undoubtedly was for those victimized by it, it represented an essential advance in the process of economic organization, an advance upon which the development of ancient civilization rested. Thus, we can justifiably speak of "the invention of slavery" as a crucial watershed for humanity.

Slavery could only occur where certain preconditions existed: there had to be food surpluses; there had to be means of subduing recalcitrant prisoners; there had to be a distinction (visual or conceptual) between them and their enslavers.[2] In many societies in which slaveholding, in some forms, was practiced, there existed no fixed slave status, only various degrees of subordination and enforced labor. In order for slave status to become institutionalized, people had to be able to form a mental concept of the possibility that such dominance could actually work. The "invention of slavery" consisted in the idea that one group of persons can be marked off as an out-group, branded enslaveable, forced into labor and subordination—and that this stigma of enslaveability combined with the reality of their status would make them accept it as a fact.[3] And, further, that such enslavement would not only last for the lifetime of the slave, but that slave status could be permanently affixed to a group of humans, formerly free, and to their offspring.

The crucial invention, over and above that of brutalizing another human being and forcing him or her to labor against their will, is the possibility of designating the group to be dominated as entirely different from the group exerting dominance. Naturally, such a difference is most obvious when those to be enslaved are members of a foreign tribe, literally "others." Yet in order to extend the concept and make the enslaved into *slaves*, somehow *other* than human, men must have known that such a designation would indeed work. We know that mental constructs usually derive from some model in reality and consist of a new ordering of past experience. That experience, which was available to men prior to the invention of slavery, was the subordination of women of their own group.

The oppression of women antedates slavery and makes it possible. We have seen in the earlier chapters, how men and women constructed social relations which gave rise to dominance and hierarchies. We have seen how the confluence of a number of factors leads to sexual asymmetry and to a division of labor which fell with unequal weight upon men and women. Out of it, kinship structured social relations in such a way that women were exchanged in marriage and men had certain rights in women, which women did not have in men. Women's sexuality and reproductive potential became a commodity to be exchanged or acquired for the service of families; thus women were thought of as a group with less autonomy than men. In some societies, such as in China, women remained marginal outsiders to their kin groups. While men "belonged in" a household or lineage, women "belonged to" males who had acquired rights in them.[4] In most societies women are more vulnerable to becoming marginal than are men. Once deprived of the protection of male kin, through death, separation, or by no longer being wanted as a sexual partner, women become marginal. At the very beginning of state formation and the establishment of hierarchies and classes, men must have observed this greater vulnerability in women and learned from it that differences can be used to separate and divide one group of

humans from another. These differences can be "natural" and biological, such as sex and age, or they can be man-made, such as captivity and branding.

The "invention of slavery" involves the development of techniques of permanent enslavement and of the concept, in the dominant as well as in the dominated, that permanent powerlessness on
the one side and total power on the other are acceptable conditions
of social interaction. As Orlando Patterson has pointed out in his
exhaustive study of the sociology of slavery, the techniques of enslavement had three characteristic features: (1) slavery originated as
a substitute for usually violent death and was "peculiarly, a conditional commutation"; (2) the slave experienced "natal alienation,"
that is, he or she was "excommunicated from all claims of birth"
and from legitimate participation in his or her own right in a social
order; (3) the "slave was dishonored in a generalized way."[5] Historical evidence suggests that this process of enslavement was at first
developed and perfected upon female war captives; that it was reinforced by already known practices of marital exchange and concubinage. During long periods, perhaps centuries, while enemy males
were being killed by their captors or severely mutilated or trans-
ported to isolated and distant areas, females and children were made
captives and incorporated into the households and society of the captors. It is difficult to know what first led men to the "conditional
commutation of death" for women and children. Most likely their
greater physical vulnerability and weakness made them appear less
of a threat in captivity than did male enemy warriors. "Natal alienation" was readily accomplished by transporting them away from
their home places, which places usually were physically destroyed.
Since their male kin had been slaughtered, these captives could have
no hope of rescue or escape. Their isolation and hopelessness increased their captors' sense of power. The process of dishonoring
could in the case of women be combined with the final act of male
dominance, the rape of captive women. If a woman had been captured with her children, she would submit to whatever condition her
captors imposed in order to secure the survival of her children. If
she had no children, her rape or sexual use would soon tend to make
her pregnant, and experience would show the captors that women
would endure enslavement and adapt to it in the hope of saving their
children and eventually improving their lot.

Most historians dealing with the subject of slavery have noted
the fact that the majority of those first enslaved were women, but

they have passed over it without giving it much significance. The article "Slavery" in the *Encyclopaedia Britannica* states:

> Warfare was the earliest source of slaves in the Ancient Near East.
> . . . Originally, captives seem to have been slaughtered; later women
> and then men were spared to serve their captors.[6]

Another historian notes:

> It may be significant that male slaves appear not only later, but also
> in far smaller numbers than do female ones. . . . Possibly, the means
> for the retention and effective employment of male captives had not
> yet been worked out, so that they were generally killed.[7]

As the Assyriologist I. M. Diakonoff points out, the keeping of male prisoners of war was dangerous:

> To force a detachment of captive slaves—i.e. former free warriors—
> to work in the field with copper hoes would demand about double the
> number of armed soldiers to watch them, because in an armed conflict
> a copper hoe was not so very different from a copper hatchet, which
> was the usual warriors' arms of that age. . . . Therefore all male
> prisoners of war were usually brained on the spot, and only female
> slaves were used in any number in the state economies.[8]

Even where the economic need for a large slave labor force existed there was not enough male labor power available among the captors to watch over the captives day and night and thus ensure their harmlessness. It would take different peoples different lengths of time to realize that human beings might be enslaved and controlled by other means than brute force.

Orlando Patterson described some of the means by which free persons were turned into slaves:

> Slaves were always persons who had been dishonored in a generalized
> way. . . . The slave could have no honor because of the origin of his
> status, the indignity and all-pervasiveness of his indebtedness, his ab-
> sence of any independent social existence, but most of all because he
> was without power except through another.[9]

One aspect of this process of "dishonoring" is the severing of family ties:

> The refusal formally to recognize the social relations of the slave had
> profound emotional and social implications. In all slaveholding socie-
> ties slave couples could be and were forcibly separated and the consen-
> sual "wives" of slaves were obliged to submit sexually to their mas-

ters; slaves had no custodial claims or powers over their children, and children inherited no claims or obligations of their parents.[10]

With typical androcentric focus, Patterson subsumes female slaves under the generic "he," ignores the historical priority of the enslavement of women, and thereby misses the significant difference implicit in the way slavery is experienced by men and women.

The impact on the conquered of the rape of conquered women was twofold: it dishonored the women and by implication served as a symbolic castration of their men. Men in patriarchal societies who cannot protect the sexual purity of their wives, sisters, and children are truly impotent and dishonored. The practice of raping the women of a conquered group has remained a feature of warfare and conquest from the second millennium B.C. to the present. It is a social practice which, like the torture of prisoners, has been resistant to "progress," to humanitarian reforms, and to sophisticated moral and ethical considerations. I suggest this is the case because it is a practice built into and essential to the structure of patriarchal institutions and inseparable from them. It is at the beginning of the system, prior to class formation, that we can see this in its purest essence.

The very concept of honor, for men, embodies autonomy, the power to dispose of oneself and decide for oneself, and the right to have that autonomy recognized by others. But women, under patriarchal rule, do not dispose of themselves and decide for themselves. Their bodies and their sexual services are at the disposal of their kin group, their husbands, their fathers. Women do not have custodial claims and power over their children. Women do not have "honor." The concept that a woman's honor resides in her virginity and in the fidelity of her sexual services to her husband was not yet fully developed in the second millennium B.C. I am arguing that the sexual enslavement of captive women was, in reality, a step in the development and elaboration of patriarchal institutions, such as patriarchal marriage, and its sustaining ideology of placing female "honor" in chastity. The cultural invention of slavery rested as much on the elaboration of symbols of the subordination of women as it did on the actual conquest of women. By subordinating women of their own group and later captive women, men learned the symbolic power of sexual control over men and elaborated the symbolic language in which to express dominance and create a class of psychologically enslaved persons. By experimenting with the enslavement of women and children, men learned to understand that all human beings have the potential for tolerating enslavement, and they developed the techniques and forms of enslavement which would enable them to make of their absolute dominance a social institution.

There is overwhelming historical evidence for the preponderance of the practice of killing or mutilating male prisoners and for the large-scale enslavement and rape of female prisoners. The earliest references to the treatment of enemy survivors in Mesopotamia date from 2500 B.C. On the Stele of the Vultures, Eannatum, the ruler of Lagash, recorded his victory over the city of Umma and described how the victors piled up thousands of enemy corpses in large heaps. Later, the second king of the Sargonic dynasty, Rimush, described the conquest of several Babylonian cities and the killing of several thousand men in each, as well as the taking of several thousand captives. An inscription of King Shu-Sin of the third dynasty of Ur (ca. 2043–2034 B.C.) describes how he settled the enemy "slaves," his booty from the defeated town Simanum, in a town on a distant frontier. This booty apparently consisted of captured civilian men and of enemy warriors, who were later freed. There are other references in various Babylonian texts to "booty" taken and offered to various temples. The term "booty" applied to goods, animals, and people. Enemy warriors were roped immediately after capture or put in woodblocks, a form of neck stocks or yoke.[11] In a study of all available sources on Bablonian captives I. J. Gelb states:

> It may be taken for granted that as long as POW's remained as slaves at the disposal of the crown, they were worked to death under the most inhumane conditions, or died because of sickness, or ran away whenever possible.[12]

There are some references in the texts to blinded war captives, who were set to work in the orchards. One of these texts is pre-Sargonic and deals with twelve male captives from a city in Elam, who were blinded. The other text, the records of the temple of the goddess Bau in Lagash, which has been earlier cited, also mentions "blind men" working in the orchards. In this case, Assyriologists have disagreed as to the meaning of the term "igi-du-nu," several suggesting that it may mean "unskilled," therefore metaphorically blind, or that it may refer to naturally blind men who were so employed. I. J. Gelb tends to think they were blinded captives and points to additional evidence from the Neo-Assyrian period that male prisoners of war were blinded.[13] The putting out of the eyes of 14,400 captives taken by the Assyrians is recorded in an inscription of Shalmaneser (ca. 1250-1200 B.C.).[14]

The Old Testament mentions a number of cases of the blinding of prisoners of war: Samson (Judges 17:21), Zedekiah (II Kings 25:7), and the story of the men of Jabesh (2 Samuel 11:2). Herodotus writes in Book IV, 2, of the Scythians blinding all prisoners of war.[15] In China, too, where slavery developed mainly out of the penal system, criminals were punished by mutilation. Mutilation generally consists of tattooing the face, amputation of nose and feet, and castration. The type of mutilation depended on the severity of the crime. It could be applied to the criminal or to members of his family. The Han law code states "the wives and children of criminals are confiscated as male and female slaves, and tattooed on the face." Persons so mutilated formed a separate class and were held to lowly tasks, living in a "slavish state."[16] Castration as a form of punishment for crimes and, later, as a means of fitting slaves for harem service, was widespread in ancient China and Mesopotamia. The practice led to the development of political eunuchism in China, Persia, ancient Rome, Byzantium, Egypt, Syria, and Africa. The practice is of interest in this discussion insofar as it illustrates the need for the visible marking and marginalization of persons in order to designate them as permanent slaves, and secondly in showing the use of sexual control in order to reinforce and perpetuate a person's enslavement.[17]

Two Mesopotamian administrative texts, written five months apart and dating from the reign of Bur-Sin (third dynasty of Ur), offer information on 197 captive women and children. In the first, rations are issued for 121 women (46 are reported dead) and for 28 children, of whom only five are reported alive. Of the 121 living women, twenty-three are denoted as sick. In the second text, 49 women and 10 children are listed as surviving and are issued rations of flour and beer. Of the 24 sick women noted in the first list, only five are listed in the second list, suggesting the possibility that these five were the only ones to survive the sickness. Since the food rations offered the prisoners were of the same standard as those for serfs, the high death and sickness rates of the prisoners indicate either that much harsher conditions prevailed at the time of the transport from the battlefield to the captive location or that there was a period of near starvation due to problems of distribution and allocation of rations.

Another of these texts describes the booty offered to the temple at Umma as consisting of 113 women and 59 children. I. J. Gelb also reports that "captive women were utilized in building the palace of Bur-Sin. This kind of hard labor was not normally performed by native women."[18]

In the ration lists of the temple Bau at Lagash dating from ca. 2350 B.C. all the temple's laborers are listed according to their status and the tasks they performed. There is a separate list of "slave women and their children." Most of them were occupied in preparing and spinning wool; some of them ground grain; others worked in the kitchen and the brewery or tended domestic animals.[19] Since they were part of the queen's household this particular group were not harem slaves or used for sexual services. In this early period there is no record of the existence of harems in general, and in the specific case of the temple Bau, no comparable records of the king's household are available. The slave women of the temple Bau were not members of families with male household heads, since such families were listed on a separate ration list. Had these women been sexually used, one might expect to find an increase in the number of children per mother as the years went by, but such seems not to have been the case. The fairly steady ratio of mothers to children—half as many children as mothers—suggests that these women had been enslaved together with their children and were simply used as laborers.[20]

Some 500 years later, the letters of King Zimri-lim of Mari, which I have earlier cited, illustrate the taking of female prisoners of war as "booty" and their incorporation into the king's household as textile workers. But in that case his selection of the most beautiful women for special service seems to indicate the existence of a harem, or at least the practice of using such women as concubines for himself and possibly for his retainers.[21]

Dating from nearly the same period as the temple Bau records, the records of the Shamas temple at Sippar show a relatively small number of slaves to total population. Of 18,000 names listed, 300 are slave names, two-thirds of them female. This predominance of female slaves over male seems to have been typical of the actual situation in Old Babylonian times. It reflects the predominant use of female slaves in private households.[22]

The Iliad, written in the eighth century B.C., reflects a social situation existing in Greece approximately 1200 B.C.[23] In Book I of *The Iliad* the practice of enslaving captured women and distributing them to the warriors as spoils is casually mentioned a number of times. King Agamemnon's concubine, Chryseis, a highborn war captive, is claimed by her father, a priest. Fearing the wrath of the gods, the Argonaut warriors urge their king to return the girl. Agamemnon reluctantly agrees, but demands another prize in compensation for Chryseis. It is pointed out to him that that is impossible, since the war booty has been distributed already. The war booty consists of captured women, and the practice is so much taken for granted that Homer does not need to explain it. Agamemnon then insists that he will take the concubine of Achilles, with these words:

> . . . But I shall take the fair-cheeked Briseis, your prize, I myself going to your shelter, that you may learn well how much greater I am than you, and another man may shrink back from likening himself to me and contending against me.[24]

Here Agamemnon states with exemplary clarity the meaning of the enslavement of women: it is to win status and honor among men. After Agamemnon carries out his threat and acquires Briseis by force, which causes Achilles to sulk in his tent and withdraw from the battle, the king does not touch her. He in fact did not actually want her but wanted to win a point of honor against Achilles—a fine example of the reification of women. Much later, when partially due to Achilles' withdrawal and the displeasure of the gods, the Greeks are faced with defeat, Agamemnon admits his fault in the quarrel with Achilles. In front of his assembled chiefs and men, the king proposes to give back Briseis and swears a great oath:

> that I never entered into her bed and never lay with her as is natural for human people, between men and women.[25]

Trying to induce Achilles to join the battle, he offers additional gifts of gold, and horses, and promises:

> I will give him seven women of Lesbos, the work of whose hands is blameless. . . . and who in their beauty surpassed the races of women.[26]

He further offers him the choice of one of his three daughters in marriage. After Troy's defeat, says Agamemnon:

> Let him choose for himself twenty of the Trojan women who are the loveliest of all after Helen of Argos.[27]

None of this impresses Achilles, who refuses all offers. When Achilles goes to sleep the poet tells us:

> and a woman lay besides him, one he had taken from Lesbos, Phorbas' daughter, Diomede of the fair colouring. In the other corner Patroklos

went to bed; with him also was a girl, Iphis the fair-girdled, whom
brilliant Achilles gave him, when he took sheer Skyros, Enyeus' cita-
del.[28]

There is no mention in *The Iliad* of enslaved male warriors.

The fate that awaits the defeated is also described by one of the
Trojan women as:

> . . . the sorrows that come to men when their city is taken: they kill
> the men, and the fire leaves the city in ashes, and strangers lead the
> children away and the deep-girdled women. . . .[29]

And Hector of Troy, speaking to his wife Andromache on the eve of
the battle, confesses that he is not so much troubled by the pain
over the certain deaths of his fellow warriors and of his father and
mother

> as troubles me the thought of you, when some bronze-armoured
> Achaian leads you off, taking away your day of liberty, in tears: and
> in Argos you must work at the loom of another and carry water from
> the spring Messeis or Hypereia, all unwilling. . . .[30]

The enslavement of female war captives and their use as concubines and war spoils continued from the time of the Homeric epic
into the modern period. Speaking of the Greece of ninth and tenth
centuries B.C., the historian M. I. Finley states:

> Slaves existed in number; they were property, disposable at will. More
> precisely, there were slave women, for wars and raids were the main
> source of supply, and there was little ground, economic or moral, for
> sparing the lives of the defeated men. The heroes as a rule killed the
> males and carried off the females, regardless of rank.[31]

The historian William Westermann, basing himself on a detailed
study of historical and literary sources, describes the practice of the
enslavement of captives throughout antiquity.[32] During the Peloponnesian war, for example, Westermann states, the Greeks killed
their male enemies instead of "the established practice of exchanging
prisoners and the release of captured males on payment of ransom.
The captive women in such cases were customarily thrown upon the
market as slaves."[33] Thucydides, in his *History of the Peloponnesian War*, cites many instances of the killing of male prisoners and
the enslavement of women. A few examples can serve as illustrations: "the number of Plataeans that perished was not less than 200
. . . and the women were sold as slaves." Later: Corcyraen men

were killed "but the women who had been captured in the fort were sold into captivity." And elsewhere: "The Athenians reduced the Scionaeons by siege, slew the adult males, made slaves of the women and children."[34]

The practice was not confined to the Greeks and Romans. Speaking of Germanic tribes in the Roman Empire, approximately in the second century A.D., E. A. Thompson writes:

> Some Germanic peoples killed off their prisoners, or at any rate, their adult male prisoners after a campaign . . . Now it is an exceedingly common practice among primitive people to kill the warriors of a beaten enemy and to enslave the womenfolk and their children. But this practice is common only at the lower stages of agricultural development. At the higher stages the frequency of the custom drops sharply and is replaced by an equally sudden rise in the practice of enslaving captured warriors.[35]

Obviously, dominance first practiced on women of one's own kind was more easily transferred to captured women than it was to men.[36]

Linguistic evidence for the fact that women were enslaved prior to men is also suggestive: The Akkadian cuneiform sign for "female slave" was "woman" plus "mountain," which seems to indicate the foreign origin of female slaves. In fact, most of the slaves came from the eastern mountains, probably the area of Subarea. According to one authority, the sign for "slave woman" appears earlier than that for "male slave."[37] This would seem to speak for the fact that women, mostly foreign war captives, were enslaved before men.

A. Bakir, describing slavery in Pharaonic Egypt, points out that the verb "slave" connotes "forced labor." The noun MR(Y)T, meaning war captives and temple servants, may also mean "weaver's comb."[38] That is interesting in light of the fact that female slaves were widely used as weavers and textile workers in Egypt and throughout the ancient world.

In a study of Greek terminology of slavery, Fritz Gschnitzer shows that the Greek word _doela (doulos)_ occurs in its feminine form twice in the Homeric epos but never in the masculine form. He comments that there were considerably more female slaves mentioned in that epos than male, explaining in a footnote that the Greeks tended to kill male prisoners and enslave the women. Interestingly, in reference to the subject to be discussed below, some writers assert that the word _doulē_ has the dual meaning of slave and concubine. Similarly the term _amphipolos_ (handmaid, waiting woman), which is confined to females in Greek usage from Mykenaen times on, is occasionally also used to denote female slaves. Gschnitzer thinks that the term was used to denote formerly free enslaved women. This would confirm the practice of enslaving conquered females and using them as domestic servants.[39]

BIOLOGICAL AND CULTURAL FACTORS predisposed men to enslave women before they had learned how to enslave men. Physical terror and coercion, which were an essential ingredient in the process of turning free persons into slaves, took, for women, the form of rape. Women were subdued physically by rape; once impregnated, they might become psychologically attached to their masters. From this derived the institutionalization of concubinage, which became the social instrument for integrating captive women into the households of their captors, thus assuring their captors not only their loyal services but those of their offspring.

Historians writing on slavery all describe the sexual use of enslaved women. Robin Winks, summarizing existing historical knowledge on the subject, states: "Free sexual access to slaves marks them off from all other persons as much as their juridical classification as property."[40]

Speaking of Babylonian slavery, Isaac Mendelsohn writes:

> In the case of the female slave the master had a right not only to her labor, but also to her body. He or a member of the family could cohabit with her freely without assuming the slightest obligation.[41]

The Babylonian slave woman could also be hired out as a prostitute for a fixed price, sometimes to a brothel owner, sometimes to private clients, with the master collecting her pay. This practice was pervasive throughout the Near East, in Egypt, Greece, and Rome of antiquity, in fact wherever slavery existed. Describing Greek slavery in the ninth and in the tenth century B.C., M. I. Finley says: "The place of the slave women was in the household, washing, sewing, cleaning, grinding meal. . . . If they were young, however, their place was also in the master's bed."[42] Slave girls staffed the brothels and filled the harems of the ancient world.

In the modern period it occurred in Africa, Latin America, the United States, and the Caribbean. The practice is worldwide; examples could be cited for every age and every slave society.

In nineteenth-century Malaya enslaved debtors became "retainers" in the creditor's household, carrying out his wishes and serving as his followers in military adventures. Female slaves or domestic servants, acquired either through debt enslavement or through raids on villages, were used as domestic workers and sexual objects, "given" by the creditor to his male retainers.[43]

In China, from the third century B.C. on until the twentieth century A.D. the "buying of concubines" was an established practice. The same end was reached through the adoption by the wealthy of children sold by their poor parents in times of famine. The trafficking in little girls, in the form of the *Mui Tsai* or "Little Sister" system of child adoption, survived into the twentieth century, despite the outlawing of slavery in 1909. As the phrase shows, it consisted mainly of a traffic in female children, raised to become prostitutes or sexual servants.[44]

A 1948 United Nations Report, describing contemporary conditions in several Muslim countries, states: "Most women slaves combine the functions of servant and concubine in any Arab home that can afford a slave."[45]

The practice of using slave women as servants and sex objects became the standard for the class dominance over women in all historic periods. Women of the subordinate classes (serfs, peasants, workers) were expected to serve men of the upper classes sexually, whether they consented or not. The feudal *droit du seigneur,* the right of the first night, which belongs to the master who has granted his serf the right to marry, institutionalized an already well-established practice.

The sexual use of servant girls by their masters is a literary subject in European nineteenth-century literature, including Czarist Russia and democratic Norway. The sexual use of black women by any white male was also characteristic of eighteenth- and nineteenth-century race relations in the United States, but it survived the abolition of slavery and became, well into the twentieth century, one of the features of race and class oppression.[46]

Thus, from its very inception, enslavement has meant something different for men and women. Both men and women, once enslaved, were totally subordinate to the power of another; they lost autonomy and honor. Male and female slaves had to perform unrewarded labor and often personal service for their masters. But for women, enslavement inevitably also meant having to perform sexual services for their masters or for those whom their masters might designate in their stead. There are, of course, in more highly developed slave systems many instances of male slaves being sexually used and abused by master or mistress, but these are exceptions. For women, sexual exploitation marked the very definition of enslavement, as it did *not* for men. Similarly, from the earliest period of class development to the present, sexual dominance of higher class males over lower class women has been the very mark of women's class oppression. Clearly, class oppression cannot ever be considered the same condition for men and women.

As SUBORDINATION OF WOMEN by men provided the conceptual model for the creation of slavery as an institution, so the patriarchal family provided the structural model. In Mesopotamian society, as elsewhere, patriarchal dominance in the family took a variety of forms: a man's absolute authority over children; authority over the wife restrained by reciprocal obligations to the wife's kin; and concubinage.

The father had the power of life and death over his children.[47] He had the power to commit infanticide by exposure or abandonment. He could give his daughters in marriage in exchange for receiving a bride price even during their childhood, or he could consecrate them to a life of virginity in the temple service. He could arrange marriages for children of both sexes. A man could pledge his wife, his concubines and their children as pawns for his debt; if he failed to pay back the debt, these pledges would be turned into debt slaves. Such power derived from a concept that a person's entire kin-group was to be held responsible for any wrongdoing of its members. Early Hittite law specified:

> If ever a servant vexes his master, either they kill him or they injure his nose, his eyes or his ears; or he [the master] calls him to account and also his wife, his sons, his brother, his sister, his relatives by marriage and his family, whether it be a male servant or a female servant.[48]

In this case, which concerns slaves (servants), the punishment seems to fall quite evenly on male or female kin.

The Code of Hammurabi, which was most likely published in its present form in the fortieth year of Hammurabi's reign, namely 1752 B.C., is, according to Driver and Miles, "not a collection of existing laws with their amendments. . . . It is a series of amendments and restatements of parts of the law in force when he wrote."[49] Driver and Miles assume the existence of a common Mesopotamian law in the third millennium B.C.[50] We can therefore reason that the social conditions reflected in these laws were generally representative of Mesopotamian society.

The Code of Hammurabi defined the treatment of debt pledges and set certain limits to their potential abuse. A man unable to satisfy a debt could pledge his wife and his children, his concubines and their children and his slaves. He could do this in two ways: either by giving his dependents as a pledge for a loan he took from a merchant in order to repay his debt or by outright sale of his debt pledge. In the first case the relative could be redeemed within a certain period of time in exchange for the money lent, but if the debtor failed to repay his debt, the pledges became ordinary slaves, liable to resale by the new owner. In the second case, the debt pledge became a slave immediately.[51] The physical abuse of debt slaves was curtailed by HC § 116, which states that if a debt pledge who was a freeman's son died from ill treatment in the creditor's house, and if such ill treatment could be proven, the creditor's son was to be killed. But if the debt pledge was a slave and not free-born, a money fine was to be levied, and the debt was to be extinguished.[52] The clear implication of this law is that any man's son was expendable for his father's crime and that children enjoyed even fewer rights than did debt pledges. The fact that no mention is made of penalties in case of the mistreatment of female debt pledges may indicate that their mistreatment was regarded with greater equanimity. On the other hand, the Code of Hammurabi (HC § 117) actually marks an improvement in the condition of debt slaves by limiting the service of the wife and children of a debtor to three years, after which they were to go free. In earlier practice they could be held for life. HC § 119 specified that a man who gave his slave-concubine, who had borne him sons, as a debt pledge even in outright sale had the right to redeem her from the new purchaser by repaying the purchase price.[53] While these provisions mark a certain improvement in the lot of female debt pledges, they actually protected the rights of husbands (debtors) against the rights of creditors. Two basic assumptions underlying these laws remained untouched: that male kin have the right of disposal over their female relatives and that a man's wife and children are part of his property to be disposed of as such.

The absolute authority of the father over his children provided men with a conceptual model of temporary dominance and dependency, due to the helplessness of youth. But such a model was unsuitable for conceptualizing permanent dominance of one human being over others. The dependency state of youth was self-terminating; youths, in their turn, would reach the age of dominance. Moreover, youths were expected to fulfill reciprocal obligations toward their aging elders. Therefore parental authority had to operate under the restraint both of the life cycle and of the future power potential of the young. The boy, observing how his father treated the grandfather, would learn for himself how to treat the father, once it was his turn. Thus, the first model of social interaction with an equal who was not quite free was provided by the social relation between husband and wife. The wife, whose sexuality had already been reified as a species of property in the marriage exchange, still had certain legal and property rights and could enforce, through the protection of her kin, certain obligations to which she was entitled. It is concubinage, evolving out of the patriarchal privileges of dominant males in the family, which represents the transitional form between dependency in marriage and unfreedom.

There is not enough historical evidence available to determine with certainty whether concubinage preceded slavery or grew out of it. While we know of many instances where men took first and secondary wives, sometimes marrying two sisters, sometimes acquiring the secondary wife later, the institutionalization of concubinage involving slave women seems to have occurred prior to the promulgation of the Code of Hammurabi. We find in this code a number of regulations pertaining to slave concubines and their rights as wives and mothers and in regard to the inheritance rights of their children. Whether the ready availability of captive women for domestic service or the increasing impoverization of formerly independent agriculturists, which tended to make more debt slaves available, contributed to the spread of concubinage cannot be established firmly on the basis of the available evidence. It seems likely that both factors were important.

Obviously, the increasing importance of keeping private property within the family spurred the development of concubinage as an institution for the preservation of patriarchal property relations. A couple's childlessness, with its implications of loss of property in the male line, could be remedied by bringing a concubine into the household. A Babylonian sales contract reads as follows:

> In the 12th year of Hammurabi, Bunene-abi and his wife Belessunu bought Shamash-nuri from her father for the price of five shekels of silver. . . . To Bunene-abi she is a wife and to Belessunu she is a slave.[54]

What is of particular interest here is that the concubine serves a dual function: she performs sexual services for the master, with the knowledge and consent of the wife, and she is a servant to the wife. This differs greatly from the relations between first and succeeding wives in many polygamous societies, in which the status of second and third wives is co-equal with that of the first wife. Each wife and her children are entitled to certain rights, to a separate dwelling place, to economic and sexual obligations the husband must fulfill in such a way as not to violate the rights of any wife. Thus, the nexus between sexual servitude to the master and economic service to the wife seems to be a distinguishing feature of concubinage under patriarchy.

The Biblical narratives of Genesis, composed between 1200 and 500 B.C., reflect a social reality similar to that described in the Babylonian sales contract (ca. 1700 B.C.).

The childless, aging Sarai urges Abram to have intercourse with her maidservant Hagar:

> And Sarai said unto Abram: "Behold now, the Lord hath restrained me from bearing; go in, I pray thee, unto my handmaid; it may be that I shall be builded up through her." And Abram harkened to the voice of Sarai.[55]

Similarly, Rachel urges her husband Jacob:

> Behold my maid Bilhah, go in unto her; that she may bear upon my knees, and I also may be builded up through her.[56]

There are several underlying assumptions implicit in these accounts: a slave woman owes sexual services to her mistress's husband, and the offspring of such intercourse counts as though it were the offspring of the mistress. All women owe sexual services to the men in whose household they live and are obliged, in exchange for "protection," to produce offspring. If they cannot do so, their female slave property may substitute for them, in the same way that a man may pay a debt by pledging the labor of his slave to the creditor. The dependent status of the "free" wife is implicit in Sarai's pathetic statement "it may be that I shall be builded up through her." The barren woman is considered faulty and worthless; only the act of bearing children will redeem her. Rachel, before offering Jacob her handmaiden, exclaims, "give me children, or else I die."[57] When at last "God harkened to her, and opened her womb," she said, "God hath taken away my reproach."[58] No clearer statement of the reification of women and of the instrumental use of wives can be made.

The Code of Hammurabi specifies an arrangement similar to the Biblical practice in the case of men married to a *naditum*, a priestess who is not allowed to bear children. The *naditum* either gives her husband her slave girl to bear her children, or, if she does not, the husband is entitled to a secondary wife, a *sugetum*, an inferior priestess or kind of "lay sister" for the purpose of his begetting sons of her.[59] If the sons are those of a slave girl they are regarded as the sons of the chief wife, as in the case of Rachel. HC § 146 deals with the case of a slave girl given by a priestess to her husband and who has borne sons and thereafter "goes about making herself equal to her mistress because she has borne sons." In that case her mistress may not sell her, but she may "count her with the slave girls." If she has not borne sons, her mistress may sell her.[60]

We see in these cases, as in the case of Shamash-nuri, the ambiguity in the concubine's position. HC § 171 specifies that a father may legitimize his sons by a slave concubine, by accepting them publicly during his lifetime. If he does not so legitimize the sons of his slave concubine, she and her sons become free after the father's death but have no inheritance rights. Clearly, the slave woman advanced her and her sons' positions by concubinage; yet she never ceased being the slave of the first wife and had publicly to acknowledge that ambiguous role.[61]

The pattern of freeing concubines who had borne sons became incorporated in Islamic law and spread throughout the world with the diffusion of Islam. It is thus one of the most common features of world slavery. Similarly, in nineteenth-century Malaya a female slave concubine was entitled to her freedom after she had borne the master's children.[62]

The Chinese case is somewhat special, in that concubines could attain the highest positions in society. During the Han dynasty, kings and high officials often married their concubines, some of whom became empresses and the mothers of kings. For this reason aristocratic families vied with one another for the privilege of offering their daughters to the court as concubines. Still, in later periods, a child born of one free and one slave parent always was considered a slave.[63]

Concubinage as a means of upward mobility for women also occurs in a somewhat different form in the pre-Colombian Inca empire (ca. 1438-1532 A.D.). As the Inca empire expanded, the conquest hierarchy consolidated its power by controlling reproduction among the conquered provinces. This took the form of the institution of *accla*—whereby virgins from the conquered areas, the *accla*, were enlisted in the service of the state, removed from their villages, set to spinning and weaving and the preparation of ritual foods. Usually selected from among the highest ranking local families, these virgins were either destined for service to the sun-god or as secondary wives of the Inca. They could also be distributed by the state to men of the nobility. They were respected and influential, and for that reason many local families took it as a great honor to contribute their daughters to such service.[64] The ambiguity of concubinage is as evident here as in the other examples cited.

The anthropologist Sherry Ortner has suggested that the development of hypergamy (upwardly mobile marriages of lower-class women to upper-class males) or vertical alliances is an important element of social control in stratified societies. Hypergamy depends on the enforced chastity of lower-class girls prior to marriage. The purity of a daughter or sister might make her eligible to become the wife or concubine of a nobleman or to be selected for temple service. Thus, female purity becomes a family asset, jealously guarded by the men in the family. Ortner suggests that this explanation makes the woman's cooperation in her own subordination plausible.[65] In the context of my argument it also illustrates the permeable boundaries between the status of wife, concubine, and slave.

There is also some linguistic evidence which would seem to show the essential connection between concubinage and female enslavement.

The Chinese word for female slave in use in the third century and second century B.C., was "pi," which also meant "humble." It was used also to describe an inferior concubine or a wife of humble origin. Summarizing the position of slaves in China of that period, the historian E. G. Pulleyblank states:: "A slave was an inferior member of his master's household and subject to the same obligations . . . as a child or a concubine."[66]

A later word for slave, in use after the second century B.C. is "nu," the sign for which is "hand" and "woman." Pulleyblank notes:

> There is another word identical in pronunciation with "nu," "slave,"
> but written differently, which appears in early texts with the meaning
> "child" or collectively "wife and children."

He cites a number of instances of this use of the word and concludes:

> There can, I think, be little doubt that the two words are identical and that the meaning "slave" is a later derivation from the original meaning child and wife and children.[67]

This makes sense as a reference to the practice of enslaving the wives and children of criminals, which is specified in the code of Shang Yang (ca. 350 B.C.).

C. Martin Wilbur notes: "The terms 'female slave' and 'concubine' sometimes appear together as though there were no great distinction between the two."[68]

Similarly, the Assyrian term "asirtu," or "esirtu," deriving from the root "eséru," to bind, is variously translated as "captive woman" and "concubine."[69]

S. I. Feigin concludes:

> The captive woman did not have the same position in all places. But nowhere was she free, and everywhere she served as a concubine. In general, the captive woman had more of an opportunity to elevate herself than did the *asiru*, the captive man.[70]

Whether one wishes to view "concubinage" as an opportunity for upward mobility or as an added form of dominance and exploitation, the institution was not only structurally significant but crucial in helping men and women define their concept of freedom and unfreedom.

In ancient civilizations, as later in history, various forms of dependency and unfreedom coexisted. Undoubtedly, patriarchal family relations, concubinage, and the enslavement of foreigners coexisted in Babylonia, China, Egypt, and elsewhere. But it is logical that the concept of hierarchy and imposed unfreedom and finally the idea of *perpetual unfreedom* as represented by the status of a permanent slave took some time to develop and evolve. In later periods of history it would take several centuries for the concept of *freedom* as an inalienable right of all human beings to evolve. In the archaic state and in the city-states of antiquity, a slave was regarded as a species of property, yet at the same time as a dependent member of a household, entitled to a degree of protection. Gradually, as slavery became the dominant system, slave status marked an inferior order of humans, who passed the permanent stigma of their status on to future generations. If that kind of slave is seen as the end product of a gradual developmental process of stratification, and if the wife under patriarchal dominance/protection is seen as the starting form of this process, then the concubine is somewhere in between these two forms.

In the period of approximately a thousand years the idea of "slavery" became actualized and institutionalized in such a way as to reflect upon the very definition of "woman." Female persons, whose sexual and reproductive services had been reified in earlier marriage exchanges, were toward the end of the period under discussion seen as persons essentially different from males in their relationship to public and private realms. As men's class positions became consolidated and defined by their relationship to property and the means of production, the class position of women became defined by their sexual relationships.

The distinction between a free married woman and a slave was expressed within degrees of unfreedom. The class difference between a wife living under the patriarchal dominance/protection of her husband and a slave living under the dominance/protection of the master was mainly that the wife could own a slave, male or female, and other property. The slave could not even own herself. The wife Belessunu, for example, could own the slave Shamash-nuri, whose work relieved her of certain arduous tasks. But Belessunu, unless she divorced her husband, could not escape entirely the domestic responsibilities and the sexual services expected of her. Shamash-nuri, on the other hand, at all times had to carry the dual oppression of slave labor and sexual slavery.[71]

Hierarchy among men rested upon property relations and was reinforced by military might. For women, their place in the hierarchy was mediated through the status of the men on whom they depended. At the bottom stood the slave woman, whose sexuality was disposed of by powerful men as though it were a marketable commodity; in the middle the slave-concubine, whose sexual performance might result in her upward mobility, the bestowal of some privileges and the winning of inheritance rights for her children; at the top the wife, whose sexual services to one man entitled her to property and legal rights. Somewhere beyond the wife ranked the exceptional women who, by virtue of their virginity and religious service, enjoyed rights otherwise reserved for men.

Let us finally, once again, turn to literature for a metaphoric elucidation of the meaning of this historical development.

The manner in which competition among men finds expression in the possession and reification of women has been illustrated in the tale of Achilles, Agamemnon, and the slave woman Briseis. The

complexities of male-female relations in a patriarchal setting of un-
bridled male power is well illustrated in another Homeric epic, *The
Odyssey*. In Odysseus' absence the suitors have been besieging his
wife, Penelope. She has defended her virtue by a ruse: telling the
suitors she would accede to one of them when she had finished her
weaving, Penelope wove assiduously all day, but spent each night
unraveling what she had woven. The endlessly weaving wife protects her virtue and domesticity with the product of her labor, performing her dual economic and sexual role to perfection. Meanwhile, roaming Odysseus engages in a variety of sexual and martial
adventures. On his return, Odysseus, rightfully angered at the threat
to his interests brought on by the suitors, accuses them:

> Ye wasted my house, and lay with the maidservants by force, and
> traitorously wooed my wife while I was yet alive. . . .[72]

In fierce contest, he slays all the suitors in the yard of his house and
then sends for the slave woman Eurycleia. Earlier, we have been told
that Eurycleia had been bought "on time" by Laertes, Odysseus'
father, for the "worth of twenty oxen":

> And he honored her even as he honored his dear wife in the halls,
> but he never lay with her, for he shunned the wrath of his lady.[73]

Eurycleia, herself a servant, has been in charge of the fifty maidservants owned by Odysseus. He commands her: "Tell me the tale of
the women in my halls, which of them dishonor me, and which be
guiltless."[74]

Eurycleia says:

> Thou hast fifty women-servants in thy halls that we have taught the
> ways of housewifery, how to card wool and to bear bondage. Of these
> twelve in all have gone the way of shame. . . .[75]

The boy, Telemachus, who was too young to protect his mother and
obviously unable to protect his maidservants, has been observing his
father's slaughter of the suitors. But now Odysseus orders him to
bring in the guilty slave women, make them carry out the dead,
then scrub the halls. Then Telemachus is to kill them "with your
long blades." But Telemachus, suddenly initiated into manhood, refuses "to take these women's lives by a clean death, these that have
poured dishonor on my head and on my mother, and have lain with
the wooers." Rather, he strangles the women by tying nooses about

their necks and drawing them up on a stout rope. The poet tells us: "They writhed with their feet for a little space, but for no long while."[76]

The virtuous slave women then rush in

> and fell about Odysseus, and embraced him and kissed him and clasped his head and shoulders and his hands lovingly . . . and a sweet longing came on him to weep and moan, for he remembered them every one.[77]

Slave women, raped by the suitors, are killed for the dishonor they have conferred upon the master's house. The youth, not strong enough to protect them, is strong enough to kill and kill them most brutally. But first, they must perform their housekeeping functions—their death is delayed until they have removed the dead and scrubbed the hall, setting the scene for the idyll of domestic bliss, which will follow once the dishonor to the household has been fittingly avenged by their own deaths.

It is somewhat startling to find the stereotype of American slavery—the joyous pickaninnies and delighted slaves hugging and kissing the returning master on the plantation—in this classical emblem. The virtuous slave women, no doubt delighted at being alive, "lovingly" kiss their master, and he in turn is moved to tears and sweet longing (presumably with sexual connotations) "for he remembered them every one."

Penelope, by craft and unceasing toil, was capable of defending her own honor, but she neither tried to nor could she have prevented the slaughter of her slave women. Class barriers unite Penelope with her husband and son. The victims of rape are guilty; they are dishonored by being dishonorable. The offense committed upon them does not count as an assault or a sexual crime but as a crime of property against the master who owns them. Finally the subordinate women, all slaves, are divided: the slave Eurycleia merely an instrument of her master's will and acting entirely in his interest; the "good" slave women divided from the "bad." No linkage of sisterhood can form under such conditions. As for the master, his love takes the form of violence and possessiveness. Killing and sweet longing are for him not incompatible. And the son of the master becomes a man in partaking in the assult on slave women.

Here the poet has offered us a domestic scene metaphoric of relations between the sexes under patriarchy. It has been reenacted in Imperial China, in Greek and Turkish peasant communities from ancient times up to the twentieth century and in the contemporary victimization of the illegitimate children of Vietnamese and Korean women and American soldiers. It was reenacted also in the wholesale casting out by their families of Bangladesh women raped by invading Pakistani soldiers.

This, in its most extreme form is the end product of a long historical process of development.

It began way back in prehistoric times, when the initial sexual division of labor imposed by biological evolutionary necessity demonstrated to men and women that distinctions could be made among people based on visible characteristics. Persons could be ascribed to one group solely by virtue of their sex. It is this psychological social potential on which the later establishment of dominance depends. Under conditions of complementarity—mutual interdependence—people would readily accept that sex-based groups would have segregate activities, privileges, and duties. Most likely, the subordination of women-as-group to men-as-group, which must have taken centuries to become firmly established, took place within a context of deference within each kinship group, the deference of the young toward the old. This form of deference which is perceived as cyclical, therefore just—each person taking their turn at subordination and dominance—formed an acceptable model for group deference. By the time women discovered that the new kind of deference exacted from them was not of the same order, it must have been so firmly established as to seem irrevocable.

As Meillassoux has pointed out, once male dominance is established, women are seen in a new way. They may, even earlier have been seen as being closer to "nature" than to "culture" and thus inferior, although not devoid of power. Once exchanged, women are no longer seen as equal human beings; rather, they become instruments for the designs of men, likened to a commodity. "Women become reified because they are conquered and protected, while men become the reifiers because they conquer and protect."[78] The stigma of belonging to a group which can be dominated reinforces the initial distinction. Before long women come to be perceived as an inferior group.

The precedent of seeing women as an inferior group allows the transference of such a stigma onto any other group which is enslaveable. The domestic subordination of women provided the model out of which slavery developed as a social institution.

Once a group has been designated as enslaved, it gathers on itself

the stigma of having been enslaved and, worse, the stigma of belonging to a group which is enslaveable.[79] This stigma becomes a
reinforcing factor which excuses and justifies the practice of enslavement in the minds of the dominant group and in the minds of the
enslaved. If this stigma is fully internalized by the enslaved—a process which takes many generations and demands the intellectual isolation of the enslaved group—enslavement then becomes to be perceived as "natural" and therefore acceptable.

By the time slavery had become widespread, the subordination
of women was a historical fact. If, by then, it was thought about at
all, it must have gathered onto it some of the stigma of slavery:
slaves, were, like women, inferior people, whom it was possible to
enslave. Women, always available for subordination, were now seen
as inferior by being like slaves.[80] The linkage between the two conditions consisted in that all women had to accept as a given the control of their sexuality and their reproductive processes by men or
male-dominated institutions. For slave women, economic exploitation and sexual exploitation were historically linked. The freedom of
other women, which was never the freedom of men, was contingent
upon the enslavement of some women, and it was always limited by
restraints upon their mobility and their access to knowledge and skills.
Conversely, for men, power was conceptually related to violence and
sexual dominance. Male power is as contingent upon the availability
of the sexual and economic services of women in the domestic realm
as it is upon the availability and smooth performance of military
manpower.

Distinctions of class and race, both first manifested in the institutionalization of slavery, rest upon the inextricable linkage of sexual dominance and economic exploitation manifested in the patriarchal family and the archaic state.

FIVE

The Wife
and the Concubine

THE THREE MAJOR PRESERVED collections of Mesopotamian law—the Codex Hammurabi (CH), the Middle Assyrian Laws (MAL), the Hittite Laws (HL)—and Biblical law are a rich source for historical analysis.[1]

The Babylonian empire over which Hammurabi reigned encompassed people of different ethnic and cultural origins and extended from the Euphrates to the banks of the Tigris, but his contemporaries considered him only as one powerful king among a number of others.[2] Hammurabi, compiling and amending the previously existing law codes of these diverse people over which he reigned, invested the laws with the authority of his office and the sanction of the god Shamash in order to expand their use and authority over his entire realm. His code, engraved on a diorite stele in ca. 1750 B.C., encompassed a large body of law already practiced for hundreds of years. Hittite laws and Middle Assyrian laws date from the 15 to the 11th century. The Covenant code was recorded somewhere between the latter part of the ninth and early part of the eighth century B.C. and was based on laws formulated and in use for as many as three hundred years earlier.

Looking at these law codes, which represent four different societies over a period of a thousand years, we might despair of the possibility of deriving any solid insights into the societies concerned, if it were not for the fact that there seems to have been a continuity of legal concepts and common law practice among them.[3] Babylonian and Assyrian law codes show considerable parallels; it is not known to what extent, if at all, Hittite law was influenced by the other two codes. The Middle Assyrian laws are considered to be amendments and clarifications of Hammurabic law. Hebrew law shows no Hittite influence, but half of the Covenant laws are parallel to Hammurabic laws and still more refer in some ways to the other Bablyonian law codes.

In using laws as sources for historical analysis we make certain methodological assumptions. We assume that laws reflect social conditions in a very specific way. The principle is well stated by J. M. Powis Smith:

> In general, it may be said that legislation does not precede the conditions of life with which it is intended to deal, but arises out of actually existing conditions and situations which it seeks to guide and control.[4]

The enactment of a law always indicates that the practice being commented on or legislated for exists and has become problematical in the society. For example, if everyone marries his cousin or if no one does, no law is required to forbid or permit the practice. But when we find a law outlawing the practice of cross-cousin marriage, we have a right to assume that (a) the custom existed and (b) it had become problematical in the society.

In the law codes under discussion we see a great deal of attention focused on the legal regulation of sexual behavior, with women being restricted much more severely than men. This is reflected in the distribution of topics with which the laws deal. Thus, of the 282 laws in the Code of Hammurabi, 73 cover subjects pertaining to marriage and sexual matters. Out of 112 surviving Middle Assyrian laws, some 59 deal with the same topics. This may indicate the existence of a social problem in that period, or it may simply be a distortion due to the incompleteness of the archaeological findings. But even if hitherto undiscovered tablets of MAL were somewhat to redress the imbalance, the heavy emphasis on the legal regulation of marriage and of the conduct of women is striking. Out of 200 Hittite laws only twenty-six deal with marriage and sexual regulation; on the other hand, they are more restrictive of women than the other law codes.

Another methodological consideration is the fact that what the law prescribes is not necessarily what was practiced. We can assume that a large part of Mesopotamian law was intended to set down ideals of behavior rather than rules and precedent for specific cases. Hammurabic law assumed "a fixed body of accepted norms" of moral and social behavior; only specific cases needed elucidation.[5] A. L. Oppenheim states flatly that CH "does not show any direct relationship to the legal practices of the time."[6] W. G. Lambert notes that Hammurabic law was often unenforceable, such as in the provision that a surgeon who performed an unsuccessful operation was punished by having his hand cut off. This could have been enforced in only a very few cases; otherwise it would soon have put an end to the profession. Further, the law was not usually observed or used, as can be seen from the fact that in the thousands of surviving texts of legal proceedings and business transactions the law is cited in only one or two cases.[7] These surviving documents, on which most of our knowledge of Babylonian society is based, are records of the sort generated mostly by upper-class people. We therefore lack the knowledge of the actuality of the lives of ordinary people, which would put the law codes into some sort of context. With these constraints in mind, it would be a mistake to interpret the law literally, that is, to deduce from the existence of a law that it described actual behavior. What the law does is to set limits to permissible behavior and offer us rough guidelines toward the social structures underlying the laws. They tell us what should or should not be done and thus better describe the *values* of a given society than its actuality.

In a period in which there were major changes taking place in property and political relations, the shifting importance of certain issues for lawmakers and compilers can tell us something about an attendant shift in values. The increasing emphasis in Mesopotamian law codes on the regulation of property crimes, the rights and duties of debtors, the control of slaves, and the regulation of the sexual conduct of women tells us that issues of gender, class, and economic power were problematic and demanded definition and that such definition linked these subjects in quite specific ways. Similarly, the severity of punishment for specific crimes is an indication of the values held by the community at the time of the codification of the laws. The Codex Hammurabi exacts the death penalty for: certain kinds of theft; housebreaking; connivance in slave escapes; faulty building construction which results in fatal accidents; black magic; kidnapping; brigandage; rape; incest; for causing certain kinds of abortions; and for adultery committed by wives.

The law reflects class and gender relations, and by comparing the different law codes we can trace shifts in these relations. Lastly, by observing facts the law takes for granted, we can learn something about the special structure and the values of the society.

MESOPOTAMIAN LAW WAS administered in the individual communities by judges and elders who formed a tribunal. Witnesses, swearing an oath to tell the truth, were probably as much bound by fear of their neighbors' censure as by respect for the abstractions of the law. The judges' decisions, which were usually recorded on clay tablets and signed by witnesses, have in many cases survived and have been used by historians in their commentaries upon the various laws. In the Old Babylonian period, women participated in the judicial process as witnesses and plaintiffs, not only as accused persons.

Underlying both CH and MAL is the concept of the *lex talionis*, the idea that the punishment must exact a physical retribution from the guilty party which mirrors the offense as much as possible. An eye for an eye, a tooth for a tooth, etc. Hammurabic law and, even more strongly, the Assyrian law codes substitute financial burdens, such as fines, and measured physical pain, such as whippings, for some of the offenses. This is generally considered an "advance," a progression to the process of symbolification of punishment.[8] Another aspect of legal thought and practice which underlies these law codes is that of substitution: a man may substitute members of his family, his servants and/or slaves to suffer the punishment for a crime he has committed. This concept tells us more about the actual power relationships in the society than the specific regulations do. Clearly at that time, men were powerful enough to *incorporate* members of their family —i.e., women, and children of both sexes— in such a way as to offer them as substitutes for themselves in case of punishment. The practice of burying servants, slaves, and retainers with a king or queen in the same tomb was an older manifestation of the power to incorporate others. That power resided at first only in the rulers who were themselves considered gods or direct emissaries of the gods. What is important for understanding the development of class hierarchy is to see this principle extended to civilian and non-royal heads-of-families and to note that such heads-of-families were, in the period under discussion, always males.

The Codex Hammurabi recognizes three distinct classes of people: the patrician, which includes priests and government officials; the burgher; and slaves. Punishment is graded by class, with the assumption that damage caused to a higher-ranking person deserves more severe punishment than that to a lower-ranking person. We will note below how the development of classes and class distinctions differs for men and women. In the discussion of Mesopotamian law it is well to remember that class status was fluid and not necessarily inherited. Old Mesopotamian society was characterized, as one of its foremost scholars, A. Leo Oppenheim, states: by "a remarkable degree of economic mobility: poor people expect to become rich; the rich are afraid of becoming poor; both dread interference from the palace administration."[9] The transition from one class status to another was swift and, in the case of debtors, often catastrophic for the family economy. Much of Hammurabic law is concerned with the plight of debtors and their families. A bad year's harvest, drought, or any number of other family disasters might compel a man to seek a loan. With the usurious interest rates which were then customary, he would soon find himself unable to repay the principal in order to meet the interest.[10] He could stave off default for a while by binding out his wife or his children to debt service. Hammurabic law limited the period of the enslavement of debt pledges to three years.[11] By earlier custom, Babylonian debtors could be enslaved for life.

The Hebrew Covenant Code (Exod. 21:2–11) provides that the male debt slave must go free after six years of service, leaving slave wife and children behind. If he chooses to stay with his family, he will be consigned to perpetual slavery. The female debt slave shall not go free as the male: she may be redeemed, given to the master's son in marriage, or married by the master himself. The law specifies that if the master does not marry her, he must treat her well or she must be released.[12] Here the assumption is that the female debt slave has, during her enslavement, been used as a concubine. Presumably, once freed, she would not be eligible for marriage and thus might be forced into the only alternative, prostitution. J. M. Powis Smith thinks "The law . . . is in reality thoughtful and considerate of the female slave, if we take into account the conditions of life to which she was subject."[13] I would rather say that Covenant law provides additional evidence of the general use of female slaves as concubines and of the sharp differences in the class position of male and female slaves. Males in Hebrew slavery could in the seventh year resume their lives as free men. Female debt slaves, on the other hand, could move a step upward into concubinage or even marriage, or a step downward into prostitution. Their fate was determined by their sexual services. We shall encounter the principle that a man's class status is determined by his economic relations and a woman's by her sexual relations in a number of other instances in this period of the formation of class society. It is a principle which has remained valid for thousands of years.

What can we learn about the social conditions of Mesopotamian women from the law codes?

Patriarchal society featured patrilineal descent, property laws guaranteeing the inheritance rights of sons, male dominance in property and sexual relations, military, political, and religious bureaucracies. These institutions were supported by the patriarchal family and in turn constantly recreated it.

Babylonian families valued the birth of sons far above the birth of daughters. Sons carried the family name forward and could enhance family property and interest by good management, military valor and/or service to temple or king. They were also deemed essential to the parents' well-being in after-life, because only they could perform certain religious rituals for the dead. Because of these considerations, childless couples, eunuchs, or single men and women, the last usually priestesses, adopted children to secure their own care in old age.

THE FATHER'S AUTHORITY over his children was unlimited, as we have seen earlier. In CH the rebellious behavior of a son striking his father was considered a grievous offense, which could be punished by cutting off the son's hand. In the case of an adopted son, who breaks the parental tie by renouncing the father who has adopted him, the penalty was to have the son's tongue cut out (CH §§ 192–193). Hebrew law is even more stringent, demanding the son's death for the offense of striking either parent.[14] It is worth noting here that in CH the major crime is that of the son's rebellion against the father, with the priestess occupying a social role somewhat akin to that of a father. Only in Hebrew law does the crime encompass both father and mother. I take this as an indication of the upgrading of the role of mother in Hebrew law.[15] The possibility of rebellious behavior on the part of a daughter is not mentioned in the laws, probably because she could easily be married off or sold if her behavior was troublesome to her parents.

The main value to a family in having daughters was their potential as brides. The bride-price received for a daughter was usually used to finance the acquisition of a bride for a son. Mesopotamian marriages were, in general, arranged by the father of the groom in negotiation with the father of the bride. Sometimes the bridegroom himself would negotiate with the bride's father. The exchange of gifts or of money, which sealed the marriage, is the subject of many laws in the Code of Hammurabi. The groom's father would pay the bride's father a betrothal gift *(biblum)* and a bridal gift *(tirhâtum)*, whereupon the couple were considered betrothed, but the bride stayed in her father's house until the marriage was completed by sexual union. In an alternate arrangement, usually made for a child bride, she was chosen by the groom's father and went to live in the father-in-law's house. Until the time the marriage was completed, she was a servant in her in-laws' house. That such an arrangement lent itself to many abuses by the father-in-law can be seen from the severe penalties in Ch §§ 155–156 against the father-in-law who raped such a girl. If the son had earlier cohabited with the girl, the father-in-law was treated as an adulterer and suffered the death penalty by drowning. If he raped the girl while she was still a virgin, the father-in-law had to pay her a fine, return any property she had brought into the marriage, such as a dowry, and return her to the house of her father.[16] It is interesting that the law says in such a case, "and a husband after her heart may marry her." This is one of the few instances when the law allows the woman some limited choice in the selection of the husband, always assuming her father is agreeable to her choice. We should also note the casual reference to the possibility of the son having intercourse with the child bride. There is no penalty on that, since she is by betrothal already his sexual property.

Marriages could also be completed by the signing of a marriage contract *(riksatum)*.[17] Such contracts could endow the wife with certain property rights, specify conditions for her rights in case of separation, and could save her from being liable to enslavement for debts her husband had incurred prior to the marriage.

After the marriage has been consummated, the father of the bride gives her a dowry (Bab. *seriktum)*, also known as "settlement" *(nudunnum)*. If a wife has sons, her *seriktum* passes to them at her death (CH §§ 162, 172). MAL § 29 makes a similar provision for a dowry which passes from mother to sons.[18] During the marriage the husband has the management of her *seriktum*; after his death the widow takes possession of it and uses it for the rest of her life, even if she remarries (CH §§ 173–174).[19] If the husband divorces his wife because she has borne no sons or because she has a disease, and he wishes to marry another woman, the first wife is entitled to stay in his house and enjoy lifelong maintenance. If this does not suit her and she chooses to leave him, she is entitled to the return of her dowry.[20] When a wife who has not given birth to sons dies, the father-in-law must return the bridal gift to the husband, and the husband must return the wife's dowry to the father-in-law.[21]

Obviously, the financial arrangements here given the force of law were possible only among propertied families. In fact, by encouraging homogamy—the marriage between partners of equal social status—these laws assured that property stayed within the class of propertied people. This was accomplished by giving children of both sexes inheritance rights, the sons inheriting at the death of the father, the daughters getting their inheritance in the form of a dowry. Strict supervision of girls to assure premarital chastity and strong family control over the selection of marriage partners further strengthened the tendency toward homogamy. Dowry and settlement money created a joint fund for the married couple, which tended to make the marriage more stable by giving each a financial interest in it. The husband enjoyed the management of his own and his wife's property during his lifetime, but he had to preserve his wife's dowry, both to guarantee an inheritance for his sons and to provide for her support in widowhood. The wife had a use-right in her dowry and therefore had every interest in investing and augmenting it, the same way the *naditum* priestess had. This accounts for the business activity of patrician women and their considerable civic and economic rights. The seeming contradiction that upper-class women had such economic rights, even as their sexual rights were increasingly restricted, is an integral aspect of the formation of the patriarchal family. The social anthropologist Jack Goody, in his thorough study of the world's marriage systems, has characterized this development as typical of Eurasian societies based on plow agriculture and featuring complex class stratification and elaborate divisions of labor. Such societies generally develop patriarchal monogamous marriages, homogamy, strong emphasis on premarital chastity, and a high degree of societal control over the sexual behavior of women. The Mesopotamian case is one of the earliest models of such a society.[22]

While it is useful to show such linkages and to classify societies the world over, showing the connection between property and gender, we should take the analysis a step further and notice that giving sons and daughters inheritance rights in order to preserve the family property does not mean that they have *equal* rights. In fact, the Mesopotamian example shows clearly that here property passes from man to man, male family head to male family head, but it passes *through* women. The wife had lifelong use-right of her dowry, but her husband (or sons) have vested rights in that property, which after her death goes to them. In case of divorce or if she did not bear sons, the dowry is returned to her father (or her brothers). A woman cannot cede or will her property, thus her rights are extremely limited. Most significantly, these rights, such as they are, depend on her sexual and reproductive services to her husband, particularly on having provided him with sons.

Where anthropologists see a strong causal link between the regulation of inheritance and marital property and that of sexual behavior, Assyriologists are more concerned with the specific cases and with how to interpret them. There are two major interpretations regarding the nature of Babylonian marriage. In the view held by Driver and Miles, Babylonian marriage law represents an advance in the rights of women by securing their economic and legal rights in marriage. In their view, the *tirhâtum* is not a bride purchase price but a symbolic gift sealing the marriage, which represents a cultural remnant of an earlier custom of bride purchase.[23] Driver and Miles do not elaborate on the origin and development of the "earlier custom" of bride purchase. They reason from the evidence of the making of marriage contracts that such contracts were, from Hammurabic times forward, the essential step in making a marriage legitimate and distinguishing it from concubinage. They show that the few extant Babylonian marriage contracts are very different in form from bills of sale. They also argue that the fact that the bride price was always far below the market price of a slave girl shows clearly that it could not represent a sale price.[24]

The contrasting view, held by Paul Koschaker and by most European Assyriologists, is that Babylonian marriage was marriage by purchase, and that the bride price was in fact an actual payment by the groom—or his family—for the bride.[25] Koschaker calls attention to the existence of two forms of marriage in the Mesopotamian region. The older form, which survived for a long time, is marriage without joint residence. The wife remains in her father's (or her mother's) house; the husband resides with her as either an occasional or permanent visitor. There are reflections of the existence of such marriage forms in the Code of Hammurabi and in the Biblical record, where it is called *beena* marriage. It is a form of marriage which allows the woman greater autonomy and which makes divorce easier for her. Koschaker thinks that CH and MAL formalized the other form, patriarchal marriage, which gradually become predominant. In this marriage system the wife resides in the husband's house and is entirely dependent on his support. Divorce is, for the wife, virtually unobtainable. Koschaker thinks that this marriage system began initially as marriage by purchase, but that it developed, approximately at the time of Gudea of Lagash (ca. 1205 B.C.), into marriage by written contract. This development was characteristic of Sumerian society; but Semitic societies retained the earlier form of patriarchal marriage. Both concepts are represented in Hammurabi's law code.[26]

> Semitic marriage by purchase stood in contrast to the Sumerian form of marriage, which had also begun as marriage by purchase, but had long ago transcended that concept. . . . Hamurapi, in his wisdom, incorporated both concepts in his law. Next to marriage by purchase he placed marriage without the *tirhâtum*, and next to *tirhâtum* the Sumerian betrothal gift, *nudunnum*.[27]

Thus Koschaker seeks to explain the contradictions in Hammurabic law, to which we have called attention. He also cautions against a vulgarized reading of his hypothesis, which would interpret it as meaning that the wife was owned as a slave. He agrees with Driver and Miles that the bride price was not the economic equivalent for the wife. But it was, he points out, its judicial equivalent. "The marriage is a marriage by purchase even when the juridic relationship resulting from it is not ownership of the wife but legal power of the husband over the wife."[28] The distinction is highly suggestive from our point of view precisely because it defines a new sort of power relationship between husband and wife, for which there was no equivalent in earlier society.

Modern anthropological evidence seems to support Koschaker's reconstruction of a historic development from marriage without joint residence to patrilocal patriarchal marriage. The former is more characteristic of nomadic and hunting and gathering tribes, while the latter occurs in connection with plow agriculture. Neither Driver and Miles nor Koschaker explain adequately the origin of marriage by purchase; they simply assume its existence and show how it devolved. An understanding of this development is only possible if we consider class as a factor. Marriage by purchase was a class phenomenon, and it did not apply equally to women of all classes.

The customary right of male family members (fathers, brother, uncles) to exchange female family members in marriage antedated the development of the patriarchal family and was one of the factors leading to its ascendancy. With the development of private property and class stratification, this customary right became of crucial economic significance. Male family heads now were under an obligation to dispose of their family members in marriage in such a way as to maximize family fortunes and keep up or improve family status. Women played an increasingly significant part in the family economy: not only as producers of economic goods, as producers of children and their caretakers, as domestic workers, but also as persons whose sexual services were turned into marketable commodities. It is the sexual and reproductive services of women which were reified, not women themselves.

Upper-class families used the marriages of their daughters to consolidate their own social and economic power. Marriages cemented military and business alliances. Fathers could dedicate some of their daughters to the service of the gods, which had the spiritual advantage of securing the blessings of the god and the economic advantage of returning the daughter's dowry, which was given to the temple, to the family after the daughter's death.[29] Thus could an excess of daughters over sons be turned to the family's advantage.

In a society where the ownership of land and herds meant high status, the purpose of marriage became the continuation of the family line through sons. The gift exchange among two wealthy families on the marriage of their children firmed up the mutual obligations of the two families and secured the passage of property to male family members. The reason the dowry was given only after the marriage was consummated was that only after the wife had shown herself capable of actually (or potentially) bearing sons was the initial purpose of the contract fulfilled. Only then was the wife, as an individual, entitled to definite economic and social rights. But the provision that her dowry must pass to her sons also signified that the sons belonged to the father's family and would carry its property forward. Women were valued mainly as procreators, and their lifelong dependency on a man was institutionalized.[30]

The same aspirations for homogamy and for upwardly mobile marriages produced quite different results in poorer families. There, lack of cash for the bride price for a son's wife could be offset by marrying off a daughter. But as the Orientalist Elena Cassin reports, "if one did not have at one's disposal a young girl who could be traded for cash by marrying her off, one was obliged to let go of part of the family's patrimony by offering as bride price a field or house."[31] Such transactions could pave the road to the family's economic ruin and lead to indebtedness and loss of status.

If such an event occurred, the family would have to use its daughters (and possibly sons) as debt pledges or sell them into slavery. Daughters sold under such circumstances might become concubines, ordinary domestic slaves, or prostitutes. They might also be purchased by a master as wives for their male slaves. In any case, the family and the daughter suffered a loss of economic and social status.

In the lower-class family, where property was insufficient or nonexistent, persons (children of both sexes) became property and were sold into slavery or degraded marriages. The main point was that they thereby gave up all property rights in their family of birth. But the arrangement whereby a son's marriage to a girl of his own class was made possible through the sale of his sister created in fact for the sister a marriage by purchase.

Seen in this light, the two opposing interpretations regarding Mesopotamian marriage can be reconciled. Marriage by purchase and marriage by contract coexisted from the time of Hammurabic law onward. The two forms of marriage applied to women of different classes. The concept that the bride is a partner in the marriage was implicit in the marriage contract of upper-class families. For lower-class women, however, marriage amounted to domestic enslavement. In Mesopotamian law, and even more strongly in Hebrew law, there are increasing distinctions being made between the first wives (upper class) and concubines (lower class). All women are increasingly under sexual dominance and regulation, but the degree of their unfreedom varies by class. As we have shown, the married wife is at one end of the spectrum, the slave woman at the other, the concubine in an intermediate position. It would be a serious misunderstanding, however, to equate the subordinate position of the wife, who had economic and legal rights and the potential of herself absolutely owning other human beings and profiting from their labor, with that of a slave. Such an interpretation mystifies and renders actual class relations invisible.

Hammurabic laws regulated sexual behavior in such a way as to sharpen the difference between the appropriation of women by enslavement and the acquisition of women by marriage. Throughout Mesopotamian law and even more strongly in Hebrew law, we can observe the sharpening distinction between first wives and concubines, between married women and slaves.

Most marriages were monogamous. We have earlier discussed the special circumstances under which a man might take a second wife (concubine): if he married a *naditum* priestess or if his wife were barren. In either case the wife might offer him a slave girl to bear his children as a substitute for herself. It was up to the husband to accept or reject such an arrangement. The ambiguous position of the concubine was reinforced in Hammurabic law, which prohibited her from "making herself equal to her mistress."[32] A slave concubine who is a mother of sons, and because of that aspired to equal status with her mistress may, according to the law, be treated as a slave, but not sold. If she is not the mother of sons and commits this offense, she may be sold.[33]

A Babylonian marriage contract with a second wife specifies that the concubine is obliged to serve the first wife, grind her daily meal, and carry her chair to the temple.[34] The Biblical story of the expulsion of Hagar, the slave woman given by the barren Sarai to Abram to bear his son, illustrates the continued practice of making a status distinction between the first wife and the slave concubine.[35]

Hebrew law, in particular, enhances the legitimate wife and mother. We need only mention the progression from Hammurabic law, which demands that sons respect their fathers, to the Ten Commandments, and to Exodus 21:15, which make it basic law that all children must respect and honor *both* parents. The strict obligations by husbands and sons toward mothers and wives in Hammurabic and Hebrew law can thus be seen as strengthening the patriarchal family, which depends on the willing cooperation of wives in a system which offers them class advantages in exchange for their subordination in sexual matters.

Male dominance in sexual relations is most clearly expressed in the institutionalization of the double standard in Mesopotamian law.

Hammurabic law specified the man's obligation to support his wife (CH §§ 133–135) and identified his obligations toward her male relatives. Marriages were generally monogamous, but men were free to commit adultery with harlots and slave women. In general, the custom of taking a second wife of a lower rank occurred only in the Old Babylonian period.[36]

The wife was legally obliged to perform her economic role to the husband's satisfaction. A man could divorce his wife or reduce her to the status of a slave and marry a second wife, if she "persists in behaving herself foolishly wasting her house and belittling her husband'' (CH § 141). In such a case the husband had to seek a court conviction before dissolving the marriage.[37] As for her sexual obligations, the bride's virginity was a condition for marriage, and any marriage arrangement could be cancelled if she was found not to be a virgin. In marriage the wife owed absolute fidelity to her husband. L. M. Epstein, in his study of sex laws and customs in the ancient world, summarizes her position:

> . . . adultery is possible only on the side of the wife, because she is the property of the husband, but not on the part of the husband. . . . the wife owes faithfulness to her own marriage; the husband owes faithfulness to another man's marriage.[38]

Here Epstein seems to agree with Koschaker that marriage constitutes wife purchase. I would argue that while the wife enjoyed considerable and specified rights in marriage, she was *sexually* the man's property. Epstein stresses that, according to the concept that "adultery was a violation of the husband's property rights," he was the only injured party and the wife's "guilt deserved the death penalty."[39] Thus CH § 129 provides drowning for both the wife and the adulterer. "If her husband wishes to let his wife live, then the king shall let his servant live."[40] This language implies that a husband who has caught his wife in the act must bring her to the king's court for judgment. In earlier practice the man and his male kin would have avenged themselves without benefit of the law. Another principle here involved is the concept that two guilty parties must receive the same punishment. If the husband chooses to be lenient with his wife, the court must let the adulterer go free. A parallel law in the Assyrian code (MAL § 15) is more specific in defining that principle: If the husband spares his wife's life and "cuts off the nose of his wife, he shall turn the man into a eunuch; and they shall disfigure his whole face. But if he spares his wife, he shall also acquit the man." Hittite laws §§ 197 and 198 provide the same penalties and specify that the husband, if he chooses to kill his wife and the adulterer, shall not be punished. If he decides to bring the case to court, he may grant both of them their lives. If he decides that they shall be punished, the penalty is up to the king, who may kill them or free them.[41]

Apart from the asymmetry in defining adultery and the cruelty of the punishment, what is remarkable about these laws is the increasing authority given to the state (king) in regard to the regulation of sexual matters. Where earlier the control of his wife's sexuality was clearly a matter of the husband's private jurisdiction, Hammurabic law involves the court, but the major decision of life or death is still up to the husband. Assyrian law curtails the husband's range of choices and specifies the nature of the punishment he may inflict. Hittite law allows the husband to kill, but removes him entirely from the process of inflicting alternate punishment. Hebrew law goes even further in that direction, insisting that the offenders must be brought to court and that "the adulterer and the adulteress shall surely be put to death" (Levit. 20:10; see also Deut. 22:22). The mode of punishment described in Ezekiel 16:38–40 is a public execution by stoning the victims.

All the law codes seek to distinguish between the guilty wife, who solicits sexual encounters inside or outside her house, and the woman who is raped. The rape of a virgin bride, who is still living in her father's house, is regarded in the same way as adultery. The rapist of such a woman is put to death, while she, provided she can prove she has resisted him, goes free (CH § 130).[42]

For women even the accusation of adultery could prove fatal. If the husband so accused his wife before a court, she could vindicate herself by taking an oath "by the life of a god" (CH § 131). If, however, the accusation came not from her husband but from others in the community, the wife could vindicate herself only by undergoing the ordeal, that is, she had to "leap into the river for her husband" (CH § 131). The river-god would then decide on her guilt or innocence.[43]

Divorce was easily obtained by the husband, who merely had to make a public declaration of his intent to divorce. The husband's privileges in regard to divorce were restricted, however, by a series of provisions regarding his wife's property and maintenance. These called for a return of her dowry, half his property, or at the least some silver, as "leaving money."[44]

It was difficult for a wife to obtain a divorce and only those without blemish might attempt it:

CH § 142

If a woman has hated her husband and states "Thou shalt not have (the natural use of) me," the facts of her case shall be determined in the district and, if she has kept herself chaste and has no fault, while her husband is given to going about out (of doors) and so has greatly belittled her, that woman shall suffer no punishment; she may take her dowry and goes [sic] to her father's house.

CH § 143

> If she has not kept herself chaste but is given to going about out (of doors), will waste her house (and) so belittle her husband, they shall cast that woman into the water.[45]

The asymmetry in the severity of the punishment for "going out of doors" is surely striking. The wife of an adulterous man, if she attempted to get a divorce, ran the risk that the husband might accuse her of various misdeeds and she might lose her life.

This double standard is carried forward in Hebrew law, which allowed a husband to divorce his wife at will but denied a woman the right to seek a divorce under any circumstances.

THE VARIOUS LAWS against rape all incorporated the principle that the injured party is the husband or the father of the raped woman. The victim was under an obligation to prove that she had resisted the rape by struggling or shouting; however, if the rape was committed in the country or in an isolated place the guilt of the rapist was taken for granted, since the woman's cries could not have been heard. Hammurabic law punishes mother-son incest with death for both parties (CH § 157) but provides only banishment from the city for the father who rapes his daughter (CH § 154). The father who rapes his son's young bride before the marriage has been consummated is fined. But if a father-in-law rapes his son's wife after the marriage has been consummated he is treated as an adulterer and gets the death penalty (CH §§ 155–156).[46]

MAL § 55 deals in detail with the rape of a virgin. If a married man rapes a virgin who lives in her father's house

> whether it was within the city or in the open country or at night in the (public) street or in a garner or at a festival of the city, the father of the virgin shall take the wife of the ravisher of the virgin (and) give her to be dishonoured; he shall not give her (back) to her husband (but) shall take her. The father shall give his daughter who has been ravished as a spouse to her ravisher.[47]

If the rapist has no wife, he must pay the price of a virgin to the father, marry the girl and know that he can never divorce her. If the girl's father does not agree to this, he shall accept the money fine and "give his daughter to whom he pleases."

Here we see the concept that rape injures the victim's father or husband carried to devastating conclusions for the women affected:

the victim of rape can expect an indissoluble marriage with the rapist; the totally innocent wife of the rapist will be turned into a prostitute. The language of the law gives us a sense of the absolute "power of disposal" of fathers in regard to their daughters.[48] This is reinforced by MAL § 56, which provides that if the man swears that the raped girl has seduced him, his wife shall be spared; he shall pay a fine to the girl's father (for robbing her of her virginity and thus debasing her value) and "the father shall treat his daughter as he pleases."[49]

It seems highly unlikely that with this escape clause any rapist would ever be convicted, unless he wished to use the occasion to rid himself of his wife. On the other hand, the description in MAL § 55 of the places in which a rape is likely to occur must somewhat alter our concept of respectable girls living in sheltered seclusion behind the walls of houses. Obviously the implication here is that girls could be encountered with some frequency in the country, at night on city streets, in granaries (possibly while purchasing food), and at festivals.

It may be indicative either of a general deterioration in the treatment of married women or of the more repressive nature of Assyrian society that, while Hammurabic law does not mention the physical chastisement of wives, MAL has three provisions, all quite brutal. MAL § 57 states that if flogging of a man's wife had been ordered "on the tablet," which means by law, it must be carried out in public. MAL § 58 reinforces this: all legally inflicted punishments of wives, such as tearing out of the breasts and cutting off the nose or ears, must be carried out by an official. The implication is that the husband may no longer, as he perhaps did in earlier times, carry out the punishment himself. This parallels the development of law regarding adultery, which we have discussed. To make the extent of the husband's power explicit, MAL § 59 states that, apart from legally prescribed penalties, ". . . a man may (may scourge) his wife, pluck (her hair), may bruise and destroy (her) ears. There is no liability therefor."[50]

This happens to be the last law on the clay tablets on which Middle Assyrian Laws §§ 1–59 are inscribed. It gives one a vivid sense of the degraded position of married women in Assyrian society compared with Old Babylonian society.

A WOMAN'S DEPENDENCY continued into widowhood. Her economic position was better if she was the mother of sons, whether first or secondary wife. Hammurabic law provided that she was to be treated with respect and to enjoy lifelong residence and maintenance in her husband's (or her son's) house. The deceased man's slave concubine was to be freed together with her sons. By implication, the childless widow or the mother of daughters was not guaranteed the same rights.[51] MAL § 46 seems to address this omission, at least partially. It gives the wife who had not been provided for in her husband's will the right to get board and lodging in her son's house. If she is a second wife, who has no sons of her own, her husband's sons shall support her. The law also refers to a case where one of her husband's sons marries the widow. This custom, which in Assyria meant that a son might marry his dead father's concubine and secondary wives, except for his mother, possibly developed from an ancient Semitic practice whereby a ruler inherited his father's wives and concubines as a token of his inheriting the kingship. These *mores* seem to reflect the concept that lower-class wives were a species of property.[52]

As we have seen, Hammurabic law had provided also that a propertied widow had the option of returning to her father's house, bringing her dowry and bridal gift with her. She might remarry, provided her sons' property rights were protected. By the time of the Middle Assyrian Laws, however, not all widows had a choice in the matter of remarriage.

A bride whose betrothed died before the marriage might be given by her father-in-law to one of his other sons. Conversely, if a man's bride died, his father-in-law may give him one of his other daughters as a wife. MAL § 33 specifies that a young widow who has no sons shall be given either to one of her husband's brothers or to his father. Only in the case where there are no male relatives available to marry her may she go "whither she wishes."[53] These laws embody the concept that the marriage exchange is not a transaction involving an individual couple but rather involving the rights of male members of one family to female members of another family.

This concept underlies the institution of the Jewish *levirate*. L. M. Epstein explains the principle involved:

> The family had paid for her [their son's widow] and the family owned her. . . . family property . . . was not allowed to lie fallow. . . . This woman . . . bought and paid for and capable of wifehood and childbearing, could not be allowed to be without a husband. . . .[54]

If the deceased had died without having a son, the widow's remarriage to a family member would provide a son who would be considered the son of her dead husband. Since the status of an unattached woman was precarious, if not impossible, the *levirate* also provided the childless widow with "protection, care and sustenance and . . . the social advantages of [continued] membership in the husband's family."[55] It is beyond the scope of our inquiry to trace the complex development of the *levirate,* as instituted in the Bible and carried forward in the Jewish tradition. But we should note that it again confirms a "class" distinction among women—the woman who had borne sons enjoyed more security and privileges than the woman who had borne only daughters, or the childless woman. Women were assigned to higher status not only by their sexual activities but by their procreative activities as well.

Laws pertaining to miscarriage and abortion offer us further insight into the relationship of sex and class. Mesopotamian law assumed that the punishment varied according to the class of the victim. In the case of women, this meant usually the class of the man who had property rights in the victim. Thus, Hammurabic law says, if a blow dealt to a patrician's daughter causes a miscarriage, the punishment is a fine of ten shekels, as against five shekels in the case of a burgher's daughter. If the blow causes the daughter's death, the punishment in the first case is the death of the aggressor's daughter; if the victim was a burgher's daughter, the punishment is a fine. Once again, according to the *lex talionis* the aggressor's daughter's life is substituted for the life of the guilty father (Ch §§ 209–214).[56]

Assyrian law covers a broader range of possible cases. MAL § 50 provides that the man who causes the miscarriage of a married woman shall see his own wife similarly treated, "the fruits of [her womb] shall be treated as [he has] treated her." If the blow struck kills the pregnant woman, the man shall be put to death. This principle holds true, whether the victim is a respectable woman or a harlot. Two other provisions are noteworthy: the first states that if the victim's husband has no son (and the wife has been struck and miscarried) the aggressor shall be put to death, and the second two, "If the fruit of the womb is a girl, he none the less pays (on the principle of) a life (for a life)."[57]

Comparing the two codes (CH and MAL), we see that the penalty for causing the death of a pregnant woman has been increased (in MAL the assailant himself must die, whereas in CH his daughter was put to death); and that, apparently, class distinctions between female victims are more strongly drawn in the later code than in the earlier one. In one specific case, the miscarriage of a "lady by birth," the crime is elevated from a civil injury to a public crime. In that case the offender must pay a large monetary fine, he shall be beaten fifty blows with rods and must serve one month of "labour for the king" (MAL § 21). Apparently the loss of a potential heir of a nobleman was considered an attack on the social order, which must be punished publicly and severely.[58] In respect to miscarriages of lower-class women, class distinctions are strongly made in the levying of fines, but when the woman's death has been caused by the injury the offender must die regardless of the woman's class status. This may indicate the development of a legal distinction between capital crimes and lesser injuries.

Hittite law is simpler and less specific. A man causing a woman's miscarriage must pay a monetary fine which is scaled according to the age of the fetus. The fine for the same injury to a slave woman is half as large as that for a free woman (HL §§17 and 18).[59] There are several parallel laws in the Hittite codes providing smaller fines for causing the miscarriage of a man's cow or mare (HL § 77A). Clearly, this is property legislation, not concern for injury to a living being, the pregnant woman.

Hebrew law combines some of the features of the various Babylonian laws. A man causing a woman's miscarriage "shall be surely fined, according as the woman's husband shall lay upon him; and he shall pay as the judges determine. But if any harm follow then thou shalt give life for life, an eye for an eye. . . ."[60] The principle underlying all of this legislation is that the crime consists in depriving the husband of a son and, in case of the wife's death, of her potential as a future bearer of his children.[61]

The political nature of this legislation can be seen most forcefully in MAL § 53, which has no precedent in CH. If a woman causes her own miscarriage

> (and) charge (and) proof have been brought against her, she shall be impaled (and) shall not be buried. . . . If that woman was concealed (?) when she cast the fruit of her womb (and) it was not told to the king. . . . [the tablet breaks off].[62]

What is striking here is, first of all, that self-induced abortion is regarded as a public crime, of which the king (the court) must be apprised. Impalement and refusal of burial are the severest penalties meted out in the Middle Assyrian legal system, and they are *public* penalties for high crimes. Why should a woman's self-adduced abortion be deemed a crime of equal severity to high treason or assault upon the king? Driver and Miles, whose commentaries on Middle Assyrian laws are considered definitive, state:

> . . . it seems inconsistent to permit the exposure of unwanted infants and to visit abortion with the severest penalties. In the case of a married mother this can be explained on the ground that it is the father who has the right to expose, while the mother has no right to deprive him by her own act of his choice of keeping alive or exposing the child.[63]

Driver and Miles go on to argue: "The reason may be . . . that the woman by her offence has caused the sacred blood of the family to flow and has thereby called down the wrath of heaven not only on herself but also on the whole community."[64] I will argue that this change in the law must be seen in the context of several other changes pertaining to the sexual control of women. The savage punishment against self-abortion has to do with the importance placed throughout the MAL on the connection between the power of the king (state) and the power of the patriarchal family-head over his wives and children. Thus, the right of the father, hitherto practiced and sanctioned by custom, to decide over the lives of his infant children, which in practice meant the decision of whether his infant *daughters* should live or die, is in the MAL equated with the keeping of social order. For the wife to usurp such a right is now seen as equal in magnitude to treason or to an assault upon the king.

WE SEE THEN, in the thousand-year span we are discussing, how patriarchal dominance moved from private practice into public law. The control of female sexuality, previously left to individual husbands or to family heads, had now become a matter of state regulation. In this, it follows, of course, a general trend toward increasing state power and the establishment of public law.

The patriarchal family, first fully institutionalized in Hammurabic law, mirrored the archaic state in its mixture of paternalism and unquestioned authority. But what is most important to understand in order to comprehend the nature of the sex/gender system under which we still live is the reverse of this process: the archaic state, from its inception, recognized its dependence on the patriarchal family and equated the family's orderly functioning with order in the public domain. The metaphor of the patriarchal family as the cell, the basic building block, of the healthy organism of the public community was first expressed in Mesopotamian law. It has been constantly reinforced both in ideology and practice over three millennia. That it still holds sway can be illustrated by the way it surfaced in the campaign against the passage of the Equal Rights Amendment in the United States of the present day.

During the second millennium B.C., class formation had taken place in such a way that for women economic status and sexual service were inextricably linked. Thus women's class position was from the outset defined differently from that of men. Structural changes had already resulted in increasing divisions between women of the upper and lower classes. It remained for the law to institutionalize this split. This can be seen dramatically in a Middle Assyrian law, which also represents the most powerful manifestation of state interest in the regulation of female sexuality, MAL § 40, regulating the public appearance of women. We will discuss this law, which in fact legislated the division of women into distinct classes according to their sexual behavior, in the next chapter. To do so, we must detour slightly and discuss the establishment of prostitution, which preceded this measure.

SIX

Veiling the Woman

"PROSTITUTION, OFTEN KNOWN AS the world's oldest profession, can be traced throughout recorded history."[1] Thus some experts and the common wisdom hold, making prostitution appear as a "natural" byproduct of human social formation, needing no explanation.

Other experts disagree. "Prostitution," as we are told in the *New Encyclopaedia Britannica*, "has not, so far as is known, been a cultural universal. In sexually permissive societies it is often rare because it is unnecessary, whereas in other societies it has been largely suppressed."[2]

In his magisterial treatment of the history of prostitution, the German physician Iwan Bloch tells us that it develops as a byproduct of the regulation of sexuality: "Prostitution appears among primitive people wherever free sexual intercourse is curtailed or limited. It is nothing else than a substitute for a new form of primitive promiscuity."[3] While this is undoubtedly true, it does not explain under what conditions prostitution arises and becomes institutionalized in a given society. It also ignores the commercial aspect of prostitution by treating it as though it were simply a variant form of sexual arrangement among consenting parties. Bloch accepts the existence of a "natural" state of promiscuity which is later supplanted by various forms of structured marriage. This nineteenth-century theory, which was elaborated by J. J. Bachofen and the American ethnologist Lewis Henry Morgan, formed the foundation of Friedrich Engels's analysis, which has influenced so much of modern feminist theory:

. . . hetaerism derives quite directly from group marriage, from the ceremonial surrender by which women purchased the right of chastity. Surrender for money was at first a religious act; it took place in the temple of the goddess of love, and the money originally went into the temple treasury. . . . Among other peoples hetaerism derives from the sexual freedom allowed girls before marriage. . . . With the rise of the inequality of property . . . wage labor appears sporadically side by side with slave labor, and at the same time, as its necessary correlate, the professional prostitution of free women side by side with the forced surrender of the slave. . . . For hetaerism is as much a social institution as any other; it continues the old sexual freedom—to the advantage of the men.[4]

A few pages later Engels refers to prostitution as "the complement" of monogamous marriage and predicts its demise "with the transformation of the means of production into social property."[5] Even as we dismiss Engels's patent Victorian bias in expecting women to be desirous of exercising their "right to chastity," we must note his insight that the origin of prostitution derives both from changing attitudes toward sexuality and from certain religious beliefs, and that changes in economic and social conditions at the time of the institutionalization of private property and of slavery affected sexual relations. No matter how many flaws and errors in scientific evidence one can show in Engels's work, he was the first to alert us to these connections and to see the essential nexus of social and sexual relations. With his formulation of the analogy between the coexistence of free and slave labor and the coexistence of the "professional prostitution of free women side by side with the forced surrender of the slave," he has pointed us toward a redefinition of the concept of "class" for men and women, which he himself unfortunately ignored in his subsequent work.

To understand the historic development of prostitution we need to follow Engels's lead and examine its relationship to the sexual regulation of all women in archaic states and its relationship to the enslavement of females. But first we must deal with the most widespread and accepted explanation of the origin of prostitution: namely, that it derives from "temple prostitution."

It is unfortunate that most authorities use the same term to cover a broad range of behavior and activities and to encompass at least two forms of organized prostitution—religious and commercial—which occur in archaic states. We are told, for example, that in Mesopotamian society (and elsewhere) sacred prostitution, which characterized ancient fertility cults and goddess worship, led to commercial prostitution.[6]

The sequence is doubtful at best. The use of the term "sacred prostitution" for any and all sexual practices connected with temple service keeps us from understanding the meaning such practices had for contemporaries. I will therefore distinguish between "cultic sexual service" and "prostitution," by which I mean commercial prostitution only.

Cultic sexual service by men and women may date back to the Neolithic period and to various cults of the Mother-Goddess or of the so-called Great Goddess in her many manifestations.[7] The archaeological evidence of the existence of female figurines, with emphasized breasts, hips, and buttocks, is abundant all over Europe, the Mediterranean, and Eastern Asia. In many places such figurines were found in what archaeologists have interpreted as shrines, but there is no way of our knowing in what manner these figurines were used or worshipped. Nor will we ever know.

In contrast, we have ample, historically valid evidence—linguistic, literary, pictorial and legal—from which we can reconstruct the worship of female goddesses and the lives and activities of priestesses in Ancient Mesopotamia and in the Neo-Babylonian period.

The ancient Babylonians thought of the gods and goddesses as actually dwelling in the temple, not as symbolically represented there. The staff of the temple, the various ranks of priests and priestesses, artisans, workmen and slaves, all worked to care for and feed the gods as they might have worked to care for and feed a lord. Daily the meals were carefully prepared and set out for the god, his bed was prepared, music was played for his entertainment. For people who regarded fertility as sacred and essential to their own survival, the caring for the gods included, in some cases, offering them sexual services.[8] Thus, a separate class of temple prostitutes developed. What seems to have happened was that sexual activity for and in behalf of the god or goddesses was considered beneficial to the people and sacred. The practices varied with the gods, the different places and different periods. There was also, especially in the later period, commercial prostitution, which flourished near or within the temple. Again, modern scholars have been confusing the issue by referring to all of this activity as prostitution and by using the term "hierodule" without distinction for various types of women engaging in cultic or commercial sexual activity.[9] It is only since 1956, when the first volume of the Chicago Assyrian Dictionary appeared, that it is possible to make more accurate use of the terms and distinguish, as the Babylonians did, different types of temple servants.

In the Old Babylonian period, the daughters of kings and rulers were appointed as high-priestesses of the Moon-God or of the goddess Ishtar. The *en* or *entu* priestesses were the counterparts of male high-priests. They wore distinctive clothing, a cap with raised rim, a folded garment, jewelry, and a staff—the same insignia and garments worn by the ruler. They lived inside the sacred shrine, had charge of temple management and affairs, performed ritual and ceremonial functions, and were usually unmarried. The *nin-dingir* priestess in ancient Sumer had a similar role. Assyriologists believe that it is this class of women who annually participated in the Sacred Marriage, impersonating or representing the goddess.

The basis for the ritual of the Sacred Marriage was the belief that fertility of the land and of people depended on the celebration of the sexual power of the fertility goddess. It is likely that this rite originated in the Sumerian city of Uruk, which was dedicated to the goddess Inanna, earlier than 3000 B.C. The Sacred Marriage was that of the goddess Inanna and either the high priest, representing the god, or the king, identified with the god Dumuzi.[10] In one typical poem, the encounter is initiated by the goddess, who expresses her eagerness for union with her lover. After their union, the land blossoms forth:

> Plants rose high by his side,
> Grains rose high by his side,
> . . . gardens flourished luxuriantly by his side.

The goddess, happy and satisfied, promises to bless the house of her husband, the shepherd/king:

> My husband, the goodly storehouse, the holy stall,
> I Inanna, will preserve you for,
> I will watch over your "house of life". . .[11]

The annual symbolic reenactment of this mythical union was a public celebration considered essential to the well-being of the community. It was the occasion of a joyous celebration, which may have involved sexual activity on the part of the worshipers in and around the temple grounds. It is important for us to understand that contemporaries regarded this occasion as sacred, as mythically significant for the well-being of the community, and that they regarded the king and the priestess with reverence and honored them for performing this "sacred" service.

The Sacred Marriage was performed in the temples of various fertility-goddesses for nearly two thousand years. The young god-lover or son of the goddess was known as Tammuz, Attis, Adonis, Baal, and Osiris in various languages. In some of these rituals, the sacred union was preceded by the death of the young god, symbolizing a season of drought or infertility which ended only by his resurrection through his union with the goddess. It was she who could make him alive, who could make him king and who could empower him to make the land fertile. Rich sexual imagery with its joyous worship of sexuality and fertility permeated poetry and myth and found expression in statuary and sculpture. Rites similar to the Sacred Marriage also flourished in classical Greece and pre-Christian Rome.[12]

While most of the information about *en* priestesses comes from the Old Babylonian period, there are many references to *nin-dingir* priestesses in the Neo-Babylonian period in Ur and Girsu. In the age of Hammurabi (1792–1750 B.C.) such priestesses could live outside the cloister, but their reputations were carefully guarded.[13]

Next in rank to the *en* and *nin-dingir* came the *naditum* priestesses. The word *naditum* means "left fallow," which is consistent with the evidence that they were forbidden child-bearing.[14] We know a good deal about the *naditum* priestesses of the god Shamash and the god Marduk during the first dynasty of Babylon. These women came from the upper levels of society; a few were kings' daughters, most were daughters of high bureaucrats, scribes, doctors, or priests. *Naditum* of the god Shamash entered a cloister at a young age and stayed unmarried. The cloister in which they lived with their servants consisted of a large complex of individual buildings within the temple. The cloister in the temple of the town of Sippar has been shown by excavation to have also contained a library and school and a graveyard.[15] The cloister housed up to two hundred priestesses at a time, but the number of *naditum* gradually declined after the age of Hammurabi.[16]

Naditu women brought rich dowries to the temple at the time of their dedication to the god. On their death, these dowries reverted back to their families of birth. They could use these dowries as capital for business transactions and to lend money at interest, and they could leave the cloister in order to take care of their various business interests. *Naditum* sold land, slaves, and houses, made loans and gifts, and managed herds and fields. The names of 185 female scribes, who served in the temple of Sippar, are known.[17] From the proceeds of their business transactions the *naditum* regularly made offerings to the gods on festival days. Since they could not have children, *naditum* often adopted children to care for them in old age. Unlike other women of their time, they could will their property to female heirs, who, most likely, were family members also serving as priestesses.

Naditum of the god Marduk were uncloistered and could get married but were not allowed to have children. It is this group of women which is particularly the subject of regulation in the Code of Hammurabi. As we have seen; a *naditum* could provide children for her husband by giving him a slave woman or a low-ranking temple servant, called *sugitum*, as a concubine or second wife. Hammurabic low elaborately provides for the inheritance rights of such children, which may indicate the importance of the *naditum* in the social order. It could also indicate that their social position had become somewhat precarious during Hammurabi's reign or that it was undergoing some kind of change. The latter fact may explain the inclusion of CH § 110, which metes out the death penalty for an uncloistered *naditum* who enters an ale house or runs such an establishment. If the "ale house" implies, as the commentator seems to think, a brothel or an inn frequented by prostitutes, the obvious meaning of the law is that she is forbidden all association with such a place. She must not only live respectably but must guard her reputation so as to be above reproach.[18] The need for recording such a law may indicate a looseness of morals among the cultic servants. It also indicates, as we will discuss below, an increased desire on the part of the lawmakers (or of the compilers of laws) to draw clear lines of distinction between respectable and non-respectable women.

Kulmashitum and *qadishtum* were lower-ranking temple servants, who are usually mentioned together in the texts. The distinction between them is not well understood. Their inheritance rights are specified in CH § 181, according to which they are entitled to one-third of their inheritance out of the paternal estate, if they were not given a dowry upon entering temple service. But they only hold use-rights in their portion of the inheritance as long as they live. Their inheritance belongs to their brothers.[19] Driver and Miles interpret the fact that the inheritance of these temple servants reverts to their brothers as indicating that they were not expected to produce children. This seems contradicted by the evidence from a number of sources that *qadishtum* not infrequently served as paid wet nurses and must therefore themselves have had children. They may have lived outside the cloister and married after they had spent a certain period of time in temple service. Or they may have been prostitutes while in the temple service. If so, their employment by wealthy people as nurses would indicate that their social role was not held in contempt. To make matters even more confusing, there are texts in which the goddess Ishtar is herself called a *qadishtu*.[20]

There are two "historic" accounts of sexual activities in and around the Babylonian temples, both of which have unduly influenced modern historians. One was written by the Greek historian Herodotus in the fifth century B.C. and purports to describe religious prostitution in the temple of the goddess Mylitta; the other was written by the Roman geographer Strabo some four hundred years later, confirming Herodotus. Here is Herodotus' account:

> Every woman born in the country must once in her life go and sit down in the precinct of Venus [Mylitta], and there consort with a stranger. . . . A woman who has once taken her seat is not allowed to return home till one of the strangers throws a silver coin into her lap, and takes her with him beyond the holy ground. . . . The silver coin may be of any size. . . . The woman goes with the first man who throws her money, and rejects no one. When she has gone with him, and so satisfied the goddess, she returns home, and from that time forth no gift however great will prevail with her. Such of the women . . . who are ugly have to stay a long time before they can fulfill the law. Some have waited three or four years in the precinct.[21]

Other than Strabo there is no confirmation for this story, and there are no known "laws" regulating or even referring to this practice. Herodotus may have mistaken the activities of prostitutes around the temple for a rite involving every Assyrian virgin. Another of Herodotus' stories, told to him by Babylonian priests, seems to have more historic foundation. It described a high tower in the temple of Marduk, at the top of which the high-priestess dwelt in a room with a couch, in which she was nightly visited by the God. The story somewhat parallels a historic account, dating from the first millennium B.C., which describes how the Neo-Babylonian king Nabu-naid dedicated his daughter as high-priestess of the moon-god Sin. He surrounded the building, in which she lived, with a high wall and furnished it with ornaments and fine furniture. This would be consistent with what we know of the living conditions of some of the royal high-priestesses and with the belief that the god visited them nightly, just as he nightly ate the meals prepared for him. Herodotus cites this as an example of "temple prostitution," and modern historians of prostitution repeat this after him, treating his accounts as facts. I interpret the function of the priestess as a significant example of sacral sexual service, whether actually carried out or symbolically reenacted.[22]

From the conflicting interpretations of the evidence we have about the activities of women in temple service it is difficult to arrive at an understanding of the social role of these women. What earlier was a purely religious cultic function may have become corrupted at a time when commercial prostitution already flourished in the temple precincts. Sexual intercourse performed for strangers in the temple to honor the fertility and sexual power of the goddess may have, customarily, been rewarded by a donation to the temple. Worshipers regularly brought offerings of food, oil, wine, and precious goods to the temple to honor the deities and in the hope of thus advancing their own cause. It is conceivable that this practice corrupted some of the temple servants, tempting them to keep all or some of these gifts for their own profit. Priests may also have encouraged or permitted the use of slave women and the lower class of temple servants as commercial prostitutes in order to enrich the temple. This brings us briefly to two other classes of female temple servants. One was the group of *secretu*, who were mentioned in the Code of Hammurabi in connection with inheritance laws. They were women of high rank, who probably lived cloistered. Driver and Miles suggest they may not have been priestesses but rather "officers" in charge of the women in the temple-harem. "Her duties correspond to those of the eunuch-chamberlain in guarding the palace-harem."[23] Other explanations are that this person was a male disguised as a woman or a woman disguised as a man. But in the Code of Hammurabi she is always referred to as a woman, the daughter of her father, the mother of an adopted child. This puzzling figure might be a person representing an earlier aspect of Mother-Goddess worship, which stressed bisexuality or aphroditism.

Finally, there was a class of *harimtu*, who were prostitutes attached to the temple. These may have been the daughters of slave women, and they were under the supervision of a minor temple official. It is unclear whether such women were considered to belong to the temple-harem. The Sippar texts list eleven such women. That small number makes it likely that they were slave women owned by priests or priestesses. These slaves' commercial earnings, like those of other slave workers, were turned over to their owners, who may then have given these sums to the temple.

By the middle of the first millennium B.C., if not earlier, there were two kinds of sexual activities carried on in or near the temples: sexual rites which were part of the religious ritual, and commercial prostitution. Temples, like the medieval churches, were centers for a wide range of commercial activities. Male and female prostitutes were visible around the temples because that is where the customers were. There was probably a geographic connection between temple and commercial prostitution. The causal connection—namely, that commercial prostitution developed out of temple prostitution—which historians have taken for granted, seems far less obvious than has generally been asserted.

There is some linguistic evidence we can pursue in order to understand the development of prostitution. *Kar.kid,* the Sumerian word for female prostitute, occurs in the earliest lists of professions in the Old Babylonian period, ca. 2400 B.C. Since it is mentioned right after *nam.luku,* which means "naditu-ship," one can assume its connection with temple service. It is of interest that the term *kur-garru,* a male prostitute or transvestite entertainer, appears on the same list but together with entertainers. This is in line with a practice connected with the cult of Ishtar, in which transvestites performed knife-throwing acts. On the same list we find the following female occupations: lady doctor, scribe, barber, cook. Obviously, prostitution is among the oldest professions although there is no evidence that it is the oldest.[24] Prostitutes continue to appear on several later lists of professions in the Middle Babylonian period. On a seventh century B.C. list there appear a variety of female entertainers as well as transvestites; midwife, nurse, sorceress, wet nurse, and "a gray-haired old lady." Prostitutes are listed again as *kar.kid* and *harimtu,* the Akkadian term. It is very interesting that among the twenty-five scribes on this list, there is no female scribe and that the doctors include no female doctors.[25]

The earliest references on clay tablet texts connect *harimtu* with taverns. There is even a sentence that reads, "When I sit in the entrance of the tavern, I, Ishtar, am a loving *harimtu.*"[26] These and other references have led to the association of Ishtar with taverns, and with ritual and commercial prostitution.

The existence of various occupational groups connected with both cultic sexual service and commercial prostitution tells us little about the meaning these occupations held to contemporaries. We can try to learn something about that by looking at the earliest-known poetic myth, "The Epic of Gilgamesh." The poem, which describes the exploits of a mythical god/king, who may actually have lived at the beginning of the third millennium B.C., has survived in several versions, the most complete of which is an Akkadian version, based on an earlier Sumerian version, written on twelve tablets at the beginning of the second millennium B.C. In the poem the hero's aggressive behavior has displeased his subjects and the gods:

> Day and night [is unbridled his arrogance.]. . . .
> Gilgamesh leaves not the maid to [her mother],
> the warrior's daughter, the noble spouse![27]

The gods create a man, "his double" to contend with Gilgamesh. This wild man, Enkidu, lives in harmony with the animals in the woods. "He knows neither people nor land." After Enkidu is discovered by a hunter, and flees, the hunter seeks counsel as to how to tame him. He is told to get a *harimtu*. The hunter brings her to the woods and tells her what to do:

> . . . and he [Enkidu] possessed her ripeness.
> She was not bashful as she welcomed his ardor.
> She laid aside her cloth and he rested upon her.
> She treated him, the savage, to a woman's task,
> as his love was drawn unto her.

After mating with her for six days, Enkidu finds that the wild beasts are afraid of him; "he now had wisdom, broader understanding." The harlot advises him:

> Come, let me lead thee [to] ramparted Uruk,
> To the holy temple, abode of Anu and Ishtar,
> Where lives Gilgamesh.[28]

Enkidu agrees, and the harlot leads him to Gilgamesh, whose best friend he becomes.

The temple harlot is an accepted part of society; her role is honorable—in fact, it is she who is chosen to civilize the wild man. The assumption here is that sexuality is civilizing, pleasing to the gods. The harlot does "a woman's task"; thus she is not set off from other women because of her occupation. She possesses a kind of wisdom, which tames the wild man. He follows her lead into the city of civilization.

According to another Gilgamesh fragment, which has only recently been published, Enkidu later regrets his entry into civilization. He curses the hunter and the *harimtu* for having removed him
from his former life of freedom in nature. He speaks an elaborate
curse against the *harimtu*:

> . . . I will curse you with a great curse . . .
> you shall not built a house for your debauch
> you shall not enter the tavern of girls
>
> . . .
>
> . . .
>
> May waste places be your couch,
> May the shadow of the town-wall be your stand
> May thorn and bramble skin your feet
> May drunkard and toper alike slap your cheek. . . .[29]

The nature of this curse tells us that the *harimtu* who mated
with Gilgamesh lived an easier and better life than the harlot who
has her stand at the town wall and is abused by her drunken customers. This would confirm the distinction we made earlier between the
woman engaged in sacral sexual service and the commercial prostitute. Such a distinction was more likely to have existed in the earlier
period than later.

It is likely that commercial prostitution derived directly from the
enslavement of women and the consolidation and formation of classes.
Military conquest led, in the third millennium B.C., to the enslavement and sexual abuse of captive women. As slavery became an established institution, slave-owners rented out their female slaves as
prostitutes, and some masters set up commercial brothels staffed by
slaves. The ready availability of captive women for private sexual
use and the need of kings and chiefs, frequently themselves usurpers
of authority, to establish legitimacy by displaying their wealth in
the form of servants and concubines led to the establishment of harems. These, in turn, became symbols of power to be emulated by
aristocrats, bureaucrats, and wealthy men.[30]

Another source for commercial prostitution was the pauperiza-
tion of farmers and their increasing dependence on loans in order to
survive periods of famine, which led to debt slavery. Children of
both sexes were given up for debt pledges or sold for "adoption."
Out of such practices, the prostitution of female family members for
the benefit of the head of the family could readily develop. Women
might end up as prostitutes because their parents had to sell them
into slavery or their impoverished husbands might so use them. Or

they might become self-employed as a last alternative to enslavement. With luck, they might in this profession be upwardly mobile through becoming concubines. By the middle of the second millennium B.C., prostitution was well established as a likely occupation for the daughters of the poor.

As the sexual regulation of women of the propertied class became more firmly entrenched, the virginity of respectable daughters became a financial asset for the family. Thus, commercial prostitution came to be seen as a social necessity for meeting the sexual needs of men. What remained problematic was how to distinguish clearly and permanently between respectable and non-respectable women. Perhaps another problem which needed solution was how to discourage men from associating socially with women now defined as "non-respectable." Both purposes were accomplished by the enactment of Middle Assyrian Law § 40.

Before proceeding to an analysis of the law, we need to understand that Assyrian society was more militaristic and its law code was generally harsher than that of Babylon. It is therefore difficult to say how representative this single law is of practices in other Mesopotamian societies. While there is no similar law to be found in the other surviving compilations of laws, Assyriologists generally assume that a common body of legal concepts prevailed in the region for nearly two thousand years. Other regulations of female sexuality also show similarities among the various law codes; thus one can assume that MAL § 40 was representative. Most importantly, the practice of veiling, on which it legislates, has been so ubiquitous and lasted for so many millennia into this century that one can justify the assumption that we are here dealing with the earliest known example of such a regulation, which was practiced in many other societies as well.[31]

MAL § 40 reads as follows:

Neither [wives] of [seigniors] nor [widows] nor [Assyrian women] who go out on the street may have their heads uncovered. The daughters of a seignior . . . whether it is a shawl or a robe or [a mantle], must veil themselves. . . . when they go out on the street alone, they must veil themselves. A concubine who goes out on the street with her mistress must veil herself. A sacred prostitute whom a man married must veil herself on the street, but one whom a man did not marry must have her head uncovered on the street; she must not veil herself. A harlot must not veil herself; her head must be uncovered. . . .[32]

The law also specifies that a slave girl must not veil herself. The veil, which was the symbol and emblem of the married woman, is here elevated to a distinguishing mark and its wearing is made a privilege. Yet the list seems curious. Veiling does not seem to distinguish the free from the unfree, nor the upper class from the lower. Harlots and unmarried sacred prostitutes may be free women, yet they are grouped with slaves. A slave concubine may be veiled, if accompanied by her mistress, but even a free-born concubine may not be veiled if she walks out alone. On closer examination we can see that the distinction between the women is based on their sexual activities. Domestic women, sexually serving one man and under his protection, are here designated as "respectable" by being veiled; women not under one man's protection and sexual control are designated as "public women," hence unveiled.

If the law did no more than setting down these rules it would represent a historical watershed for woman: the legal classification of women according to their sexual activities. But the law goes further by specifying the punishment for violators:

> . . . he who has seen a harlot veiled must arrest her, produce witnesses (and) bring her to the palace tribunal; they shall not take her jewelry away (but) the one who arrested her may take her clothing; they shall flog her fifty (times) with staves (and) pour pitch on her head.

Here, what began as a minor, seemingly petty regulation of morality is suddenly regarded as a major offense against the state. Witnesses must be secured; the accused must be brought before a "palace tribunal," that is, a court. The harlot's jewelry is left to her, presumably because it is the tool of her trade, but her punishment is harsh. It is also highly symbolic—covering her head with pitch gives her the only kind of "veil" to which her lowly state entitles her. Practically speaking, it also must have rendered her unfit for earning her living, for removing the pitch would necessitate shaving off her hair and thus disfigure her for a long time.

The law goes on to specify the punishment for a slave girl who is caught wearing a veil: she shall have her clothes taken away and have her ears cut off. One can only speculate on the meaning of the difference in punishment meted out to the harlot and the slave girl— is having one's ears cut off a lesser punishment than being beaten fifty stripes with staves? Is it harsher? If so, does it reflect the usual assumption of Mesopotamian law that the lowest ranking person shall suffer the most stringent punishment? In that case, does it tell us that a harlot has higher status than a slave? Apparently so.

The most interesting aspect of the law, however, concerns the punishment meted out to the person (the man) who fails to report a violation of the veiling law:

> If a seignior has seen a harlot veiled and has let (her) go without bringing her to the palace tribunal they shall flog that seignior fifty (times) with staves; they shall pierce his ears, thread (them) with a cord, (and) tie (it) at his back, (and) he shall do the work of the king for one full month.

The punishment for the man who does not denounce a veiled slave girl is the same, except that he shall also have his clothes taken from him by "his prosecutor." Driver and Miles, in their commentary on Assyrian law, explain that there is no corresponding law in the Babylonian law codes. They explain the meaning of the man's punishment: having his ears pierced and cord passed through them makes him appear to be bridled "perhaps so that he may be led through the streets and exposed to public ridicule."[33] They conclude that the law

> serves to distinguish ladies and other respectable women from harlots and slave girls. Further, while the law inflicts no penalty on a respectable woman who omits to wear the veil, it takes every possible means to prevent the wrongful assumption of it. . . . Wearing the veil is a privilege of the upper classes which the law is determined for some reason or other to maintain. It is conceivable that it may have been some sort of extension of the usage of the harem whereby a woman who is enclosed in private must also be enclosed in public.[34]

This analysis is astute, yet the authors admit that the purpose of the law is to them "obscure."

Quite to the contrary, the purpose of the law is devastatingly clear. We note that the state intervenes in prescribing the dress of women by passing the law and by requiring the bringing of the offender before a court, the calling of witnesses, the use of a prosecutor. We note also that, unlike the other crimes described in these laws, a woman's crime of "unauthorized veiling" or "passing herself off as being respectable" is an offense so great that its enforcement is made mandatory by savage punishment on any sympathetic and noncompliant men. We note also that the punishment is public—whipping, stripping naked in the street, being paraded in the street. Thus the matter of classifying women into respectable and not respectable has become an affair of the state.

MAL § 40 institutionalizes a ranking order for women: at the top the married lady or her unmarried daughter; beneath her, but still counted among the respectable, the married concubine, whether free-born or slave or temple prostitute; at the bottom, clearly marked off as not respectable, the unmarried temple prostitute, the harlot, and the slave woman.

The listing of the unmarried temple prostitute, presumably the *kulmashitum* and *qadishtum,* on the same level as a commercial harlot, and the *harimtu* and the temple harlot of slave origin, is a distinct declassing of the former. The sacral nature of sexual temple service is no longer the decisive factor; more and more the temple prostitute is regarded the same way as the commercial prostitute.

Why did the law apply with great severity to slave girls than to prostitutes? Slave girls were already distinguishable from free women by their hair style and possibly by a brand on their forehead. The most obvious reason would be that veiling might hide such identifying marks and thus allow a slave woman to "pass" as free. But the law also seeks to distinguish sharply between the slave woman and the slave concubine. The latter, when accompanied by her mistress—that is, by the first wife of the master—was to be treated as a respectable woman. In such a case her servile status would be clearly indicated, as we know from previously cited cases, by her walking behind her mistress, possibly carrying the mistress's stool or other belongings. Other slave women in the household, who were not concubines, would be identifiable in the street by not being veiled and thus revealing their slave marks. The immediate result of MAL § 40 would be to allow the slave concubine a publicly recognized status different from that of the ordinary slave woman in the household. This conforms to the various other legal and social practices, which place concubines in a social position intermediate between slave women and free wives.

The punishment meted out to men who were insufficiently vigilant in denouncing and persecuting women violators has other interesting implications. For one, it shows us that enforcement was a problem. If all men, or even most of them, had been eager and willing to enforce the law against women who violated it, no punishment would be needed against men who failed to do so. Did men think the law irrelevant? Did men of the lower classes think the law represented only the interest of upper-class men and were they therefore lax in their cooperation?[35] We may never know the answer to these questions, but the fact that enforcement of the veiling law met resistance indicates that is must have been problematic, for a time at least, for those who wished to see it enforced. Clearly, those who wished to see the law enforced regarded it as important to the interests of the state, which would mean of elite propertied men, bureaucrats, and possibly the class of temple officials.

How was a man to know whether the veiled woman he saw in the street was entitled to her veil? This is puzzling. It would surely be difficult, if not impossible, to distinguish one veiled woman from another, if we assume the veil covered not only her face and head but her figure as well.[36] The prohibition could therefore not have applied to total strangers. Most likely, it applied to women who were accompanied by men. A man walking out in the street with a veiled woman would presumably know her social standing. If she were veiled without being entitled to that privilege, he could be held responsible under the law. At first glance the occurrence of such an incident—a man walking in the street with a veiled harlot or slave girl—seems so far-fetched, one must wonder about the need to have a law forbidding it.

But what if the intent of the law were to discourage, even forbid, men from casually and publicly associating with prostitutes and slave women? The effect of such a law would then be to lower the social standing of these women and restrict their activities to purely commercial sexual services. The law might then represent an early instance of the many laws passed over the millennia regulating prostitution. Such laws always have fallen with unequal severity upon the prostitute and her customer. Having to appear in public unveiled would at once indentify a woman as a prostitute and mark her off from respectable women. It would also make a man's association with a prostitute an activity clearly distinguishable from his social contact with respectable women.

It is noteworthy that MAL § 40 provides punishment only for declassed women and nonconforming men. Why are there no punishments provided for women who fail to denounce violators of the veiling law? Mesopotamian law held women fully accountable for their deeds in other cases. Was it assumed that respectable women would need no incentive for cooperating with the law because it was in their interest to discourage men of their class from associating with declassed women? Or did the law represent the response of upper-class persons of both sexes against lower-class persons who attempted to blur class distinctions among women? The possibility that upper-class women had an interest in this legislation can neither be discounted nor can it be proven. What is clear is that the severity and public nature of the punishment made state intervention into private morality the dominant feature of the law.

Class formation demands visible means of distinguishing those belonging to different classes. Clothing, ornaments or their absence, and, in the case of slaves, visible marks of their status occur in all societies which make such distinctions important. It is not greatly significant whether MAL § 40 initiated such a practice regarding women or whether it is simply the earliest example for which we have historical evidence. What is important is to examine the way in which class distinctions were institutionalized for women and to distinguish it from the way in which this was done for men. The veiled wife, concubine, or virgin daughter was visibly identifiable by any man as being under the protection of another man. As such she was marked off as inviolate and inviolable. Conversely, the unveiled woman was clearly marked off as unprotected and therefore fair game for any man. This pattern of enforced visible discrimination recurs throughout historical time in the myriad of regulations which place "disreputable women" in certain districts or certain houses marked with clearly identifiable signs or which force them to register with the authorities and carry identification cards. Similarly, the way in which the unprotected slave girl is distinguished from the concubine will recur in many variations. One of them is the custom in the United States, during slavery times and after, of segregated eating facilities for black and white, except for those black people clearly identifiable as servants. Thus, black nurses and child-minders may appear in segregated places with their white charges; black valets may accompany their masters.

Men take their place in the class hierarchy based on their occupations or on their father's social status. Their class position may be expressed by the usual outward sign—clothing, residential location, ornaments or their absence. For women, from MAL § 40 forward, class distinctions are based on their relationship—or absence of such—to a man who protects them, and on their sexual activities. The division of women into "respectable women," who are protected by their men, and "disreputable women," who are out in the street unprotected by men and free to sell their services, has been the basic class division for women. It has marked off the limited privileges of upper-class women against the economic and sexual oppression of lower-class women and has divided women one from the other. Historically, it has impeded cross-class alliances among women and obstructed the formation of feminist consciousness.

THE CODE OF HAMMURABI marks the beginning of the institutional-ization of the patriarchal family as an aspect of state power. It re-flects a class society in which women's status depended on the male family head's social status and property. The wife of an impover-ished burgher could by a change of his status, without her volition or action, be turned from a respectable woman into a debt slave or a prostitute. On the other hand, a married woman's sexual behavior, such as adultery or an unmarried woman's loss of chastity, could declass her in a way in which no man could be declassed by his sexual activity. Women's class status is always differently defined than that of men of their class from that period on to the present.

From the Old Babylonian period to the time when the husband has power of life or death over the adulterous wife there have been great changes also in the authority of kings and rulers over the lives of men and women. The patriarchal head of the family at the time of Hammurabi was still somewhat restrained in his power over his wife by kinship obligations to the male head of the wife's family. By the time of the Middle Assyrian laws he is restrained mostly by the power of the state. Fathers, empowered to treat the virginity of their daughters as a family property asset, represent an authority as absolute as that of the king. Children reared and socialized within such authority will grow into the kinds of citizens needed in an ab-solutist kingship. The king's power was secured by men as abso-lutely dependent on and subservient to him as their families were dependent on and subservient to them. The archaic state was shaped and developed in the form of patriarchy.

As such, hierarchy and class privilege were organic to its func-tioning. Thus, a harlot who presumed to appear veiled on the streets was as great a threat to the social order as was the mutinous soldier or slave. The virginity of daughters and the monogamous faithful-ness of wives have become important features of the social order. With MAL § 40 the state has assumed the control of female sexual-ity, which had hitherto been left to individual heads of families or to kin groups. From 1250 B.C. on, from public veiling to the regu-lation by the state of birth control and abortion, the sexual control of women has been an essential feature of patriarchal power.

The sexual regulation of women underlies the formation of classes and is one of the foundations upon which the state rests.

SEVEN

The Goddesses

WE HAVE SEEN HOW in Mesopotamian societies the institutionalization of patriarchy created sharply defined boundaries between women
of different classes, although the development of the new gender
definitions and of the customs associated with them proceeded un-
evenly. The state, during the process of the establishment of written
law codes, increased the property rights of upper-class women, while
it circumscribed their sexual rights and finally totally eroded them.
The lifelong dependency of women on fathers and husbands became
so firmly established in law and custom as to be considered "natural" and god-given. In the case of lower-class women, their labor
power served either their families or those who owned their families'
services. Their sexual and reproductive capacities were commodified,
traded, leased, or sold in the interest of male family members. Women
of all classes had traditionally been excluded from military power
and were, by the turn of the first millennium B.C., excluded from
formal education, insofar as it had become institutionalized.

Yet, even then, powerful women in powerful roles lived on in
cultic service, in religious representation, and in symbols. There was
a considerable time lag between the subordination of women in patriarchal society and the declassing of the goddesses. As we trace
below changes in the position of male and female god figures in the
pantheon of the gods in a period of over a thousand years, we should
keep in mind that the power of the goddesses and their priestesses
in daily life and in popular religion continued in force, even as the

141

supreme goddesses were dethroned. It is remarkable that in societies which had subordinated women economically, educationally, and legally, the spiritual and metaphysical power of goddesses remained active and strong.

We have some indication of what practical religion was like from archaeological artifacts and from temple hymns and prayers. In Mesopotamian societies the feeding of and service to the gods was considered essential to the survival of the community. This service was performed by male and female temple servants. For important decisions of state, in warfare, and for important personal decisions one would consult an oracle or a diviner, who might be either a man or a woman. In personal distress, sickness, or misfortune the afflicted person would seek the help of his or her household-god and, if this was of no avail, would appeal to anyone of a number of gods or goddesses who had particular qualities needed to cure the affliction. If the appeal were to a goddess, the sick person also required the intercession and good services of a priestess of the particular goddess. There were, of course, also male gods who could benefit one in case of illness, and these would usually be served by a male priest.

For example, in Babylonia a sick man or woman would approach the Ishtar temple in a spirit of humility on the assumption that the sickness was a result of his or her transgression. The petitioner would bring appropriate offerings: food, a young animal for sacrifice, oil, and wine. For the goddess Ishtar such offerings quite frequently included images of a vulva, the symbol of her fertility, fashioned out of precious lapis lazuli stone.[1] The afflicted person would prostrate himself before the priestess and recite some appropriate hymns and prayers. A typical prayer contained the following lines:

> Gracious Ishtar, who rules over the universe,
> Heroic Ishtar, who creates humankind,
> who walks before the cattle, who loves the shepherd . . .
> You give justice to the distressed, the suffering you give
>   them justice.
> Without you the river will not open,
> the river which brings us life will not be closed,
> without you the canal will not open,
> the canal from which the scattered drink,
> will not be closed . . . Ishtar, merciful lady . . .
> hear me and grant me mercy.[2]

Mesopotamian men or women, in distress or sickness, humbled themselves before a goddess-figure and her priestly servant. In words reflecting the attitude of slave toward master, they praised and worshiped the goddess's power. Thus, another hymn to Ishtar addresses her as "mistress of the battle field, who pulls down the mountains"; "Majestic one, lioness among the gods, who conquers the angry gods, strongest among rulers, who leads kings by the lead; you who open the wombs of women . . . mighty Ishtar, how great is your strength!" Heaping praise upon praise, the petitioner continued:

> Where you cast your glance, the dead awaken, the sick arise;
> The bewildered, beholding your face, find the right way.
> I appeal to you, miserable and distraught,
> tortured by pain, your servant,
> be merciful and hear my prayer! . . .
> I await you, my mistress; my soul turns toward you.
> I beseech you: relieve my plight.
> Absolve me of my guilt, my wickedness, my sin,
> forget my misdeeds, accept my plea![3]

We should note that the petitioners regarded the goddess as all-powerful. In the symbol of the goddess's vulva, fashioned of precious stone and offered up in her praise, they celebrated the sacredness of female sexuality and its mysterious life-giving force, which included the power to heal. And in the very prayers appealing to the goddess's mercy, they praised her as mistress of the battlefield, more powerful than kings, more powerful than other gods. Their prayers to the gods similarly extolled the god's virtues and listed his powers in superlatives. My point here is that men and women offering such prayers when in distress must have thought of women, just as they thought of men, as capable of metaphysical power and as potential mediators between the gods and human beings. That is a mental image quite different from that of Christians, for example, who in a later time would pray to the Virgin Mary to intercede with God in their behalf. The power of the Virgin lies in her ability to appeal to God's mercy; it derives from her motherhood and the miracle of her immaculate conception. She has no power for herself, and the very sources of her power to intercede separate her irrevocably from other women. The goddess Ishtar and other goddesses like her had power in their own right. It was the kind of power men had, derived from military exploits and the ability to impose her will on the gods or to influence them. And yet Ishtar was female, endowed with a sexuality like that of ordinary women. One cannot help but wonder at the contradiction between the power of the goddesses and the increasing societal constraints upon the lives of most women in Ancient Mesopotamia.

UNLIKE THE CHANGES in the social and economic status of women, which have received only tangential and scattered attention in Ancient Mesopotamian studies, the transition from polytheism to monotheism and its attendant shift in emphasis from powerful goddesses to a single male god have been the subject of a vast literature. The topic has been approached from the vantage point of theology, archaeology, anthropology, and literature. Historical and artistic artifacts have been interpreted with the tools of their respective disciplines; linguistic and philosophical studies have added to the richness of interpretation.[4] With Freud and Jung and Erich Fromm, psychiatry and psychology have been added as analytic tools, focusing our attention on myth, symbols, and archetypes.[5] And recently a number of feminist scholars from various disciplines have discussed the period and the subject from yet another vantage point, one which is critical of patriarchal assumptions.[6]

Such a richness and diversity of sources and interpretations makes it impossible to discuss and critique them all within the confines of this volume. I will therefore focus, as I have done throughout, on a few analytic questions and discuss in detail a few models which, I believe, illustrate larger patterns.

Methodologically, the most problematic question is the relation between changes in society and changes in religious beliefs and myths. The archaeologist, art historian, and historian can record, document, and observe such changes, but their causes and their meaning cannot be given with any kind of certainty. Different systems of interpretation offer varying answers, none of which is totally satisfying. In the present case it seems to me most important to record and survey the historical evidence and to offer a coherent explanation, which I admit is somewhat speculative. So are all the other explanations including, above all, the patriarchal tradition.

I am assuming that Mesopoptamian religion responded to and reflected social conditions in the various societies. Mental constructs cannot be created from a void; they always reflect events and concepts of historic human beings in society. Thus, the existence of an assembly of the gods in "The Epic of Gilgamesh" has been interpreted as indicating the existence of village assemblies in pre-state Mesopotamian society. Similarly, the explanation in the Sumerian Atrahasis myth that the gods created men in order that men might serve them and relieve them of hard work can be regarded as a re-flection of social conditions in the Sumerian city-states of the first half of the third millennium B.C., in which large numbers of people worked on irrigation projects and in agricultural labor centered on the temples.[7] The relation between myth and reality is not usually that direct, but we can assume that no people could invent the con-cept of an assembly of the gods if they had not at some time expe-rienced and known a like institution on earth. While we cannot say with certainty that certain political and economic changes "caused" changes in religious beliefs and myths, we cannot help but notice a pattern in the changes of religious beliefs in a number of societies, following upon or concurrent with certain societal changes.

My thesis is that, just as the development of plow agriculture, coinciding with increasing militarism, brought major changes in kin-ship and in gender relations, so did the development of strong king-ships and of archaic states bring changes in religious beliefs and symbols. The observable pattern is: first, the demotion of the Mother-Goddess figure and the ascendance and later dominance of her male consort/son; then his merging with a storm-god into a male Creator-God, who heads the pantheon of gods and goddesses. Wherever such changes occur, the power of creation and of fertility is transfered from the Goddess to the God.[8]

The anthropologist Peggy Reeves Sanday offers some very inter-esting methodological suggestions for interpreting such changes. Sanday argues that gender symbolism in creation stories proves a reliable guide to sex roles and sexual identities in a given society. "By articulating how things were in the beginning, people . . . make a basic statement about their relationship with nature and about their perception of the source of power in the universe."[9] Sanday ana-lyzed 112 creation stories and the societies in which they occurred and found clearly defined patterns. She also found a clear correlation between gender definitions in creation stories and a people's mode of acquiring food and their child-rearing patterns:

> Where males pursue animals, fathers are more distant from childrear-ing and power is conceived as being "beyond man's dominance." When gathering is emphasized . . . fathers are closer to childrearing and notions about creative power turn to feminine or couple symbolism.[10]

In the 112 cases she studied 50 percent had creation stories fea-turing a male deity, 32 percent a divine couple, and 18 percent a female deity. In societies with masculine creation stories, 17 percent of the fathers cared for infants and 52 percent of the fathers hunted large game; in societies with couple creation stories 34 percent of the fathers cared for infants and 49 percent of them hunted; in societies with feminine creation stories 63 percent of fathers cared for infants and 28 percent hunted large game.[11]

If we applied Sanday's generalizations, which are derived from the study of contemporary primitive people, backward in time, we should expect to find major economic and social changes to occur prior to or at about the time in which we find evidence of the change in creation stories in the societies of the Ancient Near East.[12] Such changes do indeed occur in a number of societies during the second millennium B.C.

I will attempt to review these developments and then analyze their significance by focusing on the leading explanatory metaphors and symbols. These cluster around three basic questions all religions have to answer: (1) who creates life? (2) who brings evil into the world? (3) who mediates between humans and the supernatural? Or: to whom do the gods speak?

If these questions are approached by discussing changes in the leading metaphors, what we are looking at are the following changes in symbols: (1) from the vulva of the goddess to the seed of man; (2) from the tree of life to the tree of knowledge; (3) from the celebration of the Sacred Marriage to the Biblical covenants.

The pervasiveness of the veneration of the Mother-Goddess in the Neolithic and Chalcolithic periods has been confirmed by archaeological data. Marija Gimbutas reports that approximately 30,000 miniature sculptures in clay, marble, bone, copper, and gold are presently known from a total of some 3000 sites in southeastern Europe alone and that these testify to the communal worship of the Mother-Goddess. Gimbutas shows, by means of archaeological evidence, that the Neolithic cultural symbols survived into the third millennium B.C. in the Aegean area and into the second millennium B.C. in Crete.[13] E. O. James speaks of a fertility cult which "became firmly established in the religion of the Ancient Near East with the rise of agriculture in the Neolithic civilization in and after the fifth millennium B.C."[14]

There is a profusion of archaeological finds of female figurines, all emphasizing breasts, navel, and vulva, usually in a squatting position, which is the position commonly adopted in childbirth in this region. We find such a figure in the lowest layers of the excavations of Çatal Hüyük, at the level of the seventh millennium B.C., in the form of the pregnant, the birthing goddess. Her legs are parted; her navel and belly protrude; and she is surrounded by bulls' horns or stylized bulls' heads, which may symbolize male procreativity. Similar figurines have been found in sites in the Don valley of Russia, in Iraq, Anatolia, in Nineveh, Jericho, and in Southern Mesopotamia.

James, Gimbutas, and others have asserted unequivocally that these figurines are evidence of a widespread fertility cult. Such an assertion has met strong objections on methodological grounds. How can we know, in the absence of corroborating evidence, what meaning these figurines had for their contemporaries? How can we read their context and how can we be certain we interpret their symbolism correctly? Such figurines are, for example, found in great numbers in sites in ancient Israel of the eighth and seventh centuries B.C. This was a time when Yahwism was already firmly established as the main religion of Israel. Obviously the finding of such figurines is not sufficient reason to argue for the existence of widespread Mother-Goddess worship. A similar instance, illustrating the limits of generalizations based merely on archaeological evidence, is that of statues of the Virgin Mary in the Middle Ages. If an archaeologist of the future were to find thousands of such statues in the villages of Europe, she might be seriously misled, if she concluded from such a finding that a female deity was being worshiped there. On the other hand, that archaeologist would undoubtedly also have found evidence of the figure of Christ on the cross, which might affect her conclusions. Thus, the very absence of other figurative representations in comparable numbers in Neolithic sites entitles one to the conclusion that these figures had special, possibly religious meaning. Their common characteristics, their wide dispersal, and conventionalized execution suggest, at the very least, their use as amulets, possibly to help women in childbirth. Such figurines appear for thousands of years in a wide area.

Another possible interpretation is that the finding of such figures in many sites speaks to the continued existence of a popular religious practice, which coexists or stands in contrast to established religion. Such a conclusion would be warranted concerning the naked goddess figurines in Israel in the eighth century B.C. and the images of the Virgin Mary in medieval Europe.

The strongest argument in favor of the religious significance of the Neolithic female figures is the historical evidence from the fourth millennium forward derived from myths, rituals, and creation stories. In them, the Mother-Goddess is virtually universal as the dominant figure in the most ancient stories. This entitles us to read meaning back into the archaeological findings with some degree of confidence. Still, there is some danger that we may distort meaning by overgeneralizing from partial evidence. The Assyrologist A. L. Oppenheim cautions against this danger in regard to our interpretation of Mesopotamian religion in the second millennium B.C. For this period much more evidence—archaeological, literary, economic, and political—is available, yet Oppenheim considers it nearly impossible for modern scholars to reconstruct the world view and religious values of that civilization.[15] At best we can say that a profusion of female figurines with sexual features emphasizing maternity found in the Neolithic correspond to later mythological and literary material celebrating the power of female goddesses over fertility and fecundity. It is likely that this speaks to earlier Great Goddess worship, but it is not certain.

We are on firmer ground with archaeological evidence from the fourth millennium forward. Female goddess figures appear in more elaborate settings and with distinct and consistently recurring symbolic attributes. The Goddess is shown amidst pillars or trees, accompanied by goats, snakes, birds. Eggs and symbols of vegetation are associated with her. These symbols indicate that she was worshiped as a source of fertility for vegetation, animals, and humans. She is represented by the Minoan snake-goddess, with her breasts exposed. She was venerated in Sumer as Ninhursag and Inanna; in Babylon as Kubab and Ishtar; in Phoenicia as Astarte; in Canaan as Anath; in Greece, as Hekate-Artemis. Her frequent association with the moon symbolized her mystical powers over nature and the seasons. The belief system manifested in Great Goddess worship was monistic and animistic. There was unity among earth and the stars, humans and nature, birth and death, all of which were embodied in the Great Goddess.

The cults of the Great Goddess were based on the belief that it is she, in one or another of her manifestations, who creates life. But she was also associated with death. She was praised and celebrated for her virginity and her maternal qualities. The goddess Ishtar, for example, was described as free with her sexual favors, the protector of prostitutes, the patron of ale-houses, and simultaneously the virginal bride of gods (as in the Dumuzi myths). Female sexuality was sacred to her service and honored in her rituals. Ancient people saw no contradictions in these contrasting attributes. The duality of the

Goddess represented the duality observable in nature—night and day, birth and death, light and darkness. Thus, in the earliest known phases of religious worship the female force was recognized as awesome, powerful, transcendent.

The supremacy of the Goddess is also expressed in the earliest myths of origin, which celebrate the life-giving creativity of the female. In Egyptian mythology the primeval ocean, the goddess Nun, gives birth to the sun-god Atum, who then creates the rest of the universe. The Sumerian goddess Nammu creates parthenogenetically the male sky-god An and the female earth-goddess Ki. In Babylonian myth the goddess Tiamat, the primeval sea, and her consort give birth to gods and goddesses. In Greek mythology, the earth-goddess Gaia, in a virgin birth, creates the sky, Uranos. The creation of humans is also ascribed to her. In the Assyrian version of an older Sumerian myth the wise Mami (also known as Nintu), "the mother-womb, the one who creates mankind," fashions humans out of clay, but it is the male god Ea "who opened the navel" of the figures, thus completing the life-giving process. In another version of the same story, Mami, at the urging of Ea, herself finished the creative process: "The Mother-Womb, the creatress of destiny/in pairs she completed them. . . . The forms of the people Mami forms." [16]

These creation stories express concepts deriving from earlier modes of the worship of female fertility. The primal force in nature is the sea, the water, the mystery of the egg, which opens to create new life. Snake-goddess, sea-goddess, virgin-goddess, and goddess molding humans out of clay—it is the female who holds the key to the mystery.

On the other hand, we should note here that while the creative act is performed by the Goddess, the male god frequently is decisively involved in initiating the process of creation. The recognition of the necessary cooperation of the female and the male principle in the process of creation seems to be firmly established in Sumerian and Akkadian mythology.

With the domestication of animals and the development of animal husbandry, the function of the male in the process of procreation became more apparent and was better understood.[17] At a later stage of development we find the Mother-Goddess associated with a male partner, either a son or a brother, who assists her in the fertility rites by mating with her. In myth and ritual the male god is young, and he may have to die in order for rebirth to take place. It is still the Great Goddess who creates life and governs death, but there is now a more pronounced recognition of the male part in procreation.

The Sacred Marriage *(hieros gamos)* and similar annual rites, which were celebrated widely in many different societies in the fourth and third millennia B.C., expressed these beliefs. Not until the Goddess had mated with the young god and his death and rebirth had taken place, could the annual cycle of the seasons begin. The sexuality of the Goddess is sacred and confers the blessings of fertility to earth and to the people who through their ritual observances please her. The ritual of the Sacred Marriage took many forms and was widely practiced in Mesopotamia, Syria, Canaan, and the Aegean. Among its many complex meanings is that it transformed the all-encompassing fertility of the Mother-Goddess into the more domesticated fertility of the "goddess of cultivated grain."[18]

There is also, in these myths from the third and second millennia B.C., evidence that a new concept of creation enters religious thinking: Nothing exists unless it has a name. The name means existence. The gods receive their existence through name-giving, as do humans. The Babylonian "Creation Epic" *(Enuma Elish)* begins as follows:

> Firm ground below had not been called by name,
> Naught but primordial Apsu, the begetter,
> (and) Mummu-Tiamat, she who bore them all,
> Their waters commingling as a single body. . . .
> When no gods whatever had been brought into being,
> Uncalled by name, their destinies undetermined—
> Then it was that the gods were formed within them.[19]

Here the fertility principle, primarily lodged in the Mother-Goddess, requires the "commingling' with the male "begetter" before the cycle of birth can begin. But before creation can take place, there must be a concept, something "within them," which will later be "named" or "called" to life. Similarly, in "The Epic of Gilgamesh," the goddess Aruru is called by the other gods and commanded to fashion a man, a double for Gilgamesh:

> Create now his double . . .
> When Aruru heard this,
> A double of Anu she conceived within her.
> Aruru washed her hands,
> Pinched off clay and cast it on the steppe,
> [On the step]pe she created valiant Enkidu.[20]

In another Akkadian myth the god Enlil draws the likeness of a dragon on the sky, which then comes to life. As the Assyriologist Georges Contenau observes: "The creating god mentally defines the nature-to-be of his creation: when it has taken final shape in his imagination and he has given it a name, he draws its shape, whereby it acquired almost complete life."[21]

Naming has profound significance in the Old Mesopotamian belief system. The name reveals the essence of the bearer; it also carries magic power. The concept lives on through the millennia in myth and fairy tale. The person who can guess the name of another acquires power over him, as in the German fairy tale "Rumpelstilskin." A person newly endowed with power is renamed. Thus, the god Marduk, in the Babylonian creation myth, is given fifty names as tokens of his power. We will discuss later how this power of names and naming is used in the Book of Genesis. What is important to observe here is that the concept of creation has changed, at a certain period in history, from being merely the acting out of the mystic force of female fertility to being a conscious act of creation, often involving god-figures of both sexes. This element of consciousness, expressed in "the idea," "the concept," "the name" of that which will be created, may be the reflection of an altered human consciousness due to significant changes in society.

The time when these concepts first appear is the time when writing has been "invented" and with it history. Record-keeping and the elaboration of symbol systems demonstrate the power of abstraction. The name recorded enters history and becomes immortal. This must have appeared as magical to contemporaries. Writing , record-keeping, mathematical thinking, and the elaboration of various symbol systems altered people's perception of their relation to time and space. It should not surprise us to find that religious myths reflected these changes in consciousness.

From the point of view of this study, which focuses on the development and institutionalization of patriarchal gender symbols, we should notice that the symbolification of the capacity to create, as in the concept of naming, simplifies the move away from the Mother-Goddess as the sole principle of creativity.

It is, so to speak, a higher level of thinking to move away from the common-sense observable facts of female fertility and conceptualize a symbolic creativity, which can be expressed in "the name," "the concept." It is not a very big step from that to the concept of "the creative spirit" of the universe. Yet precisely that step forward in the ability to make abstractions and create symbols that can stand for abstract concepts is an essential precondition to the move toward monotheism. Until people could imagine an abstract, unseen, unknowable power which embodied such a "creative spirit," they could not reduce their numerous, anthropomorphic, contentious gods and goddesses to the One God. The transitional stage is expressed in those creation myths, which describe the "creative spirit" as the god of the air, the god of the winds, the god of thunder, who creates by bringing to life mechanically fashioned beings through his "breath of life." It seems to me likely that historic changes in society, which emphasized kingship and military leadership, would lead men to reach for a male god symbol to embody that newly realized principle of symbolic creativity. As we will see, that process continues for a period of more than a thousand years and culminates in the Book of Genesis. The fact that in Egyptian belief generativity was embodied in the male god Osiris as early as the third millennium B.C. supports the thesis that religious beliefs reflected societal conditions. Here, the early establishment of strong kingship, in which the Paraohs reigned as gods incarnate, was reflected in the power and dominance of the male gods in the creation myths.

The next major change observable in creation myths occurs contemporaneously with the rise of archaic states under strong kings. Sometime beginning in the third millennium B.C. the figure of the Mother-Goddess is replaced from the head of the pantheon of gods. She gives way to a male god, usually the god of wind and air or the god of thunder, who more and more, as time progresses, comes to resemble an earthly king of the new kind.

In this process of transformation the former Earth-Goddesses now appear as daughters and wives of vegetation-gods. The Mesopotamian Damkina, Lady of the Earth, becomes the consort of Ea or Enki, god of the waters. Similar transformations take place in the Mother-Goddesses—Ninlil, Nintu, Ninhursag, Aruru. The earliest Sumerian description of the pantheon of gods show the heaven-god An and the earth-goddess Ki presiding in unison over the other gods.[22] Out of their union springs the air-god Enlil. His chief place of worship is Nippur, a city-state in constant conflict with Eridu, whose deity is Enki. In ca. 2400 B.C. the leading gods are listed in order as An (heaven), Enlil (air), Ninhursag (queen of the mountain) and Enki (lord of the earth). Ninhursag may represent the earth-goddess Ki, now relegated to a minor position. In still later texts, ca. 2000 B.C., she is mentioned last, after Enki. The Sumerologist Samuel

Noah Kramer explains this change in the theogeny as the result of the increasing influence of priests, who are associated with particular temples and particular cities and their rulers. These priests now record the ancient myths in such a way as to serve political ends. Kramer notices the absence from the list of Namu, the Mother-Goddess, formerly hailed as creator of the universe and mother of the gods. He thinks her powers were transferred to her son Enki "in an apparent attempt to justify this bit of priestly piracy."[23]

The relationship of societal change and changes in the theogeny become even more explicit later. In the *Enuma Elish*, to which we alluded earlier (written ca. 1100 B.C.), chaos, in the form of the life-giving Tiamat, is confronted by rebellious primitive gods, who wish to create order. A terrible battle ensues, in which the rebellious gods are led by a young god, who then physically destroys Tiamat and creates, out of her carcass, the earth and the heavens. The gods now also slay Tiamat's husband, and from his blood, mixed with soil, they create humankind. It is highly significant that the young god who slays Tiamat in the epic is Marduk, the god worshipped in the city of Babylon. Marduk first emerges during the time of Hammurabi of Babylon, who has made his city-state dominant in the Mesopotamian region. In *Enuma Elish*, written down some 600 years later, some of the old mythical material is transformed into a major theological system. The young god Marduk now is elevated to supreme power among the gods. In a similar process in a period of their political dominance the Assyrians told their creation myth by putting their national god Ashur in the center of their story.[24] As one scholar observes:

> The rise of two national gods, Marduk and Ashur, to positions of supreme power in the world of gods . . . reflects the eventual crystallization of Mesopotamia into the two rival national states, each under an absolute monarch. . . . Power and decision were now centered in Marduk and Ashur, the other gods acting as their agents or as intercessors with them.[25]

In Canaanite mythology, the young storm-god Baal moves to the head of the pantheon. When, in conflict with his adversary Mot, the god of death, he descends to the underworld, all vegetation ceases on earth. Baal's sister and consort, Anath, searches for him everywhere. When she finds his dead body, she buries him and engages in a fierce battle with Mot, in which she kills him. She cuts up Mot's body, crushes it, winnows it in a sieve, grinds it in a mill, and scatters it over the fields. This symbolic treatment of Mot, as though he were grain, helps restore fertility to the earth. When Baal returns from the dead for further battles and eventual victory over Mot, Anath, who had in the myth shown all the ancient qualities of the Mother-Goddess—fierceness in battle, strength, and the power to grant fertility—now is overshadowed by him, who has become the supreme god and giver of life.[26]

We have earlier discussed how kings take over the temple of the supreme deity. Thus, in Lagash, in the earliest period of kingship, Lugalanda appointed himself chief administrator of the temple of the god Ningirsu and his wife Baranamtarra chief administrator of the temple of the goddess Bau. In a later period, such as the reign of Hammurabi, when the kingship is already well-established and embraces a vast realm, the king embodies some of the divine leadership. It is as though there were a continues flow of power, sacredness, and energy between god and king. It is not surprising that in the process the Mother-Goddess not only loses her supremacy but generally becomes domesticated and transformed into the supreme god's wife. Yet, at the same time, in some mysterious way she separates off and acquires a new life and new identity in a variety of forms, which continue to have force in popular religion. We will discuss that process below.

The changing position of the Mother-Goddess, her dethroning, takes place in many cultures and at different times, but usually it is associated with the same historical processes. In Elam the Mother-Goddess reigns supreme in the third millennium B.C., but becomes secondary in importance to her consort Humban at a later date. The same development occurred at different times in Anatolia, in Crete, and in Greece. In Egypt, where the male God early predominates, we can also find traces of a still earlier predominance of the Goddess. Isis as the "throne woman" embodied the mysterious power of kingship. As E. O. James puts it: "As such she was the source of vitality before she became the proto-type of the life-giving mother and faithful wife."[27]

A closer look at Hittite society and its development provides us with a good case study for the transition from matrilineal kinship and royal succession to patrilineal kinship and succession and its reflections in religion.

Hittite society flourished between 1700–1190 B.C. in ancient Anatolia. It combined elements of the more ancient Hatti culture with those of an Indo-European people, who overwhelmed the region probably at the end of the third millennium B.C. Early Hatti governance was based on a system in which the right of succession lodged in the *tawananna*, the prince's sister. The Hatti royal house practiced brother-sister marriage, similar to the kinship arrangement of royal families in Egypt. A male ruler married his sister, who as *tawananna* was a priestess with considerable economic and political power, such as the right to collect taxes from cities. Her male child inherited the right of succession, not because his father was the king, but because the right of succession lodged in the *tawananna*. The office was hereditary, so that the *tawananna*'s daughter, who inherited her office, inherited as important a position of power as did her brother. Later, when brother-sister marriage was outlawed, the *tawananna* continued as priestess and held the power of succession. This now meant that her brother's son would succeed to the throne.

Early in the second millennium, the first strong Hittite king, Hattusilis I, not only challenged the traditional rule of succession, by appointing his grandson over his son as his successor, which brought him in conflict with his aunt, but he also abolished the office of *tawananna* and proclaimed himself chief priest. He also began to appoint royal princesses as priestesses in the Goddess's sanctuaries.[28] We have seen earlier, how this same process occurred in Sumer during the formation of archaic states.

But the decree of Hattusilis I did not abolish the strong matrilineal tradition, and the rule of succession, that the *tawananna*'s brother's son shall be king, persisted. Hattusilis's grandson continued Hittite expansion by invading Babylon, but he was assassinated, and the kingdom was plagued by internal familial conflict and palace murders over the issue of succession. These coincided with Hurrian invasion and conquest of most of Syria.

A royal son-in-law, Telepinu, who became king, probably in line with the old matrilineal custom of accepting a ''marrying-in-man'' to the royal succession in the absence of an heir, tried to lay down patriarchal succession in his Edict, ca. 1525 B.C. The edict specified that if there were no sons available for the succession, the husband of the first-ranking daughter should become king. The edict also describes the previous period of bloodshed, which seemed to have been due the transition from one kinship system to the other. It certainly testifies to the strength of the tradition of matrilineal succession.[29]

The tradition was strong enough to survive for another 150 years, during which a new dynasty came to power. It was reflected in the quarrel of King Tuthaliya with his sister, whom he accused of having used witchcraft. The quarrel was resolved by a compromise, by which the king's son succeeded to the kingship, while the king's daughter became *tawananna* and exercised the office of the priestess to the sun-goddess. By this arrangement the right of succession was subtly shifted to the king. It was the last time in Hittite history that a brother-sister pair thus shared temporal and religious power. That these internal struggles weakened the government can be seen from the fact that the country's enemies brought it to near-extinction.

In 1380 B.C. a strong king, Suppiluliumas I, ushered in the New Hittite period of empire-building, which for nearly a hundred years would make the Hittite kingdom rival Egypt and Babylon in grandeur. He reestablished Hittite hegemony over Syria by conquering the Hurrians and extending his realm to Damascus. Most likely, his success in finally abolishing the office of the *tawananna* as the embodiment of the right of matrilineal succession is integrally connected with his strong kingship and success as an empire builder. Suppiluliumas I transformed the *tawananna* office by installing his queen in it, thus retaining the form, while transposing the content. Henceforth, succession rights were vested in the king, whose wife, not sister or daughter, was invested *by his power* in her office as *tawananna* and priestess, both now offices divested of their major and inheritable powers.

Suppiluliumas I pacified conquered areas by installing figurehead kings, who became his vassals, and to whom he married his daughters. We have seen this practice followed for similar dynastic reasons in Sumer and in Mari. It is a practice which significantly alters the relationship of women to political power, by making them tools of male power decisions and making their power dependent on their sexual and reproductive services to a particular male.

The son of Suppiluliumas I and his grandson followed in his footsteps by extending Hittite power to the Aegean and to Syria. Once again, after the grandson's death, there ensued a battle over the succession, which ended with the usurpation of the throne by the king's brother, Hattusilis III. This king, who signed treaties of friendship and mutual assistance with Egypt and Babylon, brought the kingdom to its greatest prosperity. He elevated his wife, Puduhepa, to co-ruler. It is significant that even then the old tradition of succession was so strong that the usurper-king found it necessary to write an "Apology," in which he credits his patron goddess, Ishtar, with inspiring his accession to power and with marrying his wife Puduhepa. Thus, the strong tradition of matrilineal succession and political power by women was transformed after three hundred years of struggle into the office of a powerful queen serving as her husband's stand-in in a patriarchal society.[30]

Hittite power continued for another fifty years after Hattusilis III's death and was ended about 1200 B.C. by invasions of the "sea peoples," followed a few hundred years later by Assyrian conquest of the entire region. What remained of the Hittite empire was a language, a strong artistic tradition, and hieroglyphic writing. For our purposes, however, there also remained the story of the transformation of the pantheon of gods and goddesses, which coincided with the political developments traced above.

Carol F. Justus, who by comparative linguistic means has studied the transformation of the Hittitie pantheon, has observed that the major god-figures underwent a sex change in the process, which she interprets as symbolic of political and social changes of the two sexes in Hittite society.[31]

Prior to the Hittite conquest the Indo-European inhabitants of the land had worshipped a pantheon of gods and goddesses headed by a sun-god (sawel) and a storm-god (dyew). Both figures occur in different forms in many ancient religions. The sun-god is everywhere characterized as "wide-seeing," all-encompassing. His chariot is drawn by horses across the sky. The storm-god (Sanskrit, Dyaus pitar; Greek, Zeus, Homeric, Zeu(s) pater; Latin, Jupiter) is characterized as "shining," father, begetter of men, progenitor. He is associated with the weather and with lightning. Hattic inhabitants of the region also worshipped a sun-goddess, Estan, and a storm-god, Taru.

The Hittites, synthesizing elements of both cultures, worshipped a sun-god, Istanu, who was a revised version of the sun-goddess Estan, now changed to a male. This male god was, in in the New Hittite empire, worshipped as "father" and "king." In hymns celebrating him, he is credited with establishing the custom and law of the land, and he is addressed as "father and mother of the oppressed." His epithet may well be an allusion to his origin in both a female and a male deity. His divine kingship parallels that of the Sumerian Marduk and the Assyrian Ashur, deities who ascend to heavenly kingship with the establishment of a strong kingdom on earth.

In a somewhat later Hittite period the sun-goddess Arinna is worshipped as "Queen." She echoes back to the ancient goddess Estan, who was associated with the underworld, but now her cult symbols associated her with the sun. Significantly, Queen Puduhepa, who was co-ruler with her husband at the time when patriarchal rule was firmly institutionalized, addressed this goddess as "Queen of Heaven and Earth." At a time when the *tawananna* is the wife of the king and no longer incorporates the royal line of succession, this shift in the function of the female goddess, now hailed as patron and protector of king and queen, may well serve to give heavenly legitimacy to an earthly reversal of power. It will not surprise us to learn that in a still later period the sun-goddess Arinna has become Hepat, the consort of the sun-god, who has meanwhile himself become dethroned by the storm-god Tesup. The development here is similar to the pattern we have noticed elsewhere of the sun-god being replaced by the storm-god.

Carol Justus defines the significance of these changes as follows:

> Not until the Hittite King assumed the *tawananna's* religious authority, as well as the primary right of his own son in the succession, did he in fact control the Hatti land. . . . Attempts to incorporate female spheres of authority were progressive. . . . Shifts in the pantheon from Sungoddess Estan, the Queen, to Sungod Istanu, the King, to the new King in Heaven, the Stormgod reflect the gradual absorption of female rights by patriarchal structure.[32]

What we know of religious practices in the Ancient Near East comes to us in the form of literary and religious documents preserved in clay tablets. These are overwhelmingly the product of priestly scribes associated with various temples or palaces. Even if we disregard ideological distortions and alterations in basic texts in the interests of a particular divinity or royal personage, we must understand that what we are analyzing here are those myths and texts transmitted and approved by a societal elite. The recorded versions of the myths and theogenies may have enjoyed widespread popular support, but we cannot be sure of that. The shift from the Mother-Goddess to the thunder-god may be more prescriptive than descriptive. It may tell us more about what the upper class of royal servants, bureaucrats, and warriors wanted the population to believe than what the population actually did believe.

For in the very centuries in which we have been tracing changes in the direction of patriarchal god-figures, the cult of certain goddesses flourished and diffused ever more widely. The Great Goddess may have been demoted in the pantheon of the gods, but she continued to be worshipped in her manifold manifestations. All Assyriologists testify to her enormous popularity and the persistence of her cult, in various guises, in all the major cities of the Near East for nearly two thousand years. The ancient Mother-Goddesses absorbed the features and characteristics of similar goddesses in other regions, as their cults diffused in the wake of conquests and territorial occupations.

The Egyptian Isis offers an example of the diffusion and synthesizing aspect of Great Goddess worship. As the "throne-woman" in the earliest period, she had embodied the sacred kingship and mysterious knowledge; later she became the prototype of the mother and faithful wife. She taught her brother-spouse Osiris the secrets of agriculture and restored his dismembered body to life. In the Hellenistic period she was worshipped as the Magna Mater of western Asia and the Graeco-Roman world.

In other instances, the Great Goddess herself became transformed. In the earlier period her attributes had been all-encompassing—her sexuality connected with birth, death, and rebirth; her power both for good and evil, for life and death; her aspects those of mother, warrior, protector, and interceder with the dominant male god. In the later periods her various qualities were split off and embodied in separate goddesses. Her warrior aspect diminished, probably relegated to the male god, and her qualities as a healer were more and more stressed. This does appear to reflect a change in concepts of gender in the societies in which she was worshipped.

Her erotic aspect was emphasized in the Greek goddess Aphrodite and in the Roman goddess Venus. Her quality as healer and protector of women in childbirth became embodied in the goddess Mylitta in Assyria and in Artemis, Eleithyia, and Hera in Greece. The cult of Asherah in Canaan, which coexisted for centuries with the cult of Yahweh and which is frequently condemned in the Old Testament, may have been due to the association of the goddess with protection in childbirth. To discuss her many properties and the forms in which she was worshipped would require a separate chapter.[33] Statuaries in her likeness and with her symbols are widespread, testifying to her popularity. Many of these were found not only in temples but in homes, indicating the important place of her worship in popular religion. We may be justified in regarding the extraordinary persistence of fertility and goddess cults as an expression of female resistance to the predominance of male god figures. There is as yet no hard evidence to prove this speculation, but it is difficult to explain the persistence of these female cults in any other way.

In the second millennium B.C. men and women stood in the same relation to the mysterious and awesome forces represented by the gods and goddesses. Gender distinctions were not yet used to explain the causes of evil and the problem of death. The cause of pain and human suffering was the sinfulness of men and women and their neglect of their duty toward the gods. And the kingdom of death, in Mesopotamian belief, was as likely to be governed by a female supernatural as not. The great philosophical questions: who creates human life? who speaks to God? could still be answered: human beings, men and women.

No matter how degraded and commodified the reproductive and sexual power of women was in real life, their essential equality could not be banished from thought and feeling as long as the goddesses lived and were believed to rule human life. Women must have found their likeness in the goddess, as men found theirs in the male gods. There was a perceived and essential equality of human beings before the gods, which must have radiated out into daily life. The power and mystery of the priestess was as great as that of the priest. As long as women still mediated between humans and the supernatural, they might perform different functions and roles in society than those of men, but their essential equality as human beings remained unassailed.

Illustrations

Various representations of major goddess figures are to be found in illustrations 1–13, from the earliest fertility goddesses to the powerful multifaceted Inanna/Ishtar.

Numbers 6 and 7 represent a ceremony, probably a religious festival in which the produce of the fields and of herds is offered to the goddess and her priestess. The fertility of fields and herds is represented by the images in the bottom row of the Vase from Uruk. Note the difference in status of the priestess, who is fully and formally clothed and the bearers of the offerings, who are naked.

Number 8 shows the goddess with her insignia among the other gods.

Number 10 shows the goddess bestowing her blessing and her sponsorship on worshipping dignitaries and on kings. The power of kingship is thus symbolically represented as deriving from the blessing and sponsorship of the goddess.

Number 11 shows the goddess Ishtar in her capacity as a warrior, dressed in warrior's garb and standing on a lion. Notice, in this late cylinder seal, the association of the goddess with the fruit-bearing tree.

Number 12 shows the ruler of Larsa, Gudea, holding a container spewing forth water as a symbol of his power to make the land fertile. A somewhat later representation from the palace of King Zimrilim of Mari in illustration 13 shows the goddess in an identical pose holding a similar vessel. As can be seen in the side view, the hollowed-out statue could be filled with water from the back, which could, at the appropriate moment, spew forth "miraculously." Although we cannot here demonstrate a sequential development by means of pictorial representations, we do know from prayers and hymns, that the power of the goddess to make the water flow and the land fertile had been celebrated for hundreds of years before the rulers symbolically appropriated it.

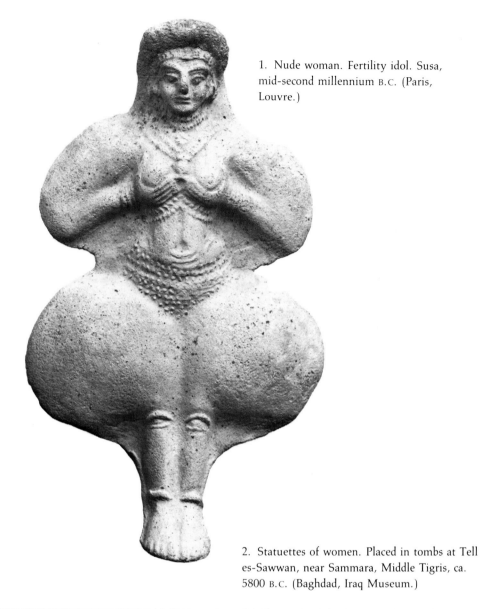

1. Nude woman. Fertility idol. Susa, mid-second millennium B.C. (Paris, Louvre.)

2. Statuettes of women. Placed in tombs at Tell es-Sawwan, near Sammara, Middle Tigris, ca. 5800 B.C. (Baghdad, Iraq Museum.)

3. Mother-Goddess giving birth. Čatal Hüyük.

4. Goddess Bau. Fragment of Stele of Gudea. Lagash, ca. 2200 B.C. (Paris, Louvre.)

5. Woman's head from Uruk. Early Sumerian, ca. 3250 B.C. (Baghdad, Iraq Museum.)

6. Alabaster vase from Uruk. Early Sumerian. (Baghdad, Iraq Museum.)

7. Detail of Uruk vase. (Baghdad, Iraq Museum.)

8. Cylinder seal of the scribe Adda. Great gods on morning of new year.
Agade period. (London, British Museum. Courtesy of the Trustees of the
British Museum.)

9. Cylinder seal. UR III/Isin period, ca. 2255–2040 B.C. (London, British
Museum. Courtesy of the Trustees of the British Museum.)

10. The goddess Ishtar, leading a king by the hand. Ca. 1700 B.C. (Friedrich-Schiller-Universität, Jena-DDR.)

11. The goddess Ishtar standing on a lion. Cylinder seal, Assyrian, 750–650 B.C. (London, British Museum. Courtesy of the Trustees of the British Museum.)

12. Gudea with flowing vase. Telloh, ca. 2200 B.C. (Paris, Louvre.)

13. Goddess with watering-bowl. Palace of King Zimrilim of Mari, ca.
2040–1870 B.C. (Hirmer Verlag.)

Illustrations 14 and 15 show women worshippers from the third millennium B.C. The strong, dignified renditions of their bodies and faces and their individualized expressions are quite remarkable. These women are represented with dignity and showing personal characteristics which, since they are not royal personages, may indicate a generally respectful attitude toward women in the society. In European art, after classical antiquity, we do not find such individualized representations of lower-class persons until the early Renaissance.

Illustration 16 comes from Anatolia and shows a spinning woman (mother) with a male child, who is holding up a stylus. On a similar relief from the same time and place, which is not shown here, we see a woman, who is seated, holding a child on her lap, who holds up a tablet and a falcon. In that representation the woman's pose and expression make it clear she is the boy's mother. These pictures indicate the distance we have come from an earlier period when women as well as men were scribes in the service of the temples. Now, the woman may be proud of her learned son, while she pursues the feminine skills of the weaver.

Illustration 17 is identified as that of a hierodule of the goddess Astarte. Because her face is unveiled in public and she displays herself in the open window of a building she is considered to represent a prostitute or possibly a religious sexual servant. The fact that this representation is part of a piece of furniture, namely, a bedstead, underscores its implicit sexual meaning.

Illustrations 18–23 shows various representations of the Tree of Life. These are arranged chronologically and derive from different places. We should notice the association of the tree with mythological creatures (18–20). In 20 and 21 the figures distinctly represent warriors, possibly one of them the king.

In illustrations 18–21 we see the Tree of Life symbol as central to the composition. Kings, servants, or various mythical creatures are shown watering or pollinating the tree. The fact that this symbol is central to palace art and also appears on cylinder seals would indicate that it was widely dispersed and recognized. The later the period, the more the symbol becomes disassociated from a realistic representation of tree or plant and from its association with the life-giving symbol of water. In 19 and 21, which come from the palace of King Ashurnarsipal II of Assyria, we can see it in its most stylized and decorative form. The fact that in this palace, which is overwhelmingly decorated with reliefs showing manly pursuits, such as war and conquest and lion hunting, the king is shown in the act of caring for and fertilizing the tree of life, adds significance to the symbol. Notice the gesture of all the male figures in the relief pointing toward the tree (20 and 21) and the winged bird, representing divine power, hovering over the tree. We interpret it as a symbolic representation of the power of creating life, now firmly and finally in the hands of the king, not of the goddess.

Illustration 22, from a large relief from the palace of King Ashurnarsipal II of Assyria shows the victory banquet of the king. It is noteworthy because it features the queen as an active participant at a public ceremony. There are various servants and entertainers, male and female, in evidence. The Tree of Life, with its symbol of fertility, the date or the pomegranate, is prominently featured.

Illustration 23 shows King Xerxes enthroned with servants, retinue, and standard bearers. In his upraised right hand he holds a flower (detail, illus. 24). It is a symbolic flower we have seen earlier in connection with the Tree of Life.

Illustrations 25, 26, and 27 represent portions of Michelangelo's Sistine Chapel ceiling and depict the story of the Creation of Man and of Woman and the story of the Fall. The power to give life is now represented by the bearded patriarchal God, the Father. The tree has become the tree of the forbidden fruit. The tempter is the snake, long associated with the goddess. The powerful images of Michelangelo more clearly represent the metaphors for gender held in the Judeo-Christian tradition than do the glosses and explanations. Adonai may be sexless and invisible; but in the popular imagination it is the bearded Father-God who creates life. And the first command to the fallen woman is that there shall be enmity between her and the snake.

14. Praying woman from Khafaje. Third millennium B.C. (Baghdad, Iraq Museum.)

15. Statuette of worshipping woman. Ca. 2900–2460 B.C. (London, British Museum. Courtesy of the Trustees of the British Museum.)

16. Spinning woman with scribe. From grave in Marash, eighth to seventh century B.C. (Adana, Museum.)

17. Astarte-hierodule. Nimrud, palace of Ashurnarsipal II (imported from Phoenicia), ca. eighth century B.C. (London, British Museum. Courtesy of the Trustees of the British Museum.)

18. Cylinder seal, Porada 609. A bird genius picks a cluster of dates from a tree. Ca. 1200 B.C. (New York, Morgan Library. Courtesy of the Trustees of The Pierpont Morgan Library.)

19. Standing eagle-headed genius in front of a palm tree. Nimrud, palace of King Ashurnarsipal II, ca. 883– 859 B.C. (Paris, Louvre.)

20. Seal of Mushezib-Ninurta. Tell Arban, northern Syria, ca. 850 B.C. (London, British Museum. Courtesy of the Trustees of the British Museum.)

21. King Ashurnarsipal II with a winged god worshipping the sacred tree. Nimrud, palace of King Ashurnarsipal II, 883–859 B.C. (London, British Museum.)

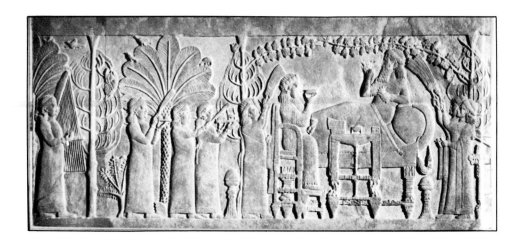

22. Victory celebration of King Ashurbanipal and Queen Ashursharrat. (London, British Museum. Courtesy of the Trustees of the British Museum.)

23. *Facing page, top.* King Xerxes, enthroned. (Persepolis, Teheran Museum.)

24. *Facing page, bottom.* Detail of flower. (Persepolis, Teheran Museum.)

27. Michelangelo, The Fall of Man and the Expulsion from the Garden of Eden. (Sistine Chapel. Alinari/Art Resource, New York.)

25. *Facing page, top.* Michelangelo, The Creation of Man. (Sistine Chapel. Alinari/Art Resource, New York.)

26. *Facing page, bottom.* Michelangelo, The Creation of Woman. (Sistine Chapel. Alinari/Art Resource, New York.)

The Patriarchs

WESTERN CIVILIZATION DRAWS many of its leading metaphors and definitions of gender and morality from the Bible. Before we consider these leading symbols, which have defined and shaped so much of our cultural heritage, we need to gain some understanding of the culture out of which the Bible came, and we need to survey, however briefly, the historic evidence within the Bible for the position of women in Hebrew society. A study of the Old Testament in its entirety would be far beyond the scope of this work. I have chosen to concentrate on the Book of Genesis, because it has provided the leading and most significant symbols concerning gender.

The use of the Bible as a historic document rests on a solid scholarly foundation, which has in the past hundred years established a close correlation between the archaeological discoveries of Ancient Near East cultures and the Biblical narrative. The Book of Genesis combines poetry and prose pieces, some of mythical, some of folkloristic character. It is by now taken for granted that earlier Sumero-Babylonian, Canaanite, and Egyptian cultural materials were adapted and transformed by the writers and redactors of the Bible and that contemporary practices, laws, and customs of neighboring peoples were reflected in its narrative. In using the Biblical text as a source for historical analysis, one must be aware of the complexity of its authorship, its purposes, and its sources.

The older tradition of ascribing the authorship of the Book of Genesis to Moses has given way, on the basis of massive internal evidence established by modern form-criticism, to the acceptance of the "documentary hypothesis." It holds that the Bible, whether one wishes to believe it divinely inspired or not, was the work of many hands. The writing of the Book of Genesis spanned a period of roughly four hundred years, from the tenth century B.C. to the fifth. It is now generally accepted that there are three main traditions of authorship and that many of the sources represent a far more ancient tradition, which the redactors reinterpreted and incorporated in the narrative.

The writing down of material which for centuries had been orally transmitted and the creation of a coherent story leading up to the Davidic monarchy was begun after the division of the kingdom. The narrative known as J (for the use of "Yahweh" and for its Judean origin) is commonly believed to have been composed in the southern kingdom of Judah in the tenth century B.C. The second author, called E for Elohist, because of the way he refers to the deity and because he is thought to represent the Ephraimite tradition, probably worked in the northern state of Israel somewhat later. Third, there is the P tradition, which includes and reinterprets the J and E narratives. While there is considerable controversy over the dating of P, scholars agree that we are dealing not with an individual but with a school of priestly redactors in Jerusalem who may have worked for hundreds of years and completed the work sometime in the seventh century B.C. The book of Deuteronomy, which is a product of the seventh century B.C., is considered to be a separate creation. The final fusion of the various elements in the Pentateuch, the Five Books of Moses, occurred around 450 B.C. under the direction of Ezra and Nehemiah, when the kingdom of Judah was under Persian domination. It represented the canonization of Jewish law and the supreme achievement of Jewish religious thought in the ancient period.[1]

In order to understand the meaning of the vast cultural transformation represented by the creation of Jewish monotheism we need to keep in mind the social conditions which are reflected in the Book of Genesis.

The patriarchal tribes of the earliest period described in Genesis lived, as had their ancestors, as nomads or semi-nomads in the desert. They raised sheep, goats, and cattle and engaged in seasonal agriculture. At various times they also lived on the outskirts of cities, under the protection of sedentary people, but keeping their own customs separate from those of their hosts. Their cohesiveness and survival depended on strong tribal ties. The smallest unit was the patriarchal family, which was comprised of a man, his wife, his sons and their wives and children, his unmarried daughters, and his servants. Several families formed a clan, a *mishpahah;* they aided each other economically and met for religious feasts. A group of clans, claiming a common ancestor and recognizing a common leader, united in a tribe. The tribes recognized a bond of blood which imposed upon them the responsibility for blood-vengeance; that is, an injury to a member of the tribe had to be avenged by the death of his attacker or by the death of a member of the attacker's family. Among nomads, in the absence of a regular judicial system, this form of retribution protected the rights and integrity of the tribes.

Members of the tribes had an obligation to care for and protect their weaker members. While some of the tribal members were richer in cattle than others, there were no great economic differences among them. Among desert nomads, a lone individual cannot survive; thus hospitality to a stranger was a basic and sacred rule.[2]

Most scholars date the patriarchal period of Biblical history to the first half of the second millennium B.C. There is useful historical evidence available for the conditions prevalent among West Semitic tribes in the documents from the royal archives of Mari, dating from ca. 1800 B.C., which illuminate actual conditions in Abraham's homeland of Haran. Documents from the city of Nuzi have also provided scholars with much information about family life, which ahs enabled them better to understand and interpret the customs reflected in Genesis.[3]

In was in Haran that Abraham had his first encounter with God, who made a covenant with him. It is this covenant which will set apart the descendants of Abraham as God's chosen people. I will discuss its symbolic significance in the next chapter. Here we should note that this mythical event marks the beginning of the Jewish religious experience and provides the energizing idea which will enable this people to survive for the subsequent four thousand years despite diaspora and frequent persecutions, and in the absence of a homeland.

Scholars generally regard Moses as the founder of Jewish monotheism and the Decalogue as its basic law. In the approximately four hundred years between Abraham and Moses, the Hebrew tribes, although they were pledged to the worship of Yahweh as their only god, continued the observance of idols in the form of household gods. The only ritual that united them was male circumcision and the prohibition against human sacrifice (as embodied in the story of Isaac).

The story of Joseph and his brothers tells of the migration of famine-stricken Hebrews into Egypt, where they dwelt peacefully until a new pharaoh, who was ill-disposed toward them, enslaved them. The Exodus from Egypt, which the Biblical story describes so vividly, has been dated by archaeological evidence as falling in the reign of Ramses II (ca. 1290–24 B.C.). Following upon the Exodus the Biblical story tells how Moses leads the people through the desert for forty years and how at Mt. Sinai he is given the tablets of the law by Yahweh. Moses' revelation of the law to the people and his destruction of the golden calf, symbol of idol worship, are the crucial points in the narrative. Yahweh's covenant with Moses confirms and reinforces all the earlier covenants and makes of Israel an entity united by a common belief and a common law. Moses dies without seeing the promised land; it is his appointed successor, Joshua, who leads the Israelites there. Scholars believe that the conquest of Canaan under Joshua was completed by 1250 B.C., which also marks the end of the Bronze Age and the beginning of the Iron Age in Palestine.[4]

The semi-nomadic tribes conquering Canaan became sedentary in a region which had been sparsely settled, due to poor soil and scarce water supply. They were able to overcome these environmental obstacles with technological innovations using iron—the storage of water in lined cisterns, deeper cultivation with iron-tipped farm tools, and the development of terracing to preserve water. They also must have experienced large-scale catastrophes brought on by war and by various epidemics, which are described in the Bible as plagues or pestilence. The combined pressure of the need for agricultural labor in settling a desert environment and the concurrent loss of population due to wars and epidemics crisis in the very period when the rudimentary principles of Jewish religious throught came into being may explain the Biblical emphasis on the family and on woman's procreative role. In such a demographic crisis women would most likely have agreed to a division of labor which gave their maternal role primacy.[5]

Permanent settlement in villages and small towns brought changes in the concept of leadership, which shifted from the tribe to the clan. In the period of Judges (ca. 1125–1020 B.C.) tribes sometimes took joint action and sometimes acted independently, but inter-tribal attachments were generally weak. Authority was wielded by elders, from among whom judges were chosen during periods of crisis. In this period, when national consciousness was essentially not yet in existence, a common religious and cultural tradition formed the bond between the tribes.

The period of warfare between Israelite tribes and Canaanites, which took place while the entire region was under Philistine dominance, is described in one of the oldest segments of the Old Testament, the Song of Deborah (Judges 4–5). It is one of only five instances in the narrative, in which a woman is shown in a leadership position and heroic role.[6] Deborah is described as a prophetess and a judge, who inspires Barak to rally the troops in resistance to the Canaanites, led by Sisera. In a passage quite exceptional in Biblical literature, she is shown to assume actual leadership over men:

> And Barak said unto her: "If thou wilt go with me, then I will go; but if thou wilt not go with me, then I will not go." And she said: "I will surely go with thee, notwithstanding the journey that thou takest shall not be for thy honour, for the Lord will give Sisera over into the hands of a woman." and Deborah arose and went with Barak to Kedish [Judges 4:8–9].

Deborah's prophecy comes true when Sisera is killed by Jael, the wife of Heber, who lures him into her tent by an offer of hospitality and, while he is sleeping, drives a tentpin into his temple with a hammer. For this heroic deed she is lauded in the Song of Deborah in these words: "Blessed above women shall Jael be,/The wife of Heber the Kenite,/Above women in the tent shall she be blessed" (Judges 5:24). Although clearly the miracle is the Lord's, who enables even a woman to kill a warrior, the passage is remarkable in its celebration of female strength, both moral (Deborah) and physical (Jael).

The Israeli victory and the need for unity against the Philistines strengthened the tendencies toward strong leadership among the twelve tribes. The first offer of kingship was made to Gideon, after his victory over the Midianties, but he declined it (ca. 1110 B.C.). Later, the tribes, as a result of their repeated defeats by the Philistines, became convinced of the need for unity and made Saul king.

Saul united the tribes, formed a standing army and defeated the Philistines. Quite similar to the Mesopotamian military leaders who ascended to kingship, he raised members of his own family to important positions and hoped to make his office hereditary. But he and his sons died in battle, and Saul was succeeded by David, who had earlier been made king of his own tribe Judah.

It was King David (ca. 1004–965 B.C.) who welded the tribes into a national state and conquered vast territories between the Mediterranean and the Red Sea. Like other archaic kings, David developed a bureaucracy and centralized administrative structure. He acquired royal land and palaces, conducted a census of the population, and made Jerusalem his capital. In moving the Ark, the center of Israelite cultic life, to Jerusalem he also made that city the center of Israelite religious life.

After a bitter struggle for succession, David was followed by Solomon, who continued the strengthening and development of the monarchy. He made many treaties and dynastic marriages with formerly hostile neighbors, thus acquiring his vast harem. He created a group of royal merchants, equipped them with a fleet, and sent them on trade missions over a vast terrain. During his reign the monarchy developed culturally and economically, but heavy taxation and increasing social stratification led to social unrest and finally a number of rebellions. After Solomon's death the monarchy split into the two kingdoms of Judah and Israel.[7]

The Dual Monarchy was under constant threat from its bigger neighbors. The kingdom of Israel lasted only a little over two hundred years and ended, after protracted warfare, when the Assyrians, under Sargon II, captured its capital, Samaria, in 722 B.C. and deported its entire population. Other important events, from the perspective of religious development were the increasing spread of the cult of Baal and Asherah during the reign of King Ahab and his foreign-born wife Jezebel and the reaction which followed upon it. Inspired by the prophets Elijah and Elisha, the sole worship of Yahweh was reestablished after a political coup and the assassination of four hundred priests of Baal in 852 B.C. Later religious revivals under the prophets Hoseah, Amos, and Isaiah introduced into Yahwism the revolutionary idea of intolerance toward other gods and cults. The bull cult was outlawed, and the concept of fertility was more firmly affixed to Yahweh by Hoseah's metaphor, which transposed the covenant idea by turning it into Yahweh's marriage with Israel, the bride. The prophets, in their inspired preaching, equated the sinfulness of Israel with "whoring." Thus patriarchal sexual metaphors became firmly embedded in religious thought.[8]

The kingdom of Judah, continuing the Davidic dynastic line, was successively invaded and fought against Egyptians, Phoenicians, Philistines, Moabites, Assyrians, and in 586 B.C. was finally subdued when the Babylonians destroyed Jerusalem, razed the temple, and deported the population.

The fall of Jerusalem marked the end of Israel's political institutions. Henceforth the survival of Israel depended on its adherence to the religion of Yahweh under the most adverse circumstances of exile, diaspora, and assimilation. This was made possible by the canonization of Jewish teaching in the Pentateuch, accomplished under the prophet Esra. The revolutionary aspect of Jewish monotheism was its absolute faith in the one, invisible, ineffable God; its rejection of ritual as proof of holiness and its demand, instead, on adherence to and the practice of ethical values. The great innovation of the synagogue as a place for religious assembly and the reading of scripture, the holy books, by any group of the faithful, instead of cultic practice monopolized by a sect of priests, made Jewish religion mobile, exportable, flexible, and communal. These were the features that made Jewish survival possible.

The very same historic conditions that created the possibility of such a cultural and conceptual advance also influenced the way in which patriarchal concepts and ideas were structured into Jewish monotheism. Let us now turn to an examination of gender as defined in Israelite practice and thought.

THE TRIBES IN CANAAN lived in a pre-state society; the period of state formation in Israel did not occur until ca. 1050 B.C. If the same pattern of development were to occur in Palestinian society as a result of state formation, which we have earlier discussed in relation to Mesopotamian society, we might expect to find stricter regulation of female sexuality and increasing exclusion of women from public activity, as the state becomes more powerful. The historical evidence seems to confirm this pattern, which we can here discuss only in outline.

The stories of the patriarchs in Genesis offer some indications of a transition from matrilocal and matrilineal to patrilocal and patrilineal family organization in some of the tribes (cf.: the marriages of Leah and Rachel. The reference to a man leaving his father and mother and cleaving to his wife in Gen. 2:24 could be so interpreted as well). Jacob's seven years of service to Laban for each of his daughters would conform to the practice of matrilocal marriage. The Assyriologist Koschaker has confirmed the existence of a form of marriage in early Mesopotamia in which the wife remained in her parents' house (or more frequently tent) and the husband resided with her as either a permanent or occasional visitor. In the Biblical narrative, matrilocal marriage is called "beena" marriage. It allowed the woman greater autonomy and gave her the right to divorce, which patrilocal marriage, known as "ba'al" marriage, abrogated. Koschaker noted that this marriage form was superseded by patriarchal marriage.[9]

The story of Jacob's courtship and of his flight from Laban's house has been interpreted as implying the transition from matrilocality to patrilocality. Even before he came to Laban's house, Jacob was pledged to return to the house of his father. In carrying out his pledge he had to overcome Laban's resistance and deception, which become more comprehensible when we understand that in a matrilocal society Laban would have been entitled to and would have taken for granted Jacob's obligation to stay in his wife's locality.[10]

Rachel's theft of the "teraphim" can also be viewed in this light. This passage has long puzzled Biblical scholars. Speiser interprets the teraphim as "house-gods" and elucidates the passage by pointing out that according to Nuzi documents, which have been found to reflect the social customs of Haran (the residence of Laban), possession of the house-gods signified legal title to an estate. Thus Rachel, believing that her father would deny her husband the legal share in his estate, took the teraphim.[11] Speiser's interpretation is not inconsistent with the idea that in transferring the teraphim from her father's house to her husband's house, Rachel's action symbolized the change from matrilocality to patrilocality.

There is no question that the predominant family structure in the Biblical narrative is the patriarchal family. Scholars have formed a fairly comprehensive picture of the social and family structure of Hebrew society which quite closely reflects that of Israel's Mesopotamian neighbors.

In the earliest period the patriarch had undisputed authority over the members of his family. The wife called her husband "ba'al" or "master"; he was similarly referred to as the "ba'al" of his house or field. In the Decalogue the wife is listed among a man's possessions, along with his servants, his ox, and his ass (Ex.20:17).[12] In this period the father also could sell his daughter into slavery or prostitution, which was later forbidden him. By the time of the monarchy, the father's power of life and death over his family members was no longer unlimited and unrestrained. In this respect we note an improvement in the position of daughters over the earlier period.

The great importance of the clan (*mishpahah*) was reinforced by property arrangements. After the settlement period, family property was the predominant form of landholding. A family's property was defined by strict boundaries and usually included the ancestral tomb. Responsibility for the maintenance and preservation of this patrimony rested upon the patriarchal head of the family. The land belonged to the clan and was considered inalienable; that is, it could not be sold to anyone and could be transferred solely by inheritance. This inheritance usually fell to the eldest son. If there was no son, it could fall to the daughters, but they had to marry within their tribe, so their portion would not be transferred out (Numbers 27:7–8 and 36:6–9). If the owner died childless, the inheritance went to his brother, uncle, or nearest kinsman. This is one of the foundations for the law of levirate, which binds a man to marry his widowed, childless sister-in-law in order to provide an heir for the deceased and to prevent alienation of the family property.[13]

The effect of these landholding patterns was to strengthen clan allegiance and to give great stability to the partriarchal-tribal organizations from one generation to the other. This strong emphasis on the patriarchal control over clan property and the way in which it was structured into the very organization of Israelite society had a great impact on the position of women.

Descent was reckoned patrilineally, with the eldest son succeeding the father in authority after the father's death. All the sons and their wives lived in the father's household until his death. The father contracted marriages for his children; in the case of sons, by paying a bride price. In the case of daughters, the father would furnish her a dowry, which took the place of her share of the inheritance. Thus, the daughters of wealthy citizens had some measure of protection from abuse, since the return of her dowry in case of divorce might be to the economic disadvantage of her husband's family. The situation of the daughters of the poorer classes was no different from the unenviable situation of Mesopotamian poor women, except for the fact that in the monarchic period and after Jewish daughters were not enslaved, slavery being the lot of foreign women and of women of conquered groups. Also, in line with the generally much more humanitarian and lenient form of slavery in Israelite society, the female slave in Deuteronomy is released in the seventh year, as is the male slave, and must be furnished with supplies and animals from the master's flock (Deut.15:12–13).

All Israelite women were expected to marry and thus passed from the control of fathers (and brothers) to that of husbands and fathers-in-law. When the husband died before his wife, his brother or another male relative assumed control over her and married her. While the custom of the levirate has frequently been interpreted as a "protective" device for the widow, it speaks most strongly to the male concern for preserving the patrimony within the family.[14]

As they did in Mesopotamian societies, Hebrew men enjoyed complete sexual freedom within and outside of marriage. The Biblical scholar Louis M. Epstein states that during the early periods the husband had free sexual use of his concubines and slave women. "If slave wives were his own, not given to him by his the primary wife, he could present them to other members of the family . . . after tiring of them himself."[15] Polygamy, which was widespread among the patriarchs, later became rare except for royalty, and monogamous marriage became the ideal and the rule.

Virginity was expected of the bride at the time of marriage, and the wife owed her husband absolute fidelity in marriage. Punishment for adultery was the death of both parties (Lev. 20:10), but the Jewish wife had less protection against false accusations of adultery than did her Mesopotamian counterpart. Divorce was obtainable by the husband, with an economic penalty, but it was never obtainable by the wife. In this respect Jewish law was more detrimental to the wife than was Hammurabic law. The same was true for legislation pertaining to rape, in which Mesopotamian law afforded somewhat more protection to the woman. Jewish law forced the rapist to marry the woman he had raped and specifies that he may not divorce her. Implicitly, this forces a woman into an indissoluble marriage with her rapist (Deut. 22:28–29).

In marriage, the wife was expected to produce offspring, namely, sons. Barrenness in a wife, which was interpreted to be failure to bear sons, was a disgrace to her and cause for divorce. Sarah, Leah, and Rachel, in despair when they find themselves barren, offer their slave women to their husbands in order that the slave woman's children be counted as their own. There is legal precedent for this custom in Hammurabic law, as there is for the different treatment accorded to the widow who is the mother of sons as against the barren widow.[16]

Adoption of kin, strangers or even slaves was as prevalent in Hebrew as it was in other Near Eastern societies, as a means of providing a man with an heir in case of childlessness and assuring care for himself in old age. Or, a man might add wives or concubines to his household, if his first wife did not bear a son. This situation, which was similar to marriage customs in Mesopotamian society as reflected in the law codes, is described in the stories of Abraham and

Hagar and Jacob and his two wives and two concubines.[17] These complex familial arrangements also raised the question of succession as a problem, since the law did not make clear, as did Hammurabic law, whether the eldest son of a slave woman would take precedence over the eldest son born to the legitimate wife. The case of Abraham and Hagar's son Ishmael is such a case, and the Biblical story clearly indicates that God's intent is that his chosen people (Abraham's seed) shall be the progeny of Isaac, the son of the legitimate marriage, and not the progeny of Ishmael, the firstborn, who is the son of the slave concubine. There is precedent in Hammurabic law § 170 for giving the heirship to the firstborn son of the first wife over the concubine's children, with the latter entitled to a lesser share in the inheritance if their father acknowledges them during his lifetime. In Ishmael's case, Abraham had already acknowledged him as his son, and yet God ordered him to expel Hagar and her son as Sarah desired, ". . . for it is through Isaac that your line shall be continued"(Gen.21:12). We may be entitled to consider this a strong divine endorsement of the primacy of the rights of legitimate sons.

AS WE COMPARE THE LEGAL and social position of women in Mesopotamian and Hebrew societies, we note similarities in the strict regulation of women's sexuality and in the institutionalization of a sexual double standard in the law codes. In general, the married Jewish woman occupied an inferior position to that of her counterpart in Mesopotamian societies. Babylonian women could own property, sign contracts, take legal action, and they were entitled to a share in the husband's inheritance. But we must also note a strong upgrading of the role of women as mothers in the Old Testament. The fifth commandment enjoins children to honor father and mother equally, and women are exalted as teachers of the young. In Proverbs, mothers and fathers are equally praised and honored in their role as parents, and the mother is described in positive terms only. This is quite in line with the general stress on the family as the basic unit of society, which we have also noted in Mesopotamian society at the time of state formation.

So far we have based our generalizations regarding the status of women on Biblical law, as do most of the scholars in the field. But the law, as we have earlier discussed, reflects reality only in a tangential way, by what it assumes as a given and by what it defines as problematical. Otherwise, the law sets norms for desirable conduct, which usually do not represent actual societal conditions. We can get glimpses of actual practice in the Biblical narrative by noting practices and values which are assumed as a given and therefore remain unexplained.

The stories of Lot in Sodom and of the origin of the Benjaminite war deal obliquely with the position of women. As told in Genesis 19, two angels in the form of two strangers come as visitors to Lot's house in Sodom. Lot makes a feast for them and invites them to stay overnight. The wicked men of Sodom surround the house and demand that he surrender the men to them, "Bring them out unto us that we may know them." Trying to calm them down, Lot steps outside the door of his house and addresses the Sodomites as follows:

> I pray you, my brethren, do not so wickedly. Behold now, I have two daughters that have not known man; let me, I pray you, bring them out unto you, and do ye to them as is good in your eyes; only to these men do nothing; forasmuch as they are come under the shadow of my roof [Gen.19:7,8].

The mob storms into the house, but the angels strike the men of the mob with blindness, then they warn Lot of the imminent destruction of the city of Sodom and tell him that he and his family would be saved, "the Lord being merciful to him." The language here indicates that Lot is not being saved for his virtue but because of God's mercy and because of Abraham. ("God remembered Abraham and sent Lot out of the midst of the overthrow, when he overthrew the cities in which Lot dwelt" (Gen. 19:29).[18]

The passage has been embarrassing to later commentators. Martin Luther praised Lot for upholding the law of hospitality, and otherwise apologized for him: "I will defend Lot and think he made his offer without sin. For knowing that the mob was not interested in them, he only tried to appease it and did not think he was exposing his daughters to any danger." John Calvin, on the other hand, thought that "Lot's great virtue was sprinkled with some imperfection . . . He does not hesitate to prostitute his daughters . . . Lot, indeed is urged by extreme necessity; yet . . . he is not free from blame."[19]

Later commentators have essentially followed these two lines of interpretation. Sarna comments that Lot's "willingness to allow his daughters to be violated" is "utterly incomprehensible" to the modern reader, "even if allowance be made for the fact that the story reflects an age and a society in which daughters were the property of their fathers."[20] I find it remarkable that E. A. Speiser, who annotates and comments on Genesis line by line, has no comment to offer regarding Lot's action. He criticizes Lot for "lacking spontaneity" and appearing "servile" in his hospitality and describes the "latent weakness in Lot's character" in his being "undecided, flustered, ineffectual." The only hint of a comment on the incident with the daughters is the sentence: "True to the unwritten code, Lot will stop at nothing in his effort to protect his guests."[21] Speiser follows Calvin's interpretation and, using a strictly textual analysis, Calvin seems quite justified in regarding Lot's offer of his daughter to the mob as merely "an imperfection," since Yahweh, to whom the crimes of Sodom are so abhorrent that he destroys the city and all its inhabitants, nevertheless saves Lot. If we analyze this Biblical story, we notice that Lot's right to dispose of his daughters, even so as to offer them to be raped, is taken for granted. It does not need to be explained; hence we can assume it reflected a historic social condition.

This assumption is strengthened by the telling of a somewhat similar story in Judges(19:1–21,25). A Levite, living in Ephraim, had a concubine from Judah, who "played the harlot against him, and went away from him unto her father's house in Beth-lehem in Judah"(Judges 19:2). After four months had passed, the Levite went after her "to speak kindly unto her," and after a prolonged stay at her father's house he proceeded toward his home, taking her with him. He stopped in Gibeah, in the land of Benjamin, but no one would offer him hospitality. Finally, he and his party were offered hospitality by a man from Ephraim. As the guests were being fed by their host, "certain base fellows" from the city surrounded the house and demanded that the Ephraimite surrender his guest to them, using almost the same words as in the Lot story, "Bring forth the man that came into thy house, that we may know him" (19:22). The host refused, saying:

> Nay, my brethren, I pray you, do not so wickedly; seeing that this man is come into my house, do not this wanton deed. Behold, here is my daughter a virgin, and his concubine; I will bring them out now, and humble ye them, and do with them what seemeth good to you; but unto this man do not so wanton a thing[19:23–24].

The men would not listen to him, so the Levite "laid hold on his concubine, and brought her forth unto them; and they knew her, and abused her all the night until the morning" and let her go at daybreak. The woman fell down at the doorstep and lay there. "And her lord rose up in the morning" and found her, and when she did not answer his call he took her upon his ass and carried her body home. There he divided her body "limb by limb into twelve pieces" and sent these "throughout all the borders of Israel" to arouse the Israelites to avenge this wicked deed(19:27–30).

This narrative is followed by a dramatic account of the Israelite council, the decision to ask for the surrender of the culprits in Gibeah, the refusal of the Benjaminites to surrender them, and the ensuing Benjaminite war. Throughout, it is clear that the insult and "wickedness" was the crime of inhospitality and the despoiling of the Levite's honor and property. The Levite's attitude toward his concubine, who in the Masoretic text is alternatively referred to as "his wife," shows not only in his willingness to surrender her to the gang rape but in his sleeping peacefully during the night of her ordeal. Nowhere in the text is there a word of censure toward him for his action or toward the host, who offers up his virgin daughter to save his guest's life and honor. On the contrary, the text assumes that no explanation for such behavior is necessary. We should note, however, that in a section written in a later period(Lev.19:29), a father is specifically forbidden such an action: "Profane not thy daughter, to make her a harlot, lest the land fall into harlotry, and the land become full of lewdness."

The earlier narrative continues, describing the total destruction of the Benjaminites with the help and counsel of God. The Israelites kill all the men, save six hundred who flee into wilderness, and they set fire to all the Benjaminite cities. Before the outbreak of the war the men of Israel had sworn: "There shall not any of us give his daughter unto Benjamin to wife" (21:1). But now they realize that their pledge will mean the loss of a tribe of Isreal. Wishing now to pacify the Benjaminite remnant without violating their pledge, the Israelites solve the problem by going to war against the people of Jabesh-Gilead, who had not responded to their call to arms against the Benjaminites. In this war the Israelites "utterly destroy every male, and every woman that hath lain by man" (Judges 21:11). That leaves four hundred virgins, and the victors give these to the men of Benjamin as wives. The two hundred remaining men of Benjamin, who lack wives, are commanded as follows:

> Behold, there is the feast of the Lord from year to year in Shiloh . . . Go and lie in the vineyards; and see, and, behold, if the daughters of Shiloh come out to dance the dances, then come ye out of the vineyards, and catch you every man his wife of the daughters of Shiloh, and go to the land of Benjamin[21:19–21].

The Benjaminites follow this command and return with their new wives to rebuild their cities in order "that a tribe not be destroyed out of Israel" (21:17). The account ends with a curious line, which one might interpret as casting some doubt on the righteousness of these proceedings: "In those days there was no king in Israel; every man did that which was right in his own eyes"(21:25).

David Bakan, in a quite ingenious construction, interprets the theme of the Benjaminite war as a conflict and victory of patrilocality over matrilocality. He notes that the crime of the concubine was to remove herself from her husband's house to her father's house and that that evil is rectified and the principle of patrilocality is affirmed by moving the four hundred virgins of Jabesh-Gilead to their husbands' homes.[22] While his argument is intriguing, it cannot be satisfactorily proven. Other modern commentators are as silent on the treatment of the women in this passage as they are in the case of Lot's daughters. For example, Louis Epstein comments on both passages that

> from these stories we get a reflection of the revulsion, which decent Jews felt to such an act [of sodomy]; in either case the host offered his daughter for rape in exchange for the strangers, pleading that "so vile a thing" be not committed. It may be taken for granted therefore that from very ancient days sodomy was considered among the Hebrews a severely immoral act.[23]

It may also be taken for granted that the honor, even the lives, of women was at the disposal of the men of their families, who regarded women as interchangeable instruments to be used for their procreative services. The men of Benjamin, whose wives and children had been killed, accept new wives from among enslaved or captured women and thus form new families. In regard to legal rights in their persons or their bodies, there is no difference between free or slave women nor between married women or virgins. The virgin daughters are as disposable as the concubine or the enslaved women captured in warfare.

The passage in Judges further corroborates the historical evidence, discussed in Chapter Four, for the origins of slavery. Even in an internecine war between the tribes of Israel, the men are slain, while the women are enslaved and raped. But the story of the Benjaminite war also demonstrates how wars are ended and enemies pacified by matrimonial arrangements, which are entirely under the control of the men of the tribe. One might regard the matrimonial exchange of the women of Jabesh-Gilead as the usual enslavement and trading of the women of defeated enemies. But what of the daughters of Shiloh, dancing at a feast of the Lord? They were not enemies, nor were their men conquered. They simply became pawns in a politically motivated effort at the pacification of a conquered enemy.

A NUMBER OF RECENT STUDIES of the role of women in the Old Testament have tried to balance the overwhelming evidence of patriarchal domination by citing a few female heroic figures or women who take independent action of one sort or another. Phyllis Trible has even asserted the existence of a "counter-culture" to the "patriarchal culture of Israel."[24] In an interpretive essay which details the various expressions of patriarchal dominance in the Old Testament, another feminist scholar, Phyllis Bird, states correctly, as her evidence shows, that women are legally and economically deemed inferior to man in the Biblical narrative and that this reflected actual conditions in Hebrew society. Nevertheless, she asserts that man in the Old Testament recognizes woman "as his opposite and equal," an assertion for which she offers precious little evidence.[25] Similarly, John Otwell concludes a book, which is full of evidence to the contrary, with the assertion that the status of women in the Old Testament was high and that they fully participated in the life of the community as wives and mothers.[26] Those who regard the Biblical narrative as showing advances for women point to the few heroic women mentioned in the narrative, speak of the role of the five female prophets mentioned in the text, stress the positive statements about women in Proverbs and the erotic richness and praise of female sexuality in the Song of Songs. Unfortunately, the historical method does not support such a construction.

The few women mentioned as having a respected or heroic role are quite overwhelmed by the many women described in servile, submissive, or subordinate roles. Clearly, the narrative, especially in the Song of Deborah and in the reference to the prophetess Huldah, lends support to the statement that women were recognized as prophetesses. But when we place these narratives in chronological order, it appears that this was so in the early period of Hebrew history, before or shortly after state formation. In the monarchy and thereafter we do not find women in such roles. That would be in line with the general pattern we have noted for other Mesopotamian cultures. The Song of Songs is so difficult to interpret and bring into historical perspective that it seems unreasonable to make inferences from it as to the actual status of women; it needs to be treated as a literary creation. Since the identity of the woman in the Song is unproven and highly controversial, it does not seem to me possible to use it as the basis for generalizations about the actual conditions of women in Hebrew society.

We are on firmer ground in observing that the Old Testament text shows a gradual restriction of women's public and economic role, a lessening of her cultic function and an ever increasing regulation of her sexuality, as the Jewish tribes move from confederacy to statehood. The laws I have discussed above derive by and large from the period of statehood. One might argue that Deuteronomic law is more favorable to women than Leviticus. The preoccupation with fighting the cult of Baal and Asherah, which persisted into the monarchic period and after and which, apparently, had its greatest and most persistent strength among women, may explain the increasingly sharp regulation of women's behavior, the excessive language of censure against women's "whoring" in Prophets and finally the pervasive use of woman-the-whore as a metaphor for the evils of sinning society. These subjects deserve close and lengthy study by Biblical and literary experts. Here we can merely call attention to them.

We will, in the next chapter, discuss the major religious and symbolic expressions of gender definition in the Book of Genesis. It remains for us to observe here the way in which Hebrew society defined the cultic community and that such definition not only excluded women in principle but historically progressed from some participation by women to their exclusion.

Louis Epstein points out that in the time of the patriarchs men and women tended the flocks together, met at the watering wells, worshipped together in the temple, shared public celebrations, ate together, and attended weddings and funerals together. Segregation in the temple begins only with the second temple, which has a "woman's court" outside the temple, but in which both men and women congregated. Epstein qualified even that development by explaining that "neither in practice nor in theory was this meant as a means of segregating the men from the women." The Jewish woman was part of the Jewish community; she could pray or study Torah: "But she was not part of the cult either as functionary or administrator or as member of the cult fellowship. . . . The Temple had a woman's court in the sense that it had a public place for those who had no share in the ritual, where women assembled as part of the public."[27]

It was considered a primary religious duty of parents to teach their sons Torah, but there was no such obligation in regard to girls. Still, Epstein reports that, as long as children were educated at home, girls were taught at the discretion of their parents. Until the fourth century A.D. there was little interference with women's attendance at public gatherings for reading of and discourse on scripture. However, formal education, which was instituted either in the second or the first century B.C., was probably limited to male students.[28]

I will show in the next chapter that from the outset the covenant community was defined as a *male* community. This would almost sequentially have led to very few opportunities for women in cultic function, since in the Mesopotamian tradition priestesses served female deities and priests served male deities. Yet Yahweh's gender identity was unspecified, especially in the earlier texts. What is significant for gender definitions in Western civilization is which metaphors, symbols, and explanation the writers of Genesis selected out of the many available sources. Similarly, what is significant for the present is not so much what the writers intended by each of their symbolic representations as what meaning future generations extracted from them. If, for example, Yahweh was not conceived or thought of as a gendered God, but rather as a principle which embodied male and female aspects, as some theologians have argued, this is significant only in showing us that there were available alternatives to the traditional patriarchal interpretation and that these alternatives were not chosen.[29] The fact is that for over 2500 years the God of the Hebrews was addressed, represented, and interpreted as a male Father-God, no matter what other aspects He may have embodied. This was, historically, the meaning given to the symbol, and therefore this was the meaning which carried authority and force. This meaning became of the utmost significance in the way both men and women were able to conceptualize women and place them both in the divine order of things and in human society.

There was therefore no inevitability in the emergence of an all-male priesthood. The prolonged ideological struggle of the Hebrew tribes against the worship of Canaanite deities and especially the persistence of a cult of the fertility-goddess Asherah must have hardened the emphasis on male cultic leadership and the tendency toward mysogyny, which fully emerged only in the post-exilic period.[30] Whatever the causes, the Old Testament male priesthood represented a radical break with millennia of tradition and with the practices of neighboring peoples. This new order under the all-powerful God proclaimed to Hebrews and to all those who took the Bible as their moral and religious guide that women cannot speak to God.

NINE

The Covenant

THE ANSWER TO THE QUESTION "Who creates life?" lies at the core of religious belief-systems. Generativity encompasses both creativity—the ability to create something out of nothing—and procreativity—the capacity to produce offspring. We have seen how religious explanations of generativity have shifted from the Mother-Goddess as the sole principle of universal fertility to the Mother-Goddess assisted in her fertility by male gods or human kings; then to the concept of symbolic creativity as expressed first in "the name," then "the creative spirit." We have seen, as well, the shift in the pantheon of gods from the all-powerful Mother-Goddess to the all-powerful Storm-God, whose female consort represents a domesticated version of the fertility goddess. It remains for the pantheon of gods to be replaced by one single powerful male God and for that God to incorporate the principle of generativity in both of its aspects. This shift, which occurs in many different forms in different cultures, occurs for Western civilization in the Book of Genesis.

The creation story in Genesis departs significantly from the creation stories of other peoples in the region. It is Yahweh who is the sole creator of the universe and all that exists in it. Unlike the chief gods of neighboring peoples, Yahweh is not allied with any female goddess nor does He have familial ties.[1] There is no longer any maternal source for the creation of the universe and for life on earth, nor is there any indication that creativity and procreativity are linked. Quite to the contrary. God's act of creation is entirely unlike anything humans can experience.

The great advance in abstract thinking represented by the symbolification of creativity into "a concept," a "name," the "breath of life" is echoed in the opening words: "And God said 'Let there be light,' And there was light" (Gen.1:3). God's word, God's breath creates. The metaphor of the divine breath as life-giving is elaborated in Genesis 2:7, "Then the Lord God formed man of the dust of the ground, and breathed into his nostrils the breath of life: and man became a living soul." Then God forms the beasts of the field and fowl of the air "and brought them unto the man to see what he would call them; and whatsoever the man would call every living creature, that was to be the name thereof" (Gen.2:19). Thus, the divine breath creates, but human naming gives meaning and order. And God gives the power of that kind of naming to Adam. If we read the Hebrew word "adam" as "humankind," then we would expect God to give the power of naming both to the male and the female of the species. But in this instance, God granted that power specifically to the human male only.[2] This might have been so simply because the female had not yet been created, but the pattern recurs after the creation of Eve, when Adam names her, as he had named the animals. "And the man said: 'This is now bone of my bone and flesh of my flesh; she shall be called Woman because she was taken out of Man' "(Gen.2:23). The naming here not only is a symbolic act of creativity, but it defines Woman in a very special way as a "natural" part of man, flesh of his flesh, in a relationship which is a peculiar inversion of the only human relationship for which such a statement can be made, namely, the relationship of mother to child. The Man here defines himself as "the mother" of the Woman; through the miracle of divine creativity a human being was created out of his body the way the human mother brings forth life out of her body. The very next sentence explains the meaning of this connectedness in human terms: "Therefore shall a man leave his father and his mother, and shall cleave unto his wife, and they shall be one flesh"(Gen.2:24). The creation of Woman out of Man's body is here taken to impose a very special interpretation upon this event—woman was created as part of man, therefore Man must cleave to her, choosing her above all other kinship relationships, and they shall be one flesh. That flesh, the Man's naming formula tells us, shall be the Man's, for he has here by the act of God's creation and by his own power of naming defined his authority over her as integral and binding. This authority also implies intimacy; it implies interdependency, and it has, in centuries of theological interpretation, been used to upgrade the marriage relationship and with it the dignity of wives. The ambiguity and complexity of this passage have given rise to greatly differing interpretations, which we will discuss below.

Name-giving is a powerful activity, a symbol of sovereignty. In Biblical times, in line with ancient Oriental tradition, it also had a magical quality, giving meaning and predicting the future. When Hagar's son is named Ishmael, his fate is predicted. Such "naming" power is given both to men and women in the Bible. Except for special circumstances, mothers or fathers choose their children's names in the Biblical narrative. But there is another kind of naming, which we might call "re-naming," which signifies the assumption of a new and powerful role for the person so re-named. We have mentioned earlier the re-naming with fifty names of the young god Marduk upon his ascendance to power. Similarly, God renames persons after important events have occurred. After the covenant He changes Abram to Abraham, "for a father of a multitude of nations have I made thee"(Gen.17:5), and Sarai to Sarah. This lends added significance to the fact that Adam, who uses the power of naming first in the creation story cited above, after the Fall renames the Woman, Eve. The impressions is given strongly and repeatedly that the male shares in the divine power of naming and re-naming.[3]

The most powerful metaphors of gender in the Bible have been those of Woman, created of Man's rib, and of Eve, the temptress, causing humankind's fall from grace. These have, for over two millennia, been cited as proof of divine sanction for the subordination of women. As such, they have had a powerful impact on defining values and practices in regard to gender relations. While it is to be expected that interpretations of a poetic, mythical, and folkloristic composite such as the Book of Genesis would vary so as to fit the needs of the interpreters, we should note that the tradition of interpretation has been overwhelmingly patriarchal and that the various feminist interpretations made by individual women in the past seven hundred years have been made against an entrenched and theologically sanctioned tradition long antedating Christianity.

There are two, seemingly contradictory versions of the creation story in Genesis. The J version appears in Genesis 2:18–25, and was written several centuries before the P version, which appears ahead of it in Genesis 1:27–29. In the J version God creates Eve out of Adam's rib, while in the P version "male and female created he them." Biblical criticism over several centuries has focused on the discrepancies between the two versions and has argued the merits of one over the other.[4]

The P version parallels the Mesopotamian *Enuma Elish* creation story in its various details and in the order of events. This might explain the androgynous statement about creation—male and female created He them—as reflecting the influence of Mesopotamian religious ideas. Some interpreters have attempted to extend that androgynous resonance to the J version by pointing out that the Hebrew word "adam," meaning humankind, stands for the generic term for humanity, including men and women, and that the capitalizing of that word in Adam is a later error, based on androcentric assumptions.[5] The effect of that "error," reprinted in tens of millions of versions of the Bible in every language, was to lend added weight to the traditional interpretations of Genesis 2:18–25.

The creation of woman from Adam's rib has been interpreted in the most literal sense for thousands of years to denote the God-given inferiority of woman. Whether that interpretation has rested upon the rib as being one of Adam's "lower" parts, and therefore denoting inferiority, or on the fact that Eve was created from Adam's flesh and bone, while he was created from earth, the passage has historically had profoundly patriarchal symbolic meaning. As an example we might cite the relatively benign interpretation of John Calvin:

> Since in the person of the man the human race had been created, the common dignity of our whole nature was without distinction. . . . The woman . . . was nothing else than an accession to the man. Certainly, it cannot be denied, that the woman also, though in the second degree, was created in the image of God . . . We may therefore conclude, that the order of nature implies that the woman should be the helper of the man. The vulgar proverb, indeed, is, that she is a necessary evil; but the voice of God is rather to be heard, which declares that woman is given as a companion and an associate to the man, to assist him to live well.[6]

Elsewhere Calvin comments: "Adam was taught to recognise himself in his wife, as in a mirror; and Eve, in her turn, to submit herself willingly to her husband, as being taken out of him."[7]

Feminists, in trying to argue this meaning away, have used a variety of ingenious interpretations. These include a clever argument by seventeen-year-old Rachel Speght, an English clergyman's daughter, who in 1617 observed that woman was created from refined matter, while Adam was created from dust. "Shee was not produced from Adam's foote, to be his low inferior nor from his head to be his superior, but from his side, near his heart to be his equall."[8] More than two centuries later the American Sarah Grimké focused her interpretation on the term "helpmeet."

> It was to give him a companion, in all respects his equal; one who was like himself a free agent, gifted with intellect and endowed with immortality, not a partaker merely of his animal gratifications, but able to enter into all his feelings as a moral and responsible being. If this had not been the case, how could she have been a help meet for him?. . . She was a part of himself, as if Jehovah designed to make the oneness and identity of man and woman perfect and complete.[9]

This somewhat circular argument, while strong in its Lutheran assumptions of the individual's free will and moral responsibility, avoids the implications of the rib image of woman's creation.

In a bold attempt to "reread (not rewrite) the Bible without the blinders" of patriarchal bias, the modern feminist theologian Phyllis Trible provides us with a challenging reinterpretation of the Creation story, which she views as "imbued with the vision of a transsexual Deity."[10] Phyllis Trible's twentieth-century reinterpretation is quite similar to Grimké's although she seems to be unaware of Grimké's work. Trible sees a similarity in Adam's creation from dust and Eve's from his rib, in that both are made of fragile material which Yahweh must process before they have life. She also considers the fact that Eve was created last as evidence of her being the culmination of creation.[11] Another feminist theologian stresses the essential similarity in the basic statement made about man and woman: "Woman is, along with man, the direct and intentional creation of God and the crown of his creation. Man and woman were made for each other. Together they constitute humankind, which is in its full and essential nature bisexual."[12] In an argument based on linguistic considerations, R. David Freedman argues that the term "make him a helpmate" should be translated to mean "a power equal to man."[13] In either case, there is little evidence in other parts of the Bible to support these optimistically feminist interpretations.

LET US CONSIDER THE VARIOUS sources of the Biblical creation story. Among the Sumerian elements incorporated and transformed in the Biblical narrative are the eating of the forbidden fruit, the concept of the tree of life, and the story of the flood.

The description of the Garden of Eden parallels the Sumerian garden of creation, which is also described as a place bordered by four great rivers. In the Sumerian creation myth, Mother-Goddess

Ninhursag allowed eight lovely plants to sprout in the garden, but the gods were forbidden to eat from them. Still, the water-god Enki ate from them, and Ninhursag condemned him to die. Accordingly, eight of Enki's organs fell ill. The Fox appealed in his behalf, and the Goddess agreed to commute the sentence of death. She created a special healing deity for each afflicted organ. When it came to the rib, she said: "To the goddess Ninti I have given birth for you." In Sumerian the word "Ninti" has a double meaning, namely, "female ruler of the rib" and "female ruler of life." In Hebrew the word "Hawwa" (Eve) means "she who creates life," which suggests that there may be a fusion of the Sumerian Ninti with the Biblical Eve. The choice of Adam's rib as the locus of Eve's creation may simply reflect the incorporation of the Sumerian myth. Stephen Langdon suggests another fascinating possibility by associating the Hebrew "Hawwa" with the Aramaic meaning of the word, which is "serpent."[14] Whether one accepts the Sumerian origin of the Creation story as a valid explanation for the metaphor of Adam's rib or not, it is significant that historically that explanation was ignored and the more sexist explanation prevailed.

The symbolism of the Genesis story suggests a dichotomy between Adam, created of dust, and Eve, successor to the ancient fertility goddesses, created out of a part of a human body, each imbued with divine substance through the intervention of Yahweh. The dichotomy becomes reinforced in the story of the Fall, when the sexual division of labor is decreed by Yahweh, this time as punishment. Adam will work in the sweat of his brow; Eve will give life in pain and raise the generations. It may be worth noting that the punishment meted out makes of man's work a burden, but it condemns to pain and suffering not women's work but woman's child-bearing body, the natural outcome of woman's sexuality.

There is another aspect to the Genesis passage which deserves our notice. The divine originator of human life, who in the Sumerian story was the goddess Ninhursag, is now Yahweh, Father-God and Lord. He may, if we credit the P version, have created "them" male and female, but he created the male exactly in his image, and he created woman another way.[15]

David Bakan, in a highly original and stimulating interpretation of the Book of Genesis, argues that the central theme of the book is the assumption of paternity by males. When men make the "scientific" discovery that conception results from intercourse between men and women, they understand that they have the power to procreate, which previously they had believed only the gods possessed. Men, in their desire "to legitimate the prerogatives the great discovery appeared to allow them," learned to distinguish between "creation" (divine) and "procreation" (male). They replaced matrilineal descent with patrilineal descent and, in order to guarantee paternal authority, demanded female virginity before marriage and absolute fidelity of the wife in marriage. With this explanation Bakan follows Engels's argument, which we have earlier discussed, but he adds: "A major metaphorical device . . . is to conceptualize the male sexual exudate as 'seed.' This way of thinking attributes all the genetic endowment to the male and none to the female." Bakan also argues that in this transition men take on the child-provider/protector role, which had been previously the female role. He calls this "the effeminization of the male."[16]

While I find Bakan's main thesis persuasive and some of his points coincide with my findings, I consider his reasoning excessively deterministic and his method ahistorical and highly subjective. A case in point is his reading of Genesis 6:1–4:

> And it came to pass, when men began to multiply on the face of the earth, and daughters were born unto them, that the sons of God saw the daughters of men that they were fair; and they took themselves wives, whomsoever they chose. And the Lord said: "My spirit shall not abide in man forever, for that he also is flesh; therefore shall his days be a hundred and twenty years." The Nephilin were in the earth in those days, and also after that, when the sons of God came in unto the daughters of men, and they bore children to them; the same were the mighty men of renown.

Bakan considers this account of divine intercourse with mortals the keystone in the arch of the development he describes in his thesis. He points out that it deals with four basic human concerns, namely, origin, death, property, and power:

> The verses indicate the origin of the men of valor. They indicate that life is terminal; although death comes only after a generous 120 years of life. They indicate prerogative of use, the essence of property, with respect to the daughters of men for the sons of God, who take whomsoever they chose. They indicate that the men who emerged from the matings were men of power.[17]

Bakan rests his case on a very difficult and controversial section of Genesis. Gerhard von Rad interprets this text quite differently. He reads "sons of God" (elohim) as "angels" and calls the union of angels with mortal women "the angel marriage." The "Nephilim," which spring from this union, are by all accounts mythological giants. Von Rad, who interprets the Bible solely as a religious document, considers this "angel marriage" one example of the sinfulness of God's creatures (from the Fall, to Lot's sin, to the Flood). The inherent sinfulness of men is illustrated in these incidents, followed by God's punishment and, finally, in the covenant, by God's redemptive mercy.[18]

E. A. Speiser considers that "the nature of the fragment is such as to discourage confident interpretation." He, too, regards the "elohim" as "divine beings" and regards their mating with human females as an abomination. He cites the striking similarity of the story of the giants with a Hurrian myth in which the storm-god Teshub must fight a formidable stone monster. Speiser offers no comment on the women in the story.[19]

I believe Bakan erred in taking the term "sons of God" literally as applying to human males. The reference to the giants of old and the similarity not only to the Hurrian myth but to the Sumerian and Greek myths of origin, which feature mythical giants in combat with gods, seem to me persuasive.[20] To my mind, what is significant in the text is the reference to human women as the daughters born to men. "When men began to multiply on the face of the earth, and daughters were born to them." It is not explained how men came to multiply, but the omission of women from the process seems to me highly significant. One would have expected the passage to read: "when mothers gave birth to men and they began to multiply." The text, written by J in the tenth century B.C., indicates that patriarchal assumptions about procreation were then already well established. The writer sees no need to explain why humans are "born to men." In fact, this is the prevailing assumption throughout Genesis. God names Isaac "the son of Abraham," and this language is used throughout. In the chronology, the "generations of the sons of Noah" are "sons of their fathers." So: "Unto Eber were born two sons" (Gen. 10:25). It is, of course, logical and to be expected, that in a patrilineal society the family line would be traced through the father, but my point is that this metaphorical means of ordering kinship was somehow transformed into a counter-factual statement about reality: not only the tracing of lineage, procreation itself has been turned into a male act. There are no mothers involved in it.

In the prayers to Ishtar, as to other fertility-goddesses, one of the praiseworthy attributes of the goddess was that "she opened the wombs of women." In Genesis, that language is used solely in reference to Yahweh: in Genesis 29:31 ("And the Lord saw that Leah was hated, and he opened her womb") and Genesis 30:22–23 ("And God remembered Rachel . . . and opened her womb. And she conceived and bore a son, and said: 'God hath taken away my reproach' "). Similarly, Eve says after she conceived and bore Cain: "I have gotten a man with the help of the Lord"(Gen.4:1). Procreativity, then, is clearly defined as emanating from God, who opens the wombs of women and blesses the seed of men. Yet, within this patriarchal frame of reference, the procreative role of the wife and mother is honored.

In the story of the Fall, the curse of mortality which has fallen on Adam and Eve is symbolically softened by giving them the immortality that comes through generation, through procreativity. In this regard, man and woman stand in the same relationship to God. One might also interpret this aspect of the Fall as indicating that woman, in her role as mother, is the carrier of God's redemptive and merciful spirit.

The decisive change in the relationship of man to God occurs in the story of the covenant, and it is defined in such a way as to marginalize woman. With the convenant humans enter historical time; henceforth their collective immortality becomes an aspect of the covenant they have made with Yahweh. Their passage through time and history is a manifestation of the carrying out of Yahweh's promise; their actions and collective behavior are interpreted and judged in the light of their covenant obligations. The convenant also, more literally, is what unites the twelve disparate tribes into a nation. Before the building of the temple, the shrine of the covenant is the center of their religious life; the ritual of the covenant, circumcision, symbolizes the rededication of each male child, each family to the covenant obligation.[21] It is neither accidental nor insignificant that women are absent from the covenant in each of its aspects.

Yahweh makes several covenants with Israel: one with Noah (Gen.9:8–17), two with Abram (Gen.15:7–18 and Gen.17:1–13), and one with Moses (Exodus 3;6:2–9,21–23). The covenant with Noah is preparatory to the other covenants: Yahweh pledges never again to send a flood to destroy the earth and its creatures, and He appoints the rainbow as "a token of the covenant." The covenant with Moses, including the Decalogue, is a concrete elaboration of the covenant relationship established with Abraham. Since it does not basically alter the concepts of gender implied in the earlier covenants, it falls beyond the scope of our investigation. The essential definition of the relationship of the chosen people to their God and of the covenant community occurs in the covenants with Abraham, and it is these we will analyze further here.

In Genesis 15 the earlier promise God has made to Abram of both land and offspring is formalized and made irrevocable by a convenant ritual. Since the Israelites are promised the actual occupation of the land only in future generations, this passage initiates their entry into historical time, their sense of passage through history as fulfillment of their destiny.[22] What is remarkable from our point of view is the language used to describe the process of generation. God expresses his purpose in these words addressed to Abram: "He that shall come forth out of thine own bowels shall be thine heir" (Gen.15:4).[23] He asks Abram to count the stars and promises him "So shall they seed be"(Gen.15:5). And "Unto thy seed I have given this land"(Gen.15:18). The male "seed" thus acquires the power and blessing of the procreativity which lodges in Yahweh. The metaphor of the male seed implanted in the female womb, the furrow, the earth, is older than the period of the writing of the Old Testament. It derives, most likely, from an agricultural context. It occurs, for example, in the story of the Courtship of Inanna and Dumuzi in the so-called Herder Wedding Song.[24] But it should be noted that the frank and graphic description of the sexual act in the Sumerian poem, in which Inanna asks "who will plow my vulva, who will plow my field?" to which question the poet answers, "May the King Dumuzi plow them for you . . ." never confuses the metaphor with the actual process. It refers, for example to Dumuzi as "he who was born from a fertile womb." What happens in Genesis is that an older metaphor becomes transformed so as to strengthen patriarchal meaning. God's blessing of Abram's "seed" lends divine sanction to the transfer of procreativity from female to male.

Yahweh's main covenant with Abram is set forth in Genesis 17, which is part of the P document. Here the covenant ritual is more formal and involves the active participation of Abram. God promises Abram, who had prostrated himself before Him, "Behold, my covenant is with thee, and thou shalt be the father of a multitude of nations"(Gen.17:5). And further:

> And I will establish My covenant between Me and thee and thy seed
> after thee through generations for an everlasting covenant, to be a
> God unto thee and to thy seed after thee [Gen.17:7].

Yahweh reiterates that He will give the land of Canaan to Abram "for an everlasting possession." It is at this point that Yahweh adds to the significance of the ritual by the re-naming of Abram and Sarai.

What does God ask of Abraham? He asks acceptance that He will be the God of Israel, He alone and no other. And He demands that His people which worship Him shall be set apart from other people by a bodily sign, a clearly identifiable token:

> This is My covenant, which ye shall keep, between Me and you and thy seed after thee: every male among you shall be circumcised. And ye shall be circumcised in the flesh of your foreskin; and it shall be a token of a covenant betwixt Me and you[Gen. 17:9–10]

We must take note of the fact that Yahweh makes the covenant with Abraham alone, not including Sarah, and that in so doing He gives divine sanction to the leadership of the patriarch over his family and tribe. Abraham incorporates the tribe and the family in a manner which Roman law at a much later period will institutionalize as *pater familias.* Sarah is mentioned in the covenant passage only as the bearer of Abraham's "seed" ("And I will bless her, and more-over I will give thee a son of her; yea, I will bless her, and she shall be a mother of nations; kings of peoples shall be of her"(Gen. 17:16). While Abraham and Sarah are equally blessed as progenitors of kings and nations, the covenant relationship is only with males—first with Abraham, then explicitly with Abraham and Sarah's son, Isaac, who is referred to only as Abraham's son. Moreover, the community of the covenenat is divinely defined as a male community, as can be seen by the selection of the symbol chosen as "token of the covenant."

Commentators have mainly focused on the form of the covenant, which bears a strong resemblance to Hittite royal treaties. In these royal treaties a vassal is obligated to keep the commands specified in the treaty by the Hittite king; it is thus a contract between unequal partners. The vassal must trust in the benevolence of the sovereign; but he is bound to carry out his treaty obligations. Usually, the treaty would be sealed by an oath and some solemn ceremony. Commentators have pointed out that there are striking formal parallels between the covenant with Moses, as described in Deuteronomy, Exodus, and Joshua, and the royal treaties. This would be in line with historic development, whereby the twelve tribes began to become consolidated into a confederacy through the Mosaic covenant, with the formal acceptance of the Decalogue, the ceremony of the ark of the covenant and male adult circumcision functioning as the binding oath and solemn ceremony. There is a strong likelihood that the emphasis on the covenant in the P document and its reiter-ation in references to God's covenant with David (II Sam. 23:1–5 and II Sam. 7:1–17) reflect the political needs at the time of the writing to legitimate the claim of David's kingship. Yahweh gave Abraham the land and promised to bless his seed and that of his descendants; Moses united the people by making them each pledge adherence to the covenant; David, by claiming direct descendance from Abraham and reasserting the claim to the land and leadership by way of the covenant with Moses, made of the tribes a nation. Land, power, and nationhood were the promise implicit in the covenant.[25]

While commentators have discussed the political and religious implications of the covenant at great length, they have not paid much attention to explaining the nature of the "token" which seals the convenant. The comments on circumcision have been uniformly unenlightening. We are told that circumcision was widely practiced in the Ancient Near East, for reasons of hygiene, as preparation for sexual life, as a sacrifice and a mark of distinction. Babylonians, Assyrians, and Phoenicians did not practice it, but some Egyptians and many Mesopotamian people did. That the practice was ancient is attested by pictorial evidence dating back to 2300 B.C. and by references to flint knives being used in the ceremony, which would mean it antedated the Bronze Age.[26] Commentators all agree that the rite underwent a decisive transformation in Israel, not only by the religious significance attached to it but by its being moved from puberty to infancy. Among most peoples, circumcision was a puberty rite, which presumably prepared men for sexual and procreative life. That fact and the way in which the Israelites transformed the rite therefore deserve closer attention.

Why was the circumcised penis chosen as the particular organ to be a "token"? If, as a number of commentators have suggested, Yahweh intended this bodily marking merely to distinguish His people from all others, why were the markings not placed on the forehead, the chest, the finger? If, as other commentators have suggested, the rite was merely hygienic, why was this particularl hygienic rite, which affected only males, chosen from among the number of possible rites and customs pertaining to health and nutrition, which could have served as well? John Calvin, for one, was conscious of the problems raised by this Biblical passage and forthrightly attempted to deal with them in his *Commentaries*:

> *Ye shall circumcise the flesh of your foreskin.* Very strange and unaccountable would this command at first sight appear. The subject

treated of, is the sacred covenant . . . and who can say that it is
reasonable for the sign of so great a mystery to consist in circumcision? But as it was necessary for Abraham to become a fool, in order
to prove himself obedient to God; so whosoever is wise, will both
soberly and reverently receive what God seems to us foolishly to have
commanded. And yet we must inquire, whether any analogy is here
apparent between the visible sign, and the thing signified.[27]

John Calvin's question concerning the sexual symbolism of circumcision is apt. I believe the key to its interpretation rests in the
various passages we have earlier cited, in which Yahweh promises to
bless Abraham's "seed." What is more logical and appropriate than
to use as the leading symbol of the covenant the organ which pro-
duces this "seed" and which "plants" it in the female womb? Nothing could better serve to impress man with the vulnerability of this
organ and with his dependence on God for his fertility (immortality). The offering of no other part of the body could have sent so
vivid and descriptive a message to man of the connection between
his reproductive capacity and the grace of God. Since Abraham and
the men of his household underwent the rite of circumcision as adults,
the act itself, which must have been painful, bespoke their trust and
faith in God and their submission to His will.

The symbolism implicit in circumcision is powerful in its patriarchal reverberations. Not only does it signify that procreativity now
lodges in God and in human males, but it also links it with land and
power. Psychoanalytic theory has suggested that the penis is the
symbol of power for men and women in Western civilization and
has regarded circumcision as a symbolic substitute for castration.
This explanation leads us to a historical reference of interest: at the
time of the writing of the Bible and earlier, priests and priestesses
of the fertility-goddess Ishtar dedicated their sexuality to the goddess. Some accepted voluntary virginity or celibacy, while others
engaged in ritual sexual intercourse in the goddess's honor. In either
case, humans sacrificed their own sexuality in order to celebrate and
enhance the fertility of the goddess. It is not inconceivable that the
rite of circumcision demanded as a token of the covenant represents
an adapatation of the old Mesopotamian rite, but transmuted as to
celebrate the fertility of the One God and His blessing of male procreativity.[28]

What is most striking is the omission of any symbolic or ritual
role for the mother in the process of procreation. God blesses Abraham's seed as though it were self-generating. The image of the breasts

of the fertility-goddess nurturing the earth and the fields has been replaced by the image of the circumcised penis signifying the covenant contract between mortal men and God. Collective immortality in the form of many generations of children, land, power, and victory over their enemies is promised to the people of the covenant, if they fulfill their obligations, among which circumcision is primary. ("And the uncircumcised male who is not circumcised in the flesh of his foreskin, that soul shall be cut off from his people; he hath broken My covenant" (Gen.17:14)).

Acceptance of monotheism, circumcision, and observance of God's laws as given to Moses are the obligations of the chosen people and will mark them off from their neighbors. But their cohesion and purity must be guaranteed by male circumcision and strict female virginity before marriage. Sexual control which assures the dominance of the father is here elevated not merely to a human social arrangement incorporated into man-made law, as, for example, in the Mesopotamian law codes—it is presented as the will of God expressed in His covenant with the men of Israel.

To the question "Who creates life?," Genesis answers, Yahweh and the God-like male he created.

IT REMAINS FOR US to discuss the third basic religious question: "What is the source of sin and death in the world?"

The ancient Mesopotamians addressed this question by breaking it into two: "How did humankind displease the gods?" and "Why does a good man suffer?" Mesopotamian concepts of the gods as rulers and of humans as their obedient servants implied that, when hardships, sickness, and defeat happened on earth, it was because human beings had somehow displeased the gods. In Mesopotamian thought death was accepted as a substantial reality; it is allotted to humankind and cannot be avoided, yet it is personified in a god or goddess. Eternal life is similarly made substantial; one can gain it by eating a certain food or "plant of life."[29]

In "The Epic of Gilgamesh" there are two segments pertinent to our question. One is the experience of the wild man, Enkidu, who lives in harmony with nature and to whom the animals speak. After he is befriended by a harlot, who "civilizes" him by having sexual intercourse with him for seven days, the animals flee him. "It was not as before/But now he had widsom, broader understanding." And the harlot says to him: "Thou art wise, Enkidu, art become like a God."[30] The acquisition of sexual knowledge separates Enkidu from nature. Human knowledge is here overlaid with sexual meanings and with the suggestion that it makes Enkidu closer to the gods than to the animals.

The second theme is man's quest for immortality. Gilgamesh, after the death of his beloved friend Enkidu, roams the earth to search for the secret of immortality. After many adventures he is offered a plant, a secret of the gods, "whereby a man may regain his life's breath," but he is robbed of it by a serpent. Although Gilgamesh is a semi-god, he is ultimately denied the secret of immortality, which is a privilege of the gods. We might note the role of the serpent, which usually is associated with the fertility-goddess, who is guarding her secret knowledge.

The Eridu school of Sumerian theology provides us with an early myth of man's fall. The god Ea has created a man, Adapa, who is skilled in navigation. "He possessed infinite knowledge which enabled him to give names to all things with the breath of life."[31] Adapa, in a quarrel with the god of the Southwind, breaks the latter's wings, for which crime he is summoned to heaven by the god Anu. Adapa's mentor, the wily god Ea, warns him not to eat or drink anything that might be offered to him in heaven. Obedient to these instructions, Adapa refuses the bread and water of life offered to him by god Anu. He is brought back to earth and held responsible for all the ills that befall humankind. "And whatsoever of ill this man has brought upon men . . . upon this man may the horror fall."[32]

In these myths the gods jealously guard their power to grant immortality. Men who aspire to divine knowledge are blamed for bringing evil into the world. We might also note that the means by which humans acquire divine knowledge is by eating and drinking certain substances and by sexual intercourse.

We find all these elements: the tree of knowledge, the forbidden fruit, the snake, with its association with the fertility-goddess and female sexuality, in the Biblical story of the Fall.

The tree of life and its fruit is early associated with the fertility-goddess. From the beginning of the third millennium B.C. on we see her depicted holding fruit or ears of corn or, alternately, a bowl from which flows the water of life. (See illus. 4 and 13.) Some of these symbols are later taken over by kings and rulers. One of the oldest of representations associating the ruler with the tree of life is a statue of Governor Gudea of Lagash (2275–60 B.C.) holding a jar dispensing the water of life in the same pose as that of the goddess Ishtar in a sculpture from Mari (see illus. 12). The Stele of Urnammu of Ur shows the king enthroned sitting before a libation vessel from which water flows and from which the tree of life grows. A mural painting from the palace in Mari depicts the investiture of King Zimri-Lim by the goddess Ishtar. A lower panel shows two goddess-like figures wearing the characteristic crown, each holding a bowl from which flows water into four great rivers. From each of the water bowls there sprouts a tree of life.[33]

The image persists for almost two thousand years. We find it on various seals (see illus. 18 and 20), and we see it on the monumental wall sculptures of the palace of Ashurbanipal of Assyria, built in the seventh century B.C. We see it in a mural depicting the king and queen feasting in an arbor (see illus. 22). The motive of the king and his attendants or some mythical genius figures watering the tree of life appears in several of the wall reliefs of that palace (see illus. 18–21).[34] The symbol was also widespread in Canaan, where Asherah, the fertility goddess, was symbolized by a stylized tree. Her cult, which was popular in Israel during the patriarchal period, took place in groves of trees.[35]

For our purposes it is worth noting the general direction of the development of this symbol, which fits into the pattern of patriarchal ascendancy we have earlier uncovered.

At first, the tree of life, with its fruit—the cassia, the pomegranate, the date, the apple—was associated with fertility-goddesses. At the time of the development of kingship, kings assume some of the services to the goddess and with them some of her power, and have themselves depicted with symbols associated with her. They carry the water-of-life jug; they water the tree of life. It is most likely that this development coincided with the change in the concept of the fertility goddess: namely, that she must have a male consort to initiate her fertility. The king of the Sacred Marriage becomes the king "watering" the tree of life. This shift is particularly striking in the panels from the palace of Ashurbanipal at Nineveh, which reveal the changes in gender definitions quite dramatically. The king and his servants are huge; they are depicted as warriors in full armor, with bulging muscles and carrying weapons. Yet the king carries a watering-pot, doing homage to the fertility principle symbolized in the tree of life. Clearly, the locus of power has shifted from female to male, but the realm of the goddess cannot be ignored; it must be honored and pacified.

Hebrew symbolism was strongly influenced by the Mesopotamian heritage and by that of Israel's Canaanite neighbors. In the story of the Fall we see all the symbolic elements of that heritage emphatically and significantly transformed.

There are in the Biblical story of paradise two trees: the tree of life and the tree of the knowledge of good and evil.—"The tree of life also in the midst of the garden, and the tree of the knowledge of good and evil"(Gen.2:9). The second reference is somewhat ambiguous and makes it appear that the two meanings have merged in one symbol—"Of every tree in the garden thou mayest freely eat; but of the tree of the knowledge of good and evil, thou shalt not eat of it; for in the day that thou eatest thereof thou shalt surely die"(Gen.2:16–17). Since eating from the tree of life is not forbidden here, one might assume the two trees have become merged. But in Gen.3:22 God specifically separates the two trees and expels Adam and Eve from the garden "lest he put forth his hand, and take also of the tree of life, and eat, and live forever."[36]

In the Biblical story the knowledge which is forbidden to humankind is of a dual nature: it is moral knowledge, the knowledge of good and evil, and it is sexual knowledge. When human beings acquire the knowledge of good and evil, they take upon themselves the obligation for making moral decisions, having lost their innocence and with it their ability to carry out the will of God without moral considerations. Fallen humanity, in this act of acquiring a higher level of "knowing," assumes the burden of distinguishing between good and evil and of choosing the good in order to be saved. The other aspect of knowledge is sexual knowledge; that is made clear in the line describing one of the consequences of the Fall, "and they knew they were naked" (Gen.3:7). In this, the consequences of Adam and Eve's transgression fall with uneven weight upon the woman. The consequence of sexual knowledge is to sever female sexuality from procreation. God puts enmity between the snake and the woman (Gen.3:15). In the historical context of the times of the writing of Genesis, the snake was clearly associated with the fertility goddess and symbolically represented her. Thus, by God's command, the free and open sexuality of the fertility-goddess was to be forbidden to fallen woman. The way her sexuality was to find expression was in motherhood. Her sexuality was so defined as to serve her motherly function, and it was limited by two conditions: she was to be subordinate to her husband, and she would bring forth her children in pain.

But there remained the tree of life, in the center of the Garden.

Implicit in the human couple's tasting the forbidden fruit of the tree of knowledge was that they would aspire to acquiring the mystery of the tree of life, the knowledge of immortality, which is reserved to God. That implication is made clear both in the earlier-cited command forbidding the fruit and in God's punishment "for dust thou art, and unto dust shalt thou return"(Gen.3:19). To aspire to the knowledge of God is the supreme hubris; the punishment for it is mortality. But God is merciful and redemptive, and so in Eve's punishment there is also a redemptive aspect. Once and forever, creativity (and with it the secret of immortality) is severed from procreativity. Creativity is reserved to God; procreativity of human beings is the lot of women. The curse on Eve makes of it a painful and subordinate lot.

But there is another side to the story of the Fall. God's curse on Adam ends with assigning him to mortality. Yet in the very next line Adam re-names his wife Eve "because she was the mother of all living." This is the profound recognition that in her now lies the only immortality to which human beings can aspire—the immortality of generation. Here is the redemptive aspect of the Biblical doctrine of the division of labor between the sexes: not only shall man work in the sweat of his brow and woman give birth in pain, but mortal men and women depend on the redemptive, life-giving function of the mother for the only immortality they shall ever experience.

It is the first act of fallen Adam thus to re-name Eve or, rather, thus to reinterpret the meaning of her name. Fallen Eve may take hope and courage from her new redemptive role as mother, but there are two conditions defining and delimiting her choices, both of them imposed upon her by God: she is to be severed from the snake, and she is to be ruled by her husband. If we understand the snake to be the symbol of the old fertility-goddess, this condition is essential to the establishment of monotheism. It will be echoed and reaffirmed in the covenant: there shall be only One God, and the fertility-goddess shall be cast out as evil and become the very symbol of sin. We need not strain our interpretation to read this as the condemnation by Yahweh of female sexuality exercised freely and autonomously, even sacredly.

The second condition is that Eve, to be honored as life-giver, shall be ruled by her husband. It is the law of patriarchy, here clearly defined and given divine sanction. We have seen an earlier development leading toward such a definition in the Code of Hammurabi and in Middle Assyrian law §40. Here we see it in the form of divine decree fully integrated into a powerful religious world-view.

We have seen how the two basic questions, "Who creates Life?" and "Who speaks to God?" were answered in different cultures, and we have shown how the answer to both questions in the Old Testament affirmed male power over women.

To the question "Who brought sin and death into the world?" Genesis answers, "Woman, in her alliance with the snake, which stands for free female sexuality." It is quite in line with such thinking that women should be excluded from active participation in the covenant community and that the very symbol of that community and that compact with God should be a male symbol.

The development of monotheism in the Book of Genesis was an enormous advance of human beings in the direction of abstract thought and the definition of universally valid symbols. It is a tragic accident of history that this advance occurred in a social setting and under circumstances which strengthened and affirmed patriarchy. Thus, the very process of symbol-making occurred in a form which marginalized women. For females, the Book of Genesis represented their definition as creatures essentially different from males; a redefinition of their sexuality as beneficial and redemptive only within the boundaries of patriarchal dominance; and finally the recognition that they were excluded from directly being able to represent the divine principle. The weight of the Biblical narrative seemed to decree that by the will of God women were included in His covenant only through the mediation of men. Here is the historic moment of the death of the Mother-Goddess and her replacement by God-the-Father and the metaphorical Mother under patriarchy.

TEN

Symbols

WESTERN CIVILIZATION RESTS upon the foundation of the moral and religious ideas expressed in the Bible and the philosophy and science developed in Classical Greece. We have shown in the preceding chapters how in the historic period, when humankind made a qualitative leap forward in its ability to conceptualize large symbol systems which explain the world and the universe, women were already so greatly disadvantaged that they were excluded from participation in this important cultural advance. To understand the implications of this fact fully we need to consider, for a moment, the importance of the creation of symbols.

Humans, like animals, preserve themselves, propagate the species, and create shelter for themselves and their offspring. Unlike animals, human beings invent tools, alter the environment, speculate about their own mortality, and make mental constructs to explain the meaning of their existence and their relationship to the supernatural. In making symbols, creating languages and symbolic systems, *Homo sapiens* becomes truly human. Erich Fromm says, "human beings are half-animal and half-symbolic."[1]

Ernst Becker explains:

Man has a symbolic identity that brings him sharply out of nature. He is a symbolic self, a creature with a name, a life history. He is a creator with a mind that soars out to speculate about atoms and infinity, who can place himself imaginatively at a point in space and con-

template bemusedly his own planet. . . . Yet, at the same
time . . . man is a worm and food for worms. . . . His body is
material . . . that is alien to him in many ways—the strangest and
most repugnant being that it aches and bleeds and will decay and die.
Man is literally split in two.[2]

Man (male) has found a way of dealing with this existential dilemma by assigning symbol-making power to himself and life-death-
nature finiteness to woman. Becker comments that by this split "man
seeks to control the mysterious processes of nature as they manifest
themselves within his own body. The body cannot be allowed to
have ascendancy over him."[3]

Above all, human beings are concerned with immortality. The
desire to survive one's own death has been the single most important force compelling humans to record the past and preserve it.
History-making is the process by which human beings record, interpret, and reinterpret the past in order to hand it down to future
generations. To do so became possible only after people learned how
to manipulate symbols.

This development took place in Mesopotamia with the invention
of writing, ca.3100 B.C. The development of a symbolic system of
number notation preceded the invention of writing. Both of these
advances were made in the course of business and trade activities.
We have shown how these activities centered in the temples and in
the courts and how the ruling elites, in establishing class society,
appropriated to themselves the control of the symbol system. Class
society, I have argued, began with the dominance of men over women
and developed into the dominance of some men over other men and
over all women. Thus, the very process of class formation incorporated an already pre-existing condition of male dominance over women
and marginalized women in the formation of symbol systems. Yet,
as we have seen, the older systems of religious and metaphysical
explanations persisted for centuries, and in those systems women
had their share of representation and symbolic power. The exclusion
of women from the creation of symbol systems became fully institutionalized only with the development of monotheism.

Hebrew monotheism conceptualized a universe created by a single force—God's will. The source of creativity, then, was the invisible, ineffable God. He created male and female in a significantly
different way, out of different substance, though each enlivened by
his divine breath. He covenanted and contracted only with males.
Circumcision as the symbol of the covenant expressed that reality.

Only males could mediate between God and humans. This was symbolically expressed in the all-male priesthood, the various ways of excluding women from the most essential and meaningful religious ritual: i.e., their exclusion from the formation of the *minyan;* their segregated seating in the temple; their exclusion as active participants from the temple service, etc. Women were denied equal access to religious learning and the priesthood, and thereby they were denied the capacity of interpreting and altering the religious belief system.

We have seen how procreativity and creativity were severed in the creation of monotheism. God's blessing of man's seed which would be planted in the passive receptacle of woman's womb symbolically defined gender relations under patriarchy. And in the story of the Fall, woman and, more specifically, female sexuality became the symbol of human weakness and the source of evil.

Jewish monotheism and Christianity, which built upon it, gave man a purpose and meaning in life by setting each life within a larger, divine plan which unfolded so as to lead man from the Fall to redemption, from mortality to immortality, from fallen man to the Messiah. Thus, in the Bible we see the development of the first philosophy of history. Human life is given meaning through its unfolding in the historical context, which context is defined as the carrying out of God's purpose and God's will. Man, endowed with free will and instructed by Holy Writ, as interpreted through male priests, could actively fulfill his destiny and affect the historical process. Men interpret God's word; men carry out the ritual, which symbolically ties the human community to God. Women's access to the purpose of God's will and to the unfolding of history is possible only through the mediation of men. Thus, according to the Bible it is men who live and move in history.

IN THE SIXTH AND FIFTH CENTURIES B.C. historical scholarship of a secular nature developed and flourished in Greece. With the writings of Thucydides and Herodotus the recording and interpretation of history became separated from religious thought, as did science and philosophy. But the construct of history was a male product and would so remain for another 2500 years.

The major definitions of gender symbols in the Old Testament had been completed by the time of the fall of Jerusalem and the Babylonian Exile in the sixth century B.C. Although we cannot deal with developments in Greece of the same period in any detail, it is important for us to look briefly at the development of Greek thought and philosophy, which forms the second root of the idea system of Western civilization. I will omit from consideration the third important symbol system, science, and its origin in Near Eastern and Greek thought, because it falls beyond the scope of this work and is beyond my capacity and training. But it is worth noting, in passing, that science also developed in such a way that women were not included in the community of participants and creators, even though there were a few exceptional female practitioners in mathematics in antiquity.[4]

As was the case in Mesopotamia and Israel, Greece of the eighth through the fifth century B.C. was a class society with slavery, and it was a thoroughly patriarchal society. Although there has been some historiographical controversy over the degree of the domestic enclosure of respectable women and the separate spheres in which men and women lived, the fact of women's legal and social subordination is undisputed.[5]

Women in Athens were excluded from participation in the political life of the city and were legally lifelong minors under the guardianship of a male. The common practice of men in their thirties marrying girls in their teens reinforced male dominance in marriage. Women were severely restricted in their economic rights, but those of the wealthier classes were somewhat protected in marriage by the provision that their dowries reverted to their natal families in case of divorce. The main function of wives was to produce male heirs and to supervise their husband's households. Many female children were exposed at birth and left to die, with the decision over their fate always made by the father. Premarital and marital chastity were strictly enforced on women, but their husbands were free to enjoy sexual gratification from lower class women, heterae, and slaves and from young men. Respectable women spent most of their life indoors, while men of their class spent most of their time in public places. The major exception to the domestic confinement of middle-class women was their participation in religious festivals and cults and their attendance at weddings and funerals.

Greek society developed the *polis*, the city-state surrounded by independent farms and governed by magistrates and laws, to its highest form. In the Archaic period (seventh and sixth centuries), which in Greece was the Iron Age, an important military development affected the social and with it the political structure of society. Greek infantry, based on the *hoplite*—the heavily armed and armored infantryman organized into tight phalanxes—replaced the horseman as the decisive force on the battlefield. The *hoplite* was a citizen-soldier, from the ranks of well-to-do farmers and the middle class, who furnished his own sword, spear, helmet, and shield. His life and military success depended on team-work within the phalanx, which fostered a spirit of egalitarianism, responsibility, and discipline. His predominance undermined the aristocratic primacy of an earlier period and fostered democratic concepts within the state and the military. As one historian put it: "The phalanx . . . was the school which made the Greek polis." William H. McNeill continues:

> The right to a voice in public affairs, formerly restricted to nobles, was broadened to include all citizens having the means to equip themselves as members of the phalanx. The "hoplite franchise" remained a conservative ideal for many Greek cities throughout the fifth century and later.[6]

This means, that, once again, citizenship was so defined so as, quite accidentally and probably, at first, unintentionally, to exclude women. If democracy was to be based on the concept of the citizen-soldier, then such exclusion seemed both inevitable and logical. Yet, Spartan society, similarly affected by the development of the hoplite phalanx, moved in the direction of suppressing all marks of inequality and difference and making of their society a garrison state of equals. The Spartan law codified under Lycurgus in the seventh century remained unchanged throughout Spartan history. It expressed the concept that the bearing of children was as important a service to the state as the service of the warrior in a law, which allowed the inscription of the name of the deceased on a tomb only of a man who had died at war and of a woman who had died in childbirth. Spartan women were occupied with gymnastics, household management, and child-rearing, while the menial housework and the making of clothing were left to non-Spartan women. All girl infants were reared to adulthood, but infanticide was practiced on weak and sickly male children. In Sparta, adultery was not as strictly proscribed as in Athenian society, and Spartan society, emphasizing the need for healthy warriors, was relatively indifferent to whether a child was born legitimately or not. In its sharp contrast in matters of sexual regulation and polity, Spartan society seemed to Greeks of other cities to represent a clear-cut choice of direction: relative equality and high status for women combined with oligarchy and unfreedom as against the strict regulation of women combined with democracy. This choice is reflected in the political thought of both Plato and Aristotle.[7]

In the Ionian city-states the development of commercial agriculture, based on a lively trade in oil and wine to far-flung colonies and trading centers, created ever sharper class division, as it gave rise to a wealthy middle class and an impoverished class of propertyless citizens and small farmers. Their discontent led in the seventh and sixth centuries to the establishment of tyrannies in many cities. For Athens, this indicated the need for corrective legislation, which would lessen class antagonism and thus safeguard the state. The laws of Draco and, later, of Solon of Athens (ca.640/635– to 560 (?) B.C.) laid the foundation of democracy in the classical age.

The class antagonisms and the insecurity of their class of poor farmers struggling to raise themselves to a middle-class level was reflected in the misogynist poetry of Hesiod and Semonides in the seventh century B.C. Hesiod in his *Works and Days* expressed the individualism of a poor man, who no longer relies on his clan or tribe for protection but expects by hard work and prudent management to increase his wealth. Restraint, self-control, and competitiveness come to be seen as virtues in such an enterprise, while the pursuit of luxurious tastes and sexual pleasures is a threat to the family economy. Hesiod's misogyny is both prescriptive and mythical. In his contrasting of the "good wife," who is chaste, hardworking, thrifty, and cheerful, and of the "bad wife" he sets standards for the definition of gender by men of his class, and he finds a convenient scapegoat for the evils of society of his day. In his recasting of the myth of Pandora, he achieves what Hebrew myth achieved in the story of the Fall—he places the blame on woman and her sexual nature for bringing evil into the world.

Hesiod's *Theogeny* defines and elaborates the ascension of the storm-god Zeus to the leading position in the Greek pantheon of gods. Certainly, Hesiod did not invent this myth of transformation, which is somewhat similar to the Mesopotamian myths we have discussed, in which male gods take over power from the forces of chaos identified with the fertility-goddesses. Hesiod's *Theogeny* reflects a change in religious and gender concepts, which had already taken place in Greek society.[8] As described by Hesiod, the conflict between the gods is expressed in terms of male-female and generational tension. In the earliest mythical period the sky-god Ouranos, trying to prevent a challenge to his rule by his son, holds his children in Gaia's (the earth-goddess's) womb. But Gaia and her son Cronos castrate Ouranos and overthrow him. Now Cronos in his turn fears that he will be overthrown by the sons his wife Rhea bears and so he swallows them each. But Rhea hides her son Zeus in a cave protected by the earth-goddess. When he is grown, Zeus fights and overthrows his father and ascends to power. To prevent his own overthrow, he swallows his wife, Metis, thus keeping her from bringing forth a son, and by this act assimilating into himself her power of procreativity. Thus, Zeus himself can give birth to Athena, who springs full-grown from his head. She comes to symbolize the forces of justice and order. We should note here not only the takeover of the male god but his assumption of the power of procreativity, which is similar to the symbolic definitions we have discussed in Genesis.

The force and importance of this symbolic downgrading of the mother is further elaborated in Aeschylus' *The Furies*, the last play in his *Oresteia* trilogy. The *Oresteia* has been interpreted by a number of critics as signifying the last defense of Mother-Goddess power against patriarchy.[9] The story concerns events following Agamemnon's sacrificial killing of his daughter Iphigenia, which propitiated the wind-gods and allowed the Greek fleet to sail to Troy and victory. Ten years later, upon his return from Troy, Agamemnon, who has returned with the Trojan princess Cassandra, now his concubine and slave, is killed by his wife, Clytemnestra, in revenge for the death of Iphigenia. Clytemnestra's son, Orestes, regarding his mother's crime as an act of rebellion against the king, kills his mother, for which crime he is hounded by the furies. To divert their anger, he argues that his action was justified and that they should have hounded his mother for her crime. The furies excuse her action by asserting the primacy of mother-right: "The man she killed was not of her own blood." Orestes asks: "But am I of my mother's?" The furies point out the obvious: "Vile wretch, she nourished you in her own womb. Do you disown your mother's blood?" The playright lets Apollo settle the argument, by asserting the claim of patriarchy:

> The mother is not the parent of the child
> Which is called hers. She is the nurse who tends the growth
> Of young seed planted by its true parent, the male. . . .

Apollo appeals to the goddess Athena to further prove his point. She obliges: "No Mother gave me birth. Therefore the father's claim and male supremacy in all things . . . wins my whole heart's loyalty." It is Athena's deciding vote, which frees Orestes and banishes the furies and with them the claims of the Mother-Goddess. Yet, the female principle has to be pacified, so the furies are given a sacred dwelling and will be worshipped as guardians of the laws.

The doctrine of male procreativity reappears in its most developed form in the work of Aristotle. It is in this form that it had its determining and shaping influence on Western science and philosophy. Aristotle elevated the counterfactual account of the origin of human life from the level of myth to the level of science by grounding it in a broad-ranging philosophical system. His theory of causation posited four factors that make a thing what it is: (1) a material cause; (2) the efficient cause (that which gives it impetus); (3) a formal cause (that which gives it form); and (4) the *telos*, the goal toward which it strives. In line with Greek philosophical thought, Aristotle considers matter of lower importance than spirit. In his explanation of the origin of human life, three of the four causes for being were attributed to the male's contribution to procreation (semen), with only the fourth and lowest, the material, being the woman's contribution. Aristotle even strongly denied that the semen contributed any material component to the embryo; He saw its contribution as spiritual, hence "more divine." "For the first principle of the movement, or efficient cause, whereby that which comes into being is male, is better and more divine than the material whereby it is female."[10] Aristotle explained that life was created by the meeting of sperm and what he called catamenia, the female discharge. However, he defined both sperm and catemenia as "semen" or "seed," with the difference that "catamenia are semen not in a pure state but in need of working up."[11] Aristotle believed that the female's colder blood prevented her blood from completing the necessary transformation into semen. It is worth noting how at every point in his explanatory system it so happens that the female's endowment or contribution is inferior to that of the male. He further postulates that the male is active and the female is passive:

> If, then, the male stands for the effective and active, and the female, considered as female, for the passive, it follows that what the female would contribute to the semen of the male would not be semen but material for the semen to work upon. This is just what we find to be the case, for the catamenia have in their nature an affinity to the primitive matter.[12]

Aristotle elaborated on the essential and important difference between the active male and the passive female sex. Without offering much evidence for his assertion, he explained that "if . . . it is the male that has the power of making the sensitive soul, it is impossible for the female to generate an animal from itself alone."[13] In a later analogy he described the process as that of a craftsman making a bed from wood or a ball from wax, the craftsman presumably being the male, the material substance being the female contribution.[14] The historian Maryanne Cline Horowitz, who has written an insightful feminist critique of Aristotle's work, comments that in Aristotle's view:

> the female passively takes on her task, laboring with her body to fulfill another's design and plan. The product of her labor is not hers. The man, on the other hand, does not labor but works . . . Aristotle implied that the male is *homo faber*, the maker, who works upon inert matter according to a design, bringing forth a lasting work of art. His soul contributes the form and model of creation.[15]

Having *a priori* and without further explanation assumed the inferiority of the female's biological equipment, Aristotle explains that a predominance of the female principle is responsible for the birth of monstrosities. Among these he lists children who do not resemble their parents and women, using this language: "The first departure [from type] is indeed that the offspring should become female instead of male; this, however, is a natural necessity."[16] Aristotle is even more explicit elsewhere:

> . . . for just as the young of mutilated parents are sometimes born mutilated and sometimes not, so also the young born of a female are sometimes female and sometimes male instead. For the female is, as it were, a mutilated male, and the catamenia are semen, only not pure; for there is only one thing they have not in them, the principle of soul.[17]

These definitions of women as mutilated males, devoid of the principle of soul, are not isolated but rather permeate Aristotle's biological and philosophical work.[18] He is quite consistent in reasoning that the biological inferiority of woman must make her inferior also in her capacities, her ability to reason and therefore her ability to make decisions. From this follows Aristotle's definition of gender and its integration into his political thought.

Aristotle's grand mental construct rests on a teleological foundation. "The nature of a thing is its end. For what each thing is when fully developed, we call its nature, whether we are speaking of a man, a horse or a family."[19]

Such a view predisposes the philosopher to reason back from that which is and to assume as a given whatever his society takes for granted. Thus "it is evident that the state is a creation of nature, and that man is by nature a political animal."[20] Aristotle's proof of this assertion lies in the fact that the individual, when isolated, is not self-sufficient. In order to make the state function properly, it must be governed by justice, which is "the principle of order in political society."[21]

The state is made up of households, and to understand properly the management of the state one must understand the management of the household: "The first and fewest possible parts of the family are master and slave, husband and wife, father and children."[22] Aristotle then discusses the institution of slavery and describes it as controversial. Some people assert that it is contrary to nature and therefore unjust. He refutes this at length, by reasoning that some are born to rule, others to be ruled. This is so because of what he sees as a natural dichotomy: the soul is by nature the ruler, the body the subject. Similarly, the mind rules the appetites. "It is clear that the rule of the soul over the body, and of the mind and the rational element over the passionate, is natural and expedient. . . . Again, the male is by nature superior, and the female inferior; and the one rules and the other is ruled; this principle, of necessity, extends to all mankind."[23] The rule of men over animals is equally natural: "And indeed the use made of slaves and of tame animals is not very different; for both with their bodies minister to the needs of life . . . . It is clear, then, that some men are by nature free, and others slaves, and that for these latter slavery is both expedient and right."[24]

Aristotle pursues the logic of his argument by describing the different ways in which a husband rules over his slaves, his wife, and his children, the difference being dependent on the nature of the persons to be ruled. "For the slave has no deliberative faculty at all; the woman has, but it is without authority, and the child has, but it is immature." Similarly, their moral virtue is different, "the courage of man is shown in commanding, of a woman in obeying."[25]

Aristotle's world-view is both hierarchical and dichotomized. Soul rules over body; rational thought over emotion; humans over animals; male over female; masters over slaves; and Greeks over barbarians. All the philosopher need do to justify the existing class relations within his society is to show how each of the subordinate groups is by "nature" designed to occupy its appropriate rank in the hierarchy. He has some difficulty doing this in the case of slaves and finds the need to justify their subordination and explain why it is "just." That is so, because even at the height of the democratic Athenian state slavery as an institution was still controversial enough to be questioned. Even some who assume that enslaving captive peoples is justified by law, says Aristotle, then question whether this can be justified in case of an unjust war. The philosopher admits that "there is some foundation for this difference of opinion."[26] But there is no difference of opinion regarding the inferiority of women. And so Aristotle uses the metaphor of the marital relationship to justify the master's dominance over the slave. Since the former appears "natural," that is, uncontroversial and therefore just, it can make the latter acceptable.

Human society is divided into two sexes: the male—rational, strong, endowed with the capacity for procreation, equipped with soul and fit to rule; the female—passionate and unable to control her appetites, weak, providing only low matter for the process of procreation, devoid of soul and designed to be ruled. And because this is so, the rule of some men over other men can be justified by ascribing to those men some of the same qualities ascribed to the female. Aristotle does just that. Slaves "with their bodies minister to the needs of life"—so do women. Slaves "participate in rational principle enough to apprehend, but not to have, such a principle"—so do women.[27] Thus, Aristotle justifies class dominance logically from his gender definitions.

The fact that sex dominance antedates class dominance and lies at its foundation is both implicit and explicit in Aristotle's philosophy. It is implicit in his choice of explanatory metaphors, which takes for granted that his audience will understand the "naturalness" of male dominance over females and consider slavery just if he can prove his analogy. It is explicit in the way he sets up his dichotomies and assigns greater value to that which men do (politics, philosophy, rational discourse) than that which women do (minister to the needs of life). And it is most explicit of all in the way his gender definitions and prescriptions are built into his discourse on politics. His great and path-breaking insight that "man is by nature a political animal" is immediately followed by his explanation that the state is made up of individual households and that the management of the household is analogous and makes a model for the management of the body politic. What he describes here is exactly the development we have been tracing in Mesopotamian society since in its inception: the patriarchal family is the form which the archaic state takes. The patriarchal family is the cell out of which the larger body of patriarchal dominance arises. Sexual dominance underlies class and race dominance.

Aristotle's grand and daring explanatory system, which encompassed and transcended most of the knowledge then available in his society, incorporated the patriarchal gender concept of the inferiority of women in such a way as to make it indisputable and, in fact, invisible. Definitions of class, of private property, of scientific explanations could and would be debated for centuries after on the basis of Aristotle's thought—but male supremacy and male dominance are here a basic foundation of the philosopher's thought and are thus elevated to the power of natural laws. This was quite an achievement, considering the opposing interpretation of female worth and potential expressed in Plato's *Republic* and his *Laws*.

In Book V of the *Republic,* Plato—in the voice of Socrates—sets down the conditions for the training of the guardians, his elite leadership group. Socrates proposes that women should have the same opportunity as men to be trained as guardians. In support of this he offers a strong statement against making sex differences the basis for discrimination:

> . . . if the difference [between men and women] consists only in women bearing and men begetting children, this does not amount to proof that a woman differs from a man in respect to the sort of education she should receive; and we shall therefore continue to maintain that our guardians and their wives ought to have the same pursuits.[28]

Socrates proposes the same education for boys and girls, freeing guardian women from housework and child-care. But this female equality of opportunity will serve a larger purpose: the destruction of the family. Plato's aim is to abolish private property, the private family, and with it self-interest in his leadership group, for he sees clearly that private property engenders class antagonism and disharmony. Therefore "men and women are to have a common way of life . . . —common education, common children; and they are to watch over the citizens in common."[29] In his philosophical writings Aristotle accepted the body vs. soul dualism of Plato, as well as his concept of the natural inequality of human beings and the justice of the stronger governing the weaker. But he was not in the least affected by Plato's (Socrates') ideas concerning women. Had he acknowledged Plato's ideas on the subject and aimed to refute them, his *dicta* on women would carry less prescriptive force. Yet, in a sense, his bypassing of Plato's ideas is quite justified, for Aristotle was writing about the state and about class and gender relations as they actually existed. Plato envisioned women as equals only in terms of a utopian state, a benevolent dictatorship of the guardians.[30] Among a carefully selected and bred elite, some women might function as equals. In the democratic polis based on slavery, about which Aristotle was writing, the very definition of citizenship had to exclude all those deemed inferior—helots, slaves, women. Thus, Aristotle's political science institutionalizes and rationalizes the exclusion of women from political citizenship as the very foundation of the democratic polity. It is this heritage, not the utopian thought of Plato, which Western civilization would use for centuries in its science, its philosophy, and its gender doctrine.

By the time men began symbolically to order the universe and the relationship of humans to God in major explanatory systems, the subordination of women had become so completely accepted that it appeared "natural" both to men and women. As a result of this historic development the major metaphors and symbols of Western civilization incorporated the assumption of female subordination and inferiority. With the Bible's fallen Eve and Aristotle's woman as mutilated male, we see the emergence of two symbolic constructs which assert and assume the existence of two kinds of human beings—the male and the female—different in their essence, their function, and their potential. This metaphoric construct, the "inferior and not quite completed female," became embedded in every major explanatory system in such a way as to take on the life and force of actuality. On the unexamined assumption that this stereotype represented reality, institutions denied women equal rights and access to privileges, educational deprivation for women became justified and, given the sanctity of tradition and patriarchal dominance for millennia, appeared justified and natural. For patriarchally organized society, this symbolic construct represented an essential ingredient in the order and structure of civilization.

The significance of this development for women is hard to overestimate. We will address some of its consequences in the second volume, when we will explore and discuss the way in which the hidden assumption of female inferiority and male dominance in the philosophies of Western civilization impeded women's ability to understand their own situation and to remedy it. But we should note, in summary, the way in which inequality among men and women was built not only into the language, thought, and philosophy of Western civilization, but the way in which gender itself became a metaphor defining power relations in such a way as to mystify them and render them invisible.

ELEVEN

The Creation of Patriarchy

PATRIARCHY IS A HISTORIC CREATION formed by men and women in a process which took nearly 2500 years to its completion. In its earliest form patriarchy appeared as the archaic state. The basic unit of its organization was the patriarchal family, which both expressed and constantly generated its rules and values. We have seen how integrally definitions of gender affected the formation of the state. Let us briefly review the way in which gender became created, defined, and established.

The roles and behavior deemed appropriate to the sexes were expressed in values, customs, laws, and social roles. They also, and very importantly, were expressed in leading metaphors, which became part of the cultural construct and explanatory system.

The sexuality of women, consisting of their sexual and their reproductive capacities and services, was commodified even prior to the creation of Western civilization. The development of agriculture in the Neolithic period fostered the inter-tribal "exchange of women," not only as a means of avoiding incessant warfare by the cementing of marriage alliances but also because societies with more women could produce more children. In contrast to the economic needs of hunting/gathering societies, agriculturists could use the labor of children to increase production and accumulate surpluses. Men-as-a-group had rights in women which women-as-a-group did not have in men. Women themselves became a resource, acquired by men much as the land was acquired by men. Women were exchanged or bought in marriages for the benefit of their families; later, they were conquered or bought in slavery, where their sexual services were part of their labor and where their children were the property of their masters. In every known society it was women of conquered tribes who were first enslaved, whereas men were killed. It was only after men had learned how to enslave the women of groups who could be defined as strangers, that they learned how to enslave men of those groups and, later, subordinates from within their own societies.

Thus, the enslavement of women, combining both racism and sexism, preceded the formation of classes and class oppression. Class differences were, at their very beginnings, expressed and constituted in terms of patriarchal relations. Class is not a separate construct from gender; rather, class is expressed in generic terms.

By the second millennium B.C. in Mesopotamian societies, the daughters of the poor were sold into marriage or prostitution in order to advance the economic interests of their families. The daughters of men of property could command a bride price, paid by the family of the groom to the family of the bride, which frequently enabled the bride's family to secure more financially advantageous marriages for their sons, thus improving the family's economic position. If a husband or father could not pay his debt, his wife and children could be used as pawns, becoming debt slaves to the creditor. These conditions were so firmly established by 1750 B.C. that Hammurabic law made a decisive improvement in the lot of debt pawns by limiting their terms of service to three years, where earlier it had been for life.

The product of this commodification of women—bride price, sale price, and children—was appropriated by men. It may very well represent the first accumulation of private property. The enslavement of women of conquered tribes became not only a status symbol for nobles and warriors, but it actually enabled the conquerors to acquire tangible wealth through selling or trading the product of the slaves' labor and their reproductive product, slave children.

Claude Lévi-Strauss, to whom we owe the concept of "the exchange of women," speaks of the reification of women, which occurred as its consequence. But it is not women who are reified and commodified, it is women's sexuality and reproductive capacity which is so treated. The distinction is important. Women never became "things," nor were they so perceived. Women, no matter how exploited and abused, retained their power to act and to choose to the same, often very limited extent, as men of their group. But women *always and to this day* lived in a relatively greater state of un-freedom than did men. Since their sexuality, an aspect of their body, was controlled by others, women were not only actually disadvantaged but psychologically restrained in a very special way. For women, as for men of subordinate and oppressed groups, history consisted of their struggle for emancipation and freedom from necessity. But women struggled against different forms of oppression and dominance than did men, and their struggle, up to this time, has lagged behind that of men.

The first gender-defined social role for women was to be those who were exchanged in marriage transactions. The obverse gender role for men was to be those who did the exchanging or who defined the terms of the exchanges.

Another gender-defined role for women was that of the "stand-in" wife, which became established and institutionalized for women of elite groups. This role gave such women considerable power and privileges, but it depended on their attachment to elite men and was based, minimally, on their satisfactory performance in rendering these men sexual and reproductive services. If a woman failed to meet these demands, she was quickly replaced and thereby lost all her privileges and standing.

The gender-defined role of warrior led men to acquire power over men and women of conquered tribes. Such war-induced conquest usually occurred over people already differentiated from the victors by race, ethnicity, or simple tribal difference. In its ultimate origin, "difference" as a distinguishing mark between the conquered and the conquerors was based on the first clearly observable difference, that between the sexes. Men had learned how to assert and exercise power over people slightly different from themselves in the primary exchange of women. In so doing, men acquired the knowledge necessary to elevate "difference" of whatever kind into a criterion for dominance.

From its inception in slavery, class dominance took different forms for enslaved men and women: men were primarily exploited as workers; women were always exploited as workers, as providers of sexual services, and as reproducers. The historical record of every slave society offers evidence for this generalization. The sexual exploitation of lower-class women by upper-class men can be shown in antiquity, under feudalism, in the bourgeois households of nineteenth- and twentieth-century Europe, in the complex sex/race relations between women of the colonized countries and their male colonizers—it is ubiquitous and pervasive. For women, sexual exploitation is the very mark of class exploitation.

At any given moment in history, each "class" is constituted of two distinct classes—men and women.

The class position of women became consolidated and actualized through their sexual relationships. It always was expressed within degrees of unfreedom on a spectrum ranging from the slave woman, whose sexual and reproductive capacity was commodified as she herself was; to the slave-concubine, whose sexual performance might elevate her own status or that of her children; then to the "free" wife, whose sexual and reproductive services to one man of the upper classes entitled her to property and legal rights. While each of these groups had vastly different obligations and privileges in regard to property, law, and economic resources, they shared the unfreedom of being sexually and reproductively controlled by men. We can best express the complexity of women's various levels of dependency and freedom by comparing each woman with her brother and considering how the sister's and brother's lives and opportunities would differ.

Class for men was and is based on their relationship to the means of production: those who owned the means of production could dominate those who did not. The owners of the means of production also acquired the commodity of female sexual services, both from women of their own class and from women of the subordinate classes. In Ancient Mesopotamia, in classical antiquity, and in slave societies, dominant males also acquired, as property, the product of the reproductive capacity of subordinate women—children, to be worked, traded, married off, or sold as slaves, as the case might be. For women, class is mediated through their sexual ties to a man. It is through the man that women have access to or are denied access to the means of production and to resources. It is through their sexual behavior that they gain access to class. "Respectable women" gain access to class through their fathers and husbands, but breaking the sexual rules can at once declass them. The gender definition of sexual "deviance" marks a woman as "not respectable," which in fact consigns her to the lowest class status possible. Women who withhold heterosexual services (such as single women, nuns, lesbians) are connected to the dominant man in their family of origin and through him gain access to resources. Or, alternatively, they are declassed. In some historical periods, convents and other enclaves for single women created some sheltered space, in which such women could function and retain their respectability. But the vast majority of single women are, by definition, marginal and dependent on the protection of male kin. This is true throughout historical time up to the middle of the twentieth century in the Western world and still is true in most of the underdeveloped countries today. The group of independent, self-supporting women which exists in every society is small and usually highly vulnerable to economic disaster.

Economic oppression and exploitation are based as much on the commodification of female sexuality and the appropriation by men of women's labor power and her reproductive power as on the direct economic acquisition of resources and persons.

The archaic state in the Ancient Near East emerged in the second millennium B.C. from the twin roots of men's sexual dominance over women and the exploitation by some men of others. From its inception, the archaic state was organized in such a way that the dependence of male family heads on the king or the state bureaucracy was compensated for by their dominance over their families. Male family heads allocated the resources of society to their families the way the state allocated the resources of society to them. The control of male family heads over their female kin and minor sons was as important to the existence of the state as was the control of the king over his soldiers. This is reflected in the various compilations of Mesopotamian laws, especially in the large number of laws dealing with the regulation of female sexuality.

From the second millennium B.C. forward control over the sexual behavior of citizens has been a major means of social control in every state society. Conversely, class hierarchy is constantly reconstituted in the family through sexual dominance. Regardless of the political or economic system, the kind of personality which can function in a hierarchical system is created and nurtured within the patriarchal family.

The patriarchal family has been amazingly resilient and varied in different times and places. Oriental patriarchy encompassed polygamy and female enclosure in harems. Patriarchy in classical antiquity and in its European development was based upon monogamy, but in all its forms a double sexual standard, which disadvantages women, was part of the system. In modern industrial states, such as in the United States, property relations within the family develop along more egalitarian lines than those in which the father holds absolute power, yet the economic and sexual power relations within the family do not necessarily change. In some cases, sexual relations are more egalitarian, while economic relations remain patriarchal; in other cases the pattern is reversed. In all cases, however, such changes within the family do not alter the basic male dominance in the public realm, in institutions and in government.

The family not merely mirrors the order in the state and educates its children to follow it, it also creates and constantly reinforces that order.

It should be noted that when we speak of relative improvements in the status of women in a given society, this frequently means only that we are seeing improvements in the degree in which their situation affords them opportunities to exert some leverage within the system of patriarchy. Where women have relatively more economic power, they are able to have somewhat more control over their lives than in societies where they have no economic power. Similarly, the existence of women's groups, associations, or economic networks serves to increase the ability of women to counteract the dictates of their particular patriarchal system. Some anthropologists and historians have called this relative improvement women's "freedom." Such a designation is illusory and unwarranted. Reforms and legal changes, while ameliorating the condition of women and an essential part of the process of emancipating them, will not basically change patriarchy. Such reforms need to be integrated within a vast cultural revolution in order to transform patriarchy and thus abolish it.

The system of patriarchy can function only with the cooperation of women. This cooperation is secured by a variety of means: gender indoctrination; educational deprivation; the denial to women of knowledge of their history; the dividing of women, one from the other, by defining "respectability" and "deviance" according to women's sexual activities; by restraints and outright coercion; by discrimination in access to economic resources and political power; and by awarding class privileges to conforming women.

For nearly four thousand years women have shaped their lives and acted under the umbrella of patriarchy, specifically a form of patriarchy best described as paternalistic dominance. The term describes the relationship of a dominant group, considered superior, to a subordinate group, considered inferior, in which the dominance is mitigated by mutual obligations and reciprocal rights. The dominated exchange submission for protection, unpaid labor for maintenance. In the patriarchal family, responsibilities and obligations are

not equally distributed among those to be protected: the male children's subordination to the father's dominance is temporary; it lasts
until they themselves become heads of households. The subordination of female children and of wives is lifelong. Daughters can escape
it only if they place themselves as wives under the domi-
nance/protection of another man. The basis of paternalism is an unwritten contract for exchange: economic support and protection given
by the male for subordination in all matters, sexual service, and unpaid domestic service given by the female. Yet the relationship frequently continues in fact and in law, even when the male partner
has defaulted on his obligation.

It was a rational choice for women, under conditions of public
powerlessness and economic dependency, to choose strong protectors
for themselves and their children. Women always shared the class
privileges of men of their class *as long as they were under "the
protection" of a man.* For women, other than those of the lower
classes, the "reciprocal agreement" went like this: in exchange for
your sexual, economic, political, and intellectual subordination to men
you may share the power of men of your class to exploit men and
women of the lower class. In class society it is difficult for people
who themselves have some power, however limited and circumscribed, to see themselves also as deprived and subordinated. Class
and racial privileges serve to undercut the ability of women to see
themselves as part of a coherent group, which, in fact, they are not,
since women uniquely of all oppressed groups occur in all strata of
the society. The formation of a group consciousness of women must
proceed along different lines. That is the reason why theoretical for-
mulations, which have been appropriate to other oppressed groups,
are so inadequate in explaining and conceptualizing the subordination of women.

Women have for millennia participated in the process of their
own subordination because they have been psychologically shaped
so as to internalize the idea of their own inferiority. The unaware-
ness of their own history of struggle and achievement has been one
of the major means of keeping women subordinate.

The connectedness of women to familial structures made any development of female solidarity and group cohesiveness extremely
problematic. Each individual woman was linked to her male kin in
her family of origin through ties which implied specific obligations.
Her indoctrination, from early childhood on, emphasized her obligation not only to make an economic contribution to the kin and

household but also to accept a marriage partner in line with family interests. Another way of saying this is to say that sexual control of women was linked to paternalistic protection and that, in the various stages of her life, she exchanged male protectors, but she never outgrew the childlike state of being subordinate and under protection.

Other oppressed classes and groups were impelled toward group consciousness by the very conditions of their subordinate status. The slave could clearly mark a line between the interests and bonds to his/her own family and the ties of subservience/protection linking him/her with the master. In fact, protection by slave parents of their own family against the master was one of the most important causes of slave resistance. "Free" women, on the other hand, learned early that their kin would cast them out, should they ever rebel against their dominance. In traditional and peasant societies there are many recorded instances of female family members tolerating and even participating in the chastisement, torture, even death of a girl who had transgressed against the family "honor." In Biblical times, the entire community gathered to stone the adulteress to death. Similar practices prevailed in Sicily, Greece, and Albania into the twentieth century. Bangladesh fathers and husbands cast out their daughters and wives who had been raped by invading soldiers, consigning them to prostitution. Thus, women were often forced to flee from one "protector" to the other, their "freedom" frequently defined only by their ability to manipulate between these protectors.

Most significant of all the impediments toward developing group consciousness for women was the absence of a tradition which would reaffirm the independence and autonomy of women at any period in the past. There had never been any woman or group of women who had lived without male protection, as far as most women knew. There had never been any group of persons like them who had done anything significant for themselves. Women had no history—so they were told; so they believed. Thus, ultimately, it was men's hegemony over the symbol system which most decisively disadvantaged women.

MALE HEGEMONY OVER the symbol system took two forms: educational deprivation of women and male monopoly on definition. The former happened inadvertently, more the consequence of class dominance and the accession of military elites to power. Throughout historical times, there have always been large loopholes for women of the elite classes, whose access to education was one of the major aspects of their class privilege. But male dominance over definition has been deliberate and pervasive, and the existence of individual highly educated and creative women has, for nearly four thousand years, left barely an imprint on it.

We have seen how men appropriated and then transformed the major symbols of female power: the power of the Mother-Goddess and the fertility-goddesses. We have seen how men constructed theologies based on the counterfactual metaphor of male procreativity and redefined female existence in a narrow and sexually dependent way. We have seen, finally, how the very metaphors for gender have expressed the male as norm and the female as deviant; the male as whole and powerful, the female as unfinished, mutilated, and lacking in autonomy. On the basis of such symbolic constructs, embedded in Greek philosophy, the Judeo-Christian theologies, and the legal tradition on which Western civilization is built, men have explained the world in their own terms and defined the important questions so as to make themselves the center of discourse.

By making the term "man" subsume "woman" and arrogate to itself the representation of all of humanity, men have built a conceptual error of vast proportion into all of their thought. By taking the half for the whole, they have not only missed the essence of whatever they are describing, but they have distorted it in such a fashion that they cannot see it correctly. As long as men believed the earth to be flat, they could not understand its reality, its function, and its actual relationship to other bodies in the universe. As long as men believe their experiences, their viewpoint, and their ideas represent all of human experience and all of human thought, they are not only unable to define correctly in the abstract, but they are unable to describe reality accurately.

The androcentric fallacy, which is built into all the mental constructs of Western civilization, cannot be rectified simply by "adding women." What it demands for rectification is a radical restructuring of thought and analysis which once and for all accepts the fact that humanity consists in equal parts of men and women and that the experiences, thoughts, and insights of both sexes must be represented in every generalization that is made about human beings.

TODAY, HISTORICAL DEVELOPMENT has for the first time created the necessary conditions by which large groups of women—finally, all women—can emancipate themselves from subordination. Since women's thought has been imprisoned in a confining and erroneous patriarchal framework, the transforming of the consciousness of women about ourselves and our thought is a precondition for change.

We have opened this book with a discussion of the significance of history for human consciousness and psychic well-being. History gives meaning to human life and connects each life to immortality, but history has yet another function. In preserving the collective past and reinterpreting it to the present, human beings define their potential and explore the limits of their possibilities. We learn from the past not only what people before us did and thought and intended, but we also learn how they failed and erred. From the days of the Babylonian king-lists forward, the record of the past has been written and interpreted by men and has primarily focused on the deeds, actions, and intentions of males. With the advent of writing, human knowledge moved forward by tremendous leaps and at a much faster rate than ever before. While, as we have seen, women had participated in maintaining the oral tradition and religious and cultic functions in the preliterate period and for almost a millennium thereafter, their educational disadvantaging and their symbolic dethroning had a profound impact on their future development. The gap between the experience of those who could or might (in the case of lower-class males) participate in the creating of the symbol system and those who merely acted but did not interpret became increasingly greater.

In her brilliant work *The Second Sex*, Simone de Beauvoir focused on the historical end product of this development. She described man as autonomous and transcendent, woman as immanent. But her analysis ignored history. Explaining "why women lack concrete means for organizing themselves into a unit" in defense of their own interests, she stated flatly: "They [women] have no past, no history, no religion of their own."[1] De Beauvoir is right in her observation that woman has not "transcended," if by transcendence one means the definition and interpretation of human knowledge. But she was wrong in thinking that therefore woman has had no history. Two decades of Women's History scholarship have disproven this fallacy by unearthing an unending list of sources and uncovering and interpreting the hidden history of women. This process of creating a history of women is still ongoing and will need to continue for a long time. We are only beginning to understand its implications.

The myth that women are marginal to the creation of history and civilization has profoundly affected the psychology of women and men. It has given men a skewed and essentially erroneous view of their place in human society and in the universe. For women, as shown in the case of Simone de Beauvoir, who surely is one of the best-educated women of her generation, history seemed for millennia to offer only negative lessons and no precedent for significant action, heroism, or liberating example. Most difficult of all was the seeming absence of a tradition which would reaffirm the independence and autonomy of women. It seemed that there had never been any woman or group of women who had lived without male protection. It is significant that all the important examples to the contrary were expressed in myth and fable: amazons, dragon-slayers, women with magic powers. But in real life, women had no history—so they were told and so they believed. And because they had no history they had no future alternatives.

In one sense, class struggle can be described as a struggle for the control of the symbol systems of a given society. The oppressed group, while it shares in and partakes of the leading symbols controlled by the dominant, also develops its own symbols. These become in time of revolutionary change, important forces in the creation of alternatives. Another way of saying this is that revolutionary ideas can be generated only when the oppressed have an alternative to the symbol and meaning system of those who dominate them. Thus, slaves living in an environment controlled by their masters and physically subject to the masters' total control, could maintain their humanity and at times set limits to the masters' power by holding on to their own "culture." Such a culture consisted of collective memories, carefully kept alive, of a prior state of freedom and of alternatives to the masters' ritual, symbols, and beliefs. What was decisive for the individual was the ability to identify him/herself with a state different from that of enslavement or subordination. Thus, all males, whether enslaved or economically or racially oppressed, could still identify with those like them—other males—who showed transcendent qualities in the symbol systems of the master. No matter how degraded, each male slave or peasant was like to the master in his relationship to God. This was not the case for women. Quite the contrary—in Western civilization up to the time of the Protestant Reformation no woman, no matter how elevated or privileged, could feel her humanity reinforced and confirmed by imagining persons like her—female persons—in positions of intellectual authority and in direct relationship to God.

Where there is no precedent, one cannot imagine alternatives to existing conditions. It is this feature of male hegemony which has been most damaging to women and has ensured their subordinate status for millennia. The denial to women of their history has reinforced their acceptance of the ideology of patriarchy and has undermined the individual woman's sense of self-worth. Men's version of history, legitimized as the "universal truth," has presented women as marginal to civilization and as the victim of historical process. To be so presented and to believe it is almost worse then being entirely forgotten. The picture is false, on both counts, as we now know, but women's progress through history has been marked by their struggle against this disabling distortion.

Moreover, for more than 2500 years women have been educationally disadvantaged and deprived of the conditions under which to develop abstract thought. Obviously thought is not based on sex; the capacity for thought is inherent in humanity; it can be fostered or discouraged, but it cannot ultimately be restrained. This is certainly true for thought generated by and concerned with daily living, the level of thought on which most men and women operate all their lives. But the generating of abstract thought and of new conceptual models—theory formation—is another matter. This activity depends on the individual thinker's education in the best of existing traditions and on the thinker's acceptance by a group of educated persons who, by criticism and interaction, provide "cultural prodding." It depends on having private time. Finally, it depends on the individual thinker being capable of absorbing such knowledge and then making a creative leap into a new ordering. Women, historically, have been unable to avail themselves of all of these necessary preconditions. Educational discrimination has disadvantaged them in access to knowledge; "cultural prodding," which is institutionalized in the upper reaches of the religious and academic establishments, has been unavailable to them. Universally, women of all classes had less leisure time then men, and, due to their child-rearing and family service function, what free time they had was generally not their own. The time of thinking men, their work and study time, has since the inception of Greek philosophy been respected as private. Like Aristotle's slaves, women "who with their bodies minister to the needs of life" have for more than 2500 years suffered the disadvantages of fragmented, constantly interrupted time. Finally, the kind of character development which makes for a mind capable of seeing new connections and fashioning a new order of abstractions has been exactly the opposite of that required of women, trained to accept their subordinate and service-oriented position in society.

Yet there have always existed a tiny minority of privileged women, usually from the ruling elite, who had some access to the same kind of education as did their brothers. From the ranks of such women have come the intellectuals, the thinkers, the writers, the artists. It is such women, throughout history, who have been able to give us a female perspective, an alternative to androcentric thought. They have done so at a tremendous cost and with great difficulty.

Those women, who have been admitted to the center of intellectual activity of their day and especially in the past hundred years, academically trained women, have first had to learn "how to think like a man." In the process, many of them have so internalized that learning that they have lost the ability to conceive of alternatives. The way to think abstractly is to define precisely, to create models in the mind and generalize from them. Such thought, men have taught us, must be based on the exclusion of feelings. Women, like the poor, the subordinate, the marginals, have close knowledge of ambiguity, of feelings mixed with thought, of value judgments coloring abstractions. Women have always experienced the reality of self and community, known it, and shared it with each other. Yet, living in a world in which they are devalued, their experience bears the stigma of insignificance. Thus they have learned to mistrust their own experience and devalue it. What wisdom can there be in menses? What source of knowledge in the milk-filled breast? What food for abstraction in the daily routine of feeding and cleaning? Patriarchal thought has relegated such gender-defined experiences to the realm of the "natural," the non-transcendent. Women's knowledge becomes mere "intuition," women's talk becomes "gossip." Women deal with the irredeemably particular: they experience reality daily, hourly, in their service function (taking care of food and dirt); in their constantly interruptable time; their splintered attention. Can one generalize while the particular tugs at one's sleeve? He who makes symbols and explains the world and she who takes care of his bodily and psychic needs and of his children—the gulf between them is enormous.

Historically, thinking women have had to choose between living a woman's life, with its joys, dailiness, and immediacy, and living a man's life in order to think. The choice for generations of educated women has been cruel and costly. Others have deliberately chosen an existence outside of the sex-gender system, by living alone or with other women. Some of the most significant advances in women's thought were given us by such women, whose personal struggle for an alternative mode of living infused their thinking. But such women, for most of historical time, have been forced to live on the margins of society; they were considered "deviant" and as such found it difficult to generalize from their experience to others and to win influence and approval. Why no female system-builders? Because one cannot think universals when one's self is excluded from the generic.

The social cost of having excluded women from the human enterprise of constructing abstract thought has never been reckoned. We can begin to understand the cost of it to thinking women when we accurately name what was done to us and describe, no matter how painful it may be, the ways in which we have participated in the enterprise. We have long known that rape has been a way of terrorizing us and keeping us in subjection. Now we also know that we have participated, although unwittingly, in the rape of our minds.

Creative women, writers and artists, have similarly struggled against a distorting reality. A literary canon, which defined itself by the Bible, the Greek classics, and Milton, would necessarily bury the significance and the meaning of women's literary work, as historians buried the activities of women. The effort to resurrect this meaning and to re-evaluate women's literary and artistic work is recent. Feminist literary criticism and poetics have introduced us to a reading of women's literature, which finds a hidden, deliberately "slant," yet powerful world-view. Through the reinterpretations of feminist literary critics we are uncovering among women writers of the eighteenth and nineteenth centuries a female language of metaphors, symbols, and myths. Their themes often are profoundly subversive of the male tradition. They feature criticism of the Biblical interpretation of Adam's fall; rejection of the goddess/witch dichotomy; projection or fear of the split self. The powerful aspect of woman's creativity becomes symbolized in heroines endowed with magical powers of goodness or in strong women who are banished to cellars or to live as "the madwoman in the attic." Others write in metaphors upgrading the confined domestic space, making it serve, symbolically as the world.[2]

For centuries, we find in the works of literary women a pathetic, almost desperate search for Women's History, long before historical studies as such exist. Nineteenth-century female writers avidly read the work of eighteenth-century female novelists; over and over again they read the "lives" of queens, abbesses, poets, learned women. Early "compilers" searched the Bible and all historical sources to which they had access to create weighty tomes with female heroines.

Women's literary voices, successfully marginalized and trivialized by the dominant male establishment, nevertheless survived. The voices of anonymous women were present as a steady undercurrent in the oral tradition, in folksong and nursery rhymes, tales of powerful witches and good fairies. In stitchery, embroidery, and quilting women's artistic creativity expressed an alternate vision. In letters, diaries, prayers, and song the symbol-making force of women's creativity pulsed and persisted.

All of this work will be the subject of our inquiry in the next volume. How did women manage to survive under male cultural hegemony; what was their influence and impact on the patriarchal symbol system; how and under what conditions did they come to create an alternate, feminist world-view? These are the questions we will examine in order to chart the rise of feminist consciousness as a historical phenomenon.

Women and men have entered historical process under different conditions and have passed through it at different rates of speed. If recording, defining, and interpreting the past marks man's entry into history, this occurred for males in the third millennium B.C. It occurred for women (and only some of them) with a few notable exceptions in the nineteenth century. Until then, all History was for women pre-History.

Women's lack of knowledge of our own history of struggle and achievement has been one of the major means of keeping us subordinate. But even those of us already defining ourselves as feminist thinkers and engaged in the process of critiquing traditional systems of ideas are still held back by unacknowledged restraints embedded deeply within our psyches. Emergent woman faces a challenge to her very definition of self. How can her daring thought—naming the hitherto unnamed, asking the questions defined by all authorities as "non-existent"—how can such thought coexist with her life as woman? In stepping out of the constructs of patriarchal thought, she faces, as Mary Daly put it, "existential nothingness." And more immediately, she fears the threat of loss of communication with, approval by, and love from the man (or the men) in her life. Withdrawal of love and the designation of thinking women as "deviant" have historically been the means of discouraging women's intellectual work. In the past, and now, many emergent women have turned to other women as love objects and reinforcers of self. Heterosexual feminists, too, have throughout the ages drawn strength from their friendships with women, from chosen celibacy, or from the separation of sex from love. No thinking man has ever been threatened in his self-definition and his love life as the price for his thinking. We should not underestimate the significance of that aspect of gender control as a force restraining women from full participation in the process of creating thought systems. Fortunately, for this generation of educated women, liberation has meant the breaking of this emotional hold and the conscious reinforcement of our selves through the support of other women.

Nor is this the end of our difficulties. In line with our historic gender-conditioning, women have aimed to please and have sought to avoid disapproval. This is poor preparation for making the leap into the unknown required of those who fashion new systems. Moreover, each emergent woman has been schooled in patriarchal thought. We each hold at least one great man in our heads. The lack of knowledge of the female past has deprived us of female heroines, a fact which is only recently being corrected through the development of Women's History. So, for a long time, thinking women have refurbished the idea systems created by men, engaging in a dialogue with the great male minds in their heads. Elizabeth Cady Stanton took on the Bible, the Church fathers, the founders of the American republic. Kate Millet argued with Freud, Norman Mailer, and the liberal literary establishment; Simone de Beauvoir with Sartre, Marx, and Camus; all Marxist-Feminists are in a dialogue with Marx and Engels and some also with Freud. In this dialogue woman intends merely to accept whatever she finds useful to her in the great man's system. But in these systems woman—as a concept, a collective entity, an individual—is marginal or subsumed.

In accepting such dialogue, thinking woman stays far longer than is useful within the boundaries or the question-setting defined by the "great men." And just as long as she does, the source of new insight is closed to her.

Revolutionary thought has always been based on upgrading the experience of the oppressed. The peasant had to learn to trust in the significance of his life experience before he could dare to challenge the feudal lords. The industrial worker had to become "class-conscious," the Black "race-conscious" before liberating thought could

develop into revolutionary theory. The oppressed have acted and
learned simultaneously—the process of becoming the newly conscious person or group is in itself liberating. So with women.

The shift in consciousness we must make occurs in two steps:
we must, at least for a time, be woman-centered. We must, as far
as possible, leave patriarchal thought behind.

To BE WOMAN-CENTERED MEANS: asking if women were central to
this argument, how would it be defined? It means ignoring all evidence of women's marginality, because, even where women appear
to be marginal, this is the result of patriarchal intervention; frequently also it is merely an appearance. The basic assumption should
be that it is inconceivable for anything ever to have taken place in
the world in which women were not involved, except if they were
prevented from participation through coercion and repression.

When using methods and concepts from traditional systems of
thought, it means using them from the vantage point of the centrality of women. Women cannot be put into the empty spaces of patriarchal thought and systems—in moving to the center, they transform the system.

To STEP OUTSIDE OF PATRIARCHAL THOUGHT MEANS: Being skeptical
toward every known system of thought; being critical of all assumptions, ordering values and definitions.

Testing one's statement by trusting our own, the female experience. Since such experience has usually been trivialized or ignored,
it means overcoming the deep-seated resistance within ourselves
toward accepting ourselves and our knowledge as valid. It means
getting rid of the great men in our heads and substituting for them
ourselves, our sisters, our anonymous foremothers.

Being critical toward our own thought, which is, after all, thought
trained in the patriarchal tradition. Finally, it means developing intellectual courage, the courage to stand alone, the courage to reach
farther than our grasp, the courage to risk failure. Perhaps the greatest challenge to thinking women is the challenge to move from the
desire for safety and approval to the most "unfeminine" quality of
all—that of intellectual arrogance, the supreme hubris which asserts
to itself the right to reorder the world. The hubris of the god-
makers, the hubris of the male system-builders.

The system of patriarchy is a historic construct; it has a beginning; it will have an end. Its time seems to have nearly run its

course—it no longer serves the needs of men or women and in its inextricable linkage to militarism, hierarchy, and racism it threatens the very existence of life on earth.

What will come after, what kind of structure will be the foundation for alternate forms of social organization we cannot yet know. We are living in an age of unprecedented transformation. We are in the process of becoming. But we already know that woman's mind, at last unfettered after so many millennia, will have its share in providing vision, ordering, solutions. Women at long last are demanding, as men did in the Renaissance, the right to explain, the right to define. Women, in thinking themselves out of patriarchy add transforming insights to the process of redefinition.

As long as both men and women regard the subordination of half the human race to the other as "natural," it is impossible to envision a society in which differences do not connote either dominance or subordination. The feminist critique of the patriarchal edifice of knowledge is laying the groundwork for a correct analysis of reality, one which at the very least can distinguish the whole from a part. Women's History, the essential tool in creating feminist consciousness in women, is providing the body of experience against which new theory can be tested and the ground on which women of vision can stand.

A feminist world-view will enable women and men to free their minds from patriarchal thought and practice and at last to build a world free of dominance and hierarchy, a world that is truly human.

APPENDIX

Definitions

IN UNDERTAKING THIS WORK I AM part of a group effort by feminist thinkers in a variety of disciplines to rectify the neglect of women as subject of discourse and their exclusion as participants in the formation of systems of ideas. The exclusion of women from symbol-making and definition has appeared to men and women to stand outside of history, and therefore it has acquired a prescriptive force far greater than that used against any other subordinate group. The way this has come about and the way it has affected history have been discussed in more detail in this volume. What we already know is that the ahistoricity of this practice has prevented women from "coming into consciousness" as women, and it thus has been one of the major props of the system of patriarchal dominance. It is only in this century that for a small group of women—still only a tiny minority considered on a global scale—the preconditions of educational access and equity have at last become available, so that women themselves could begin to "see" and hence define their predicament.

Those of us engaged in this enterprise of redefinition face the threefold challenge of correctly defining, of deconstructing existing theory, and of constructing a new paradigm. We not only face the difficulty of not having an appropriate language, but also unique problems as women in transcending our traditional training and our deeply rooted and historically conditioned psychology.

Whatever the field of knowledge in which we work, we have to face the inadequacy of language and concepts to the task at hand. All philosophies and systems of thought in which we are trained

231

have either ignored or marginalized women. Thus, the only way they can conceptualize "women-as-group" is to compare them with various other groups, usually oppressed groups, and to describe women in terms appropriate to such groups. But the comparison is not apt; the terms do not fit. The tools we have at our disposal are inadequate.

The mode in which abstract thought is cast and the language in which it is expressed are so defined as to perpetuate women's marginality. We women have had to express ourselves through partriarchal thought as reflected in the very language we have had to use. It is a language in which we are subsumed under the male pronoun and in which the generic terms for "human" is "male." Women have had to use "dirty words" or "hidden words" to describe our own body experiences. The vilest insults in every language refer to parts of the female body or to female sexuality.

More, the difficulties with vocabulary and with definition are pervasive, and feminist thinkers have valiantly struggled with them. It is exceedingly difficult, possibly even futile, to attempt to change language and usage in the short range. Words are socially created cultural constructs; they cannot come to life unless they represent concepts accepted by large numbers of people. Words created for the use of a small sect of the initiated often obscure more than they illuminate—the language becomes a technical jargon understandable only to those in the inner circle of the enlightened. For those of us wishing to deconstruct the androcentric assumptions inherent in the language we use and to express adequately concepts appropriate to half the human race, the problem of redefining and renaming marks the scope and the limits of our enterprise. In order to continue to be comprehended and to be expressive of women's experience our efforts at renaming must be conservative or our words will be incomprehensible to those to whom and of whom we speak. I have therefore tried, wherever possible to use common and long accepted words, but to define their usage clearly. On the other hand, the need to redefine and rethink inevitably must affect our language. Perhaps as a writer and poet, I am a conservative in regard to language and thus shy away from newly coined words, although I recognize their power to shock thought out of worn and well-used ruts, and thus to teach.

The confusion of differing interpretations of certain concepts basic to feminist thought reflects, with considerable accuracy, the state of feminist thought. The rebellion against women's intellectual marginality is occurring with the force of spring floods, breaking out of rock and ground in different places and in a great variety of courses. It is too soon to expect unanimity or even a common vocabulary and, I suspect, we may never attain it, any more than all men have learned to speak in a language comprehensible to one another. Still, ever so often a concept, a definition, a particular term attains acceptance and wider currency. Such new language becomes a token, an indicator of changed consciousness and new thinking. So we must use the language of the patriarchs, even as we think our way out of patriarchy. But that language is also our language, women's language, as the civilization, although patriarchal, is also ours. We must reclaim it, transform it, recreate it and in the doing transform thought and practice so as to create a new, a common, and gender-free language.

For the time being, paying attention to the words we use and how we use them is a way of taking our thought seriously. Which means, it is an essential beginning.

For my purposes three concepts have been particularly difficult to define and properly name: (1) that concept describing the historical situation of women; (2) that describing various forms of women's autonomous strivings; and (3) that describing the goal of women's strivings.

What word describes women's historical position in society?

Oppression of women is the term commonly used by women writers and thinkers and by feminists. The term "oppression," meaning forceful subordination, has been used to describe the subject condition of individuals and of groups, as in "class oppression" or "racial oppression." The term inadequately describes paternalistic dominance, which, while it has oppressive aspects, also involves a set of mutual obligations and is frequently not perceived as oppressive. The term "oppression of women" inevitably conjures up comparison with the other oppressed groups and leads one to think in terms of comparing the various degrees of oppression as though one were dealing with similar groups. Are Blacks, female and male, more oppressed than white women? Is the oppression of colonials in any way comparable to that experienced by middle-class suburban housewives? Such questions are misleading and irrelevant. The differences in the status of women and that of members of oppressed minority groups, or even majority groups such as "the colonized," are so essential that it is inappropriate to use the same term to describe all of them. The dominance of one half of humankind over the other is qualitatively different from any other form of dominance, and our terminology should make that clear.

The word "oppression" implies victimization; indeed, those who apply it to women frequently conceptualize women-as-a-group primarily as victims. This way of thinking of women is misleading and ahistorical. While all women have been victimized in certain aspects of their lives and some, at certain times, more than others, women are structured into society in such a way that they are both subjects and agents. As we discussed earlier, the "dialectic of women's history," the complex pull of contradictory forces upon women, makes them simultaneously marginal and central to historical events. Trying to describe their condition by the use of a term which obscures this complexity is counter-productive.

The word "oppression" focuses on a wrong; it is subjective in that it represents the consciousness of the subject group that they have been wronged. The word implies a power struggle, defeat resulting in the dominance of one group over the other. It may be that the historical experience of women includes "oppression" of this kind, but it encompasses considerably more. Women, more than any other group, have collaborated in their own subordination through their acceptance of the sex-gender system. They have internalized the values that subordinate them to such an extent that they voluntarily pass them on to their children. Some women have been "oppressed" in one aspect of their lives by fathers or husbands, while they themselves have held power over other women and men. Such complexities become invisible when the term "oppression" is used to describe the condition of women as a group.

The use of the phrase **subordination of women** instead of the word "oppression" has distinct advantages. Subordination does not have the connotation of evil intent on the part of the dominant; it allows for the possibility of collusion between him and the subordinate. It includes the possibility of voluntary acceptance of subordinate status in exchange for protection and privilege, a condition which characterizes so much of the historical experience of women. I will use the term "paternalistic dominance" for this relation. "Subordination" encompasses other relations in addition to "paternalistic dominance" and has the additional advantage over "oppression" of being neutral as to the causes of subordination. The complex sex/gender relations of men and women over five millennia cannot be ascribed to a simple single cause—the greed for power of men. It is therefore better to use fairly value-free terms in order to enable us to describe the various and varied sex/gender relations, which were constructed by both men and women in different times and different places.

The use of the word **deprivation** has the advantage over both of the other terms of being objective, but it has the disadvantage of masking and hiding the existence of power relations. Deprivation is the observed absence of prerogatives and privileges. It focuses attention on that which is denied, not on those who do the denying. Deprivation can be caused by a single individual, groups of people, institutions, natural conditions and disasters, ill health, and many other causes.

When one conceptualizes women as being central, not marginal, to the history of humankind, it becomes obvious that all three words describe women at some period of history and in some places or groups. It is also obvious that each word is appropriate to specific aspects of women's status at a given time or place. Thus, men and women on the American western frontier were **deprived** of adequate health care and educational opportunities due to frontier conditions. American women in the urban Northeast before the Civil War can be described as being *oppressed,* in that they were denied legal rights such as the ballot, and sexual freedom, such as the right to control their reproduction. Discriminatory practices in employment and in education constitute *oppression,* since such restrictions, at the time, were enforced in order to benefit specific groups of men, such as their employers and male professionals. Women were *deprived* economically, by being channeled into sex-segregated employment. Married women can be said to have been *subordinate* to men in their legal rights and their property rights. Women in general were subordinate to men in voluntary associations and in institutions, such as in the churches. On the other hand, middle-class women of that period were increasingly dominant within the family, due to the separation of male and female "spheres." The key to understanding the complexity of their situation is that increased domestic autonomy took place within a societal structure which restricted and deprived women in various ways.

The effort to affix one descriptive label to all the different aspects of women's situation has confused the interpretation of Women's

History. It is impossible, and no one has attempted, to describe the status of "men" during any given period of history in one appropriate word. It is no more possible to do so for women. The status of women as opposed to that of men at any given time and place must be closely differentiated as to its specific aspects and its relation to different social structures. Therefore, a variety of appropriate terms must be used in order to highlight these differences, which is the practice I have followed throughout.

What is the appropriate word to describe the strivings or the discontent of women?

Feminism is the term commonly and quite indiscriminately used. Some of the currently used definitions are: (a) a doctrine advocating social and political rights for women equal to those of men; (b) an organized movement for the attainment of these rights; (c) the assertion of the claims of women as a group and the body of theory women have created; (d) belief in the necessity of large-scale social change in order to increase the power of women. Most persons using the term incorporate all the definitions from (a) to (c), but the necessity for basic social change in the system to which women demand equal access is not necessarily accepted by feminists.

I have long argued the need for a more disciplined definition of the term. I then called attention to the useful distinction between "woman's rights" and the concept "woman's emancipation."[1]

Woman's rights movement means a movement concerned with winning for women equality with men in all aspects of society and giving them access to all rights and opportunities enjoyed by men in the institutions of that society. Thus, the women's rights movement is akin to the civil rights movement in wanting equal participation for women in the status quo, essentially a reformist goal. The nineteenth-century woman's rights and suffrage movement is an example of this kind.

The term **Woman's Emancipation** means: freedom from oppressive restrictions imposed by sex; self-determination; and autonomy.

Freedom from oppressive restrictions imposed by sex means free-

---

[1] I follow the nineteenth-century spelling for Woman's Rights movement and the twentieth-century spelling for the current women's emancipation movement.

dom from biological and societal restrictions. Self-determination means being free to decide one's own destinay; being free to define one's social role; having the freedom to make decisions concerning one's body. Autonomy means earning one's own status, not being born into it or marrying it; it means financial independence; freedom to choose one's lifestyle and sexual preference—all of which implies a radical transformation of existing institutions, values, and theories.

Feminism can include both positions, and twentieth-century feminism generally has done so, but I believe for greater accuracy we would do well to distinguish between *woman's rights feminism* and *women's emancipation feminism*. The striving for women's emancipation predates the woman's rights movement. It is not always a movement, for it can be a level of consciousness, a stance, an attitude, as well as the basis for organized effort. Women's emancipation has, of course, nowhere been reached as yet, while women in various places have won many rights. By using the two definitions instead of the one, we can in historical studies distinguish more sharply the level of consciousness and the goals of the women we are studying.

Emancipation has a specific historical derivation from Roman civil law—*e + manus + capere*—to come out from under the hand of, to free from paternalistic dominance—which fits the situation of women with far greater precision than does "liberation." I therefere prefer the word "emancipation."

I try to follow the practice of using *woman's rights* for *women's emancipation* whenever appropriate and confine my use of the word *feminism* to those occasions when both levels of consciousness and activity are evident.

What word describes the goal of women's strivings?

Woman's liberation is the commonly used term. My objections to the use of this term are the same as to the use of "oppresssion." The term conjures up political liberation movements of other groups, such as colonials and racial minorities. It implies victimization and a subjective consciousness in a group striving to correct a wrong. While the latter concept certainly needs to be included in any adequate definition, the former should be avoided.

It is obvious from this discussion that the terms we use depend largely on how we define women-as-a group. What are women, over and above being half of every human population?

Women are a **Sex.** Women are a separate group due to their biological distinctiveness. The merit of using the term is that it clearly defines women, not as a subgroup or a minority group, but as half of the whole. Men are the only other sex. Obviously, we are here not referring to sexual activity, but to a biological given. Persons belonging to either sex are capable and can be grouped according to a broader variety of sexual preferences and activities.

Gender is the cultural definition of behavior defined as appropriate to the sexes in a given society at a given time. Gender is a set of cultural roles. It is a costume, a mask, a straitjacket in which men and women dance their unequal dance. Unfortunately, the term is used both in academic discourse and in the media as interchangeable with "sex." In fact, its widespread public use probably is due to it sounding a bit more "refined" than the plain word "sex" with its "nasty" connotations. Such usage is unfortunate, because it hides and mystifies the difference between the biological given—sex—and the culturally created—gender. Feminists above all others should want to point up that difference and should therefore be careful to use the appropriate words.

Sex-gender system is a very useful term, introduced by the anthropologist Gayle Rubin, which has found wide currency among feminists. It refers to the institutionalized system which allots resources, property, and privileges to persons according to culturally defined gender roles. Thus, it is sex which determines that women should be child-bearers, it is the sex-gender system which assures that they should be child-rearers.

What word describes the system under which women have lived since the dawn of civilization and are living now?

The problem with the word **patriarchy,** which most feminists use, is that it has a narrow, traditional meaning—not necessarily the one feminists give it. In its narrow meaning, patriarchy refers to the system, historically derived from Greek and Roman law, in which the male head of the household had absolute legal and economic power over his dependent female and male family members. People using the term that way often imply a limited historicity for it: patriarchy began in classical antiquity and ended in the nineteenth century with the granting of civil rights to women and married women in particular.

This usage is troublesome because it distorts historical reality. The patriarchal dominance of male family heads over their kin is much older than classical antiquity; it begins in the third millennium B.C. and is well established at the time of the writing of the Hebrew Bible. Further, it can be argued that in the nineteenth century male dominance in the family simply takes new forms and is not ended. Thus, the narrow definition of the term "patriarchy" tends to foreclose accurate definition and analysis of its continued presence in today's world.

Patriarchy in its wider definition means the manifestation and institutionalization of male dominance over women and children in the family and the extension of male dominance over women in society in general. It implies that men hold power in all the important institutions of society and that women are deprived of access to such power. It does *not* imply that women are either totally powerless or totally deprived of rights, influence, and resources. One of the most challenging tasks of Women's History is to trace with precision the various forms and modes in which patriarchy appears historically, the shifts and changes in its structure and function, and the adaptations it makes to female pressure and demands.

If patriarchy describes the institutionalized system of male dominance, paternalism describes a particular mode, a subset of patriarchal relations.

Paternalism, or more accurately *Paternalistic Dominance,* describes the relationship of a dominant group, considered superior, to a subordinate group, considered inferior, in which the dominance is mitigated by mutual obligations and reciprocal rights. The dominated exchange submission for protection, unpaid labor for maintenance. In its historical origins, the concept comes from family relations as they developed under patriarchy, in which the father held absolute power over all the members of his household. In exchange, he owed them the obligation of economic support and protection. The same relationship occurs in some systems of slavery; it can occur in economic relations, such as the *padrone* system of southern Italy or the system used in some contemporary Japanese industries. As applied to familial relations, it should be noted that responsibilities and obligations are not equally distributed among those to be protected: the male children's subordination to the father's dominance is temporary; it lasts until they themselves become heads of households. The subordination of female children and of wives is lifelong. Daughters can escape it only if they place themselves as wives under the dominance/protection of another man. The basis of "paternalism" is an unwritten contract for exchange: economic support and protection given by the male for subordination in all matters, sexual service and unpaid domestic service given by the female.

Sexism defines the ideology of male supremacy, of male superiority and of beliefs that support and sustain it. Sexism and patriarchy mutually reinforce one another. Clearly, sexism can exist in societies where institutionalized patriarchy has been abolished. An example would be socialist countries with constitutions guaranteeing women absolute equality in public life but in which social and familial relations are nevertheless sexist. The question whether patriarchy can exist, even when private property is abolished, is one currently debated by and dividing Marxists and feminists. I tend to think that wherever the patriarchal family exists, there is patriarchy constantly being reborn, even when in other parts of society patriarchal relations have been abolished. However one may think about this, the fact is that, as long as sexism as an ideology exists, patriarchal relations can easily be re-established, even when legal changes have occurred to outlaw them. We know that civil rights legislation has been ineffective, as long as racist beliefs have flourished. So with sexism.

Sexism stands in the same relation to paternalism as racism does to slavery. Both ideologies enabled the dominant to convince themselves that they were extending paternalistic benevolence to creatures inferior and weaker than themselves. But here the parallel ends, for slaves were driven to group solidarity by racism, while women were separated from one another by sexism.

The slave saw, in his world, other kinds of hierarchy and inequality: that of white men inferior in rank and class to his master; that of white women inferior to white men. The slave experienced his oppression as one kind within a system of hierarchy. Slaves could see clearly that their condition was due to the exploitation of their race. Thus race, the factor on which oppression was based, became also the force unifying the oppressed.

For the maintenance of paternalism (and slavery) it is essential to convince subordinates that their protector is the only authority capable of fulfilling their needs. It is therefore in the interest of the master to keep the slave in ignorance of his past and of future alternatives. But slaves kept alive an oral tradition—a body of myth, folklore, and history—which spoke of a time prior to their enslavement and defined a previous time of freedom. This offered an alternative to their present state. Slaves knew that their people had not always been slaves and that others like them were free. This knowledge of the past, their separate cultural tradition, the power of their religion and their group solidarity enabled slaves to resist oppression and secure the reciprocity of rights implicit in their status.

Eugene Genovese, in his superb study of slave culture, shows how paternalism, while it softened the harshest features of the system, also tended to weaken the individual's ability to see the system in political terms. He says: "It was not that the slaves did not act like men. Rather, it was that they could not grasp their collective strength as people and act like political men."[2] That they could not become conscious of their collective strength was due to paternalism.

This description has great significance for an analysis of the position of women, since their subordination has been primarily expressed in the form of paternalistic dominance within the structure of the family. This structural condition made any development of female solidarity and group cohesiveness extremely difficult. In general we can observe that women deprived of group support and of an accurate knowledge of the past history of women experienced the full and devastating impact of cultural modeling through sexist ideology, as expressed in religion, law, and myth.

On the other hand it was easier for women to maintain a sense of self-worth, because they so obviously shared the world and its tasks with men. Certainly this was so in pre-industrial society, when the complementarity of men and women's economic efforts was clearly visible. It was more difficult to maintain a sense of self-worth in

[2] Eugene Genovese, *Roll, Jordan, Roll: The World the Slaves Made* (New York, 1974), p. 149. Note how in this quote Genovese subsumes women under the term "men" and thus loses them. Male slaves could not become political men, because they were slaves; female slaves could not become political persons because they were women and slaves. Genovese, who is conscious of women's role in history and supportive of Women's History, is here entrapped by the sexism structured into the language.

industrial society, because of the complexity of the technological world in which men operated and because of the commodity nature of all market transactions, from which women as housewives were largely excluded. It is no accident that, worldwide, feminist movements begin only after industrialization.

The ground out of which such movements develop is woman's culture, yet another concept that deserves definition.

Woman's Culture is the ground upon which women stand in their resistance to patriarchal domination and their assertion of their own creativity in shaping society. The term implies an assertion of equality and an awareness of sisterhood. Woman's culture frequently takes the form of redefinition of the goals and strategies of mass movements in terms women deem appropriate. In the nineteenth century United States woman's culture led to a self-conscious definition of the moral superiority of women as a rationale for their enfranchisement.

The term has also been used in its anthropological sense to encompass the familial and friendship networks of women, their affective ties, their rituals. It is important to understand that woman's culture is never a subculture. It would hardly be appropriate to define the culture of half of humanity as a subculture. Women live their social existence within the general culture. Whenever they are confined by patriarchal restraint or segregation into separateness (which always has subordination as its purpose), they transform this restraint into complementarity and redefine it. Thus, women live a duality—as members of the general culture and as partakers of woman's culture.

When historical conditions are right and women have both the social space and the social experience in which to ground their new understanding, ***feminist consciousness*** develops. Historically, this takes place in distinct stages: (1) the awareness of a wrong; (2) the development of a sense of sisterhood; (3) the autonomous definition by women of their goals and strategies for changing their condition; and (4) the development of an alternate vision of the future.

The recognition of a wrong becomes political when women realize that it is shared with other women. In order to remedy this collective wrong, women organize in political, economic, and social life. The movements they organize inevitably run into resistance, which forces the women to draw on their own resources and strength. In the process, they develop a sense of sisterhood. This process also leads to new forms of woman's culture, forced upon women by the resistance they encounter, such as sex-segregated or separatist institutions or modes of living. Based on such experiences, women begin to define their own demands and to develop theory. At a certain level, women make the shift from androcentricity, in which they have been schooled, to "woman-centeredness." In the field of scholarship, Women's Studies seeks to find a new framework of interpretation from within women's historical culture, leading to their emancipation.

It is only through the discovery and acknowledgment of their roots, their past, their history, that women, like other groups, become enabled to project an alternate future. The new vision of women demands that women be placed at the center, not only of events, where we have always been, but of the thinking work of the world. Women are demanding, as men did during the Renaissance, the right to define, the right to decide.

Notes

INTRODUCTION

1. Joan Kelly, "The Doubled Vision of Feminist Theory: A Postscript to the "Women and Power" Conference, *Feminist Studies*, vol. 5, no. 1 (Spring 1979), 221-22.

CHAPTER ONE. ORIGINS

1. See Chapters Ten and Eleven for a detailed discussion of this position.

2. See, for example, George P. Murdock, *Our Primitive Contemporaries* (New York, 1934); R. B. Lee and Irven De Vore (eds.), *Man, the Hunter* (Chicago, 1968).

Margaret Mead, *Male and Female* (New York, 1949), while breaking new ground by showing the existence of wide varieties in societal attitudes toward sex roles, accepts the universality of sexual asymmetry.

3. See Lionel Tiger, *Men in Groups* (New York, 1970), chap. 3; Robert Ardrey, *The Territorial Imperative: A Personal Inquiry into the Animal Origins of Property and Nations* (New York, 1966); Alison Jolly, *The Evolution of Primate Behavior* (New York, 1972); Marshall Sahlins, "The Origins of Society," *Scientific American*, vol. 203, no. 48 (Sept. 1960), 76–87.

For a male-centered explanation, which values men negatively and blames their aggressive impulses for the development of warfare and the subordination of women, see Marvin Harris, "Why Men Dominate Women," *Columbia* (Summer 1978), 9–13, 39.

4. Simone de Beauvoir, *The Second Sex* (New York, 1953; 1974 reprint ed.), pp. xxxiii–xxxiv.

5. Peter Farb, *Humankind* (Boston, 1978), chap. 5; Sally Slocum, "Woman the Gatherer: Male Bias in Anthropology," in Rayna R. Reiter, *Toward an Anthropology of Women* (New York, 1975), pp. 36–50. For an interesting viewpoint revising Slocum, see

245

Michelle Z. Rosaldo, "The Use and Abuse of Anthropology: Relections on Feminism and Cross-Cultural Understanding," *SIGNS*, vol. 5, no. 3 (Spring 1980), 412–13, 213.

6. Michelle Zimbalist Rosaldo and Louise Lamphere, "Introduction," in M. Z. Rosaldo and L. Lamphere, *Woman, Culture and Society* (Stanford, 1974), p. 3. For an extended discussion, see Rosaldo, "A Theoretical Overview," *ibid.*, pp. 16–42; L. Lamphere, "Strategies, Cooperation, and Conflict Among Women in Domestic Groups," *ibid.*, pp. 97–112. See also Slocum in Reiter, *Anthropology of Women*, pp. 36–50, and articles by Patricia Draper and Judith K. Brown, also in Reiter.

For an example of complementarity of the sexes, see Irene Silverblatt, "Andean Women in the Inca Empire," *Feminist Studies*, vol. 4, no. 3 (Oct. 1978), 37–61.

A thorough review of the literature on this question and an interesting interpretation of it can be found in Peggy Reeves Sanday, *Female Power and Male Dominance: On the Origins of Sexual Inequality* (Cambridge, Eng., 1981).

7. M. Kay Martin and Barbara Voorhies, *Female of the Species* (New York, 1975), esp. chap. 7; Nancy Tanner and Adrienne Zihlman, "Women in Evolution, Part I: Innovation and Selection in Human Origins," *SIGNS*, vol. 1, no. 3 (Spring 1976), 585–608.

8. Elise Boulding, "Public Nurturance and the Man on Horseback," in Meg Murray (ed.), *Face to Face: Fathers, Mothers, Masters, Monsters—Essays for a Non-sexist Future* (Westport, Conn., 1983), pp. 273–91.

9. William Alcott, *The Young Woman's Book of Health* (Boston, 1850) and Edward H. Clarke, *Sex in Education or a Fair Chance for Girls* (Boston, 1878), are typical of nineteenth-century attitudes.

A recent discussion of nineteenth-century views of women's health can be found in Mary S. Hartman and Lois Banner (eds.), *Clio's Consciousness Raised: New Perspectives on the History of Women* (New York, 1974). See articles by Ann Douglas Wood, Carroll Smith-Rosenberg, and Regina Morantz.

10. The unconscious patriarchal bias built into so-called scientific psychological experiments was first exposed by Naomi Weisstein, "Kinder, Küche, Kirche as Scientific Law: Psychology Constructs the Female," in Robin Morgan (ed.), *Sisterhood Is Powerful: An Anthology of Writings from the Women's Liberation Movement* (New York, 1970), pp. 205–20.

11. For the traditional Freudian view see: Sigmund Freud, "Female Sexuality" (1931), in *The Standard Edition of the Complete Psychological Works of Sigmund Freud*, vol. 21 (London, 1964); Ernest Jones, "Early Development of Female Sexuality," *International Journal of Psycho-Analysis*, vol. 8 (1927), 459–72; Sigmund Freud, "Some Physical Consequences of the Anatomical Distinction Between the Sexes" (1925), in *Standard Edition*, vol. 19 (1961); Erik Erikson, *Childhood and Society* (New York, 1950); Helene Deutsch, *Psychology of Women*, vol. 1 (New York, 1944). See also the discussion of the revisionist Freudian position in Jean Baker Miller (ed.), *Psychoanalysis and Women* (Harmondsworth, Eng., 1973).

12. See, for example, Ferdinand Lundberg and Marynia Farnham, M.D., *Modern Women: The Lost Sex* (New York, 1947).

13. Edward O. Wilson, *Sociobiology: The New Synthesis* (Cambridge, Mass., 1975), especially the last chapter, "Man: From Sociobiology to Sociology."

14. Ruth Bleier, *Science and Gender: A Critique of Biology and Its Theories on Women* (New York, 1984), chap. 2. See also Marian Lowe, "Sociobiology and Sex Differences," *SIGNS*, vol. 4, no. 1 (Autumn 1978), 118–25.

A special issue of SIGNS, "Development and the Sexual Division of Labor," vol. 7, no. 2 (Winter 1981), addresses the question from a feminist point of view, both empirically and theoretically. See especially Maria Patricia Fernandez Kelly, "Development and the Sexual Division of Labor: An Introduction," pp. 268–78.

15. For an illuminating summary of the impact of demographic changes on women, see Robert Wells, "Women's Lives Transformed: Demographic and Family Patterns in America, 1600-1970," in Carol Ruth Berkin and Mary Beth Norton (eds.), *Women of America, A History* (Boston, 1979), pp. 16–36.

16, These critiques are best summarized in a series of review essays in *SIGNS*. Cf.: Mary Brown Parlee, "Psychology," vol. 1, no. 1 (Autumn 1975), 119–38; Carol Stack *et al.*, "Anthropology," *ibid.*, 147–60; Reesa M. Vaughter, "Psychology," vol. 2, no. 1 (Autumn 1976), 120–46; Louise Lamphere, "Anthropology," vol. 2, no. 3 (Spring 1977), 612–27.

17. Gayle Rubin, "The Traffic in Women: Notes on the 'Political Economy' of Sex," in Reiter, *Anthropology of Women*, p. 159.

18. Frederick Engels, *The Origin of the Family, Private Property and the State*, ed. Eleanor Leacock (New York, 1972).

19. J. J. Bachofen, *Myth, Religion and Mother Right*, trans. Ralph Manheim (Princeton, 1967); and Lewis Henry Morgan, *Ancient Society*, ed. Eleanor Leacock (New York, 1963; reprint of 1877 edition).

20. Engels, *Origin*, p. 218.

21. For a survey of the division of labor by sex in 224 societies, see Murdock, *Our Primitive Contemporaries* (New York,1934), and George P. Murdock, "Comparative Data on the Division of Labor by Sex," in *Social Forces*, vol. 15, no. 4 (May 1937), 551–53. For a thorough evaluation and feminist critique of these data see Karen Sacks, *Sisters and Wives: The Past and Future of Sexual Equality* (Westport, Conn., 1979), chaps. 2 and 3.

22. Engels, *Origin*, pp. 220–21.

23. *Ibid.*, p. 137, first quote; pp. 120–21, second quote.

24. An opposing biological-deterministic theory is offered by Mary Jane Sherfey, M.D., *The Nature and Evolution of Female Sexuality* (New York, 1972). Sherfey argues that it was women's unlimited orgasmic capacity and their perpetual estrus which posed a problem for emergent community life in the Neolithic period. Women's biology fostered conflict among males and inhibited group cooperation, which caused men to institute incest taboos and male sexual dominance in order to control the socially destructive potential of female sexuality.

25. Engels, *Origin*, p. 129.

26. Claude Lévi-Strauss, *The Elementary Structures of Kinship* (Boston, 1969), p. 481.

27. Gayle Rubin, "Traffic in Women," in Reiter, *Anthropology of Women*, p. 177.

28. For a feminist critique of Lévi-Strauss's theory see Sacks, *Sisters*, pp. 55–61.

29. Sherry Ortner, "Is Female to Male as Nature Is to Culture?" in Rosaldo and Lamphere, *Woman, Culture and Society*, pp. 67–88.

30. *Ibid.*, pp. 73–74.

31. The debate is well defined in two essay collections: Sherry B. Ortner and Harriet Whitehead (eds.), *Sexual Meanings: The Cultural Construction of Gender and Sexuality* (New York, 1981), and Carol MacCormack and Marilyn Strathern (eds.), *Nature, Culture and Gender* (Cambridge, Eng., 1980).

32. Johann Jacob Bachofen, *Das Mutterrecht: Eine Untersuchung über die Gynai-kokratie der alten Welt nach ihrer religiösen und rechtlichen Natur* (Stuttgart, 1861). Cited hereafter as *Mother Right*.

33. Cf. Charlotte Perkins Gilman, *Women and Economics* (New York, 1966 "Reprint of 1898 edition"); Helen Diner, *Mothers and Amazons: The First Feminine History of Culture* (New York, 1965); Elizabeth Gould Davis, *The First Sex* (New York, 1971); Evelyn Reed, *Women's Evolution* (New York, 1975).

34. Robert Briffault, *The Mothers: A Study of the Origins of Sentiments and Institutions,* 3 vols. (New York, 1927); see also Joseph Campbell "Introduction" to Bachofen, *Mother Right*, pp. xxv–vii.

35. Bachofen, *Mother Right*, p. 79.

36. Cf. ECS speeches in Ellen DuBois (ed.), *Elizabeth Cady Stanton and Susan B. Anthony: Correspondence, Writings, Speeches* (New York, 1981).

37. For this shift in attitudes toward women, see Mary Beth Norton, *Liberty's Daughters: The Revolutionary Experience of American Women, 1750–1800* (Boston, 1980), chaps. 8, 9, and the conclusion; and Linda Kerber, *Women of the Republic: Intellect and Ideology in Revolutionary America* (Chapel Hill, 1980), chap. 9.

38. The idea of woman's special aptitude for reform and community service appears throughout Jane Addams's work. It informed the thought of Mary Beard, who substantiated it with historical evidence in *Women's Work in Municipalities* (New York, 1915). For examples of the modern maternalist position see Adrienne Rich, *Of Woman Born: Motherhood as Experience and Institution* (New York: 1976); and Dorothy Dinnerstein, *The Mermaid and the Minotaur* (New York, 1977). Mary O'Brien, *The Politics of Reproduction* (Boston, 1981), constructs an explanatory theory in which reproductive labor is paralleled to economic labor within a Marxist framework.

The position underlies the ideology of the woman's peace movement and is expressed by feminist-ecologists like Susan Griffin, *Woman and Nature: The Roaring Inside Her* (New York, 1978); and Robin Morgan, *The Anatomy of Freedom: Feminism, Physics, and Global Politics* (New York, 1982).

A different maternalist argument is offered by Alice Rossi in "A Biosocial Perspective on Parenting," *Daedalus,* vol. 106, no. 2 (Spring 1977), 1–31. Rossi accepts sociobiological arguments and uses them for feminist ends. She calls for a restructuring of social institutions to enable women to perform their mothering and nurturant functions without giving up their striving for equality and opportunity. Rossi has accepted uncritically the ahistoricity and unscientific claims of sociobiology and differs from most feminists in not advocating that men share equally in child-rearing. But her position deserves attention as a variety of maternalist thought and because of her role as a pioneer of feminist criticism in the field of sociology.

39. Martin and Voorhies, *Female of the Species,* p. 187, describe economic patterns in such societies.

40. The literature is well surveyed in N. Tanner and A. Zihlman (see note 7 above); and in Sacks, *Sisters and Wives,* chaps. 2 and 3.

41. Martin and Voorhies, *Female of the Species,* p. 190. For examples of such scholarly disagreements see fn. 43 below and Leacock on Eskimos, and, for different interpretations: Jean L. Briggs, "Eskimo Women: Makers of Men," in Carolyn J. Matthiasson, *Many Sisters: Women in Cross-Cultural Perspective* (New York, 1974), pp. 261–304; and Elise Boulding, *The Underside of History: A View of Women Through Time* (Boulder, Colo., 1976), p. 291.

42. Eleanor Leacock, "Women in Egalitarian Societies," in Renate Bridenthal and Claudia Koonz, *Becoming Visible: Women in European History* (Boston, 1977), p. 27.

43. For a detailed description and analysis of the position of Iroquois women see Judith K. Brown, "Iroquois Women: An Ethnohistoric Note," in Reiter, *Anthropology of Women*, pp. 235–51. The analysis in Martin and Voorhies, *Female of the Species*, pp. 225–29, is interesting for stressing the powerful position of Iroquois women without defining it as matriarchy.

Eleanor Leacock's similar assertion of the existence of matriarchy is challenged by Farb, pp. 212–13, and Paula Webster, "Matriarchy: A Vision of Power," in Reiter, *Anthropology*, pp. 127–56.

44. Martin and Voorhies, *Female of the Species*, p. 214. See also David Aberle, "Matrilineal Descent in Crosscultural Perspective," in Kathleen Gough and David Schneider (eds.), *Matrilineal Kinship* (Berkeley, 1961), pp. 657–727.

45. For a thorough survey of the entire literature about amazons, see Abby Kleinbaum, *The Myth of the Amazons* (New York, 1983). The author concludes that amazons never existed, but that the myth of their existence served to reinforce patriarchal ideology.

46. Regardless of family structure and kinship arrangements, high status for women does not necessarily mean power. Rosaldo has argued persuasively that even in cases where women have formal power, they do not have authority. She cites the Iroquois as an example. In that matrilineal society some women held prestigious positions and sat in the Council of Elders, but only men could be chiefs. An example of a patriarchally organized culture in which women had economic power is the Jewish *shtetl* of the early twentieth century. Women conducted business, earned money, and controlled family finances; they had a strong influence on politics through gossip, the making of marriage alliances, and through the influence exerted over their sons. Yet women were deferential to their fathers and husbands and idolized the scholar—by definition a male—as the highest status person in the community. See Michelle Rosaldo, "A Theoretical Overview," in Rosaldo and Lamphere, *Woman, Culture and Society*, pp. 12–42.

47. The following description is based on James Mellaart, *Çatal Hüyük: A Neolithic Town in Anatolia* (New York, 1967). Also: James Mellaart, "Excavations at Çatal Hüyük, 1963, Third Preliminary Report," *Anatolian Studies*, vol. 14 (1964), 39–120; James Mellaart, "Excavations at Çatal Hüyük, 1965, Fourth Preliminary Report," *Anatolian Studies*, vol. 16 (1966), 165–92; Ian A. Todd, *Çatal Hüyük in Perspective* (Menlo Park, 1976).

48. Lawrence Angel,"Neolithic Skeletons from Çatal Hüyük," *Anatolian Studies*, vol. 21 (1971), 77–98,80. The ochre painting of skeletons was made possible because the corpses were apparently first left out for the vultures, who cleaned them of flesh, and were then buried. Various wall paintings at the site illustrate the process.

49. Mellaart, "Fourth Preliminary Report." It should be noted that Mellaart's speculations and interpretations are far more restrained in his reports on the dig than in his later book. See also Todd, *Çatal Hüyük in Perspective*, pp. 44–45.

50. Purushottam Singh, *Neolithic Cultures of Western Asia* (London, 1974), pp. 65–78, 85–105.

51. Todd, *Çatal Hüyük in Perspective*, p. 133.

52. Anne Barstow, "The Uses of Archeology for Women's History: James Mellaart's Work on the Neolithic Goddess at Çatal Hüyük," *Feminist Studies*, vol. 4, no. 3 (Oct. 1978), 7–18.

53. Ruby Rohrlich-Leavitt, "Women in Transition: Crete and Sumer," in Bridenthal and Koonz, *Becoming Visible,* pp. 36–59; and Ruby Rohrlich, "State Formation in Sumer and the Subjugation of Women," *Feminist Studies,* vol. 6, no. 1 (Spring 1980), 76–102. My references concern mostly the latter essay.

54. Angel, (see note 48), pp. 80–96.

55. Todd, *Čatal Hüyük in Perspective,* p. 137.

56. Paula Webster, after surveying all the evidence in favor of matriarchy, concluded that it could not be proven, but explained that women needed "a vision of matriarchy" to help them shape their own future against the overwhelming evidence of their powerlessness and subordination. See Paula Webster, "Matriarchy: A Vision of Power," in Reiter, *Anthropology of Women,* pp. 141–56; also: Joan Bamberger, "The Myth of Matriarchy: Why Men Rule in Primitive Society," in Rosaldo and Lamphere, *Woman, Culture and Society,* pp. 263–80.

CHAPTER TWO. A WORKING HYPOTHESIS

1. My concepts here are grounded in the approach first formulated by Mary Beard in *Woman as Force in History* (New York, 1946). I have elaborated on this theme throughout my historical work. See especially Gerda Lerner, *The Majority Finds Its Past: Placing Women in History* (New York, 1979), chaps. 10–12.

2. See Paula Webster, "Matriarchy: A Vision of Power," in Rayna Reiter, *Toward an Anthropology of Women* (New York, 1975), pp. 141–56, for a thorough discussion of the psychological needs of contemporary women to have a vision of matriarchy in the distant past.

3. Michelle Rosaldo, "The Use and Abuse of Anthropology: Reflections on Feminism and Cross-Cultural Understanding," *SIGNS,* vol. 5, no. 3 (Spring 1980), 393.

Rosaldo elaborates on these views in her unpublished paper, "Moral/Analytical Dilemmas Posed by the Intersection of Feminism and Social Science," prepared for the Conference on the Problem of Morality in the Social Sciences, Berkeley, March 1980. The following statement seems to me particularly apt: "By challenging the view that we are either victims of cruel social rule or the unconscious products of a natural world that (most unfortunately) demeans us, feminists have highlighted our need for theories that attend to the ways that actors shape their worlds; to interactions in which significance is conferred, and to the cultural and symbolic forms in terms of which expectations are organized, desires articulated, prizes conferred, and outcomes given meaning" (p. 18).

4. See Nancy Makepeace Tanner, *On Becoming Human* (Cambridge, Eng., 1981), pp. 157–58. See also Nancy Tanner and Adrienne Zihlman, "Women in Evolution, Part I: Innovation and Selection in Human Origins," *SIGNS,* vol. 1, no. 3 (Spring 1976), 585–608.

5. Ruth Bleier, *Science and Gender: A Critique of Biology and Its Theories on Women* (New York, 1984), chap. 3, esp. pp. 55 and 64–68. The same point is made in Clifford Geertz, "The Impact of the Concept of Culture on the Concept of Man," in *The Interpretation of Cultures* (New York, 1973), pp. 33–54.

6. *Ibid.,* pp. 144–45; quote, p. 145.

7. Cf. Chapter One above, fn. 11. Also: Karen Horney, *Feminine Psychology* (New York, 1967); Clara Thompson, *On Women* (New York, 1964); Harry Stack Sullivan, *The Interpersonal Theory of Psychiatry* (New York, 1953), chaps. 4–12.

8. Conversely, one of the first powers men institutionalized under patriarchy was the power of the male head of the family to decide which infants should live and which infants should die. This power must have been perceived as a victory of law over nature, for it went directly against nature and previous human experience.

9. Information about prehistoric populations is unreliable and can be expressed only in rough quantitative terms. Cipolla thinks that "indirect evidence supports the view that Paleolithic populations had very high mortality. Since the species survived, we must admit that primitive man also had very high fertility. A study of 187 Neanderthal fossil remains reveals that one-third died before reaching the age of 20. An analysis of 22 fossil remains of the Asiatic Sinanthropus population revealed that 15 died when less than 14 years old, 3 before age 29 and 3 between the ages of 40 and 50." Carlo M. Cipolla, *The Economic History of World Population* (New York, 1962), pp. 85–86.

Lawrence Angel, "Neolithic Skeletons from Čatal Hüyük," *Anatolian Studies*, vol. 21 (1971), 77–98; quote on p. 80.

In contemporary hunting/gathering societies we find infant mortality rates as high as 60 percent in the first year. See F. Rose, "Australian Marriage, Land Owning Groups and Institutions," in R. B. Lee and Irven DeVore (eds.), *Man, the Hunter* (Chicago, 1968), p. 203.

10. Cf. Karen Sacks, *Sisters and Wives: The Past and Future of Sexual Equality* (Urbana, 1982), chap. 2.

There is, additionally, the possibility that menstruation presented an obstacle to women's hunting, not because it physically incapacitated women, but because of the effect of the scent of blood on the animal. This possibility came to my attention during a recent trip to Alaska. The National Park Service in its leaflets to campers and back-packers advises menstruating women to stay away from the wilderness areas, since grizzly bears are attracted by the scent of blood.

11. The anthropologist Marvin Harris argues to the contrary that "hunting is an intermittent activity and there is nothing to prevent lactating women from leaving their infants in someone else's care for a few hours once or twice a week." Harris argues that man's hunting specialty arose from his warfare training and that it is in men's warfare activities that we must seek the cause for male supremacy and sexism. Marvin Harris, "Why Men Dominate Women," *Columbia* (Summer 1978), 9–13, 39. It is unlikely and we have no evidence to show that organized warfare preceded big-game hunting, but I would argue that in any case both hunting and military activities would not be chosen by women for the reasons I have cited.

For a feminist interpretation of the same material, which makes no concessions to "biological determinism," see Bleier, *Science and Gender*, chaps. 5 and 6.

12. Cf. M. Kay Martin and Barbara Voorhies, *Female of the Species* (New York, 1975), pp. 77–83; Sacks, *Sisters and Wives*, pp. 67–84; Ernestine Friedl, *Women and Men: An Anthropologist's View* (New York, 1975), pp. 8, 60–61.

13. Simone de Beauvoir, *The Second Sex* (New York, 1953; 1974 reprint ed.).

14. While there is no hard proof for these claims to the originality of woman's contributions, neither is there proof for man's inventiveness. Both claims rest on speculation. For our purposes, it is important to allow ourselves the freedom to speculate on woman's contributions as equals. The only danger in this exercise is that we may claim for our speculations, because they sound convincing and logical, that they represent actual proof. This is what men have done; we should not repeat that mistake.

Elise Boulding, *The Underside of History: A View of Women Through Time* (Boulder, Colo., 1976), chaps. 3 and 4. See also V. Gordon Childe, *Man Makes Himself* (New York, 1951), pp. 76–80.

For a somewhat similar synthesis based on later anthropological work see Tanner and Zihlman, and Sacks, cited above in notes 4 and 10.

15. Nancy Chodorow, *The Reproduction of Mothering: Psychoanalysis and the Sociology of Gender* (Berkeley, 1978), p. 91.

16. *Ibid.*, p. 169. For a similar analysis based on different evidence see Carol Gilligan, *In a Different Voice: Psychological Theory and Women's Development* (Cambridge, Mass., 1982).

17. Chodorow, *The Reproduction of Mothering*, pp. 170, 173.

18. Adrienne Rich, in her analyses of "the institution of motherhood under patriarchy" and of "enforced heterosexuality," and Dorothy Dinnerstein, in her interpretation of Freudian thought, come to similar conclusions. See Adrienne Rich, *Of Woman Born: Motherhood As Experience and Institution* (New York, 1976); Adrienne Rich, "Compulsory Heterosexuality and Lesbian Existence," *SIGNS*, vol. 5, no. 4 (Summer 1980), 631–60; Dorothy Dinnerstein, *The Mermaid and the Minotaur: Sexual Arrangements and Human Malaise* (New York, 1977).

M. Rosaldo in "Dilemmas" (see note 3, above) criticizes these psychological theories because they slight or ignore the social context in which parenting takes place. Although I admire Chodorow's and Rich's work I agree with this criticism and add to it that in both cases generalizations applicable to middle-class people in industrialized nations are made to appear as universal.

19. Lois Paul, "The Mastery of Work and the Mystery of Sex in a Guatemalan Village," in M. Z. Rosaldo and Louise Lamphere, *Woman, Culture and Society* (Stanford, 1974), pp. 297–99.

20. Cf.: Sigmund Freud, *Civilization and Its Discontent* (New York, 1962); Susan Brownmiller, *Against Our Will: Men, Women and Rape* (New York, 1975); Elizabeth Fisher, *Woman's Creation, Sexual Evolution and the Shaping of Society* (Garden City, N.Y., 1979), pp. 190, 195.

21. My thinking on the subject of the rise and consequences of male warfare were influenced by Marvin Harris, "Why Men Dominate Women," and by a stimulating exchange of letters and dialogue with Virginia Brodine.

22. Claude Lévi-Strauss, *The Elementary Structures of Kinship* (Boston, 1969), p. 115.

For a contemporary illustration of the workings of this process and of the way the girl indeed "cannot alter its nature," see Nancy Lurie (ed.), *Mountain Wolf Woman, Sister of Crashing Thunder* (Ann Arbor, 1966), pp. 29–30.

23. C. D. Darlington, *The Evolution of Man and Society* (New York, 1969), p. 59.

24. Boulding, *Underside*, chap. 6.

25. See, for example, the case of the Lovedu in Sacks, *Sisters and Wives*, chap. 5.

26. Cf. Maxine Molyneux, "Androcentrism in Marxist Anthropology," *Critique of Anthropology*, vol. 3, nos. 9–10 (Winter 1977), 55–81.

27. Peter Aaby, "Engels and Women," *Critique of Anthropology*, vol. 3, nos. 9–10 (Winter 1977), 39–43.

28. *Ibid.*, p. 44. Aaby's explanation allows also for the case, inexplicable by Meillassoux's thesis, of societies which progress directly from relatively egalitarian sexual division of labor to patriarchal dominance by way of extended war activities. See, for example, the development of Aztec society described in June Nash, "The Aztecs and the

Ideology of Male Dominance," *SIGNS*, vol. 4, no. 2 (Winter 1978), 349–62. For Inca society, see Irene Silverblatt, "Andean Women in the Inca Empire," *Feminist Studies*, vol. 4, no. 3 (Oct. 1978), 37–61.

29. Aaby, "Engels on Women," p. 47. It may be noted that Aaby's argument sustains Darlington's evolutionary thesis. See p. 47, above.

30. Rayna Rapp Reiter, "The Search for Origins: Unraveling the Threads of Gender Hierarchy," *Critique of Anthropology*, vol. 3, nos. 9–10 (Winter 1977), 5–24; Robert McC. Adams, *The Evolution of Urban Society* (Chicago, 1966); Robert Carneiro, "A Theory of the Origin of the State," *Science*, vol. 169, no. 3947 (Aug. 1970), 733–38.

CHAPTER THREE. THE STAND-IN WIFE AND THE PAWN

1. My generalizations about archaic state formation are based on the following: Charles Redman, *The Rise of Civilization: From Early Farmers to Urban Society in the Ancient Near East* (San Francisco, 1978); Robert Carneiro, "A Theory of the Origin of the State," *Science*, vol. 169, no. 3947 (August 1970), 733–38; V. Gordon Childe, *Man Makes Himself* (London, 1936); Morton Fried, "On the Evolution of Social Stratification and the State," in Stanley Diamond (ed.), *Culture and History*, (New York, 1960), pp. 713–31; Jacquetta Hawkes and Sir Leonard Woolley, *History of Mankind*, vol. I (New York, 1963); Robert McC. Adams, *The Evolution of Urban Society* (Chicago, 1966); Robert McC. Adams, *Heartland of the Cities: Surveys of Ancient Settlement and Land Use on the Central Flood Plain of the Euphrates* (Chicago, 1981); Elman Service, *Origins of the State and Civilization: The Process of Cultural Evolution* (New York, 1975); *Cambridge Ancient History* (hereafter referred to as CAH), vol. I, pt. 1, "Prolegomena and Prehistory," ed. by I. E. S. Edwards, C. J. Gadd, N. G. L. Hammond (Cambridge, Eng., 1970, 3rd edition), chap. 13: C. J. Gadd, "The Cities of Babylon." Henry T. Wright and Gregory A. Johnson, "Population, Exchange, and Early State Formation in Southwestern Iran," *American Anthropologist*, vol. 77, no. 2 (Spring 1975), 267–89.

2. For the various theories of origin see Frederick Engels, *The Origin of the Family, Private Property and the State*, ed. Eleanor Leacock (New York, 1972); Childe, *Man Makes Himself*; Karl Wittfogel, *Oriental Despotism* (New Haven, 1957), p. 18; Carneiro, "A Theory . . ."; Adams, *Urban Society*, pp. 14, 42.

For a detailed historiographic discussion of these theories see Redman, *Rise of Civilization*, chap. 7.

3. Rayna Rapp Reiter, "The Search for Origins: Unraveling the Threads of Gender Hierarchy," *Critique of Anthropology*, vol. 3, nos. 9–10 (Winter 1977), 5–24; quote on p. 9.

Other feminist writers on the subject are Ruby Rohrlich-Leavitt, "Women in Transition: Crete and Sumer," in Renate Bridenthal and Claudia Koonz (eds.), *Becoming Visible: Women in European History* (Boston, 1977), pp. 36–59; Ruby Rohrlich, "State Formation in Sumer and the Subjugation of Women," *Feminist Studies*, vol. 6, no. 1 (Spring 1980), 76–102; Germaine Tillion, "Prehistoric Origins of the Condition of Women in 'Civilized' Areas," *International Social Science Journal*, vol. 29, no. 4 (1977), 671–81.

4. Redman, *Rise of Civilization*, p. 229.

5. My description follows the many-factor-systems ecological model developed by Redman in *Rise of Civilization*, pp. 229–36.

6. Denise Schmandt-Besserat, "The Envelopes That Bear the First Writing," _Technology and Culture_, vol. 21, no. 3 (1980), 357–85; Denise Schmandt-Besserat, "Decipherment of the Earliest Tablets," _Science_, vol. 211 (16 Jan. 1981), 283–85.

7. The name of this ruler is, according to most recent scholarship, being read as Uruinimgina. Since he has been widely cited in books addressed to the general reader as Urukagina, I have decided to use the older reading in this book in order to avoid unnecessary confusion.

8. Some writers have speculated that the exclusion of women from ruling elites was due to their exclusion from the military. Cf. Elise Boulding, "Public Nurturance and the Man on Horseback," in Meg Murray (ed.), _Face to Face: Fathers, Mothers, Masters, Monsters: Essays for a Nonsexist Future_ (Westport, Conn., 1983). A similar conclusion is reached by the anthropologist Marvin Harris in "Why Men Dominate Women," _Columbia_ (Summer 1978), 9–13, 39.

9. Adams, _Urban Society_, p. 79.

10. Irene Silverblatt, "Andean Women in the Inca Empire," _Feminist Studies_, vol. 4, no. 3 (Oct. 1978), 37–61.

11. _CAH_, vol. I, pt. 2, p. 115.

12. The information on the royal graves at Ur is based on the account of Sir Leonard Woolley in P. R. S. Moorey, _Ur of the Chaldees: A Revised and Updated Version of Sir Leonard Woolley's Excavations at Ur_ (Ithaca, N.Y., 1982), pp. 51–121. The number of royal graves is variously given as sixteen in Wooley and Moorey (p. 60) and seventeen in the leaflet "Royal Graves at Ur," Western Asiatic Antiquities, The British Museum (no publishing place or date).

See also an earlier edition, Sir Charles Leonard Woolley, _Excavations at Ur_ (London, 1954), and Shirley Glubok (ed.), _Discovering the Royal Tombs at Ur_ (London, 1969).

13. Her name was formerly read Shub-ad.

14. Glubok, _Discovering the Royal Tombs_, pp. 48–49.

15. _Ibid._, pp. 43–49, 71–83.

16. Quoted in _ibid._, p. 80.

17. _Ibid._, pp. 47–49.

18. Redman, _Rise of Civilization_, pp. 297–98.

19. _Ibid._, pp. 304–6.

20. The information on the rule of Lugalanda and Urukagina is based on P. Anton Deimel, _Sumerische Tempelwirtschaft zur Zeit Urukaginas und seiner Vorgaenger_ (Rome, 1931), pp. 75–112; A. I. Tyumenev, "The Working Personnel on the Estate of the Temple BaU in Lagos During the Period of Lugalanda and Urukagina (24–25th century B.C.)," in I. M. Diakonoff (ed.), _Ancient Mesopotamia: Socio-economic History: A Collection of Studies by Soviet Scholars_ (Moscow, 1969), pp. 93–95; C. J. Gadd, "The Cities of Babylon," _CAH_, I, pp. 35–51, and C. C. Lambert-Karlovsky, "The Economic World of Sumer," in Denise Schmandt-Besserat (ed.), _The Legacy of Sumer: Invited Lectures on the Middle East at the University of Texas at Austin_ (Malibu, 1976), pp. 62–63. For evidence of the slave purchases of Baranamtarra, see Otto Edzard Dietz, "Sumerische Rechtsurkunden des 3. ten Jahrtausends, aus der Zeit vor der III. ten Dynastie von Ur," _Bayerische Akademie der Wissenschaften, Phil.-Hist. Klasse, Abhandlungen Neue Folge_, Heft 67 (München, 1968), nos. 40, 41, 45.

21. There is some controversy over the nature of his ascendance to power. Deimel claims that Urukagina killed Lugalanda and his queen, while Tyumenev claims that both stayed alive and "Baramantarra lived two years after Urukagina's advent to power, en-

joying a position of considerable eminence." Tyumenev, in Diakonoff, *Ancient Meso-potamia*, p. 93.

22. The first view is represented by the Soviet scholar V. V. Struve, who cites an increase in the number of freemen entitled to rations from communally held temple lands in the second year of Urukagina's reign, which he describes as "a victory for the Lugash freemen over the rich, a sort of democratic revolution." Struve, in Diakonoff, *Ancient Mesopotamia*, pp. 17–69 and 127–72; quote on p. 39. This evidence seems unconvincing and could certainly be explained as the effort by a usurper to broaden the base of his support. The second explanation is favored by A. I. Tyumenev, "The State Economy of Ancient Sumer," *ibid.*, pp. 70–87; and Deimel, *Sumerische Tempelwirt-schaft*, p. 75.

23. Kazuya Maekawa, "The Development of the É-MÍ in Lagash during the Early Dynastic III," *Mesopotamia*, vols. 8–9 (1973–74), 77–144; 137–42.

24. I am indebted to Professor Jerrold Cooper of the Department of Near Eastern Studies, Johns Hopkins University, Baltimore, for calling his translation of this text to my attention and giving me the benefit of his interpretation. The translation appears in Jerrold Cooper, *Reconstructing History from Ancient Inscriptions: The Lagash-Umma Border Conflict* (Sources from the Ancient Near East, vol. 2/1 (Malibu, 1983), p. 51. Professor Cooper interprets this statement as hyperbole, part of Urukagina's justification for his usurpation of power.

Another authoritative translation emphasizes the difficulty of this text. It reads: "Women of former times each had two men; as regards the women of today, this prac-tice . . . has been dropped." (Translated from the German by Gerda Lerner). H. Steible, *Altsumerische Bau-und Weihinschriften*, 2 vols. (Wiesbaden, 1982). Quote from Uru-kagina # 6, vol. I, pp. 318–19; commentary, vol. II, pp. 158–59.

25. Translation by Professor Jerrold Cooper. The question mark indicates that the translation of the word is uncertain.

Steible reads the passage as follows: "If a woman to a man . . . speaks!, her remarks . . . and these . . . will be hung up on the city gate" (tr. from German by Gerda Lerner). The meaning of one word, which can be read as "nose, mouth or teeth," is considered so uncertain by Steible that he omits it. The comment "hung up on the city gate" occurs in other contexts to indicate a ceremony of public shaming. The difficulty of the passage as interpreted by two experts should make us especially cautious in inter-pretation.

26. Rohrlich, "State Formation," *Feminist Studies* (Spring 1980), 97.

27. Following the first interpretation, C. J. Gadd states that Urukagina enacted "cer-tain remission of fees formerly exacted on the occasion of divorces, thus curbing unlaw-ful connexions of women, who in consequence of these fines became wives of another without ceasing to be married to the former husband." Gadd in *CAH*, I, chap. 13, p. 51. Redman, *Rise of Civilization*, p. 306, follows a similar interpretation. I am indebted for the second interpretation to Professor Anne Kilmer, Department of Near Eastern Studies, University of California, Berkeley.

28. Bernard Frank Batto, *Studies on Women at Mari* (Baltimore, 1974), p. 8.

29. Deimel, *Sumerische Tempelwirtschaft*, pp. 36–37, 85, 88–89, 98, 110–11.

30. Tyumenev in Diakonoff, *Ancient Mesopotamia*, pp. 115–17. After the second year of Urukagina's reign the total personnel list stays at approximately 1000 a year. See also Gadd, *CAH*, I, p. 39, and Maekawa, "The Development of the É-MÍ . . . ," *passim*.

31. William Hallo, "The Women of Sumer," in Schmandt-Besserat, *Legacy of Sumer*, p. 29.

32. *Ibid.* Also: William Hallo and J. J. A. van Dijk (trans.), *The Exaltation of Inanna* (New Haven, 1968).

33. Hallo, "Women of Sumer," in Schmandt-Besserat, *Legacy of Sumer*, p. 30.

34. *Ibid.*, p. 31.

35. For an interesting study of medieval princesses fulfilling these roles see Elise Boulding, *The Underside of History: A View of Women Through Time* (Boulder, Colo., 1976), pp. 429–39.

36. Hallo, "Women of Sumer," in Schmandt-Besserat, *Legacy of Sumer*, p. 30.

37. *Ibid.*, p. 34.

38. Batto, *Women at Mari*, pp. 5, 137–38.

39. *Ibid.*, p. 137.

40. *Ibid.*, pp. 24–25.

41. *Ibid.* For references to this practice in the Bible see 2 Samuel 16:20–23 and Genesis 49:3–4. For the suggestions that a similar fate befell the wives and daughters of Zimri-Lim after his defeat, see Jack M. Sasson, "The Thoughts of Zimri-Lim," *Biblical Archaeologist*, vol. 47, no. 2 (June 1984), p. 115.

42. Batto, *Women at Mari*, pp. 51–2.

43. *Ibid.*, p. 20.

44. *Ibid.*, p. 16.

45. *Ibid.*, p. 27. *Ugbabatum* were the highest ranking priestesses at Mari, although elsewhere they were outranked by other ranks of priestesses. Batto thinks the term "status document" refers to a tablet on which captives were assigned their roles. Wara-ilisu may have been a more important official than merely a harem guard. Batto suggests, from other evidence, he may have been a controller, which was an important bureaucratic office.

The term "Subarean veil" is not explained by Batto and other interpreters of this passage. In investigating the matter myself, I found no reference to this phrase, but I found that Subartu was an area in the north of Babylon, from which slaves were frequently acquired. One might be justified in considering a "Subarean veil" as designating a veil appropriate to a Subarean slave woman. For this, see J. J. Finkelstein, "Subartu and Subarians in Babylonian Sources," *Journal of Cuneiform Studies*, vol. 9 (1955), 1–7.

Jack Sasson translates this passage "Teach them Subarean dancing." (Personal communication to Gerda Lerner.) It seems to me that the veiling of these women should be viewed in light of the well-established practice of veiling women as part of the marriage ceremony or veiling a concubine to make her a wife. While this practice is confirmed for Babylon and Sumer, it is quite possible that it was also practiced in Mari. In that case, the reference to the "Subarean veil" might have the symbolic significance of incorporating these women to their proper place in the harem.

46. The text cited here is from W. H. Roemer, *Frauenbriefe über Religion, Politik und Privatleben in Mari*. Untersuchungen zu G. Dossin, Archives Royales de Mari X, Paris, 1967 (Neukirchen-Venyn, 1971). (Trans. Gerda Lerner).

Batto (P. 84) translates this passage as follows: "There is (other) booty here before me; I myself will select girls for the veil from among the booty which is here and I will send (them to you)."

47. Jack Sasson suggests that Kirum was the secondary wife, and Shibatum the first,

and that the former remained childless while Shibatum bore twins. Professor Sasson reads the name 'Shimatum."

48. Batto, *Studies*, pp. 42–28; citation, p. 43.

49. The end of Kirum's first letter and the second letter are cited in full in Jack M. Sasson, "Biographical Notices on Some Royal Ladies from Mari," *Journal of Cuneiform Studies*, vol. 25, no. 2 (Jan. 1973), 59–104; citation, pp. 68–69.

50. Reference and citation, Sasson, *ibid.*

51. Batto, *Studies*, pp. 48–51; citation, pp. 48–49.

52. *Ibid.*, p. 39. The same incident is treated in Sasson, *Royal Ladies*, pp. 61–66.

53. Batto, *Studies*, chap. 5; citation, p. 96.

54. *Ibid.*, p. 99. I am indebted to Professor Jack Sasson for a somewhat different translation of this passage: "I am the daughter of a king! You are a queen! Since even soldiers treat well whom they acquire as booty, should you not *me* also, when you and your husband have entered me into a cloister?"

55. Batto, p. 100.

56. *Ibid.*, p. 106 fn. 44.

57. *Ibid.*, pp. 100–101.

58. *Ibid.*, pp. 67–73. For the suggestion that she may have been a relative of the king, I am indebted to Professor Sasson (personal correspondence).

59. Norman Yoffee, *The Economic Role of the Crown in the Old Babylonian Period* (Malibu, 1977), p. 148.

CHAPTER FOUR. THE WOMAN SLAVE

1. *The New Encyclopaedia Britannica*, 15th ed. (Chicago, 1979), vol. 16, "Slavery, Serfdom and Forced Labour," pp. 855, 857.

2. My generalizations on slavery are mainly based on the following sources: David Brion Davis, *The Problem of Slavery in Western Culture* (Ithaca, N.Y., 1966); David Brion Davis, *The Problem of Slavery in the Age of Revolution: 1770-1823* (Ithaca, N.Y., 1975); Carl Degler, *Neither Black Nor White; Slavery and Race Relations in Brazil and the United States* (New York, 1971); Moses I. Finley, "Slavery," *Encyclopedia of the Social Sciences* (New York, 1968), vol. 14, 307–12; Moses I. Finley, *Slavery in Classical Antiquity* (Cambridge, Eng., 1960); Eugene D. Genovese, *Roll Jordan Roll: The World the Slaves Made* (New York, 1974); Winthrop D. Jordan, *White Over Black: American Attitudes Toward the Negro, 1550–1812* (Chapel Hill, 1968); Herbert S. Klein, *Slavery in the Americas: A Comparative Study of Virginia and Cuba* (Chicago, 1967); Gunnar Myrdal, *American Dilemma: The Negro Problem and Modern Democracy* (New York, 1944); Suzanne Miers and Igor Kopytoff (eds.), *Slavery in Africa: Historical and Anthropological Perspectives* (Madison, 1977); Orlando Patterson, *Slavery and Social Death: A Comparative Study* (Cambridge, Mass., 1982).

3. Other authors have approached the subject similarly: "The slave is an outsider: that alone permits not only his uprooting but also his reduction from a person to a thing which can be owned." Robin Winks (ed.), *Slavery: A Comparative Perspective* (New York, 1972), pp. 5–6.

Also: Patterson, *Slavery and Social Death*, pp. 5, 7; Finley, "Slavery," pp. 307–12; *Encyclopedia of the Social Sciences*, pp. 308–9.

"Slaves [in Africa] have one thing in common: all are strangers in a new setting." Miers and Kopytoff, *Slavery in Africa*, p. 15.

4. James L. Watson, "Transactions in People: The Chinese Market in Slaves, Servants and Heirs," in James L. Watson (ed.), *Asian and African Systems of Slavery* (Berkeley, 1980), pp. 231–2.

5. Patterson, *Slavery and Social Death*, pp. 5, 6, 10.

6. *The New Encyclopaedia Britannica*, vol. 16, p. 855.

7. Robert McC. Adams, *The Evolution of Urban Society* (Chicago, 1966), pp. 96–97.

8. Igor M. Diakonoff, "Socio-economic Classes in Babylonia and the Babylonian Concept of Social Stratification," which is published as a component of D. O. Edzard, "Gesellschaftsklassen im alten Zweistromland und in den angrenzenden Gebieten—XVIII Rencontre assyriologique internationale, Muenchen, 29. Juni bis 3. Juli 1970" (München, Bayerische Akademie der Wissenschaften, Phil.-Hist. Klasse, Abhandlungen, Neue Folge, Heft 75 (1972), p. 45.

9. Patterson, *Slavery and Social Death*, p. 10.

10. *Ibid.*, p. 6.

11. I. J. Gelb, "Prisoners of War in Early Mesopotamia," *Journal of Near Eastern Studies*, vol. 32 (1973), 74–77.

12. *Ibid.*, p. 94.

In surveying the historiography on the question whether the majority of the prisoners of war in Mesopotamia were enslaved, Orlando Patterson shows that until a decade ago the affirmative view was held, but that recent scholarship, both Russian and Western, seems in agreement that prisoners of war were kept as prisoners for a short time and then released and resettled. This view is held by I. I. Semenov and by I. J. Gelb. Patterson himself thinks that while this is true for the majority of prisoners of war, "at all times some prisoners of war were used as slaves . . . and by the neo-Babylonian period there is reason to believe that the majority were being enslaved." Patterson, *Slavery and Social Death*, pp. 109–10.

13. Gelb, "Prisoners of War," p. 91.

On the "igi-du-nu," see V. V. Struve, "'The Problem of the Genesis, Development and Disintegration of the Slave Societies of the Ancient Orient," in I. M. Diakonoff (ed.), *Ancient Mesopotamia: Socio-economic History: A Collection of Studies by Soviet Scholars* (Moscow, 1969), pp. 23–24. For a different interpretation, see A. I. Tyumenev, in Diakonoff, *ibid.*, p. 99, fn. 36.

14. *Ibid.*, p. 23. (Struve).

15. Gelb, "Prisoners of War," p. 91.

16. E. G. Pulleyblank, "The Origins and Nature of Chattel Slavery in China," *Journal of Economic and Social History of the Orient*, vol. 1, pt. 2 (1958), 190. The quotation from the Han law code is cited in C. Martin Wilbur, "Slavery in China during the Former Han Dynasty; 206 B.C.–A.D. 25," *Anthropological Series, Publications of Field Museum of Natural History*, Vol. 34 (Jan. 15, 1943), p. 84. Other instances of slave mutilation are cited, *ibid.*, p. 286.

17. C. W. W. Greenidge, *Slavery* (London, 1958), p. 29.

18. Gelb uses the name Bur-Sin. This name is now being transcribed 'Amar-Su'en. "Prisoners of War," p. 89.

19. P. Anton Deimel, *Sumerische Tempelwirtschaft zur Zeit Urukaginas und seiner Vorgaenger* (Rome, 1931), pp. 88–89.

For a detailed discussion of the Temple BaU ration lists, see essays by V. V. Struve and A. I. Tyumenev, in Diakonoff (ed.), *Ancient Mesopotamia . . .* , pp. 17–69 and 88–126.

20.   *List of Female Slaves and Their Children*
                           (based on A. I. Tyumenev in Diakonoff, p. 116)

	Women	Children
Year I of Urukagina	93	42
II	143	89
III	141	65
IV	128	57
V	128	60
VI	173	48

Since the list does not tell us how many of the women were childless we cannot determine the number of children per woman. But the fact that the total number of children does not greatly increase in five years seems to indicate that these women were not sexually used. If one considers the generally high rate of infant mortality, the number of children actually seems to decline as the number of women increases. This might have been due to the death or sale of the children. Figures from four other temples in Lagash during year V of Urukagina show 104 slave women and 51 children of the goddess Nanse; 10 slave women and 3 children of the god Nindar; 16 slave women and 7 children of the god Dumuzi and 14 slave women and 7 children of the goddess Ninmar. Diakonoff, p. 123. These figures consistently show the same ratio as the figures above: less than half the number of children than the number of women.

21. Bernard Frank Batto, *Studies on Women at Mari* (Baltimore, 1974), p. 27, Doc. 126.

22. Rivkah Harris, *Ancient Sippar: A Demographic Study of an Old-Babylonian City (1894–1595 B.C.)*, (Nederlands Historisch-Archelogisch Institute te Istanbul, 1975), p. 333.

23. For the dating of *The Iliad* see Moses I. Finley, *The World of Odysseus* (London, 1964), p. 26.

24. Richmond Lattimore, trans., *The Iliad of Homer* (Chicago, 1937), I, pp. 184–88.

25. *Ibid.*, IX, 132–34.

26. *Ibid.*, IX, 128–29.

27. *Ibid.*, IX, 139–40.

28. *Ibid.*, IX, 664–68.

29. *Ibid.*, IX, 593; see also: XVI, 830–32.

30. *Ibid.*, 450–59.

31. Moses I. Finley, *The World of Odysseus* (Meridian paperback edition; New York, 1959), p. 56.

32. William L. Westermann, *The Slave Systems of Greek and Roman Antiquity* (Philadelphia, 1955), pp. 26, 28, 63.

33. *Ibid.*, p. 7.

34. Thucydides, *History of the Peloponnesian War* (Cambridge, Mass., 1920), III,68, 2; IV, 48, 4; V, 32, 1.

See also O. Patterson, *Slavery and Social Death*, "The primitive practice of massacring the men and enslaving only the women and children was clearly attested in numerous instances" (p. 121).

35. E. A. Thompson, "Slavery in Early Germany," in Moses I. Finley, *Slavery in Classical Antiquity*, pp. 195–96.

36. In his worldwide survey of slavery O. Patterson finds "What determined sexual

bias in the taking of captives was not the level of development of the society or the degree of structural dependence on slavery, but the use to which slaves were to be put . . . purely military considerations and the problem of security in the captor's society. It is obvious that women and children were easier to take than men; they were also easier to keep and to absorb in the community. In addition, in most pre-modern societies women were highly productive laborers . . ." Patterson, *Slavery and Social Death*, pp. 120–21.

In surveying 186 slave societies which he selected from the Murdock sample, Patterson found that "female slaves outnumber males in 54 percent of all slaveholding societies . . . ; they are equal in number to men in 17 percent; and number less than males in only 29 percent of the sampled societies" (p. 199). This conclusion lends support to my thesis that women were more easily and readily enslaved than men in most slaveholding societies.

37. Adams, *Urban Society*, p. 96.

38. Abd el-Mohsen Bakir, *Slavery in Pharaonic Egypt* (Cairo, 1952), p. 25.

39. Fritz Gschnitzer, *Studien zur griechischen Terminologie der Sklaverei:* "Untersuchungen zur aelteren, insbesondere Homerischen Sklaventerminologie" (Wiesbaden, 1976), pp. 8, 10, fns. 25, 114–15. The fact that both *doulos* and *amphipolos* applied to males appear only centuries later, corroborates the linguistic evidence I have cited from other cultures to show that women were enslaved considerably earlier than men.

40. Winks, *Slavery*, p. 6.

41. Isaac Mendelsohn, *Legal Aspects of Slavery in Babylonia, Assyria and Palestine: A Comparative Study; 3000–500* B.C. (Williamsport, Pa., 1932), p. 47.

42. Finley, *Odysseus*, p. 57 (Meridian edition).

43. John M. Gullick, "Debt Bondage in Malaya," in Winks, *Slavery*, pp. 55–57.

44. Greenidge, *Slavery*, p. 47. See also Watson, "Transactions in People," in Watson, *Slavery*, 225, 231–33, 244.

45. Greenidge, *Slavery*, p. 30.

46. There is a large literature on the subject of rape and sexual exploitation of women. See: Susan Brownmiller, *Against Our Will: Men, Women and Rape* (New York, 1975). On rape and marital violence, Wini Breines and Linda Gordon, "The New Scholarship on Family Violence" *SIGNS*, vol. 8, no. 3 (Spring 1983), 490–531; Jane R. Chapman and Margaret Gates (eds.), *Victimization of Women* (Beverly Hills, 1978); Murray Straus, Richard Gelles, and Suzanne Steinmetz, *Behind Closed Doors: Violence in the American Family* (Garden City, N.Y., 1980); Miriam F. Hirsch, *Women and Violence* (New York, 1981).

On sexual relations of servants and masters see: Lawrence Stone, *The Family, Sex and Marriage in England, 1500–1800*, (New York, 1977); Edward Shorter, *Making of the Modern Family* (New York, 1975); Joan Scott and Louise Tilly, "Women's Work and the Family in Nineteenth Century Europe," *Comparative Studies in Society and History*, vol. 17 (1975), 36–64; Joan Scott, Louise Tilly, and Miriam Cohen, "Women's Work and European Fertility Patterns," *Journal of Interdisciplinary History*, vol. 6, no. 3 (1976), 447–76; John R. Gillis, "Servants, Sexual Relations and the Risks of Illegitimacy in London, 1801–1900," *Feminist Studies*, vol. 5, no. 1 (Spring 1979), 142–73.

My remarks on the sexual use of slave women by white men are based on extensive readings in slave narratives and primary sources on U.S. slavery. See Gerda Lerner, "Black Women in the United States," in Lerner, *The Majority Finds Its Past: Placing Women in History* (New York, 1979), pp. 63–83 and 191, fns. 15 and 16.

47. Patterson noted that societies with more female slaves than male tended to be the ones in which household production prevailed. "In such societies the master, as *patria potestas*, usually had the power to discipline to the point of death all members of the household, not only slaves but wives, children, junior kinsmen, and retainers. . . . [the female slave] may have been killed with impunity, for she belonged 'in blood and bone,' but under the master's potestas this happened no more frequently than it did to 'free' persons." O. Patterson, *Slavery and Social Death*, p. 199.

48. Cited in Jacquetta Hawkes and Sir Leonard Woolley, *History of Mankind*, Vol. I, "Prehistory and the Beginnings of Civilization" (New York, 1963), p. 475.

49. G. R. Driver and John C. Miles, *The Babylonian Laws, edited with Translation and Commentary*, 2 vols. (Oxford, 1952, 1955), vol. I, p. 36, and "Chronological Table" for a discussion of the dating of the Code of Hammurabi. The reign of Hammurabi is dated by Driver and Miles 1711–1669 B.C.; 1801–1759 B.C. by Ungnad, and 1704–1662 B.C. by Boehl.

Quotation in Driver-Miles, *BL*, I: 45.

50. *Ibid.*, I: 11.

51. *Ibid.*, I: 212–13.

52. HC § 116, *ibid.*, II: 47. Commentary on the law I: 215–19.

53. HC § 117–§ 119, *ibid.*, II, p. 49. Commentary, I:217–20.

54. M. Schorr, *Urkunden des altbabylonischen Zivil-und Processrechts* (Leipzig, 1913), No. 77, p. 121, as cited in Isaac Mendelsohn, *Legal Aspects of Slavery*, p. 23.

In commenting on this document, Driver and Miles interpret its background as follows: "a wife Belizumu seems to be a *naditum* [priestess; G. L.], as she had no children and has bought a concubine for her husband." Driver-Miles, *BL*, I: 333, fn. 1.

55. *The Holy Scriptures According to the Masoretic Text* (Philadelphia, 1958), Genesis 16:2.

56. Genesis 30:3

57. *Ibid.*, 30:7

58. *Ibid.*, 30:23

59. HC § 144 and § 145, Driver-Miles, *BL*, II: 57. Commentary, *BL*, I: 304–5.

60. HC § 146, *BL*, II:: 57. Commentary, *BL*, I: 305–6. Driver and Miles comment on the Biblical parallels (I: 333, fn. 8). See also below Chapter 5, fns. 32–33.

61. HC § 171, *BL*, II: 67. Commentary, *BL*, I: 324–34.

62. Patterson, *Slavery and Social Death*, pp. 144–45. The information on Malaysian concubinage is from Gullick, in Winks, *Slavery*, pp. 55–57.

63. Wilbur, "Slavery in China," pp. 133, 163, 183. Also, Patterson, *Slavery and Social Death*, pp. 141–42.

64. Irene Silverblatt, "Andean Women in the Inca Empire," *Feminist Studies*, vol. 4, no. 3 (Oct. 1978), 48–50.

65. Sherry B. Ortner, "The Virgin and the State," *Feminist Studies*, vol. 4, no. 3 (Oct. 1978), pages 19–36.

66. Pulleyblank (note 16, above), pp. 203–4, 218.

67. *Ibid.*, pp. 194–95.

68. Wilbur, "Slavery in China," p. 162.

69. Jastrow, Luckenbill, and Geers translate the term as "captive women," Ebeling and Schorr as "concubine." Ehelohlf translates the term as "an enclosed one" and remarks: "Obviously a term for a category of women who stand in the middle between free mistresses and unfree slave women." All of the above are cited in Samuel I. Feigin,

"The Captives in Cuneiform Inscriptions," *American Journal of Semitic Languages and Literatures*, vol. 50, no. 4 (July 1934), 229–30.

70. *Ibid.*, 243.

71. If it is the case, as Driver and Miles interpreted, that Belizumu was a *naditum* priestess, she would not be permitted to bear children, but presumably had sexual intercourse with her husband, using contraceptive methods. The principle of the wife having to submit to sexual regulation imposed by her husband and by society remains the same in either case.

72. S. H. Butcher (trans.), *The Odyssey of Homer* (London, 1917), 23: 38–39.

73. *Ibid.*, 1: 430.

74. *Ibid.*, 22: 418–20.

75. *Ibid.*, 23: 420–24.

76. *Ibid.*, 23: 445–72.

77. *Ibid.*, 23: 498–501.

78. Peter Aaby, "Engels and Women," *Critique of Anthropology: Women's Issue*, vol. 3, nos. 9 and 10 (1977), 39, paraphrasing Meillassoux.

79. For a detailed discussion on how the fact of once having been enslaved leads to the loss of social prestige and to the contempt for and marginalization of formerly enslaved persons, see Patterson, *Slavery and Social Death*, pp. 249–50.

80. Aristotle, *Politics*, Vol. I, 2–7.

CHAPTER FIVE. THE WIFE AND THE CONCUBINE

1. I have read the Codex Hammurabi in the following editions:: G. R. Driver and John C. Miles, *The Babylonian Laws*, 2 vols. (Oxford, Vol. I, 1952; Vol. II, 1955), hereafter referred to as Driver-Miles, *BL*. "The Code of Hammurabi," Theophile J. Meek (trans.), in James B. Pritchard (ed.), *Ancient Near Eastern Texts Relating to the Old Testament* (2nd edition, Princeton, 1955). Also consulted: David H. Müller, *Die Gesetze Hammurabis und ihr Verhältnis zur mosaischen Gesetzgebung* (Wien, 1903); J. Kohler and F. E. Peiser, *Hammurabi's Gesetz* (Leipzig, 1904), vol. I. All textual quotes are from Driver-Miles.

"The Middle Assyrian Laws" (Theophile J. Meek, trans.), in Pritchard; "The Assyrian Code," Daniel D. Luckenbill and F. W. Geers (trans.), in J. M. Powis Smith, *The Origin and History of Hebrew Law* (Chicago, 1931); G. R. Driver and John C. Miles, *The Assyrian Laws* (Oxford, 1935); all textual quotes from Driver-Miles, *AL*.

"The Hittite Laws" (Albrecht Goetze, trans.), in Pritchard; all quotes from that text. Also, "The Hittite Code" (Arnold Walther, trans.), in Smith.

Johann Friedrich, *Die Hethitischen Gesetze* (Leiden, 1959). I will cite in full in the footnotes the text of those laws I consider important for my argument and give number references for the others.

2. C. J. Gadd, *CAH*, vol. 2, pt. 1, chap. 5. Gadd cites the letter of an emissary of King Zimri-lim of Mari to semi-nomadic tribes on the Euphrates, who addressed some local chieftains as follows: "There is no King who is mighty by himself. Ten or fifteen Kings follow Hammurabi, the man of Babylon, a like number Rim-Sin of Larsa, a like number Ibalpiel of Eshnunna, a like number Amutpiel of Qatana, and twenty follow Yarimlim of Yamkhad"(pp. 181–82). Nevertheless, it was Hammurabi who defeated Rim-Sin of Larsa and a coalition of Elam, Gutium, Assyria, and Eshnunna, although he could never defeat Assyria herself. Later he also defeated King Zimri-Lim of Mari.

3. My generalizations are based on Smith, *Origin*, pp. 15–17, and Driver-Miles, *BL*, I, pp. 9, 41–45.

4. Smith, *Origin*, p. 3.

5. W. B. Lambert, "Morals in Ancient Mesopotamia," *Vooraziatisch Egypt Genootschap "Ex Oriente Lux" Jaarbericht*, no. 15 (1957–58), 187; Driver-Miles, *AL*, pp. 52–53. See also: J. J. Finkelstein, "Sex Offenses in Babylonian Laws," *Journal of the American Oriental Society*, vol. 86 (1966).

6. A. Leo Oppenheim, *Ancient Mesopotamia* (Chicago, 1964), p. 158.

7. Lambert, "Morals in Ancient Mesopotamia," p. 187.

8. A. S. Diamond argues that the *lex talionis* represents an advance over the earlier legal concept of pecuniary penalties to next of kin for damages done. He cites, for example, the laws of Ur-Nammu (ca. 300 years earlier than Hammurabic law), in which all sanctions for personal injury are pecuniary. Corporal law, according to his view, becomes established with the advent of strong states, which remove the authority of settling disputes, mostly by the payment of damages, from contending kin groups to the authority of the state. Thus offenses become criminalized, and in the absence of jails, death or mutilation becomes the appropriate punishment. He explains the prevalence of pecuniary punishment in the Assyrian and Hittite law codes as due to their "simpler culture" and "more backward stage" of development. A. S. Diamond, "An Eye for an Eye," *Iraq*, vol. 19, pt. 2 (Autumn 1957), 155, 153.

9. Oppenheim, *Ancient Mesopotamia*, p. 87.

10. Driver-Miles, *BL*, I, pp. 174–76. CH Law § 50 specifies 33½ percent interest on the loan of grain and 20 percent interest on the loan of money. Driver and Miles consider this to be fairly representative and point out that Assyrian interest rates were also fixed at 25–33½ percent. (This reference is on p. 176.)

11. CH § 117 "If a man has become liable to arrest under a bond and has sold his wife his son or his daughter or gives (them) into servitude for 3 years they shall do work in the house of him who has bought them or taken them in servitude; in the fourth year their release shall be granted." Driver-Miles, *BL*, II, pp. 47–49. See also, below, Chapter Six, for a discussion of this topic.

12. I have used *The Holy Scriptures According to the Masoretic Text* (Philadelphia, 1917) as my source for Biblical citations. (Exod. 21:2–11, Deut. 15:12–15, 18). For comment see Driver-Miles, *BL*, I, p. 221. The Nuzi records confirm the frequent use of slaves as concubines or as the wives of slaves of their masters. In Nuzi record V 437, for example, a man disposes of his sister to a man who will give her as a wife to his slave. The contract provides that if her slave husband dies, she shall be married to another slave husband, if he dies to yet another, and so on to the fourth. This record comes from a society in which elite women held great delegated power and propertied women could engage in business and sales transactions, which frequently involved slave sales and the sales of children. Cyrus H. Gordon, "The Status of Women Reflected in the Nuzi Tablets," *Zeitschrift für Assyriologie*, Neue Folge, Band IX (1936), 152, 160, 168.

13. Smith, *Origin*, p. 20.

14. CH § 195—"If a son strikes his father, they shall cut off his forehand." Driver-Miles, *BL*, II, p. 77.

CH §§ 192–193 "If the (adopted) son of a chamberlain or the (adopted) son of an epicene states to the father who has brought him up or the mother who has brought him up 'Thou are not my father' (or) 'Thou art not my mother,' they shall cut out his tongue." Driver-Miles, *BL*, II, pp. 75–77. Note: The word "epicene" (votary) designates here a *Sal-zikrum* priestess. Such priestesses, since they were forbidden to have natural children, frequently adopted children in order to secure their services in old age. From this it is clear that the "father" and "mother" mentioned in CH § 192 are not a married couple, but the reference is to two different cases, one in which the son was adopted by a chamberlain, another in which a son was adopted by a *Sal-zikrum* priestess. See Driver-Miles, *BL*, I, pp. 401–5.

15. "And he that smiteth his father, or his mother, shall surely be put to death" (Exod. 21:15). Comment and reference to Hebrew law, Exod. 21:15. Driver-Miles, *BL*, I, pp. 407–8.

16. CH § 155 "If a man has chosen a bride for his son and his son has (carnally) known her, (and if) thereafter he himself lies in her bosom and they catch him, they shall bind that man and shall cast him into the water" (Driver-Miles, *BL*, II, p. 61).

CH § 156—"If the man has chosen a bride for his son and his son has not (carnally) known her and he himself lies in her bosom, he shall pay her ½ maneh of silver and further shall make good to her anything that she has brought from the house of her father, and a husband after her heart may marry her." *Ibid.*

17. The subject is controversial. Driver and Miles regard the contract as essential to making an upper-class marriage legitimate. Others consider it optional. For details of this discussion see fn. 20, below. For a detailed discussion of the marriage contract see Samuel Greengus, "The Old Babylonian Marriage Contract," *Journal of the American Oriental Society*, vol. 89 (1969), 505–32.

18. CH § 162—"If a man has taken a wife (and) she has borne him sons, and that woman has then gone to (her) fate, her father shall not bring a claim (against him) for dowry; her dowry belongs to her sons" (Driver-Miles, *BL*, II, p. 63).

CH § 172—"If her husband has not made her a settlement, they shall make good her dowry to her and she shall take a share like (that of) one heir from the property of her husband's house. If her sons persist in persecuting her to make her go out of the house, the judges shall determine the facts of her case and lay a penalty on the sons; that woman shall not go out of her husband's house. If that woman sets her face to go out, she shall surrender the settlement which her husband gave her to her sons; she shall take her dowry which she brought from her father's house, and a husband after her heart may marry her." *Ibid.*, p. 67.

MAL § 29—"If a woman has entered her husband's house, her dowry or whatever she has brought from her father's house or what her father-in-law has given her on her entry are reserved for her sons; her father-in-law's sons shall not claim (it). But, if her husband survives (?) her, he may give (it in) what (shares) he will to his sons." Driver-Miles, *AL*, p. 399.

Commentary on CH § 162 and § 172, Driver-Miles, *BL*, I, pp. 344, 351–52. Commentary on MAL § 29, Driver-Miles, *AL*, pp. 189–90, 205–11.

I am indebted to Dr. Anne Kilmer, Department of Oriental Studies, University of California at Berkeley, for alerting me to the fact that the word "sons" here may mean both sons and daughters, i.e., children of either sex.

19. CH § 173—"If that woman, in the house that she has entered, bears sons to her latter husband, after that woman dies the sons of the former and of the latter husband shall divide her dowry." Driver-Miles, *BL*, II, p. 67.

CH § 174—"If she does not bear sons to her latter husband, then the sons of her first husband shall take her dowry." *Ibid.*, p. 69.

Commentary, *BL*, I, pp. 350–53.

20. CH § 148—"If a man has married a wife and ague attacks her, (and) he sets his face to marry another woman, he may marry (her). He shall not divorce his wife whom ague has attacked; she shall dwell in his house which he has built, and he shall continue to maintain her so long as she lives."

CH § 149—"If that woman does not consent to dwell in the house of her husband, he shall make good to her her dowry which she brought from the house of her father and so she shall go (away)." Driver-Miles, *BL*, II, p. 59. Commentary, I, pp. 309–11.

21. CH § 163—"If a man has married a wife and she has not provided him with sons, (and) that woman has then gone to (her) fate, if his father-in-law renders to him the bridal gift which that man has brought to the house of his father-in-law, her husband shall bring no claim for the dowry of that woman; her dowry belongs to her father's house."

CH § 164—"If this father-in-law does not render the bridal gift to him, he shall deduct the full amount of her bridal gift from her dowry and shall render (the residue of) her dowry to her father's house." Driver-Miles, *BL*, II, p. 63. Commentary, I, pp. 252–59.

22. Driver and Miles argue that the dowry is a substitute for the woman's inheritance. They point to the fact that a priestess, if no dowry has been given to her, is entitled to one share of her father's inheritance at his death. This may mean "that every woman has the right to inherit if no *seriktum* is given to her." *BL*, I, p. 272.

Jack Goody in *Production and Reproduction: A Comparative Study of the Domestic Domain* (London, 1976) has connected the phenomenon of what he calls "diverging devolution," the transmission of property to children of both sexes, with status stratification. Goody regards the giving of a dowry to a woman as equivalent to her inheriting part of the family property. Goody contrasts a "diverging devolution" system of inheritance (prevalent in Eurasian countries) with the African system, in which a deceased man's estate is not called upon to support the surviving spouse. Women bring no dowry into the marriage and get nothing when the marriage is dissolved. See Goody, pp. 7, 11, 14–22.

In a worldwide comparison of societies, showing the connection between woman's work and marriage structures, Esther Boserup comes to similar findings as Goody. Esther Boserup, *Women's Role in Economic Development* (London, 1970).

23. The debate is summarized in Driver-Miles, *BL*, I, pp. 259–65. It is continued and broadened in Driver-Miles, *AL*, pp. 142–60. For Koschaker's views see Paul Koschaker, *Rechtsvergleichende Studien zur Gesetzgebung Hammurapis, Königs von Babylon* (Leipzig, 1917), pp. 130–85. All quotes from this book translated by Gerda Lerner.

24. Driver-Miles, *BL*, I, p. 263, on marriage contracts; Driver-Miles, *AL*, p. 145, on sales price of slaves. During the first Babylonian dynasty the bride price for a free girl was 5 to 30 shekels; 5 shekels for a manumitted slave girl. At the same time the purchase price of a slave girl was 33⅓ to 84 shekels. Driver-Miles, *AL*, p. 145. On the other hand, the Nuzi tablets show that "the average sum paid for a normal able-bodied girl is 40 shekels of silver, whether . . . as wife or handmaid." Gordon (note 12, above), p. 156.

25. "Koschaker . . . his views seem to have obtained almost universal acceptance," Driver-Miles, *AL*, p. 142.

26. Koschaker, *Rechtsvergleichende*, pp. 150–99; Driver and Miles, *AL, pp.* 138–61. On *beena* marriage, see also Elizabeth Mary MacDonald, *The Position of Women As Reflected in Semitic Codes of Law* (Toronto, 1931), pp. 1–32, esp. 5–10, 24).

27. Koschaker, *Rechtsvergleichende*, pp. 182–83.

28. *Ibid.*, pp. 198–99. Koschaker also uses philological evidence in favor of his position (pp. 153–54). In Sumerian the word "marriage" is different for man and woman. A man "takes a wife," but a woman is described as "entering a man's house." Koschaker argues that the word for marriage applied to the man derives directly from "to take, to grab, to take possession of" and this fact supports his interpretation of marriage by purchase. Although they agree elsewhere that the woman "is the object, not the subject of marriage," Driver and Miles refute Koschaker by showing that the verb in question means "having possession," but that it never means "to purchase". When the object has been acquired by purchase the acquirer is said "to take" or "to take away" the thing in question. Driver-Miles, *BL*, I, pp. 263–64.

29. Rivkah Harris describes the role of cloistered *naditum* priestesses in the temple of the god Shamash in the family economy. A priestess entered temple service bringing a dowry with her, which, on her death, returned to her family. CH § 178 and CH § 179 provide that the priestess is to receive a full share of the paternal estate equal to that of a son, unless she has been given such a dowry. If she is given a dowry, she has full rights over it during her lifetime, and she may bestow her estate on whom she chooses. Driver-Miles, *BL*, II, pp. 71–73.

Rivkah Harris comments: "For the first time in Mesopotamian history there is a concentration of wealth in the hands of a wider range of private individuals, in addition to the continuing affluence of the temple and palace. . . . It would, of course, be in the interest of these families to prevent the diffusion of their wealth which occurred when a girl married and took her dowry to another family." The institution of the *naditum* "served the economic function of keeping a girl unmarried until her death when her share of the family property would revert to the family." Harris, *Ancient Sippar: A Demographic Study of an Old-Babylonian City (1894–1595 B.C.)* (Istanbul, 1975), p. 307.

30. For a discussion of the function of gift exchange as a means of creating a network of mutual obligations, see Marcel Mauss, *The Gift: Forms and Functions of Exchange in Archaic Societies* (London, 1954). For the connection between inheritance and class, see Goody, *Production and Reproduction*, chap. 8.

31. Elena Cassin, "Pouvoir de la femme et structures familiales," *Revue d'Assyriologie et d'Archeologie Orientale*, vol. 63, no. 2 (1969), 130 (translation by Gerda Lerner).

32. CH § 145—"If the man has married a priestess and she has not provided him with sons and so he sets his face to marry a lay-sister, that man may marry a lay-sister (and) take her into his house; that lay-sister shall not then make herself equal to the priestess." Driver and Miles, *BL*, II, p. 57. Commentary, I, pp. 372–73. The fact that CH §§ 145–147 refer to the marriage of a *naditum* priestess and not to an ordinary marriage, does not alter the principle of the class distinction herein made between the concubine or the second wife and the primary wife. It is noteworthy that the second wife is considered lower in class and status regardless of whether she is a free woman (as in CH § 145) or a slave (CH §§ 146–147).

33. CH § 146—"If a man has married a priestess and she has given a slave-girl to her husband and she bears sons, (if) thereafter that slave-girl goes about making herself equal to her mistress, because she has borne sons her mistress shall not sell her; she may put the mark (of a slave) on her and may count her with the slave-girls." CH § 147—"If she has not borne sons, her mistress may sell her". Driver and Miles, *BL*, II, p. 57. Commentary, *BL*, I, pp. 372–73.

34. M. Schorr, *Urkunden des altbabylonischen Zivil und Prozessrechts*, Vorderasiatische Bibliothek (Leipzig), pp. 4–5, as cited in Driver-Miles, *BL*, I, p. 373, fn. 8.

35. Genesis 16:1–16; 21:1–21. See also below, Chapter Six.

36. CH §§ 133–135, Driver-Miles, *BL*, II, p. 53. Commentary, *BL*, I, pp. 284–98. Oppenheim, *Ancient Mesopotamia*, p. 77.

37. CH § 141—"If a married lady who is dwelling in a man's house sets her face to go out (of doors) and persists in behaving herself foolishly wasting her house (and) belittling her husband, they shall convict her and, if her husband then states that he will divorce her, he may divorce her; nothing shall be given to her (as) her divorce-money (on) her journey. If her husband states that he will not divorce her, her husband may marry another woman; that woman shall dwell as a slave-girl in the house of her husband." Driver-Miles, *BL*, II, pp. 56–57. Commentary, I, pp. 299–301.

38. Louis M. Epstein, *Sex Laws and Customs in Judaism* (New York, 1948), p. 194.

39. *Ibid.*, pp. 194–95.

40. CH § 129—"If a married lady is caught lying with another man, they shall bind them and cast them into the water; if her husband wishes to let his wife live, then the king shall let his servant live." Driver-Miles, *BL*, II, p. 51. Commentary, I, pp. 281–82.

41. MAL § 15—"If a man has taken a man with his wife (and) charge (and) proof have been brought against him, both of them shall surely be put to death; there is no liability therefor. If he has taken and brought (him) either before the king or before the judges (and) charge (and) proof have been brought against him, if the woman's husband puts his wife to death, then he shall put the man to death; (but) if he has cut off his wife's nose, he shall make the man a eunuch and the whole of his face shall be mutilated. Or, if he has allowed his wife to go free, the man shall be allowed to go free." Driver-Miles, *AL*, p. 389.

HL § 197—"If a man seizes a woman in the mountains, it is the man's crime and he will be killed. But if he seizes her in (her) house, it is the woman's crime and the woman shall be killed. If the husband finds them, he may kill them, there shall be no punishment for him."

HL § 198—"If he brings them to the gate of the palace and declares: 'My wife shall not be killed' and thereby spares his wife's life, he shall also spare the life of the adulterer and shall mark his head. If he says, 'Let them die both of them!' . . . The king may order them killed, the king may spare their lives." Goetze (trans.) in Pritchard, *Ancient Near Eastern Texts*, p. 198.

Hebrew Law. See Deut. 22:23–28 and Levit. 20:10.

Commentary, Driver Miles, *AL*, pp. 36–50. Commentary on Biblical law concerning rape in Epstein, *Sex Laws*, pp. 179–83.

42. CH § 130—"If a man has stopped the cries of (?) a married lady, who has not known a man and is dwelling in her father's house, and has then lain in her bosom and they catch him, that man shall be put to death; that woman then goes free." Driver-Miles, *BL*, II, p. 53.

43. CH § 131—"If the husband of a married lady has accused her but she is not caught lying with another man, she shall take an oath by the life of a god and return to her house." *Ibid.*

CH § 132—"If a finger has been pointed at the married lady with regard to another man and she is not caught lying with the other man, she shall leap into the holy river for her husband." *Ibid.*

Commentary, Driver and Miles, *BL*, I, pp. 282–84; Epstein, *Sex Laws*, pp. 196–201.

It is worth noting that in case the husband does not catch the adulterous pair in the act, he cannot punish the man, since there is only circumstantial evidence against him. But he can punish the wife on the basis of the same circumstantial evidence, forcing her to take a public oath, or in the case described in CH § 132, forcing her to undergo the ordeal. Driver and Miles, in the reference cited above, call attention to this example of a double standard of justice. In their commentary on the practice of the ordeal by water, Driver and Miles state that it is unknown how the outcome was determined. Some authorities think that the person's innocence was proven by her floating, her guilt by drowning. If that is so, Driver and Miles point out that this would be the reverse of the Semitic practice, which also prevailed in Europe in the Christian era, by which it was held that the water would accept the innocent and reject the guilty. Thus, if the victim drowned, she would presumably be proven innocent; if she floated, she would be proven guilty. The aims of justice were served, at least in some historically verifiable instances, by tying cords to the victim—those who were proved innocent by drowning could then be rescued by being pulled to safety. See Driver-Miles, *AL*, pp. 86–106.

44. CH § 138—"If a man wishes to divorce his first wife who has not borne him sons, he shall give her money to the value of her bridal gift and shall make good to her the dowry which she has brought from her father's house and (so) divorce her."

CH § 139—"If there is no bridal gift, he shall give her 1 maneh of silver for divorce-money."

CH § 140—"If (he is) a villein, he shall give her ⅓ maneh of silver." All three, Driver-Miles, *BL*, II, p. 55.

Commentary, Driver-Miles, *BL*, I, pp. 290–98. Driver and Miles cite Old-Assyrian and Old-Babylonian legal documents which state that "the husband says to his wife, 'Thou art not my wife,' gives her divorce-money and leaves her." Sometimes he solemnicizes the divorce by cutting the fringe of her garment. *Ibid.*, p. 291.

45. Both laws, Driver-Miles, *BL*, II, p. 57.

46. CH § 157—"If a man after (the death of) his father lies in his mother's bosom, they shall burn both of them." *Ibid.*, p. 61.

CH § 154—"If a man (carnally) knows his daughter, they shall banish that man from the city." *Ibid.*, p. 61.

For CH § 155 and CH § 156, see fn. 16 above. Commentary, Driver-Miles, *BL*, I, pp. 318–20.

47. MAL § 55 full text, Driver-Miles, *AL*, p. 423. Commentary, *AL*, pp. 52–61. For comparative Hebrew law see Exodus 22:16–17. Finkelstein in "Sex Offenses" cites a Nippur trial in which a man raped a slave girl in a granary, denied the crime, which was confirmed by witnesses. He was found guilty and had to pay the owner of the slave girl ½ a minah of silver. There was no discussion in the trial of whether the slave girl was willing or had been raped. Finkelstein comments: "The slave girl is not considered a legal person" (pp. 359–60).

48. Finkelstein comments as follows on MAL § 155: "We may safely ignore—as a piece of typically Assyrian 'calculated frightfulness'—the further stipulation by which the wife of the attacker is to be handed over to the father of the raped girl for (sexual) degradation . . ." (p. 357). There is no evidence whatever offered for this counsel to ignore a part of the law which offends contemporary sensibilities.

See Claudio Saporetti, "The Status of Women in the Middle Assyrian Period," *Monographs on the Ancient Near East*, vol. 2, fascicle 1 (Malibu, Calif., 1979), pp. 1–20, esp. p. 10, for an interpretation of MAL § 55 which does not minimize its repressive character and cites private examples of private contracts which show the low status of women of the lower classes. Saporetti throughout shows the "woman's total and absolute dependence" on father and husband (p. 13).

49. MAL § 56—"If a virgin has given herself to a man, the man shall swear (to this, and) his wife shall not be touched. The seducer shall give 'the third' the price of a virgin (in) silver (and) the father shall treat (his) daughter as he pleases." Driver-Miles, *AL,* pp. 423–25.

50. Commentary on text, *AL,* p. 425. "The chastisement of the wife then to which this section relates is that which a husband may inflict by virtue of his domestic authority or marital control. . . . the Babylonian code has no sections expressly dealing with the discretionary power which it clearly allows a husband in certain cases against his wife . . ." (p. 292).

51. CH §§ 171 and 172. Driver-Miles, *BL,* II, p. 67. Commentary I, pp. 334–35.

52. MAL § 46—"If a woman whose husband is dead does not go forth from her house on her husband's death, (and) if her husband has assigned her nothing in writing, she shall dwell in a house belonging to her sons where she chooses; her husband's sons shall provide her with food; they shall enter into a covenant for her for (the provision of) her food and her drink as (for) a bride whom they love. If she is a second (wife and) she has no sons, she shall dwell with one (of her husband's sons and) they shall provide her with food in common; if she has sons (and) the sons of the former (wife) do not agree to provide her with food, she shall dwell in a house belonging to her own sons where she chooses, (and) her own sons too shall provide her with food and she shall do their work. But if indeed among her sons (there is one) who has taken her (as his spouse), he who takes her (as his spouse) shall surely provide her with food and her (own) sons shall not provide her with food." Driver and Miles, *AL,* p. 415. It is worth noting that the widowed mother, in exchange for being supported by her sons, is expected to "do their work," presumably housework and the production of textiles.

The ancient Semitic practice is discussed in Driver-Miles, *BL,* I, p. 321. For instances of it see II Samuel 16:21–22 and I Kings 2:21–22.

53. MAL §§ 30, 31. Driver-Miles, *AL,* pp. 399–401.

MAL § 33—"[If] a woman is still dwelling in her father's house (and) her husband is dead and [she] has sons, [she shall dwell in a] house [belonging to them where she chooses. If] she has no [son, her father-in-law shall give her] to whichever [of his sons] he likes. . . . or, if he pleases, he shall give her as a spouse to her father-in-law. If her husband and her father-in-law are [indeed] dead and she has no son, she becomes (in law) a widow; she shall go whither she pleases" (*AL,* p. 401). It is worth noting that this law applies only to a particular class of widow, namely, the one who, though married, still lives in her father's house. This would usually refer to a child-bride only. In this case, both her father and her father-in-law have the right to dispose of her in a *levirate* marriage. Saporetti discusses the woman as widow in Assyrian society, with some attention to the special and exceptional case of the *almattu* widow, who was a free woman without sons (unless they were minors), whose father-in-law had also died, thus making her subject to no one's tutelage. Such a woman may cohabit with someone, taking her possessions with her, and eventually become a legitimate wife. She also may be considered head of a household. Saporetti stresses that this position is exceptional and contrasts with the generally degraded position of widows in ancient Near Eastern society. Saporetti, "The Status of Women . . . ," pp. 17–20.

54. Louis M. Epstein, *Marriage Laws in the Bible and the Talmud* (Cambridge, Mass., 1942), p. 77.

55. *Ibid.,* p. 79.

56. CH §§ 209–214. Driver-Miles, *BL*, II, p. 79. Commentary, I, pp. 413–16. The authors comment that these laws make class distinctions among women and that the person receiving the payment "for the loss of the unborn child . . . must be the husband or master" (p. 415).

57. The relevant MAL laws are:

MAL § 21—"If a man has struck a lady by birth and has caused her to cast the fruit of her womb (and) charge (and) proof have been brought against him, he shall pay 2 talents 30 manehs of lead; he shall be beaten 50 blows with rods (and) shall do labour for the king for 1 full month." Driver-Miles, *AL*, p. 393.

MAL § 50, cited in the text. *AL*, p. 419.

MAL § 51—"If a man has struck a married woman who does not rear her children and has caused her to cast the fruit of her womb, this punishment (shall be inflicted): he shall pay 2 talents of lead." *AL*, p. 421.

MAL § 52—"If a man has struck a harlot and caused her to cast the fruit of her womb, blow for blow shall be laid upon him, (thus) he pays (on the principle of) a life (for a life)." *AL*, p. 421. Each of these laws refers to a different class of women: MAL § 21 to a lady, MAL § 50 to a burgher's wife, MAL § 51 to a woman who for reasons of ill health or by selling her children does not rear them, therefore is not considered to have suffered as great a loss as the other women; and MAL § 52, a harlot. In her case children had great value since they were reared for sale or to become harlots and helped to support a woman who had no male provider. Commentary, *AL*, pp. 106–15.

58. See fn. 57, MAL § 21 above, for text of the law. Driver and Miles, *AL*, p. 108: ". . . the assault in this case is regarded to some extent as an offence against the state . . ."

59. HL § 17 (earlier version)—"If anyone causes a free woman to miscarry, if (it is) the 10th month, he shall give 10 shekels of silver, if (it is) the 5th month, he shall give 5 shekels of silver and pledge his estate as security."

HL § 17 (later version)—"If anyone causes a free woman to miscarry, he shall give 20 shekels of silver."

HL § 18 (earlier version) "If anyone causes a slave woman to miscarry, if (it is) the 10th month, he shall give five shekels of silver."

HL § 18 (later version) "If anyone causes a slave-girl to miscarry, he shall give ten shekels of silver." Albrecht Goetze (trans.) in Pritchard, *Ancient Near Eastern Texts*, p. 190.

60. Exodus 21:22.

61. That is why, according to the *lex talionis*, the offender's wife or daughter must suffer the same penalty and why, in Hebrew law, the same principle is invoked, if the mother's potential as a childbearer has been affected.

62. MAL § 53. Driver-Miles, *AL*, p. 421, Commentary, *AL*, pp. 115–17.

63. *Ibid.*, p. 116.

64. *Ibid.*, p. 117.

CHAPTER SIX. VEILING THE WOMAN

1. *Encyclopedia Americana* (Danbury, Conn., 1979), vol. 22, p. 169.

2. *New Encyclopaedia Britannica* (Chicago, 1979), vol. 15, p. 76.

3. Iwan Bloch, *Die Prostitution*, vol. 1 (Berlin, 1912), pp. 70–71. Quote translated by Gerda Lerner.

4. Frederick Engels, *Origin of the Family, Private Property and the State* (New York, 1970), pp. 129–30. Engels's reference to temple prostitution is based on his uncritical acceptance of the account of Herodotus. See page 129.

5. *Ibid.*, pp. 138–39.

6. *New Encyclopaedia Britannica*, vol. 25, p. 76; *Encyclopedia Americana*, vol. 22, pp. 672–74; *Encyclopedia of the Social Sciences*, vol. 13 (New York, 1934), p. 553; Vern and Bonnie Bullough, *The History of Prostitution: An Illustrated Social History* (New York, 1978), pp. 19–20; Bloch, *Die Prostitution*, vol. 1, pp. 70–71; F. Henriques, *Prostitution and Society* (London, 1962), chap. 1; William Sanger, *A History of Prostitution* (New York, 1858), pp. 40–41; Geoffrey May, "Prostitution," *Encyclopedia of the Social Sciences*, vol. 13, pp. 553–59; Max Ebert, *Reallexicon der Vorgeschichte*, vol. 5 (Berlin, 1926), p. 323; Erich Ebeling and Bruno Meissner, *Reallexicon der Assyriologie* (Berlin, 1971); article "Geschlechtsmoral," article "Hierodulen," vol. 4, pp. 223, 391–93.

7. Marija Alseikaite Gimbutas, *Goddesses and Gods of Old Europe* (Berkeley, 1982); Edwin O. James, *The Cult of the Mother Goddess: An Archaeological and Documentary Study* (London, 1959). See Chapter Nine for a fuller discussion of this topic.

8. A. Leo Oppenheim, *Ancient Mesopotamia: Portrait of a Dead Civilization* (Chicago, 1964), pp. 187–92.

9. Vern L. Bullough, "Attitudes Toward Deviant Sex in Ancient Mesopotamia," in Vern L. Bullough, *Sex, Society and History* (New York, 1976), pp. 17–36, makes the same observation (pp. 22–23).

10. For discussion of the Sacred Marriage see Samuel Noah Kramer, *The Sacred Marriage Rite: Aspects of Faith, Myth and Ritual in Ancient Sumer* (Bloomington, 1969), p. 59; Thorkild Jacobsen, *Toward the Image of Tammuz and Other Essays on Mesopotamian History and Culture*, ed. William L. Moran (Cambridge, Mass., 1970); Judith Ochshorn, *The Female Experience and the Nature of the Divine* (Bloomington, 1981), p. 124. Also W. G. Lambert, "Morals in Ancient Mesopotamia," *Vooraziatisch Egypt Genootschap, "Ex Oriente Lux," Jaarbericht*, no. 15 (1957–58), 195.

11. Both quotes, Kramer, *Sacred Marriage Rite*, p. 59.

12. Thorkild Jacobsen, *Toward the Image of Tammuz*, pp. 73–101.

13. My comments about the female cultic servants are mostly based on the thorough study by Johannes Renger, "Untersuchungen zum Priestertum in der altbabylonischen Zeit," *Zeitschrift für Assyriologie und vorderasiatische Archeologie*, Neue Folge, Band 24 (Berlin, 1967) 1. Teil, pp. 110–88. Hereafter referred to as *ZA*.

14. G. R. Driver and J. C. Miles, *The Babylonian Laws*, 2 vols. (London: vol. 1, 1952; vol. 2, 1955). Hereafter referred to as *BL*. They think that the *naditum*, although unmarried, may not have made a vow of chastity, "for it is likely that she was in some temples, as for instance, those of Ishtar, a sacral prostitute." (*BL*, I, p. 366).

15. *BL*, I, p. 359.

16. The most complete study of these women is Rivkah Harris, *Ancient Sippar: A Demographic Study of an Old-Babylonian City (1894–1595 B.C.)* (Istanbul, 1975). Reference to their numbers, p. 304. See also Renger, note 13 above, pp. 156–68. Renger, Driver and Miles, and Benno Landsberger regard the *naditu* as priestesses, but Harris sees no evidence of their performing any religious function. She says their position was that of "daughter-in-law to the God Shamash and his bride Aja." As such they performed all the customary ritual services of daughters-in-law. Harris regards their function as "cultic" in that their lives were dedicated to the service of the god. See Harris, pp. 308–9.

17. *Ibid.*, p. 285.

18. *BL*, II, p. 45. Commentary, *BL*, I, pp. 205–6. It also illustrates, incidentally, that contemporaries regarded cultic sexual services rendered by priestesses in quite a different light from commercial prostitution. Renger comments as follows on this passage: "The interests of the state, as expressed in legal practice and in the Codex Hammurabi were directed toward guaranteeing the financial independence of a *naditu* in order to avoid that she would turn to prostitution due to her insufficient income. That is also why she lived in the *gagum* (cloister)." Renger, *ZA*, p. 156. Translation by Gerda Lerner.

19. *BL*, II, p. 73. Commentary, *BL*, I, pp. 369–70. The authors translate *kulmashitum* as "hierodule" and *qadishtum* as "votaress."

20. Harris, *Ancient Sippar*, p. 327. Some Orientalists make no distinction between these two kinds of temple servants and translate both as "hierodule" and describe them as being engaged in "sacred prostitution." Driver and Miles point out that there is no evidence for or against this interpretation, but there are cases when the goddess Ishtar herself has been referred to as a *qadishtum*. *BL*, I, pp. 369–70. For examples of differing translations of the word *qadishtu*, see Paul Koschaker, *Rechtsvergleichende Studien zur Gesetzgebung Hammurapis, Königs von Babylon* (Leipzig, 1917), p. 189 fn; *BL*, I, p. 369.

21. Herodotus, *Historia* (trans. A. D. Godley), Loeb Classical Library (Cambridge, Mass., 1920), Book I, p. 199.

22. *BL*, I, pp. 361–62.

23. *Ibid.*, pp. 368–69.

24. "Old Babylonian Proto-Lu list," B. Landsberger, E. Reiner, M. Civil (eds.), *Materials for the Sumerian Lexicon*, vol. 12 (Rome, 1969), pp. 58–59. I am greatly indebted to Dr. Anne D. Kilmer of the Department of Near Eastern Studies, University of California, Berkeley, for her help in pointing out these lists to me and translating them.

25. *Ibid.*, Canonical Series *lu-sha*, pp. 104–5.

26. *Assyrian Dictionary of the Oriental Institute of the University of Chicago* (Chicago, 1968), vol. 6, pp. 101–2.

27. "The Epic of Gilgamesh" in James B. Pritchard, *Ancient Near Eastern Texts Relating to the Old Testament* (2nd edition, Princeton, 1955), p. 74.

28. All citations from *ibid.*, pp. 74–75.

29. C. J. Gadd, "Some Contributions to the Gilgamesh Epic," *Iraq*, vol. 28, part II (Autumn 1966), quote, p. 108.

30. For a detailed treatment of the subject see Chapter Six.

31. My interpretations of the Middle Assyrian Laws, hereafter referred to as MAL, are based on extensive reading in all the various extant translations of Mesopotamian law compilation. For MAL I have read "The Middle Assyrian Laws," Theophile J. Meek, (trans.) in James B. Pritchard (ed.), *Ancient Near Eastern Texts*, 2nd ed.; D. D. Luckenbill and F. W. Geers (trans.) in J. M. Powis Smith, *The Origin and History of Hebrew Law* (Chicago, 1931); G. R. Driver and J. C. Miles, *The Assyrian Laws* (Oxford, 1935). All textual quotes are from Driver-Miles, *AL*. The declassing of the prostitute in the Assyrian code was noted in a footnote by Isaac Mendelsohn in his study of slavery. He cited several examples of legal texts which show that prostitution was a recognized and established institution in the Ancient Near East. "Though not a very honorable profession, no disgrace was attached to the person practicing it. The professional prostitute was a free-born independent woman and the law protected her economic position. . . . The degradation of the prostitute to the level of the slave in Assyria and in NeoBabylonia was due to the fact that the majority of the prostitutes at that time were female slaves

leased by their owners to individuals and to public houses." Isaac Mendelsohn, *Slavery in the Ancient Near East* (New York, 1949), fn. 57, pp. 131–32.

32. All quotations below of MAL§ 40 from Pritchard, *Ancient Near Eastern Texts*, p. 183.

33. Driver and Miles, *AL*, p. 134.

34. *Ibid.*

35. In Pritchard *awilum* is read as "seignior," but other translators use the term "burgher" and indicate it might mean "noble" as well. Thus, both upper— and middle-class men of property might have been included in the term.

36. We may leave unquestioned the implied assumption that every man would know, if he saw them unveiled, who were the harlots and who were the respectable women.

CHAPTER SEVEN. THE GODDESSES

1. Reference to the offering of a vulva is found in Erich Ebeling, "Quellen zur Kenntnis der babylonischen Religion," *Mitteilungen der vorderasiatischen Gesellschaft* (E.V.) 23. Jahrgang (Leipzig, 1918), Part II, p. 12. (Translation Gerda Lerner.)

2. *Ibid.*

3. Heinrich Zimmern, "Babylonische Hymnen und Gebete in Auswahl,'" *Der Alte Orient*, 7. Jahrgang, Heft 3 (Leipzig, 1905), quotes, pp. 20–21.

4. William Foxwell Albright, *From the Stone Age to Christianity: Monotheism and the Historical Process* (Baltimore, 1957); Henri Frankfort et al., *Before Philosophy* (Baltimore, 1963); John Gray, *Near Eastern Mythology* (London, 1969); Jane Ellen Harrison, *Mythology* (New York, 1963); Thorkild Jacobsen, *Toward the Image of Tammuz and Other Essays on Mesopotamian History and Culture* (Cambridge, Mass., 1970); Walter Jayne, *The Healing Gods of Ancient Civilizations* (New Haven, 1925); Alfred Jeremias, *Handbuch der altorientalischen Geisteskultur* (Berlin, 1929); E. O. James, *The Ancient Gods: The History and Diffusion of Religion in the Ancient Near East and the Eastern Mediterranean* (London, 1960); Samuel Noah Kramer, *The Sacred Marriage Rite: Aspects of Faith, Myth and Ritual in Ancient Sumer* (Bloomington, 1969); Samuel Noah Kramer, *Sumerian Mythology: A Study of Spiritual and Literary Achievement in the Third Millennium* B.C. (New York, 1961); Theophile J. Meek, *Hebrew Origins* (New York, 1960); H. W. F. Saggs, *The Encounter with the Divine in Mesopotamia and Israel* (London, 1978); Arthur Ungnad, *Die Religion der Babylonier und Assyrer* (Jena, 1921); Hugo Winckler, *Himmels und Weltenbild der Babylonier* (Leipzig, 1901).

5. Sigmund Freud, *Moses and Monotheism: Three Essays* in *Complete Psychological Works* (London, 1963–74), vol. 23, pp. 1–137; Erich Fromm, *The Forgotten Language: An Introduction to the Understanding of Dreams, Fairy Tales and Myths* (New York, 1951); Robert Graves, *The White Goddess: A Historical Grammar of Poetic Myth* (New York, 1966); Erich Neumann, *The Great Mother: An Analysis of the Archetype* (Princeton, 1963).

6. Judith Ochshorn, *The Female Experience and the Nature of the Divine* (Bloomington, 1981); Carole Ochs, *Behind the Sex of God* (Boston, 1977); Peggy Reeves Sanday, *Female Power and Male Dominance: On the Origins of Sexual Inequality* (Cambridge, Eng., 1981); Merlin Stone, *When God Was a Woman* (New York, 1976).

7. Thorkild Jacobsen, "Primitive Democracy in Ancient Mesopotamia," *Journal of*

Near Eastern Studies, vol. 2, no. 3 (July 1943), 162, 165; for a number of examples of this kind of correspondence of myth and social reality, see Saggs, *Encounter*, pp. 167–68.

8. For a full discussion and overview see Edwin O. James, *The Cult of the Mother-Goddess: An Archaeological and Documentary Study* (London, 1959), pp. 228–53.

9. Sanday, *Female Power*, p. 57.

10. *Ibid.*, p. 73.

11. *Ibid.*, pp. 61, 66.

12. One can raise many objections to making such an methodological leap, especially since it implies assumptions about cause and effect in history, which are exceedingly difficult to substantiate. We do not know enough, if anything, about Mesopotamian child-rearing practices, and careful historical tracing of variations in big and small game hunting are beyond the scope of this book. Still, Sanday's sampling offers cross-cultural evidence of similar patterns of change in creation myths in various cultures and thereby strengthens my thesis.

13. Marija Gimbutas, *Goddesses and Gods of Old Europe* (Berkeley, 1982), p. 18. See also, James, *Mother-Goddess*, pp. 1–46. Stone, *When God Was a Woman*, discusses the long history of Great Goddess worship in detail.

14. E. O. James, *The Ancient Gods*, p. 47.

15. A. L. Oppenheim, *Ancient Mesopotamia* (Chicago, 1964), chap. 4.

16. See myth of "Atrahasis," in James B. Pritchard, *Ancient Near Eastern Texts Relating to the Old Testament* (Princeton, 1950), p. 100.

17. In support of this explanation, see, for example, James, *Mother-Goddess*, p. 228. "With the establishment of husbandry and the domestication of flocks and herds, how-ever, the function of the male in the process of generation became more apparent and vital as the physiological facts concerning paternity were more clearly understood and recognized. Then the mother-goddess was assigned a male partner, either in the capacity of her son and lover, or of brother and husband. Nevertheless, although he was the begetter of life he occupied a subordinate position to her, being in fact a secondary figure in the cultus." See also Elizabeth Fisher, *Woman's Creation: Sexual Evolution and the Shaping of Society* (Garden City, N.Y., 1979), chap. 19.

18. James, *Mother-Goddess*, p. 228; E. O. James, *Myth and Ritual in the Ancient Near East* (London, 1958), pp. 114–17.

19. Pritchard, *Ancient Near Eastern Texts*, pp. 60–61.

20. *Ibid.*, p. 74.

21. Georges Contenau, *Everyday Life in Babylon and Assyria* (London, 1954), p. 197. See also: Jeremias, *Geisteskultur*, pp. 33–34.

22. The Sumerian word "anki" means "universe."

23. Samuel Noah Kramer, "Poets and Psalmists; Goddesses and Theologians: Literary, Religious and Anthropological Aspects of the Legacy of Sumer," in Denise Schmandt-Besserat, *The Legacy of Sumer: Invited Lectures on the Middle East at the University of Texas at Austin* (Malibu, 1976), p. 14.

24. Edward Chiera, *They Wrote on Clay* (Chicago, 1938), pp. 125–27.

25. Jacobsen, *Tammuz*, pp. 20–21.

26. James, *Ancient Gods*, pp. 87–90.

27. James, *Mother-Goddess*, p. 241.

28. Shoshana Bin-Nun, *The Tawananna in the Hittite Kingdom* (Heidelberg, 1975),

pp. 158–59. See also O. R. Gurney, "The Hittites," in Arthur Cotterell, *The Encyclopaedia of Ancient Civilizations* (New York, 1980), pp. 111–17. Hattusilis I left a written testament, which documents these historic changes.

29. Carol F. Justus, "Indo-Europeanization of Myth and Syntax in Anatolian Hittite: Dating of Texts as an Index," *Journal of Indo-European Studies*, vol. 2 (1983), 59–103. Reference to Telepinu, pp. 63, 74.

30. *Ibid.*, p. 63.

31. My argument here is based entirely on Justus's work. See *ibid.*, pp. 67–92.

32. *Ibid.*, pp. 91–92.

33. She has been fully discussed and the myths pertaining to her have been interestingly analyzed in every major work on Mesopotamian religion. See, among others: Gray, *Near Eastern Mythology*; William Hallo, *The Exaltation of Inanna* (New Haven, 1968); Jacobsen, *Tammuz*; James, *Mother-Goddess*; James, *Myth and Ritual*; Morris Jastrow, *The Civilization of Babylon and Assyria* (Philadelphia, 1915); Jayne, *Healing Gods*; Jeremias, *Geisteskultur*; Kramer, *Mythology*; Bruno Meissner, *Babylonien and Assyrien*, 2 vols. (Heidelberg, 1920); Ochshorn, *Female Experience and the Divine*; Stone, *When God Was a Woman*; Merlin Stone, *Ancient Mirrors of Womanhood: Our Goddess and Heroine Heritage*, 2 vols. (New York, 1979); Diane Wolkstein and Samuel Noah Kramer, *Inanna: Queen of Heaven and Earth* (New York, 1983).

CHAPTER EIGHT. THE PATRIARCHS

1. My comments on the history of the Pentateuch are based on the article "Pentateuch" in *Encyclopaedia Judaica* (Jerusalem, 1978, 4th ptg.), vol. 13, pp. 231–64. I have relied for my subsequent generalizations and interpretation of specific passages on the following: E. A. Speiser, *The Anchor Bible: Genesis* (Garden City, N.Y., 1964); Nahum M. Sarna, *Understanding Genesis* (New York, 1966); Gerhard von Rad, *Genesis: A Commentary*, transl. of German edition (Philadelphia, 1961); Theophile J. Meek, *Hebrew Origins* (New York, 1960); William F. Albright, *From the Stone Age to Christianity: Monotheism and the Historical Process* (Baltimore, 1940); William F. Albright, *Archaeology and the Religion of Israel* (Baltimore, 1956); Roland de Vaux, O.P., *Ancient Israel: Its Life and Institutions* (New York, 1961); paperback edition 2 vols., New York, 1965).

2. De Vaux, *Ancient Israel*, I, pp. 4–14.

3. My generalizations are based on the article "History" in the *Encyclopaedia Judaica*, vol. 8, pp. 571–74; and Tykva Frymer-Kensky, "Patriarchal Family Relationships and Near Eastern Law," *Biblical Archaeologist*, vol. 44, no. 4 (Fall 1981).

4. *Oxford Bible Atlas*, ed. Herbert G. May with the assistance of R. W. Hamilton and G. N. S. Hunt (London, 1962), pp. 15–17.

5. My interpretation here is based on Carol Meyers, "The Roots of Restriction: Women in Early Israel," *Biblical Archaeologist*, vol. 41, no. 3 (Sept. 1978), 95–98. Her argument runs parallel to the theoretical positions taken by Aaby and Sanday.

6. The other four are merely references to Miriam, Huldah, Noadiah as "prophetess" (Exod. 15:20; 2 Kings 22:14f. There is also an incident in which "a wise woman of Abel" prophesies. II Sam. 20:14–22.)

7. *Encyclopaedia Judaica*, vol. 8, pp. 583–92.

8. See Meek, *Hebrew Origins*, pp. 217–27, for a more detailed exposition of this viewpoint.

9. Paul Koschaker, *Rechtsvergleichende Studien zur Gesetzgebung Hammurapis, Königs von Babylon* (Leipzig, 1917), pp. 150–84. See also Elizabeth Mary MacDonald, *The Position of Women as Reflected in Semitic Codes of Law* (Toronto, 1931), pp. 1–32; De Vaux, *Ancient Israel*, I, pp. 19–23, 29.

10. David Bakan, *And They Took Themselves Wives: The Emergence of Patriarchy in Western Civilization* (San Francisco, 1979), pp. 94–95.

11. Speiser, *Anchor Bible*, pp. 250–51. A similar position is taken by M. Greenberg, "Another Look at Rachel's Theft of the Teraphim," *Journal of Biblical Literature*, vol. 81 (1962), 239–48.

Savina J. Teubal, *Sarah the Priestess: The First Matriarch of Genesis* (Athens, Ohio, 1984), assumes the existence of a basic conflict between "matriarchs" (Sarah, Rebecca, Rachel) and patriarchs in which only the patriarchal side is told in the Bible. She postulates a struggle on the part of these women to uphold the social mores of their tribes, which were matrilineal, as against the pressure of the patriarchs to institute patrilineality. In this light, she considers Rachel's action to be based on her "right" to the teraphim, because she is the youngest daughter and in some matrilineal societies descent is traced through the youngest daughter. Her interesting speculation seems to me here to be based on such narrow evidence that I do not find it persuasive, especially since she tries to elevate the Biblical foremothers into powerful "matriarchs" in the face of overwhelming contradictory evidence. Yet her attention to the many traces of matriliny and matrilocality in the Biblical text is important and should be further pursued by scholars in the field.

12. It should be noted that in the Deuteronomy version of the Decalogue the order is reversed: the command "Thou shalt not covet thy neighbor's wife" is placed before the command against coveting the neighbor's other possessions. Julias A. Bewer considers this a significant departure from the earlier usage and interprets it as "elevating her from her former position of mere property." See Julius A. Bewer, *The Literature of the Old Testament* (New York, 1962), p. 34.

13. De Vaux, *Ancient Israel*, I, pp. 166–67. See also A. Malamat, "Mari and the Bible: Some Patterns of Tribal Organization and Institutions," *Journal of the American Oriental Society*, vol. 82, no. 2 (1962), 143–49, for a discussion of the close parallels between conditions reflected in the Mari documents and those described in the Bible. Malamat shows how these economic conditions and concepts differed from those prevailing in other Mesopotamian societies.

14. If the widow were permitted to marry outside of the family, as was the Babylonian widow, she might take her widow's share of the inheritance with her.

15. Louis M. Epstein, *Marriage Laws in the Bible and the Talmud* (Cambridge, Mass., 1942), pp. 7, 38–39.

16. My generalizations about the status of Jewish women in the pre-exilic period are based on the following sources: De Vaux, *Ancient Israel*, chaps. 1–3; Louis Epstein, *Sex Laws and Customs in Judaism* (New York, 1948); Epstein, *Marriage Laws*; MacDonald, *Semitic Codes of Law*; Frymer-Kensky, "Patriarchal Family Relationships," 209–14; Phyllis Trible, "Depatriarchalizing in Biblical Interpretation," *Journal of the American Academy of Religion*, vol. 41 (1973), 31–34; and Trible, "Woman in the Old Testament," *The*

Interpreter's Dictionary of the Bible, Supplementary Volume, ed. K. R. Crim (Nashville, 1976), pp. 963–66.

17. I have discussed these two stories in more detail earlier.

18. For this interpretation, see Sarna, *Understanding Genesis,* p. 150.

19. Oskar Ziegner, *Luther und die Erzvaeter: Auszuege aus Luther's Auslegungen zum ersten Buch Moses mit einer theologischen Einleitung* (Berlin, 1952), p. 90 (translation by Gerda Lerner); John Calvin, *Commentaries on the First Book of Moses Called Genesis* (trans. by Rev. John King) (Grand Rapids, Mich., 1948), I, pp. 499–500.

20. Sarna, *Understanding Genesis,* p. 150.

21. Speiser, *Anchor Bible,* p. 143.

22. Bakan, *And They Took Themselves Wives,* pp. 97–101.

23. Epstein, *Sex Laws,* p. 135.

24. Trible, "Woman in the OT," p. 965.

25. Phyllis Bird, "Images of Women in the Old Testament," in Rosemary Ruether (ed.), *Religion and Sexism* (New York, 1974), pp. 41–88, citation, p. 71.

26. John Otwell, *And Sarah Laughed: The Status of Woman in the Old Testament* (Philadelphia, 1977).

27. Epstein, *Sex Laws,* pp. 78, 80–81.

28. *Ibid.,* pp. 86–87; De Vaux, *Ancient Israel,* I, 48–50.

29. Judith Ochshorn, *The Female Experience and the Nature of the Divine* (Bloomington, 1981), chaps. 5 and 6. Ochshorn discusses the question of the gendered nature of God in all its complexity and directs our attention to the profound ambivalence of the Biblical text regarding this question.

30. Meyers, "The Roots of Restriction . . . ," pp. 100–102. See also Ochshorn, *Female Experience,* pp. 196–97.

CHAPTER NINE. THE COVENANT

1. William F. Albright, *From the Stone Age to Christianity* (Baltimore, 1940), p. 199; E. O. James, *Myth and Ritual in the Ancient Near East* (London, 1958), p. 63.

2. In his highly respected commentary Gerhard von Rad, *Genesis: A Commentary* (Philadelphia, 1961; trans. of German edition, 1956), the author comments: "This naming is thus both an act of copying and an act of appropriate ordering, by which man intellectually objectifies the creatures for himself. . . . Namegiving in the ancient Orient was primarily an exercise of sovereignty, of command" (p. 81). See also Roland de Vaux, O.P., *Ancient Israel: Its Life and Institutions* (New York, 1961; paperback edition, 2 vols., 1965), I, pp. 43–46; Speiser, *The Anchor Bible: Genesis* (Garden City, N.Y., 1966), pp. 126–27; Sarna, *Understanding Genesis* (New York, 1966), pp. 129–30; Alfred Jeremias, *Handbuch der Altorientalischen Geisteskultur* (Berlin, 1929), pp. 33–34.

3. Phyllis Trible attempts to interpret the passage "and she shall be called woman" (Gen. 2:23) not as Adam's naming of Eve but as his recognition of sexuality and gender, a sort of definition. When discussing the contradictory passage in 3:20, where "the man called his wife's name 'Eve'," which, as she recognizes, is an assertion of his rule over her, she explains it as his "corrupting a relationship of mutuality and equality." Trible, "Depatriarchalizing in Biblical Interpretation," *Journal of the American Academy of Religion,* vol. 41 (March 1973), p. 38 and quote on p. 41. I find this explanation uncon-

vincing and strained, although I sympathize with Trible's effort to offer an alternate reading to the patriarchal one.

4. The modern and generally accepted interpretation is that both versions were written independently one of the other and that both derive from a body of much older traditions. See E. A. Speiser, *Genesis,* pp. 8–11; Nahum M. Sarna, *Understanding Genesis,* pp. 1–16.

5. For the latest feminist version of this argument see Maryanne Cline Horowitz "The Image of God in Man—Is Woman Included?" *Harvard Theological Review,* vol. 72, nos. 3–4 (July–Oct. 1979), 175–206.

6. John Calvin, *Commentaries on the First Book of Moses called Genesis* (trans. Rev. John King) (Grand Rapids, Mich., 1948), vol. I, p. 129.

7. *Ibid.,* pp. 132–33.

8. Rachel Speght, *A Mouzell for Melastomus, the Cynical Bayter and foule-mouthed Barker against Evah's Sex* (London, 1617).

9. Sarah M. Grimké, *Letters on the Equality of the Sexes and the Condition of Woman* (Boston, 1838), p. 5.

10. Phyllis Trible, "Depatriarchalizing," pp. 31, 42.

11. *Ibid.,* pp. 36–37.

12. Phyllis Bird, "Images of Women in the Old Testament," in Rosemary Radford Ruether (ed.), *Religion and Sexism* (New York, 1974), p. 72.

13. R. David Freedman, "Woman, a Power Equal to Man: Translation of Woman as a 'Fit Helpmate' for Man Is Questioned," *Biblical Archaeologist,* vol. 9, no. 1 (Jan./Feb. 1983), 56–58.

14. Stephen Langdon, *The Sumerian Epic of Paradise, the Flood and the Fall of Man,* University of Pennsylvania, University Museum Publications of the Babylonian Section, vol. 10, no. 1 (Philadelphia, 1915), pp. 36–37. I. M. Kikawada draws an interesting parallel between the name of Eve, "mother of all living" and the attribute "mistress of all the gods" given to the Creator-Goddess, Mami, in the Babylonian Atrahasis epic. See I. M. Kikawada, "Two Notes on Eve," *Journal of Biblical Literature,* vol. 19 (1972), p. 34.

15. Maryanne Cline Horowitz, agreeing with Phyllis Trible's interpretation, argues strongly that the concept "image of God in man and woman" invites "us to transcend both the masculine and the feminine metaphors for God which abound in the Bible and to transcend our historical selves and social institutions in recognition of the Holy One." Horowitz, "Image of God," p.175. I agree that the text is ambiguous enough to "open up" the possibility of a less "misogynist" interpretation, but I believe the overwhelming weight of the gender symbols in the Bible falls on the side of patriarchal interpretations and, as noted above, it is these which have prevailed for over 2000 years.

16. David Bakan, *And They Took Themselves Wives: The Emergence of Patriarchy in Western Civilization* (New York, 1979), pp. 27–28. For a similar psychological explanation of men's need for symbolic authority and dominance, see Mary O'Brien, *The Politics of Reproduction* (Boston, 1981).

17. Bakan, *And They Took Themselves Wives,* p. 28.

18. Von Rad, *Genesis,* pp. 113–16.

19. Speiser, *Anchor Bible,* pp. 44–46.

20. James, *Myth and Ritual,* pp. 154–74.

21. Delbert R. Hillers, *Covenant: The History of a Biblical Idea* (Baltimore, 1969), pp. 66, 74–80.

22. Sarna, *Understanding Genesis*, pp. 122–24.

23. Compare this with the parthenogenetic birth of Athena out of the head of Zeus.

24. See Thorkild Jacobsen, *The Treasures of Darkness: A History of Mesopotamian Religion* (New Haven, 1976), p. 46.

25. For a full and highly illuminating discussion of the covenant, see Hillers, *Covenant, passim*; for reference to the three separate convenants see especially chap. 5. See also G. Mendenhall, "Covenant Forms in Israelite Tradition," *Biblical Archaeologist*, vol. 17 (1954), 50–76.

26. Sarna, *Understanding Genesis*, pp. 131–33; De Vaux, *Ancient Israel*, I, pp. 46–48; Robert Graves and Raphael Patai, *Hebrew Myths: The Book of Genesis* (New York, 1983), p. 240; articles "Circumcision" in *Encyclopedia Judaica*, vol. 5, p. 567, and *The Interpreter's Bible* (New York, 1962), pp. 629–31. Michael V. Fox, "The Sign of the Covenant: Circumcision in the Light of the Priestly 'ôt' Etiologies," *La Revue Biblique*, vol. 81 (1974), 557–96. Fox considers circumcision to be a *cognition* sign, "whose function it is to remind God to keep his promise of posterity." In this regard it is a symbol like the rainbow in the covenant with Noah.

27. Calvin, *Commentaries*, p. 453.

28. This interpretation is supported in the article on circumcision in *The Interpreter's Bible*, p. 630.

29. H. and H. A. Frankfort, "Myth and Reality," in Henri Frankfort, John A. Wilson, Thorkild Jacobsen, William A. Irwin, *The Intellectual Adventure of Ancient Man* (Chicago, 1946), pp. 14–17.

30. James B. Pritchard, *Ancient Near Eastern Texts Relating to the Old Testament* (Princeton, 1950), p. 75, both citations.

31. As cited in Langdon, *The Sumerian Epic*, pp. 44–46. Note the parallel to Adam's "naming" in Genesis.

32. *Ibid.*

33. Anton Moortgat, *Die Kunst des alten Mesopotamien: Sumer und Akkad* (Köln, 1982), Stele of Urnammu, vol. 1, pp. 117, 127, pictures 196, 203; Mari murals are on pp. 121–22.

34. John Gray, *Near Eastern Mythology* (London, 1969), pp. 62–63.

The subject is also treated in G. Widengren, *The King and the Tree of Life in Ancient Near Eastern Religion*, Uppsala Universitets Arsskift, no. 4 (Uppsala, 1951), and in Ilse Seibert, "Hirt-Herde-König," *Deutsche Akademie der Wissenschaften zu Berlin*, Schriften der Sektion für Altertumswissenschaft, no. 53 (Berlin, 1969).

35. André Lemaire, "Who or What Was Yahweh's Asherah?," *Biblical Archaeology Review*, vol. 10, no. 6, (Nov./Dec. 1984), pp. 42–51.

36. There is a vast literature of interpretation of this text, which we cannot hope to render here. Two differing opinions on the subject of the two—or the one—trees are offered in Speiser, *Anchor Bible*, p. 20, who suggests that the original text refered only to the tree of knowledge. He also calls attention to the Gilgamesh passages and Adapa story we have discussed. His analysis supports mine on the sexual connotations of the "knowledge of good and evil."

Sarna, *Understanding Genesis*, pp. 26–28, emphasizes the significance of what he considers a deliberate shift from the tree of life to the tree of knowledge. He sees in it a deliberate dissociation of the Bible from the preoccupation with the quest for immortality in Mesopotamian literature. He thinks the Bible meaning is "Not magic . . . but human action is the key to a meaningful life."

Arthur Ungnad discusses the parallels between the two trees in paradise with the trees at the gate of the palace of the god of heaven in Mesopotamian myth, one, the tree of life, the other, the tree of truth or knowledge. Ungnad explains the ambiguity of the Biblical passage as indicating that the road to the tree of knowledge is by way of the tree of life. When human beings begin to think and reason about life and God, they may next arrogate to themselves the secret of immortality, which is reserved for God. It is to prevent this that Adam and Eve are expelled from paradise. See: Arthur Ungnad, "Die Paradisbäume," *Zeitung der deutschen morgenlaendischen Gesellschaft*, LXXIX, Neue Folge, vol. 4, pp. 111–18.

CHAPTER TEN. SYMBOLS

1. Erich Fromm, *The Heart of Man: Its Genius for Good and Evil* (New York, 1964), pp. 116–17.

2. Ernst Becker, *The Denial of Death* (New York, 1973), p. 26.

3. Fromm, *Heart*, p. 32.

4. For a feminist analysis of the problem, see Evelyn Fox Keller, *Reflections on Gender and Science* (New Haven, 1985).

5. Cf.: A. W. Gomme, "The Position of Women in Athens in the Fifth and Fourth Centuries," *Classical Philology*, vol. 20, no. 1 (Jan. 1925), 1–25; Donald Richter "The Position of Women in Classical Athens," *Classical Journal*, vol. 67, no. 1 (Oct.–Nov. 1971), 1–8. My own generalizations are based on Sarah B. Pomeroy, *Goddesses, Whores, Wives, and Slaves* (New York, 1975), chap. 4; Marylin B. Arthur, "Origins of the Western Attitude Toward Women," in John Peradotto and J. P. Sullivan (eds.), *Women in the Ancient World: The Arethusa Papers* (Albany, 1984), pp. 31–37; Helene P. Foley "The Conception of Women in Athenian Drama," in Helene P. Foley (ed.), *Reflections of Women in Antiquity* (New York, 1981), pp. 127–32; S. C. Humphreys, *The Family, Women and Death: Comparative Studies* (London, 1983), pp. 1–78; Victor Ehrenberg, *From Solon to Sokrates: Greek History and Civilization During the Sixth and Fifth Centuries* B.C. (London, 1973); Victor Ehrenberg, *The People of Aristophanes: A Sociology of Old Attic Comedy* (Oxford, 1951), pp. 192–218; Ivo Bruns, *Frauenemanzipation in Athen, ein Beitrag zur attischen Kulturgeschichte des fünften und vierten Jahrhunderts* (Kiliae, 1900).

6. William H. McNeill,, *The Rise of the West: A History of the Human Community* (Chicago, 1963), Mentor Books edition, both quotes, p. 221.

7. My generalizations on Spartan society are based on McNeill, *Rise of the West*, p. 220; Pomeroy, *Goddesses*, pp. 36–40, and Raphael Sealey, *A History of the Greek City States: 700–338* B.C. (Berkeley, 1976).

8. For a somewhat different interpretation of Hesiod's work and its meaning for women, see Arthur, "Origins," pp. 23–25. For the creation myths, see Robert Graves, *The Greek Myths*, Vol.. I (New York, 1959),, pp. 37–47.

9. Cf: Kate Millet, *Sexual Politics* (Garden City, N.Y., 1969), pp. 111–15; Erich Fromm, "The Theory of Mother Right and Its Relevance for Social Psychology," in Erich Fromm, *The Crisis of Psychoanalysis* (Greenwich, Conn., 1970); reprint of hardcover edition, p. 115. I am indebted for the suggestion of the Aeschylus passage to a lecture by Marylin Arthur, "Greece and Rome: The Origins of the Western Attitude Toward Woman," 1971. This lecture was later developed into the article cited above in fn. 5, but the relevant passages were not included in the article.

10. *The Works of Aristotle,* trans. by J. A. Smith and W. D. Ross (Oxford, 1912), *De Generatione Animalium,* II, 1 (732a, 8–10). Hereafter *G.A.*

11. G.A. I, 20 (728b, 26–27).

12. G.A. I, 20 (729a, 28–34).

13. G.A. II, 5 (741a, 13–16).

14. G.A. I, 21 (729b, 12–21).

15. Maryanne Cline Horowitz, "Aristotle and Woman," *Journal of the History of Biology,* vol. 9, no. 2 (Fall 1976), p. 197.

16. G.A. IV, 3 (767b, 7–9).

17. G.A. II, 3 (737a, 26–31).

18. For a thorough discussion of this topic see Horowitz, "Aristotle and Woman," *passim.*

19. Aristotle, *Politica* (trans. by Benjamin Jowett). In W. D. Ross (ed.), *The Works of Aristotle* (Oxford, 1921) Hereafter *Pol.,* I, 2, 1252a, 32–34.

20. *Ibid.,* 12531, 1–2.

21. *Ibid.,* 1253a, 39–40.

22. *Ibid.,* 1253, 5–7.

23. *Ibid.,* 1254b, 4–6, 12–16.

24. *Ibid.,* 1254b, 24–26; 1255a, 2–5.

25. *Ibid.,* 1260a, 11–13, 24–25.

26. *Ibid.,* 1255b, 4–5.

27. *Ibid.,* 1254b, 25; 21–23 It is worth noting (1260a) that Aristotle grants women, unlike slaves, "deliberative faculty," but states that it is without authority.

28. Plato's *The Republic,* (trans. B. Jowett), (New York: Random House, n.d., paperback ed.), V, 454.

29. *Ibid.,* 466.

30. This cursory discussion in no way does justice to the complexities and possibilities of Plato's work for generating thought on the emancipation of women. The subject deserves to be further explored by specialists. I have based my generalizations on Alban D. Winspear, *The Genesis of Plato's Thought* (New York, 1940), esp. chaps. 10 and 11; Paul Shorey, *What Plato Said* (Chicago, 1933); A. E. Taylor, *Plato: The Man and His Work* (London, 1955); Dorothea Wender, "Plato: Misogynist, Phaedophile, and Feminist," in Peradotto and Sullivan, *Arethusa Papers,* pp. 213–28.

CHAPTER ELEVEN. THE CREATION OF PATRIARCHY

1. Simone de Beauvoir, *The Second Sex* (New York, 1953), introduction, xxii, both quotes. De Beauvoir based this erroneous generalization on the androcentric historical scholarship available to her at the time of the writing of her book, but has to date not corrected it.

2. Sandra M. Gilbert and Susan Gubar, *The Madwoman in the Attic: The Woman Writer and the Nineteenth Century Literary Imagination* (New Haven, 1984)

Bibliography

I. THEORY AND HISTORY

1. *General and History*

Books

Alcott, William. *The Young Woman's Book of Health*. Boston: Tappan, Whittmore & Mason, 1850.

Bachofen, Johann J. *Das Mutterrecht. Eine Untersuchung über die Gynaikokratie der alten Welt nach ihrer religiösen und rechtlichen Natur*. Stuttgart: Krais & Hoffman, 1861.

————. *Myth, Religion and Mother Right: Selected Writings of J. J. Bachofen*. Trans. Ralph Manheim. Princeton: Princeton University Press, 1967. Introduction by Joseph Campbell.

Beard, Mary R. *Woman as Force in History*. New York: Macmillan, 1946.

————. *Women's Work in Municipalities*. New York: Appleton, 1915.

Becker, Ernest. *The Denial of Death*. New York: Macmillan, 1973.

Berkin, Carol Ruth, and Mary Beth Norton (eds.). *Women of America: A History*. Boston: Houghton Mifflin, 1979.

Bleier, Ruth. *Science and Gender: A Critique of Biology and Its Theories on Women*. New York: Pergamon Press, 1984.

Borgese, Elisabeth. *Ascent of Woman*. New York: Braziller, 1963.

Boserup, Esther. *Women's Role in Economic Development*. New York: St. Martin's Press, 1970.

Boulding, Elise. *The Underside of History: A View of Women Through Time*. Boulder, Colo.: Westview Press, 1976.

Bridenthal, Renate, and Claudia Koonz. *Becoming Visible: Women in European History*. Boston: Houghton Mifflin, 1977.

Briffault, Robert. *The Mothers: The Matriarchal Theory of Social Origins*. New York: Macmillan, 1931.

283

Brownmiller, Susan. *Against Our Will: Men, Women, and Rape.* New York: Simon & Schuster, 1975.

Carroll, Berenice. *Liberating Women's History: Theoretical and Critical Essays in Women's History.* Urbana: University of Illinois Press, 1976.

Chodorow, Nancy. *The Reproduction of Mothering: Psychoanalysis and the Sociology of Gender.* Berkeley: University of California Press, 1978.

Cipolla, Carlo M. *The Economic History of World Population.* New York: Penguin, 1962.

Clarke, Edward H. *Sex in Education, or A Fair Chance for Girls.* Boston, 1878.

Davis, Elizabeth Gould. *The First Sex.* New York: Putnam, 1971.

De Beauvoir, Simone. *The Second Sex.* New York: Knopf, 1953; rpt. New York: Vintage Books, 1974.

Deutsch, Helene. *The Psychology of Women, a Psychoanalytic Interpretation.* 2 vols. New York: Grune & Stratton, 1944–45 [1962–63].

Diner, Helen. *Mothers and Amazons: The First Feminine History of Culture.* New York: Julian Press, 1965.

Dinnerstein, Dorothy. *The Mermaid and the Minotaur: Sexual Arrangments and Human Malaise.* New York: Harper & Row, 1977.

DuBois, Ellen (ed.). *Elizabeth Cady Stanton and Susan B. Anthony, Correspondence, Writings, Speeches.* New York: Schocken, 1981.

Eisenstein, Zillah, R., (ed.). *Capitalist Patriarchy and the Case for Socialist Feminism.* New York: Monthly Review, 1979.

Elshtain, Jean Bethke. *Public Man, Private Woman: Women in Social and Political Thought.* Princeton: Princeton University Press, 1981.

Engels, Frederick. *The Origin of the Family, Private Property and the State.* Ed. Eleanor Leacock. New York: International Publishers, 1972. The text of this edition is essentially the English translation by Alex West as published in 1942, but it has been revised against the German text as it appears in K. Marx and F. Engels, *Werke,* vol. 21 (Berlin: Dietz Verlag, 1962).

Erikson, Erik. *Childhood and Society.* New York: W. W. Norton, 1950. First edition.

Figes, Eva. *Patriarchal Attitudes.* New York: Stein and Day, 1970.

Firestone, Shulamith. *The Dialectic of Sex: The Case for Feminist Revolution.* New York: Bantam Books, 1970.

Fisher, Elizabeth. *Woman's Creation: Sexual Evolution and the Shaping of Society.* Garden City, N.Y.: Doubleday, 1979.

Foreman, Ann. *Femininity as Alienation: Women and the Family in Marxism and Pyschoanalysis.* London: Pluto Press, 1977.

Freud, Sigmund. *Civilization and Its Discontent.* Newly trans. and ed. by James Strachey. New York: W. W. Norton, 1961, 1962.

———. "Moses and Monotheism: Three Essays." In *Complete Psychological Works.* Vøl. 23. London: Hogarth Press, 1963–64.

———. *The Standard Edition of the Complete Psychological Works of Sigmund Freud.* Vols. 19 and 21. London: 1961 and 1964.

Fromm, Erich. *The Crisis of Psychoanalysis.* Greenwich, Conn.: Fawcett, 1970.

———. *The Forgotten Language: An Introduction to the Understanding of Dreams, Fairy Tales, and Myths.* New York: Rinehart, 1951.

———. *The Heart of Man: Its Genius for Good and Evil.* New York: Harper & Row, 1964.

Gage, Matilda Joslyn. *Women, Church and State*. Perspective Press, 1980. Reprint of 1893 ed.

Geertz, Clifford. *The Interpretation of Cultures*. New York: Basic Books, 1973.

Gilbert, Sandra M., and Susan Gubar. *The Madwoman in the Attic: The Woman Writer and the Nineteenth-Century Literary Imagination*. New Haven: Yale University Press, 1984.

Gilligan, Carol. *In a Different Voice: Psychological Theory and Women's Development*. Cambridge: Harvard University Press, 1982.

Gilman, Charlotte Perkins. *Women and Economics*. New York: Harper & Row, 1966. Reprint of 1898 ed.

Gimbutas, Marija. *Goddesses and Gods of Old Europe*. Berkeley: University of California Press, 1982.

Griffin, Susan. *Woman and Nature: The Roaring Inside Her*. New York: Harper & Row, 1978.

Hartman, Mary S., and Lois Banner (eds.). *Clio's Consciousness Raised: New Perspectives on the History of Women*. New York: Harper & Row, 1974.

Hays, Hoffman Reynolds. *The Dangerous Sex*. New York: Putnam, 1964.

Heilbrun. Carolyn G. *Toward a Recognition of Androgyny*. New York: Harper & Row, 1973.

Horney, Karen. *Feminine Psychology*. New York: W. W. Norton, 1967.

Jaggar, Alison M. *Feminist Politics and Human Nature*. Sussex, Eng.: Rowman & Allanheld, 1983.

Janeway, Elizabeth. *Man's World, Woman's Place: A Study in Social Mythology*. New York: Morrow, 1971.

——. *Powers of the Weak*. New York: Knopf, 1980.

Janssen-Jurreit, Marielouise. *Seximus: Über die Abtreibung der Frauenfrage*. München: Fischer, 1979.

——. *Sexism: The Male Monopoly on History and Thought*. New York: Farrar, Straus and Giroux, 1980.

Keller, Evelyn Fox. *Reflections on Gender and Science*. New Haven: Yale University Press, 1985.

Keohane, Nannerl O., Michelle Z. Rosaldo, and Barbara Gelpi (eds.). *Feminist Theory: A Critique of Ideology*. Chicago: University of Chicago Press, 1982.

Kerber, Linda. *Women of the Republic: Intellect and Ideology in Revolutionary America*. Chapel Hill: University of North Carolina Press, 1980.

Klein, Viola. *The Feminine Character: History of an Ideology*. Urbana: University of Illinois Press, 1972. Reprint of 1946 ed.

Kleinbaum, Abby Wettan. *The War Against the Amazons*. New York: McGraw-Hill, 1983.

La Follette, Suzanne. *Concerning Women*. New York: Boni & Liveright, 1926.

Lakoff, Robin. *Language and Woman's Place*. New York: Harper & Row, 1975.

Lundberg, Ferdinand, and Marynia Farnham. *Modern Woman: The Lost Sex*. New York: Harper & Bros., 1947.

Memmi, Albert. *Dominated Man: Notes Towards a Portrait*. Boston: Beacon Press, 1968.

Miller, Casey, and Kate Swift. *Words and Women*. Garden City, N.Y.: Doubleday, 1977.

Miller, Jean Baker (ed.). *Psychoanalysis and Women*. Harmondsworth, Eng.: Penguin Books, 1947.

———. *Toward a New Psychology of Women*. Boston: Beacon Press, 1976.

Millett, Kate. *Sexual Politics*. Garden City, N.Y.: Doubleday, 1969.

Mitchell, Juliet. *Woman's Estate*. New York: Random House, 1971.

Morgan, Robin (ed.). *Sisterhood Is Powerful: An Anthology of Writings from the Women's Liberation Movement*. New York: Vintage Books, 1970.

———. *The Anatomy of Freedom: Feminism, Physics and Global Politics*. Garden City, N.Y.: Doubleday, 1982.

Neuman, Erich. *The Great Mother: An Analysis of the Archetype*. Princeton: Princeton University Press, 1963.

Norton, Mary Beth. *Liberty's Daughters: The Revolutionary Experience of American Women, 1750–1800*. Boston: Little, Brown, 1980.

O'Brien, Mary. *The Politics of Reproduction*. Boston: Routledge & Kegan Paul, 1981.

Reed, Evelyn. *Woman's Evolution: From Matriarchal Clan to Patriarchal Family*. New York: Pathfinder, 1975.

Rich, Adrienne. *On Lies, Secrets, and Silences: Selected Prose, 1966–1978*. New York: W. W. Norton, 1979.

———. *Of Woman Born: Motherhood as Experience and Institution*. New York: W. W. Norton, 1976.

Rowbotham, Sheila. *Woman's Consciousness, Man's World*. New York: Penguin, 1973.

Schur, Edwin M. *Labeling Women Deviant: Gender, Stigma, and Social Control*. New York: Random House, 1984.

Sherfey, Mary Jane. *The Nature and Evolution of Female Sexuality*. New York: Random House, 1966.

Sullivan, Harry Stack. *The Interpersonal Theory of Psychiatry*. New York: W. W. Norton, 1953.

Swerdlow, Amy, and Hanna Lessinger (eds.). *Class, Race and Sex: The Dynamics of Control*. Boston: G. K. Hall, 1983.

Thompson, Clara. *On Women*. New York: New American Library, 1964.

Thompson, William Irwin. *The Time Falling Bodies Take To Light: Mythology, Sexuality and the Origins of Culture*. New York: St. Martin's Press, 1981.

Vaerting, M. and M. *The Dominant Sex*. London: Allen and Unwin, 1923.

Veblen, Thorstein. *The Theory of the Leisure Class (1899)*. New York: Mentor Books, 1962.

Weinbaum, Batya. *The Curious Courtship of Women's Liberation and Socialism*. Boston: South End Press, 1978.

Wilson, E. O. *Sociobiology: The New Synthesis*. Cambridge, Mass.: Belknap Press, 1975.

Woolf, Virginia. *A Room of One's Own*. New York: Harcourt Brace Jovanovich, 1929.

Articles

Boulding, Elise. "Public Nurturance and the Man on Horseback." In Meg Murray (ed.). *Fathers, Mothers, Masters, Monsters: Essays for a Non-Sexist Future*, Westport, Conn.: Westview Press, 1983, pp. 273–91.

———. "Women and Social Violence." *International Social Science Journal*, vol. 30, no. 4 (1978), 801–15.

Catalyst. Special Issue on "Feminist Thought." nos. 10–11 (Summer 1977).

Heilbrun, Carolyn. "On Reinventing Womanhood." *Columbia* (Fall 1979), 31–32.

Jones, Ernest. "Early Development of Female Sexuality." *International Journal of Psychoanalysis*, vol. 8 (1927), 459–72.

Kelly-Gadol, Joan. "The Social Relations of the Sexes: Methodological Implications of Woman's History." *SIGNS*, vol. 1, no. 4 (Summer 1976), 809–24.

Nochlin, Linda. "Why Have There Been No Great Women Artists?" *Art News*, vol. 69, no. 9 (Jan. 1971), 24–39.

Parlee, Mary Brown. Review Essay: "Psychology." *SIGNS*, vol. 1, no. 1 (Autumn 1975), 119–38.

Rossi, Alice S. "A Biosocial Perspective on Parenting." *Daedalus*, vol. 106, no. 2 (Spring 1977), 1–31.

Silverblatt, Irene. "Andean Women in the Inca Empire." *Feminist Studies*, vol. 4, no. 3 (Oct. 1978), 37–61.

Stern, Bernard J. "Women, Position of in Historical Society." In *Encyclopedia of Social Sciences*, Edwin R. Seligman (ed.), vol. 15. New York: Macmillan, 1935, pp. 442–46.

Tillion, Germaine. "Prehistoric Origins of the Condition of Women in 'Civilized' Societies," *International Social Science Journal*, vol. 69, no. 4 (1977), 671–81.

Vaughter, Reesa M. Review Essay: "Psychology." *SIGNS*, vol. 2, no. 1 (Autumn 1976), 120–46.

2. *Anthropology*

Books

Ardrey, Robert. *The Territorial Imperative: A Personal Inquiry into the Animal Origins of Property and Nations.* New York: Atheneum, 1966.

Childe, V. Gordon. *Man Makes Himself.* London: Watts, 1936.

Farb, Peter. *Humankind.* Boston: Houghton Mifflin, 1977.

Friedl, Ernestine. *Women and Men: An Anthropologist's View.* New York: Holt, Rinehart & Winston, 1975.

Goody, Jack. *Production and Reproduction: A Comparative Study of the Domestic Domain.* London: Cambridge University Press, 1976.

Hrdy, Sarah Blaffer. *The Woman That Never Evolved.* Cambridge: Harvard University Press, 1981.

Jolly, Alison. *The Evolution of Primate Behavior.* New York: Macmillan, 1972.

Lee, R. B., and Irven DeVore (eds.). *Man, the Hunter.* Chicago: Aldine, 1968.

Leith-Ross, Sylvia. *African Women: A Study of the Ibo of Nigeria.* London: Routledge, 1937.

Lévi-Strauss, Claude. *The Elementary Structures of Kinship.* Boston: Beacon Press, 1969.

Marshak, Alexander. *The Roots of Civilization: The Cognitive Beginnings of Man's First Art, Symbol and Notation.* New York: McGraw-Hill, 1971.

Martin, M. Kay, and Barbara Voorhies. *Female of the Species.* New York: Columbia University Press, 1975.

Matthiasson, Carolyn J. *Many Sisters: Women in Cross-Cultural Perspective.* New York: Macmillan, 1974.

Mauss, Marcel. *The Gift: Forms and Functions of Exchange in Archaic Societies.* London: Cohen & West Ltd., 1954.

Mead, Margaret. *Male and Female: A Study of the Sexes in a Changing World*. New York: Morrow, 1949.

———. *Sex and Temperament in Three Primitive Societies*. New York: Laurel, 1971.

Morgan, Elaine. *The Descent of Woman*. New York: Stein and Day, 1972.

Morgan, Lewis Henry. *Ancient Society*. New York: World, 1963. Reprint of 1877 ed.

Murdock, George P. *Our Primitive Contemporaries*. New York: Macmillan, 1934.

Ortner, Sherry B., and Harriet Whitehead (eds.). *Sexual Meanings: The Cultural Construction of Gender and Sexuality*. New York: Cambridge University Press, 1981.

Reiter, Rayna Rapp. *Toward an Anthropology of Women*. New York: Monthly Review, 1978.

Rohrlich-Leavitt, Ruby (ed.). *Women Cross-Culturally: Change and Challenge*. Chicago: Aldine, 1975.

Rosaldo, Michelle, and Louise Lamphere. *Women, Culture & Society*. Stanford: Stanford University Press, 1974.

Sacks, Karen. *Sisters and Wives: The Past and Future of Sexual Equality*. Urbana: University of Illinois Press, 1982.

Sanday, Peggy Reeves. *Female Power and Male Dominance: On the Origins of Sexual Inequality*. Cambridge: Cambridge University Press, 1981.

Schneider, David M., and Kathleen Gough (eds.). *Matrilinial Kinship*. Berkeley: University of California Press, 1962.

Tanner, Nancy Makepeace. *On Becoming Human*. Cambridge: Cambridge University Press, 1981.

Tiger, L. *Men in Groups*. New York: Random House, 1969.

Articles

Aaby, Peter. "Engels and Women." *Critique of Anthropology*, vol. 3, nos. 9–10, (1977), 25–53.

Harris, Marvin. "Why Men Dominate Women." *Columbia*, vol. 21 (Summer 1978), 9–13, 39.

Lamphere, Louise. Review Essay: "Anthropology." *SIGNS*, vol. 2, no. 3 (1977), 612–27.

Lee, Richard B. "What Hunters Do for a Living, or, How To Make Out on Scarce Resources." In *Man the Hunter*, eds. R. B. Lee and Irven DeVore. Chicago: Aldine, 1968, 30–48.

Meillassoux, Claude. "From Reproduction to Production: A Marxist Approach to Economic Anthropology." *Economy and Society*, no. 1 (1972), 93–105.

———. "The Social Organisation of the Peasantry: The Economic Basis of Kinship." *Journal of Peasant Studies*, vol. 1, no. 1 (1973).

Molyneux, Maxine. "Androcentrism in Marxist Anthropology." *Critique of Anthropology*, vol. 3, nos. 9–10 (1977), 55–81.

Moore, John. "The Exploitation of Women in Evolutionary Perspective." *Critique of Anthropology*, vol. 3, nos. 9–10 (1977), 83–100.

Murdock, George P. "Comparative Data on the Division of Labor by Sex." *Social Forces*, vol. 15, nos. 1–4 (May 1937), 551–53.

Ortner, Sherry B. "The Virgin and the State." *Feminist Studies*, vol. 4, no. 3 (Oct. 1978), 19–35.

Rapp, Rayna. "Review of Claude Meillassoux, 'Femmes, Greniers et Capitaux.' " *Dialectical Anthropology*, vol. 3 (1977), 317–23.

Reiter, Rayna Rapp. "The Search for Origins: Unravelling the Threads of Gender Hierarchy." *Critique of Anthropology*, vol. 2, nos. 9–10 (1977), 5–24.

Rosaldo, M. Z. "The Use and Abuse of Anthropology: Reflections on Feminism and Cross-Cultural Understanding." *SIGNS*, vol. 5, no. 3 (Spring 1980), 389–417.

Safa, H., and E. Leacock (eds.). "Development and the Sexual Division of Labor." Special Issue, *SIGNS*, vol. 7, no. 2 (Winter 1981).

Sahlins, Marshall. "The Origins of Society." *Scientific American*, vol. 203, no. 48 (Sept. 1960), 76–87.

Silverblatt, Irene. "Andean Women in the Inca Empire." *Feminist Studies*, vol. 4, no. 3 (Oct. 1978), 37–61.

Stack, Carol, *et al.* Review Essay: "Anthropology." *SIGNS*, vol. 1, no. 1 (Autumn 1975), 147–60.

Tanner, Nancy, and Adrienne Zihlman, "Women in Evolution, Part I: Innovation and Section in Human Origins." *SIGNS*, vol. 1, no. 3 (Spring 1976), Part 1, pp. 585–608.

Tiffany, Sharon. "The Power of Matriarchal Ideas." *International Journal of Women's Studies*, vol. 5, no. 2 (1982), 138–47.

————. "Women, Power, and the Anthropology of Politics: A Review." *International Journal of Women's Studies*, vol. 2, no. 5 (1979), 430–42.

Wolf, Eric. "They Divide and Subdivide, and Call it Anthropology." *New York Times* (Nov. 30, 1980), sect. 4, p. 9.

II   THE ANCIENT NEAR EAST

1. *Primary Sources*

Books

The Code of Hammurabi in the following editions:

Driver, G. R., and John C. Miles. *The Babylonian Laws*. 2 vols. Oxford: Clarendon Press. vol. I, 1952; vol. II, 1955.

Kohler, J., and F. E. Peiser, *Hammurabi's Gesetz: Übersetzung, Juristische Wiedergabe, Erläuterung*. Leipzig: Pfeiffer, 1904.

Meek, Theophile J. Trans. In James B. Pritchard, 1955.

Mueller, David. *Die Gesetze Hammurabis und ihr Verhältnis zur mosaischen Gesetzgebung*. Wien: A. Holder, 1903.

The Hittite laws in the following editions:

Friedrich, Johannes. *Die Hethitischen Gesetze*. Leiden: E. J. Brill, 1959.

Goetze, Albrecht. Trans. In Pritchard, 1955.

Walther, Arnold. "The Hittite Code." In J. M. Powis Smith, 1931.

The Middle Assyrian laws in the following editions:

Driver, G. R., and John C. Miles. *The Assyrian Laws*. Oxford: Clarendon Press, 1935.

Luckenbill, Daniel D., and F. W. Geers. Trans. In J. M. Powis Smith, *The Origin and History of Hebrew Law*. Chicago: University of Chicago Press, 1931.

Meek, Theophile. Trans. In James B. Pritchard, 1955.

Falkenstein, Adam. *Archaische Texte aus Uruk.* (Ausgrabungen der Deutschen For-
    schung in Uruk-Warka). Vol. 2, no. 111, Berlin, 1936.
———. "Neusumerische Gerichtsurkunden," *Bayerische Akademie der Wissenschaften,*
    Phil.-historische Abteilung, Neue Folge, Heft 39, 40, 44.
———. *Sumerische Götterlieder.* Heidelberg: (Winter 1959).
Pritchard, James B. *Ancient Near Eastern Texts Relating to the Old Testament.* Prince-
    ton: Princeton University Press, 1950.
———. *Ancient Near Eastern Texts Relating to the Old Testament.* 2nd ed. Trans. and
    annotators W. F. Albright and others. Princeton: Princeton University Press, 1955.
———. *The Ancient Near East: Supplementary Texts and Pictures Relating to the Old*
    Testament. Princeton: Princeton University Press, 1969.
Roemer, W. H. *Frauenbriefe über Religion, Politik und Privatleben in Mari.* Untersu-
    chungen zu G. Dossin, Archives Royales de Mari X, Paris, 1967. Neukirchen-
    Venuyn: Butzon & Bercker Kevelaer, 1971.
Singh, Purushottam. *Neolithic Cultures of Western Asia.* London: Seminar Press, 1974.
Steible, H. *Altsumerische Bau- und Weihinschriften.* 2 vols. Wiesbaden: Franz Steiner,
    1982.
Wolkenstein, Diane, and Samuel Noah Kramer. *Inanna: Queen of Heaven and Earth:*
    Her Stories and Hymns from Sumer. New York: Harper & Row, 1983.
Zimmern, Heinrich. "Babylonische Hymnen und Gebete in Auswahl." *Der alte Orient.*
    7 Jahrgang, Heft 3, pp. 1–32. Leipzig: J. C. Hinrichs, 1905.

Articles

Angel, Lawrence. "Neolithic Skeletons from Čatal Hüyük." *Anatolian Studies,* vol. 21
    (1971), 77–98.
Dietz, Otto Edzard. "Sumerische Rechtsurkunden des 3. Jahrtausends, aus der Zeit vor
    der III. Dynastie von Ur." *Bayerische Akademie der Wissenschaften, Phil.-Hist.*
    Klasse, Abhandlungen, Neue Folge, Heft 67. München, Verlag der Bayerischen
    Akademie der Wissenschaften, 1968.
Ebeling, Erich. "Quellen zur Kenntnis der babylonischen Religion." *Mitteilungen der*
    vorderasiatischen Gesellschaft (E. V.), 1918, I, 23. Jahrgang. Leipzig: J. C. Hin-
    richs, 1918, pp. 1–70.
Parker B. "The Nimrud Tablets, 1952—Business Documents." *Iraq,* vol. 16 (1954), 29–
    58.

Reports

Mellaart, James. "Excavations at Čatal Hüyük: 1963, Third Preliminary Report." *Ana-*
    tolian Studies, vol. 14 (1964), 39–120.
———. "Excavations at Čatal Hüyük: 1965, Fourth Preliminary Report." *Anatolian*
    Studies, vol. 16 (1966), 165–192.

2. Reference Works

Books

The Assyrian Dictionary of the Oriental Institute of the University of Chicago. Chicago:
    Oriental Institute; and Glückstadt: J. J. Augustin, 1968.

Cotterell, Arthur. *The Encyclopedia of Ancient Civilizations*. New York: Mayflower Books, 1980.

Ebeling, Erich, and Bruno Meissner. *Reallexicon der Assyriologie*. 6 vols. Berlin & Leipzig: De Gruyter, 1932.

Ebert, Max. *Reallexicon der Vorgeschichte*. vol. 4, (erste Hälfte). Berlin: De Gruyter, 1926.

Edwards, I. E. S. *et al* (eds.). *The Cambridge Ancient History*. vol. 1, pt. 1: *Prolegomena and Prehistory*. 3rd ed. Cambridge, 1970.

———. vol. 1, pt. 2: *Early History of the Middle East*. 1971.

———. vol. 2, pt. 1: *The Middle East and the Aegean Region, c. 1800–1380 B.C.* 1973.

———. vol. 2, pt. 2: *The Middle East and the Aegean Region, c. 1380–1000 B.C.*, 1975.

Landsberger, Benno, E. Reiner, and M. Civil. (eds.). *Materials for the Sumerian Lexicon (MSL)*. vol. 12. Rome: Pontifical Bibilical Institute, 1969.

3. Secondary Works

Books

Adams, Robert McCormick. *The Evolution of Urban Society*. Chicago: Aldine, 1966.

———. *Heartland of the Cities: Surveys of Ancient Settlement and Land Use on the Central Flood Plain of the Euphrates*. Chicago: University of Chicago Press, 1981.

Andrae, Walter. *Die archaischen Ishtar-Tempel in Assur*. Wissenschaftliche Veröffentlichungen der deutschen Orientgesellschaft. No. 39, Leipzig, 1922.

Batto, Bernard Frank. *Studies on Women at Mari*. Baltimore: Johns Hopkins University Press, 1974.

Bin-Nun, Shoshana R. *The Tawananna in the Hittite Kingdom*. Heidelberg: Carl Winter, 1975.

Bottero, Jean, Elena Cassin, and Jean Vercoutter (eds.). *Near East: The Early Civilizations*. London: Weidenfeld and Nicolson, 1967.

Chiera, Edward. *They Wrote on Clay*. Chicago: University of Chicago Press, 1938.

Contenau, Georges. *Everyday Life in Babylon and Assyria*. London: Edward Arnold Ltd., 1954.

Darlington, C. D. *The Evolution of Man and Society*. New York: Simon & Schuster, 1969.

Deetz, James. *Invitation to Archaeology*. Garden City, N.Y.: Natural History Press, 1967.

Deimel, P. Anton. *Sumerische Tempelwirtschaft zur Zeit Urukaginas und seiner Vorgänger*. Roma: Pontificio Instituto Biblico, 1931.

Diakonoff, I. M. (ed.). *Ancient Mesopotamia: Socio-economic History, A Collection of Studies by Soviet Scholars*. Moscow: Nauka Publishing House, 1969.

Driver, G. R. *Canaanite Myths and Legends*. Edinburgh: T & T Clark, 1956.

Frankfort, Henri, *et al*. *Before Philosophy*, Baltimore: Penguin Books, 1963.

Frankfort, Henri, John A. Wilson, Thorkild Jacobsen, and William A. Irwin. *The Intellectual Adventure of Ancient Man: An Essay on Speculative Thought in the Ancient Near East*. Chicago: University of Chicago Press, 1946.

Gadd, C. J. *Teachers and Students in the Oldest Schools*. London, 1956.

Glubok, Shirley, (ed.). *Discovering the Royal Tombs at Ur*. London: Macmillan, 1969.

Hallo, William W., and J. J. A. van Dijk. *The Exaltation of Inanna*. New Haven: Yale University Press, 1968.

Harris, Rivkah. *Ancient Sippar: A Demographic Study of an Old Babylonian City (1894–1595 B.C.).* Istanbul: Historisch-Archeologisch Instituut, 1975.

Hawkes, Jacquetta, and Sir Leonard Woolley. *History of Mankind.* Vol. I, *Prehistory and the Beginnings of Civilization.* New York: Harper & Row, 1963.

Jacobsen, Thorkild. *The Treasures of Darkness: A History of Mesopotamian Religion.* New Haven: Yale University Press, 1976.

———. *Toward the Image of Tammuz and Other Essays on Mesopotamian History and Culture.* Ed. William L. Moran. Cambridge: Harvard University Press, 1970.

James, Edwin O. *The Cult of the Mother-Goddess: An Archaeological and Documentary Study.* London: Thames & Hudson, 1959.

———. *Myth and Ritual in the Ancient Near East.* London: Thames & Hudson, 1958.

Jastrow, Morris. *The Civilization of Babylon and Assyria.* Philadelphia: Lippincott, 1915.

Jayne, Walter A., M.D. *The Healing Gods of Ancient Civilizations,* New Haven: Yale University Press, 1925.

Jeremias, Alfred. *Handbuch der altorientalischen Geisteskultur.* Berlin: De Gruyter, 1929.

Koschaker, Paul. *Quellenkritische Untersuchungen zu den altassyrischen Gesetzen.* Leipzig: J. C. Hinrich, 1921.

———. *Rechtsvergleichende Studien zur Gesetzgebung Hammurapis, Königs von Babylon.* Leipzig: Veit & Co., 1917.

Kraeling, Carl H., and Robert McC. Adams. *City Invincible: A Symposium on Urbanization and Cultural Development in the Ancient Near East.* Chicago: University of Chicago Press, 1960.

Kramer, Samuel Noah. *From the Tablets of Sumer.* Indian Hills, Colo.: Falcon Wing Press, 1956.

———. *History Begins at Sumer.* 3rd rev. ed. Philadelphia: University of Pennsylvania Press, 1981.

———. *The Sacred Marriage Rite: Aspects of Faith, Myth and Ritual in Ancient Sumer.* Bloomington: Indiana University Press, 1969.

———. *Sumerian Mythology: A Study of Spiritual and Literary Achievement in the Third Millennium B.C.* Rev. ed. New York: Harper & Bros., 1961.

———. *The Sumerians.* Chicago: University of Chicago Press, 1963.

Langdon, Stephen. *Sumerian Epic of Paradise, the Flood and the Fall of Man.* Philadelphia: University Museum, 1915.

Lansing, Elizabeth. *The Sumerians: Inventors & Builders.* London: Cassell, 1974.

Lesko, Barbara S. *The Remarkable Women of Egypt.* Berkeley: B. C. Scribe Publications, 1978.

MacQueen, James G. *Babylon,* London: Robert Hale Ltd., 1964.

Matthiae, Paolo. *Ebla: An Empire Rediscovered.* Garden City, N.Y.: Doubleday, 1981.

Meissner, Bruno. *Babylonien & Assyrien.* 2 vols. Heidelberg: Carl Winter, 1920.

Mellaart, James. *Çatal Hüyük: A Neolithic Town in Anatolia.* New York: McGraw-Hill, 1967.

———. *Earliest Civilizations of the Near East.* New York: McGraw-Hill, 1965.

Messerschmidt, Leopold. *Die Hettiter.* Leipzig: J. C. Hinrich, 1902.

Ministry of Information, Government of Iran. *Persepolis, Pasargadae, and Naghsh-e-Rustam.* Teheran: Offset Press, 1966.

Moorey, P. R. S. *Ur of the Chaldees: A Revised and Updated Version of Sir Leonard Woolley's Excavations at Ur.* Ithaca, N.Y.: Cornell University Press, 1982.

Murray, Margaret Alice. *The Genesis of Religion.* London: Routledge & Kegan Paul, 1963.

Oppenheim, A. Leo. *Ancient Mesopotamia: Portrait of a Dead Civilization.* Chicago: University of Chicago Press, 1964.

Redman, Charles. *The Rise of Civilization: From Early Farmers to Urban Society in the Ancient Near East.* San Francisco: W. H. Freeman, 1978.

Saggs, H. W. F. *The Greatness That Was Babylon.* London: Sidgewick and Jackson, 1962.

Schmandt-Besserat, Denise, (ed.). *The Legacy of Sumer; Invited Lectures on the Middle East at the University of Texas at Austin.* Malibu, Calif.: Undena Publications, 1976.

Schmandt-Besserat, Denise, and S. M. Alexander. *The First Civilization: The Legacy of Sumer.* Austin: University of Texas Press, 1975.

Schreier, Josephine. *Göttinnen: Ihr Einfluss von der Urzeit bis zur Gegenwart.* München: C. Verlag Frauenoffensive, 1977.

Service, Elman, *Origins of the State and Civilization: The Process of Cultural Evolution.* New York: W. W. Norton, 1975.

Todd, Ian, *Čatal Hüyük in Perspective.* Menlo Park: Cummings Publishing Co., 1976.

Welskopf, Elizabeth. *Die Produktionsverhältnisse im alten Orient und in der grieschisch-römischen Antike.* Berlin: Deutsche Akademie der Wissenschaften, 1957.

Widengren, G. *The King and the Tree of Life in Ancient Near Eastern Religion.* Uppsala Universitets Arsskrift, no. 4, 1951.

Winckler, Hugo. *Himmels-und Weltenbild der Babylonier.* Leipzig: J. C. Hinrich, 1901.

Woolley, C. Leonard. *The Sumerians.* Oxford: Clarendon Press, 1928.

Woolley, Sir Charles Leonard. *Excavations at Ur: A Record of Twelve Years' Work.* London: Ernest Benn Ltd., 1954.

Articles

Albenda, Pauline. "Western Asiatic Women in the Stone Age: Their Image Revealed." *Biblical Archaeologist,* vol. 46, no. 2 (Spring 1983), 82–88.

Barstow, Anne. "The Uses of Archeology for Women's History: James Mellaart's Work on the Neolithic Goddess at Čatal Hüyük." *Feminist Studies,* vol. 4, no. 3 (Oct. 1978), 7–18.

Bottero, Jean. "La Femme dans la Mesopotamie ancienne." chap. 1, In *Historie mondiale de la femme,* Ed. Pierre Grimal. Paris: Nouvelle Librarie de France, 1965.

Carneiro, Robert. "A Theory of the Origin of the State." *Science,* vol. 169, no. 3947 (Aug. 1970), 733–35.

Cassin, Elena. "Pouvoirs de la femme et structures familiales." *Revue d'Assyriologie et d'Archéologie Orientale,* vol. 63, no. 2 (1969), 121–48.

Diakonoff, Igor M. "Socio-economic Classes in Babylonia and the Babylonian Concept of Social Stratification." In Dietz, Otto Edzard, *Gesellschaftsklassen im alten Zweistromland und in den angrenzenden Gebieten*—XVIII Recontre Assyriologique Internationale, München, 29 Juni bis 3 Juli 1970. München, Bayerische Akademie der Wissenschaften, Philosophisch-Historische Klasse, Abhandlungen, Neue Folge, Heft 75, 1972.

Diamond, A.S., "An Eye for an Eye." *Iraq,* vol. 19, pt. 2 (Autumn 1957), 151–55.

Dougherty, Raymond Philip. "The Shirkutu of Babylonian Deities." *Yale Oriental Series,* vol. 5, pt. 2. New Haven: Yale University Press, 1923.

Durand, Jean-Marie. "Trois Etudes sur Mari." *Mari: Annales de Recherches Interdisciplinaires,* vol. 3 (1904), 127–72.

Ebeling, Erich. "Quellen zur Kenntnis der babylonischen Religion." *Mitteilungen der vorderasiatischen Gesellschaft* (E. V.), 1918, I, 23 Jahrgang. Leipzig: J. C. Hinrichs, 1918, pp. 1–70.

Finkelstein, J. J. "Sex Offenses in Babylonian Laws." *Journal of the American Oriental Society*, vol. 86 (1966), 355–372.

––––––. "Subartu and Subarians in Old Babylonian Sources." *Journal of Cuneiform Studies*, vol. 9 (1955), 1–7.

Fried, Morton. "On the Evolution of Social Stratification and the State." In Stanley Diamond (ed.). *Culture and History*. New York: Columbia University Press, 1960.

Gadd, C. J. "Some Contributions to the Gilgamesh Epic." *Iraq*, vol. 28, pt. 2 (Autumn 1966), 105–21.

Gordon, Cyrus H. "The Status of Women Reflected in the Nuzi Tablets." *Zeitschrift für Assyriologie*, Neue Folge, Band IX (1936), 147–69.

Greengus, Samuel. "The Old Babylonian Marriage Contract." *Journal of the American Oriental Society*, vol. 89 (1969), 505–32.

Grosz, K. "Dowry and Bride Price in Nuzi." In *Studies on the Civilization and Culture of Nuzi and the Hurrians*. Ed. David I. Owen and Martha A. Morrison. Winona Lake, Ind: Eisenbrauns, 1981, pp. 161–82.

Harris, Rivkah. "Biographical Notes on the *Naditu* Women of Sippur." *Journal of Cuneiform Studies*, vol. 16 (1962), 1–12.

Jacobsen, Thorkild. "Primitive Democracy in Ancient Mesopotamia." *Journal of Near Eastern Studies*, vol. 2, no. 3 (July 1943).

Justus, Carol F. "Indo-Europeanization of Myth and Syntax in Anatolian Hittite: Dating of Texts As an Index." *Journal of Indo-European Studies*, vol. 2 (1983), 59–103.

Koschaker, Paul. "Fratriarchat, Hausgemeinschaft und Mutterrecht in Keilschriftrechten." *Zeitschrift für Assyriologie*, Neue Folge, Band 7 (Band 41) Berlin and Leipzig, (1939), 1–89.

Kramer, Samuel Noah. "The Weeping Goddess: Sumerian Prototypes of the *Mater Dolorosa*." *Biblical Archaeologist*, vol. 46, no. 2 (Spring 1983), 60–80.

Kraus, F. R. "Le Role des temples depuis la troisième dynastie d'Ur jusqu'a la premiere Dynastie de Babylone." *Cahiers d' Histoire Mondiale*, vol. 1, no. 3 (Jan. 1954), 518–45.

La Fay, Howard. "Ebla: Splendor of an Unknown Empire." *National Geographic*, vol. 154, no. 6. (Dec. 1978).

Lambert, W. G. "Morals in Ancient Mesopotamia." *Vooraziatisch Egypt Genootschap "Ex Oriente Lux" Jaarbericht*, no. 15 (1957–58), 184–96.

Leacock, Eleanor. "Women in Egalitarian Societies." In Renate Bridenthal and Claudia Koonz. *Becoming Visible*, pp. 11–35.

Maekawa, Kunio. "The Development of the E-MI in Lagash during the Early Dynastic III." *Mesopotamia*, vols. 8–9 (1973–74), 77–144.

Meissner, Bruno. "Aus dem altbabylonischen Recht." *Der alte Orient*, Jahrgang 7, Heft 1. Leipzig: J. C. Hinrich, 1905, pp. 3–32.

Millard, Alan R. "In Praise of Ancient Scribes." *Biblical Archaeologist*, vol. 45, no. 3 (Summer 1982).

Morrison, Martha A. "The Family of Silva Tesub *marsarr*." *Journal of Cuneiform Studies*, vol. 31, no. 1 (Jan. 1979), 3–29.

Oppenheim, A. Leo. "The Golden Garments of the Gods." *Journal of Near Eastern Studies*, vol. 8 (1949).

———. "A Note on the Scribes of Mesopotamia." *Studies in Honor of Benno Landsberger on His 75th Birthday, April 25, 1965.* Chicago: University of Chicago Press, 1965.

———. " 'Siege-Documents' from Nippur." *Iraq,* vol. 17 (1955), pages 69–89.

Perlman, Alice, and Polly Perlman. "Women's Power in the Ancient World." *Women's Caucus, Religious Studies,* vol. 3 (Summer 1975), 4–6.

Postgate, J. N. "On Some Assyrian Ladies." *Iraq,* vol. 41 (1979), 89–103.

Rapp, Rayna. "Women, Religion and Archaic Civilizations." *Feminist Studies,* vol. 4, no. 3 (Oct. 1978), 1–6.

Renger, Johannes. "Untersuchungen zum Priestertum in der altbabylonischen Zeit." *Zeitschrift für Assyriologie und vorderasiatische Archeologie,* Neue Folge, Band 24. Berlin: De Gruyter, 1967, 1. Teil, 110–88.

Rohrlich, Ruby. "State Formation in Sumer and the Subjugation of Women." *Feminist Studies,* vol. 6, no. 1 (Spring 1980), pp. 76–102.

Rorhlich-Leavitt, Ruby. "Women in Transition: Crete and Sumer," in Bridenthal and Koonz, *Becoming Visible,* pp. 36–59.

Rowton, M. B. "Urban Autonomy in a Nomadic Environment." *Journal of Near Eastern Studies,* vol. 32 (1973), 201–15.

Saporetti, Claudio. "The Status of Women in the Middle Assyrian Period." In *Monographs on the Ancient Near East,* vol. 2, no. 1. Malibu, Calif.: Undena Publ., 1979.

Sasson, Jack M. "Biographical Notices on Some Royal Ladies from Mari." *Journal of Cuneiform Studies,* vol. 25, no. 2 (Jan. 1973), 59–104.

———. "Thoughts of Zimri-Lim." *Biblical Archaeologist,* vol. 47, no. 2 (June 1984), 111–20.

Schmandt-Besserat, Denise. "Decipherment of the Earliest Tablets." *Science,* vol. 211 (16 Jan. 1981), 283–85.

———. "The Envelopes That Bear the First Writing." *Technology and Culture,* vol. 21, no. 3 (1980), 357–85.

Seibert, Ilse. "Hirt-Herde-König." *Deutsche Akademie der Wissenschaften zu Berlin,* Schriften der Sektion für Altertumswissenschaft, no. 53. Berlin: Akademie Verlag, 1969.

Wright, Henry T., and Gregory A. Johnson. "Population, Exchange, and Early State Formation in Southwestern Iran." *American Anthropologist,* vol. 77, no. 2 (Spring 1975), 267–89.

Yoffee, Norman. "The Economic Role of the Crown in the Old Babylonian Period." *Bibliotheca Mesopotamia.* Ed. G. Bucellati, vol. 5 Malibu, Calif.: Undena Publ., 1977.

III SLAVERY

Books

Bakir, Abd el-Mohsen. *Slavery in Pharaonic Egypt.* Cairo, 1952.

Davis, David Brion. *The Problem of Slavery in the Age of Revolution, 1770–1823.* Ithaca, New York: Cornell University Press, 1975.

———. *The Problem of Slavery in Western Culture.* Ithaca, New York: Cornell University Press, 1966.

Degler, Carl. *Neither Black nor White: Slavery and Race Relations in Brazil and the United States.* New York: Macmillan, 1971.

Finley, Moses I. *Aspects of Antiquity.* London: Chatto & Windus, 1968.

———. *Slavery in Classical Antiquity: Views and Controversies.* Cambridge: Heffer & Sons, 1960.

Genovese, Eugene D. *Roll, Jordan, Roll: The World the Slaves Made.* New York: Pantheon, 1974.

Greenidge, Charles W. W. *Slavery.* London: Allen & Unwin, 1958.

Jordan, Winthrop D. *White Over Black: American Attitudes Toward the Negro, 1550–1812.* Chapel Hill: University of North Carolina Press, 1968.

Klein, Herbert S. *Slavery in the Americas: A Comparative Study of Virginia and Cuba.* Chicago: University of Chicago Press, 1967.

Mendelsohn, Isaac. *Legal Aspects of Slavery in Babylonia, Assyria and Palestine: A Comparative Study, 3000–500 B.C.* Williamsport, Pa.: The Bayard Press, 1932.

———. *Slavery in the Ancient Near East.* New York: Oxford University Press, 1949.

Miers, Suzanne, and Igor Kopytoff (eds.). *Slavery in Africa: Historical and Anthropological Perspectives.* Madison: University of Wisconsin Press, 1977.

Myrdal, Gunnar. *American Dilemma: The Negro Problem and Modern Democracy.* New York: Harper & Row, 1944.

Patterson, Orlando. *Slavery and Social Death: A Comparative Study.* Cambridge: Harvard University Press, 1982.

Watson, James L. *Asian and African Systems of Slavery.* Berkeley: University of California Press, 1980.

Westerman, William L. *The Slave Systems of Greek and Roman Antiquity.* Philadelphia: American Philosophical Society, 1955.

Wiedemann, Thomas. *Greek and Roman Slavery.* Baltimore: Johns Hopkins University Press, 1981.

Winks, Robin (ed.). *Slavery: A Comparative Perspective.* New York: New York University Press, 1972.

Articles

Feigin, Samuel I. "The Captives in Cuneiform Inscriptions." *American Journal of Semitic Languages and Literatures,* vol. 50, no. 4 (July 1934).

Finley, Moses I. "Slavery." In *Encyclopedia of the Social Sciences.* Vol. 14. New York: Macmillan and the Free Press, 1968, pp. 307–18.

Gelb, I. J. "Prisoners of War in Early Mesopotamia." *Journal of Near Eastern Studies,* vol. 32 (1973), 70–98.

Harris, Rivkah. "Notes on the Slave Names of Old Babylonian Sippar." *Journal of Cuneiform Studies,* vol. 29, no. 1 (Jan. 1977), 46–51.

Pulleyblank, E. G. "The Origins and Nature of Chattel Slavery in China." *Journal of Economic and Social History of the Orient,* vol. 1, pt. 1 (1958), 201–5.

Siegel, Bernard. "Slavery During the 3rd Dynasty of Ur." *Memoirs of the American Anthropological Association,* New Series, vol. 49, no. 1.

———. "Some Methodological Considerations for a Comparative Study of Slavery." *American Anthropologist,* New Series, vol. 47, no. 2 (April–June 1945), 357–92.

"Slavery, Serfdom and Forced Labor." In *New Encyclopaedia Britannica.* 15th ed. vol. 16, (Chicago, 1979), *Macropaedia,* pp. 853–66.

Wilbur, C. Martin. "Slavery in China during the Former Han Dynasty, 206 B.C.–A.D. 25." *Publications of Field Museum of National History*, Anthropological Series, vol. 34 (15 Jan. 1943).

IV PROSTITUTION

Books

Bloch, Iwan. *Die Prostitution*. Vol. 1. Berlin: L. Marcies, 1912.

Bullough, Vern L. *Sex, Society and History*. New York: Science History Publications, 1976.

Bullough, Vern L., and Bonnie Bullough, *The History of Prostitution: An Illustrated Social History*. New York: Crown, 1978.

Henriques, Fernando. *Prostitution and Society*. Vol. 1. London: MacGibbon and Kee, 1962.

————. *Stews and Strumpets: A Survey of Prostitution*. London: MacGibbon and Kee, 1961.

La Croix, Paul. *History of Prostitution*, Chicago: Pascal Covici, 1926.

Sanger, William W. *A History of Prostitution*. 1858; rpt. New York: Medical Publishing Co., 1898.

Articles

Ebert, Max, "Prostitution." In *Reallexicon der Vorgeschichte*, Vol. V, erste Hälfte. Berlin: De Gruyter, 1926, p. 323.

May, Geoffrey. "Prostitution." In *Encyclopedia of the Social Sciences*, Vol. 13, New York: Macmillan, 1934, pp. 553–59.

"Prostitution." In *Encyclopedia Americana*, International Edition, Vol. 22. Danbury, Conn.: Americana Corp., 1979, pp. 672–74.

"Prostitution." In *New Encyclopaedia Britannica*, Vol. 15. Chicago: Helen Hemingway Benton Publishers, 1979, p. 76.

Reference

"Geschlechtsmoral" and "Hierodulen," in Erich Ebeling and Bruno Meissner, *Reallexicon der Assyriologie*, vol. 4, Berlin: De Gruyter, 1971, pp. 223, 391–93.

V RELIGION, OLD TESTAMENT, ANCIENT ISRAEL

1. *Primary Sources*

Books

Calvin, John. *Commentaries on the First Book of Moses called Genesis*. Vol. I. Trans. John King. Grand Rapids, Mich.: Eerdmans, 1948.

Grimké, Sarah M. *Letters on the Equality of the Sexes and the Condition of Women*. Boston: Isaac Knapp, 1838.

The Holy Scriptures According to the Masoretic Text. Philadelphia: Jewish Publication Society of America, 1917.

Sasson, Jack M. *Ruth: A New Translation with a Philological Commentary and a For-malist-Folklorist Interpretation.* Baltimore: Johns Hopkins University Press, 1979.

Speght, Rachel. *A Mouzell for Melastomus, the Cynical Bayter and foule-mouthed Bar-ker against Evah's Sex.* London: Thomas Archer, 1617.

Stanton, Elizabeth Cady, and the Revising Committee. *The Woman's Bible.* 1898; rpt. Seattle: Coalition Task Force on Women and Religion, 1974.

Zeigner, Oskar. *Luther und die Erzväter: Auszüge aus Luther's Auslegungen zum ersten Buch Moses mit einer theologischen Einleitung.* Berlin: Evangelische Verlagsan-stalt, 1962.

2. Reference Works

Books

Baly, Dennis. *Geography of the Bible: A Study in Historical Geography.* New York: Harper & Row, 1977.

Encyclopaedia Judaica. 16 vols. Jerusalem: Keter Publishing House, 1971–72.

"Hebrew Religion." *Encyclopaedia Britannica,* 11th ed., vol. XIII, New York: Encyclo-paedia Britannica Co., 1910.

Harris, Rivkah. "Women in the Ancient Near East." In *The Interpreter's Dictionary of the Bible, Supplementary Volume,* ed. K. R. Crim, Nashville: Abingdon, 1976, pp. 960–63.

The Interpreter's Dictionary of the Bible, Supplementary Volume. ed. K. R. Crim. Nashville: Abingdon, 1976.

Trible, Phyllis. "Women in the Old Testament." In *The Interpreter's Dictionary of the Bible, Supplementary Volume,* ed. K. R. Crim.

3. Secondary Works

Books

Albright, William Foxwell. *Archaeology and the Religion of Israel.* Baltimore: Johns Hopkins University Press, 1956.

——. *From the Stone Age to Christianity: Monotheism and the Historical Process.* Baltimore: Johns Hopkins University Press, 1940.

Bakan, David. *And They Took Themselves Wives: The Emergence of Patriarchy in Western Civilization.* New York: Harper & Row, 1979.

Bewer, Julius August. *The Literature of the Old Testament.* New York: Columbia Uni-versity Press, 1933. First ed. 1922.

Carmichael, Calum M. *Women, Law, and the Genesis Traditions.* Edinburgh: Edinburgh University Press, 1979.

Daly, Mary. *Beyond God the Father: Toward a Philosophy of Women's Liberation.* Boston: Beacon Press, 1973.

——. *The Church and the Second Sex.* New York: Harper & Row, 1975.

De Vaux, Roland O. *Ancient Israel: Its Life and Institutions.* New York: McGraw-Hill, 1961; paperback edition, 2 vols., 1965.

Driver, Samuel R. *An Introduction to the Literature of the Old Testament.* New York: Meridian Books, 1960.

Epstein, Louis M. *Marriage Laws in the Bible and the Talmud.* Cambridge: Harvard University Press, 1942.

————. Sex Laws and Customs in Judaism. New York: Bloch, 1948.

Freud, Sigmund. "Moses and Monotheism: Three Essays." In *Complete Psychological Works.* vol. 23. London: 1963–64, pp. 1–137.

Fiorenza, Elisabeth Schussler. *In Memory of Her: A Feminist Theological Reconstruction of Christian Origins.* New York: Crossroads, 1983.

Goldenberg, Naomi, R. *Changing of the Gods: Feminism and the End of Traditional Religions.* Boston: Beacon Press, 1979.

Gottwald, Norman K. *The Tribes of Yahweh: A Sociology of the Religion of Liberated Israel, 1250–1050 B.C.* Maryknoll, N.Y.: Orbis Books, 1979.

Graves, Robert. *The White Goddess: A Historical Grammar of Poetic Myth* (Amended and enlarged edition.) New York: Farrar, Straus and Giroux, 1983.

Graves, Robert, and Raphael Patai. *Hebrew Myths: The Book of Genesis.* New York: Greenwich House, 1983.

Gray, John. *Near Eastern Mythology.* London: Hamlyn, 1969.

Harris, Kevin. *Sex, Ideology and Religion: The Representation of Women in the Bible.* Totowa, N.J.: Barnes & Noble Books, 1984.

Harrison, Jane Ellen. *Mythology.* New York: Harcourt, Brace and World, 1963.

Hillers, Delbert R. *Covenant: The History of a Biblical Idea.* Baltimore: Johns Hopkins University Press, 1969.

Hoch-Smith, Judith, and Anita Spring. *Women in Ritual and Symbolic Roles.* New York: Plenum Press, 1978.

James, E. O. *The Ancient Gods: The History and Diffusion of Religion in the Ancient Near East and the Eastern Mediterranean.* London: Weidenfeld and Nicolson, 1960.

MacDonald, Elizabeth Mary. *The Position of Women as Reflected in Semitic Codes of Law.* Toronto: University of Toronto Press, 1931.

May, Herbert G., (ed.). *Oxford Bible Atlas.* London: Oxford University Press, 1962.

Meek, Theophile James. *Hebrew Origins.* New York: Harper Torchbooks, 1960.

Monro, Margaret T. *Thinking About Genesis.* Chicago: Henry Regnery, 1966; London: Longmans, Green, 1953.

Negev, Abraham. *Archeological Encyclopedia of the Holy Land.* New York: Putnam, 1972.

Ochs, Carol. *Behind the Sex of God: Toward a New Consciousness—Transcending Matriarchy and Patriarchy.* Boston: Beacon Press, 1977.

Ochshorn, Judith. *The Female Experience and the Nature of the Divine.* Bloomington: Indiana University Press, 1981.

Otwell, John. *And Sarah Laughed: The Status of Women in the Old Testament.* Philadelphia: Westminster Press, 1977.

Pagels, Elaine. *The Gnostic Gospels.* New York: Random House, 1979.

Ruether, Rosemary Radford, (ed.). *Religion and Sexism: Images of Woman in the Jewish and Christian Traditions.* New York: Simon Schuster, 1974.

Saggs, H. W. F. *The Encounter with the Divine in Mesopotamia and Israel.* London: Athlone Press, 1978.

Sarna, Nahum M. *Understanding Genesis.* New York: McGraw-Hill, 1966.

Smith, W. Robertson. *Kinship and Marriage in Early Arabia* (1903); reprint Boston: Beacon Press, n.d.

Speiser, E. A. *Genesis.* Garden City, N.Y.: Doubleday, 1964.

Stone, Merlin. *Ancient Mirrors of Womanhood.* Vol. I, *Our Goddess and Heroine Heritage.* New York: New Sibylline Books, 1979.

———. *When God Was a Woman.* New York: Harcourt Brace Jovanovich, 1976.

Teubal, Savina J. *Sarah the Priestess: The First Matriarch of Genesis.* Athens, Ohio: Swallow Press, 1984.

Von Rad, Gerhard. *Genesis: A Commentary.* Philadelphia: Westminster Press, 1961. (Translation of German edition, 1956.)

Wellhausen, Julius. *Prolegomena to the History of Ancient Israel.* New York: Meridian Books, 1965.

Ungnad, Arthur. *Die Religion der Babylonier und Assyrer.* Jena: E. Diderichs, 1921.

Articles

Farians, Elizabeth. "Phallic Worship: The Ultimate Idolatry." In J. Plaskow and Joan Arnold (eds.). *Women and Religion.* Rev. ed. Missoula, Mont.: Scholars Press, American Academy of Religion, 1974.

Fox, Michael V. "The Sign of the Covenant: Circumcision in the Light of the Priestly 'ôt Etiologies." *La Revue Biblique,* vol. 81 (1974), 557–96.

Freedman, R. David. "Woman, a Power Equal to Man." *Biblical Archaeology Review,* vol. 9, no. 1 (Jan./Feb. 1983), 56–58.

Frymer-Kensky, Tikva. "Patriarchal Family Relationships and Near Eastern Law." *Biblical Archaeologist,* vol. 44, no. 4 (Fall 1981), 209–14.

Greenberg, Moshe. "Another Look at Rachel's Theft of the Teraphim" *Journal of Biblical Literature,* vol. 81 (1962), 239–48.

Horowitz, Maryanne Cline. "The Image of God in Man—Is Woman Included?" *Harvard Theological Review,* vol. 72, nos. 3–4 (July–Oct. 1979), 175–206.

Kikawada, I. M. "Two Notes on Eve." *Journal of Biblical Literature,* vol. 91 (1972), 33–37.

Lemaire, André. "Mari, the Bible, and the Northwest Semitic World." *Biblical Archaeologist,* vol. 47, no. 2 (June 1984), 101–8.

———. "Who or What Was Yahweh's Asherah? Startling New Inscriptions from Two Different Sites Reopen the Debate about the Meaning of Asherah," *Biblical Archaeology,* vol. 10, no. 6 (Nov./Dec. 1984), 42–52.

Malamat, A. "Mari and the Bible: Some Patterns of Tribal Organization and Institutions." *Journal of the American Oriental Society,* vol. 82, no. 2 (April–June 1962), 143–49.

Mendenhall, G. "Ancient Oriental and Biblical Law." *Biblical Archaeologist,* vol. 17 (1954), 26–46.

Mendenhall, G. E. "Covenant Forms in Israelite Tradition." *Biblical Archaeologist,* vol. 17 (1954), 50–76.

Meyers, Carol. "The Roots of Restriction: Women in Early Israel." *Biblical Archaeologist,* vol. 41, no. 3 (Sept. 1973), 91–103.

Meyers, Eric M. "The Bible and Archaeology." *Biblical Archaeologist,* vol. 47, no. 1 (March 1984), 36–40.

Morrison, Martha A. "The Jacobs and Laban Narratives in Light of Near Eastern Sources." *Biblical Archaeologist,* vol. 46, no. 3 (Summer 1983), 155–64.

Pardee, Dennis, and Jonathan Glass. "Literary Sources for the History of Palestine and Syria: The Mari Archives." *Biblical Archaeologist*, vol. 47, no. 2 (June 1984), 88–100.

Segel, M. H. "The Religion of Israel Before Sinai." *Jewish Quarterly Review*, vol. 52 (1961–62), 41–68.

Speiser, E. A. "The Biblical Idea of History in Its Common Near Eastern Setting." *Israel Exploration Journal*, vol. 7, no. 4 (1957), 201–16.

———. "3000 Years of Bible Study." *The Centennial Review*, vol. 41 (1960), 206–22.

Tadmor, Miriam. "Female Cult Figurines in Late Canaan and Early Israel: Archeological Evidence." In Tomoo Ishida (ed.) *Studies in the Period of David and Solomon and other Essays*. Winona Lake, Ind.: Eisenbrauns, 1982, pp. 139–73.

Trible, Phyllis. "The Creation of a Feminist Theology." *New York Times Book Review*, vol. 88 (May 1, 1983), 28–29.

———. "Depatriarchalizing in Biblical Interpretation." *Journal of the American Academy of Religion*, vol. 41, no. 1 (March 1973), 30–48.

VI   ANCIENT GREECE

1. *Primary Sources*

Books

Aristotle, *Politica*. Benjamin Jowett (trans.). *The Works of Aristotle*, W. D. Ross (ed.). Oxford: Clarendon Press, 1921.

———. Plato, *The Republic*. Benjamin Jowett (trans.). New York: Random House, n.d. *The Iliad of Homer*. Richmond Lattimore (trans.). Chicago: University of Chicago Press, 1937.

———. *The Odyssey of Homer*. Richmond Lattimore (trans.). London: Macmillan, 1975.

Euripides. Robert W. Cirrigan (trans.). New York: Dell, 1965.

Lefkowitz, Mary R., and Maureen B. Fant. *Women's Life in Greece and Rome: A Sourcebook in Translation*. Baltimore: Johns Hopkins University Press, 1982.

Herodotus, *Historia*. Trans. A. D. Godley. Loeb Classical Library. Cambridge: Harvard University Press, 1920.

The Odyssey of Homer. S. H. Butcher (trans.). London: Macmillan, 1917.

The Works of Aristotle J. A. Smith and W. D. Ross. (trans.). Oxford: Clarendon Press, 1912.

Thucydides, *History of Peloponnesian War*. 4 vols. Translated by Charles F. Smith. Cambridge: Harvard University Press, 1920.

2. *Secondary Works*

Books

Bruns, Ivo, *Frauenemanzipation in Athen, ein Beitrag zur attischen Kulturgeschichte des fünften und vierten Jahrhunderts*. Kiliae: Libraria Academica, 1900.

Ehrenberg, Victor. *From Solon to Socrates: Greek History and Civilization During the 6th and 5th Centuries* B.C.. London: Methuen, 1973.

———. *The People of Aristophanes: A Sociology of Old Attic Comedy.* Oxford: Basil Blackwell, 1951.

Foley, Helen, ed. *Reflections of Women in Antiquity.* New York: Gordon & Breach Science Publications, 1981.

Graves, Robert. *The Greek Myths.* 2 vols. New York: George Braziller, 1959.

Humphreys, S. C. *The Family, Women and Death: Comparative Studies.* London: Routledge & Kegan Paul, 1983.

Marrou, H. I. *A History of Education in Antiquity.* New York: 1956.

McNeill, William H. *The Rise of the West: A History of the Human Community.* Chicago: University of Chicago Press, 1963.

Peradotto, J., and J. P. Sullivan. *Women in the Ancient World: The Arethusa Papers.* Albany: S.U.N.Y. Press, 1984.

Pomeroy, Sarah B. *Goddesses, Whores, Wives, and Slaves: Women in Classical Antiquity.* New York: Schocken, 1975.

Sealey, Raphael. *A History of the Greek City States: 700–338 B.C.* Berkeley: University of California Press, 1976.

Selfman, Charles. *Women in Antiquity.* London: Thames & Hudson, 1936.

Shorey, Paul. *What Plato Said.* Chicago: University of Chicago Press, 1933.

Taylor, Alfred E. *Plato: The Man and His Work.* London: Methuen, 1926.

Thomson, George. *Aeschylus and Athens: A Study in the Social Origins of Drama.* London: Lawrence and Wishart, 1941.

Winspear, Alban D. *Genesis of Plato's Thought.* New York: Dryden, 1940. Reprinted by Russell & Russell.

Articles

Arthur, Marylin B. "Origins of the Western Attitude Toward Women." In John Peradatto and J. P. Sullivan (eds.), *Women in the Ancient World: The Arethusa Papers* (Albany, 1984), pp. 31–37.

Dover, K. J. "Classical Greek Attitudes to Sexual Behavior." *Arethusa,* vol. 6, no. 1 (1973), 59–73.

Gomme, A. M. "The Position of Women in Athens in the Fifth and Fourth Centuries." *Classical Philology,* vol. 20, no. 1 (Jan. 1925), 1–25.

Havelock, Christine Mitchell. "Mourners on Greek Vases: Remarks on the Social History of Women." In *The Greek Vases: Papers based on lectures presented to a symposium at Hudson Valley Community College at Troy, New York, in April of 1979,* ed. Stephen L. Hyatt. Latham, N.Y.: Hudson-Mohawk Association of Colleges and Universities, 1981, pp. 103–18.

Horowitz, Maryanne Cline. "Aristotle and Woman." *Journal of the History of Biology,* vol. 9, no. 2 (Fall 1976), 183–213.

Pomeroy, Sarah B. "Selected Bibliography on Women in Antiquity." *Arethusa,* vol. 6 (1973), 127–57.

Richter, Donald. "The Position of Women in Classical Athens." *Classical Journal,* vol. 67, no. 1 (1971), 1–8.

Warren, Larissa Bonfante. "The Women of Etruria." *Arethusa,* vol. 6, no. 1 (Spring 1973), 91–101.

Zeitlin, Froma I. "Travesties of Gender and Genre in Aristophanes' *Thesomorporiazousae.*" In *Reflections of Women in Antiquity,* ed. Helene Foley, New York: Gordon & Breach Science Publications, 1981.

VII ART

Books

Akurgal, Ekrem. *The Art of the Hittites*. New York: Harry N. Abrams, 1962.

Amiet, Pierre. *Art of the Ancient Near East*. New York: Harry N. Abrams, 1980.

Bittel, Kurt. *Die Hethiter: die Kunst Anatoliens von Ende des 3 bis zum Anfang des 1. Jahrtausends, vor Christus*. München: Beck, 1976.

Broude, Norma, and Mary D. Garrard. *Feminism and Art History: Questioning the Litany*. New York: Harper & Row, 1982.

Goldscheider, Ludwig. *Michelangelo*. London: Phaidon, 1959.

Moortgat, Anton. *Die Kunst des alten Mesopotamien; Die klassiche Kunst Vorderasiens*. 2 vols. Köln: Dumont, 1982 & 1984.

Parrot, André. *Sumer: The Dawn of Art*. New York: Golden Press, 1961.

Seibert, Ilse. *Woman in Ancient Near East*. Leipzig: Edition Leipzig, 1974.

Strommenger, E., and M. Hirmer. *The Art of Mesopotamia*. London: Thames & Hudson, 1964.

Strommenger, Eva. *5000 Years of Mesopotamian Art*. New York: Harry N. Abrams, 1962.

Index

Aaby, Peter, 51-53, 275n
Abortion, Mesopotamian laws pertaining to, 119-121
Abraham, 170, 172, 182, 188-189
  as patriarch, 190
Abram. *See also* Abraham
  covenant with Yahweh, 163, 188-190
  re-naming of, 190
Abstract thought, women's exclusion from constructing, 224-225
Adam
  naming of, in Bible, 183
  power of naming given to, 181-182
Adams, Robert McC., 55, 58
Addams, Jane, 28, 248n
Addu-duri, 74
Adonis, 127
Adoption, in Jewish society, 170
Adultery
  accusation of, Mesopotamian laws about, 115, 267n-268n
  in Israelite society, 170
  in Mesopotamian law, 114-115, 267n, 268n
  in Sparta, 203
Aeschylus
  The Furies, 205
  The Oresteia, 205
Aggression, male, hypotheses of origin, 45-46
Agriculture

development of, 50-51, 212
and kinship shifts, 49-50
and women's status, theory about, 34
Altruism, as feminine principle, 27
Amazons, 249n
American women
  19th-c., 28
  in young republic, status of, 27-28
Amphipolos, 86-87, 260n
Amutpiel of Qatana (king), 262n
An (sky-god), 149, 152
Anath, 148, 153-154
Androcentric fallacy, of Western symbol systems, 220
Androcentricity
  in history, 12-13, 15, 36
  in sciences, 21
Angel, Lawrence, 34-35
Animal husbandry
  and evolution of Creator-god, 149-150, 274n
  history of, 46
  and institutionalized aggression, 46
  and social relations, 50-51
Anthropology, uses for women's history, 37
Anu (god), 194
Aphrodite, 159
Archaeology, uses, for women's history, 31, 249n

Archaic state, 212, 216
  formation, 54
  origin, 53-55
  and patriarchy, 9
  prefigured in patriarchal family, 209, 212
Arinna (sun-goddess), 157, 158
Aristotelian philosophy
  doctrine of male procreativity, 205-208
  sex dominance in philosophy of, 209
  on slavery, 208-209
  status of women in, 10, 205-209
Artemis, 159
Aruru (goddess), 150, 152
Asherah (goddess), 159, 166, 177, 178, 195
Ashur (god), 153, 157
Astarte, 148
Athena, parthenogenetic birth of, 205
Atrahasis myth, 144-145
Attis, 127
Atum (sun-god), 149
Aztec society, 252n

Baal, 127, 153, 154, 166, 177
Bachofen, J. J., 21, 22, 26-27, 123
  Das Mutterrecht, 26
Bakan, David, 175, 185-186
Bakir, A., 86
Baranamtarra, 62, 154, 254n-255n
Barrenness, in Jewish society, 170
Barstow, Anne, 34
Batto, Bernard Frank, 69, 70, 73
Bau (goddess), 154
  temple of, 62, 64
    personnel lists, 65
    ration lists, 83, 258n-259n
    slave women of, 83
Beard, Mary, 250n
Becker, Ernst, 199
Belessnu, 96
Belizumu, 262n
Benjamites, wives, 174-175
Benjamite war, 173-175
Bewer, Julius A., 276n
Bible
  documentary hypothesis, 162
  gender symbols in, 278n
  as historic document, 161, 201
Biblical law, 101
Bird, Phyllis, 176
Bleier, Ruth, 39

Bloch, Iwan, 123
Boulding, Elise, 18, 43, 48
Bride price, 106, 109, 110, 169, 213, 265n
Briffault, Robert, 26
Bronze Age, women's status in, 31
Brownmiller, Susan, 46
Burial customs, as evidence of social relations, 56

Calvin, John
  on circumcision, 191-192
  on creation of woman, 183
  interpretation of story of Lot, 172-173
Canaan, tribes in, 163-164, 167
Cassin, Elena, 111
Castration, of criminals and slaves, 82
Čatal Hüyük, 32-35, 56, 146-147
  animal husbandry in, 46
  ochre painting of skeletons in, 32-33, 249n
Chastity. *See also* Virginity
  and female honor, 80
  premarital, 108
Childbearing, and childrearing, association of, 42
Child bride, 107, 269n
Children
  as economic asset, 50
  exchange of, 48
  patriarchal father's power over, 89, 90, 106, 117, 121, 140, 202, 251n
China
  concubines in, 93
  linguistic connection between concubinage and female enslavement, 94-95
  oppression of women in, 77
  slavery in, 82, 88
Chodorow, Nancy, 43-44
Christianity, 201
Circumcision, 188, 190-193, 279n
  symbolism of, 192, 200
City-state, 145. *See also* Polis
  formation, 66
Civilization, rise of, 54
Class
  and gender, 213
  for men, 8-9, 215
  status, and Mesopotamian law, 105

of women, 122, 139-141, 215
    defined by their sexual relation-
        ships, 8-9, 96, 215
    and women's role in family econ-
        omy, 111
Class distinctions
    in Mesopotamian laws, 119-120, 270n
    for women, 139-141
Class dominance, 214
Class formation, 122, 139
    early, as shift from kin-based soci-
        ety, 55
Class society, 55, 200, 218
Class struggle
    sex relations as, 24
    as struggle for control of symbol
        systems, 222
Code of Hammurabi, 89, 101-104, 110,
    128, 130, 140, 197-198
    classes of people recognized in, 104
    dating, 261n
    sec. 50, 263n
    sec. 110, 128
    sec. 116, 90
    sec. 117, 90, 263n
    sec. 119, 90
    sec. 129, 114, 267n
    sec. 130, 115, 267n
    sec. 131, 115, 267n
    sec. 132, 267n
    sec. 133-135, 113, 267n
    sec. 138, 268n
    sec. 139, 268n
    sec. 140, 268n
    sec. 141, 114, 267n
    sec. 142, 115
    sec. 143, 116
    sec. 145, 266n
    sec. 146, 92, 266n
    sec. 147, 266n
    sec. 148, 265n
    sec. 149, 265n
    sec. 154, 116, 268n
    sec. 155, 264n, 268n
    sec. 155-156, 107, 116
    sec. 156, 264n, 268n
    sec. 157, 116, 268n
    sec. 162, 107, 264n
    sec. 163, 265n
    sec. 164, 265n
    sec. 170, 171
    sec. 171, 93, 269n
    sec. 172, 107, 264n, 269n

sec. 173, 264n
sec. 173-174, 107
sec. 174, 264n
sec. 181, 128
sec. 192, 264n
sec. 192-193, 106, 263n
sec. 195, 263n
sec. 209-214, 119, 270n
Codex Lipit-Ishtar, 68
Codex Ur-Nammu, 68
Concubinage, 87, 88. *See also* Enslave-
    ment; Slavery
    and birth of sons, status of mother
        in, 93
    and female enslavement, linguistic
        connection of, 94-95
    institutionalization of, 91-92
Concubine, Levite's, story of, 173-174
Concubines, 128, 215. *See also* En-
    slavement; Slavery; Slaves
    class of, 112, 113, 266n
Contenau, Georges, 151
Cosmogony, and archaic state, 54
Covenant community, 178
    women's status in, 10, 188
Covenant law, 101-102
    and debt slaves, 105
    status of mother in, 106
Covenants, Biblical, 163, 188-189, 191,
    279n
Creation, and name-giving, 150-151
Creation Epic, Babylonian. *See Enuma
    Elish*
Creation stories, 149, 274n
    Biblical, sources of, 184-185
    gender symbolism in, 145-146
    in Genesis, 180-183
    male gods in, 151-152
    Sumerian, reflected in Biblical ac-
        counts, 184-185
Creative spirit, 151-152, 180
Creativity, 180, 186
    emanating from God, 200
    reserved to God, 197
    symbolization, in monotheism, 10
Creator-God
    evolution of, 149-150, 274n
    male, transfer of power to, from fe-
        male deities, 145
Cronos, 204
Cultic servants, female, 271n
Cultic sexual service, 125, 272n
Cultural prodding, 223

Culture, 24
  development of, by women, theory
    of, 26-27

Damkina, 152
Darlington, C. D., 47, 253*n*
Darwinism, and explanations of wom-
    en's inferiority, 18-19
David (king), 165-166
  God's covenant with, 191
Death, Mesopotamian concept of, 193
de Beauvoir, Simone, 3, 17, 43, 46, 227,
    281*n*
  The Second Sex, 221-222
Deborah, Song of, 165, 176
Debt pledges, 89-90, 105, 112, 133, 213
Decalogue, 163, 190, 276*n*
Democracy, foundation of, 203-204
Demographic changes, effects on women,
    20, 247*n*
Deprivation, definition, 235
Deuteronomy, 162, 177
Diakonoff, I. M., 79
Diamond, A. S., 263*n*
Dinnerstein, Dorothy, 28, 248*n*
Diviners, 142
Divorce, 169
  in Ancient Greece, 202
  in Israelite society, 170
  in Mesopotamian law, 107, 109-110,
    113, 115-116, 267*n*, 268*n*
  taxation on, in Mesopotamia, 64, 255*n*
Double standard, 171
  institutionalization, under Mesopo-
    tamian law, 113
Doulos, 86-87, 260*n*
Dowry, 107-108, 115, 169, 264*n*, 265*n*,
    266*n*
  of *naditu* women, 127-128
  of priestesses, 111
  of temple servants, 128
  wife's use-right of, 108-109
Draco, 204
Driver, G. R., 89-90, 109, 110, 121, 128,
    136, 261*n*, 266*n*, 268*n*
Droit du seigneur, 88
Dumuzi (god), 126

Ea (god), 149, 152, 194
Eannatum, 81
Earth-goddess, 149, 152

Education
  of Jewish women, 178
  of women
    in ancient Mesopotamia, 67-68
    in Plato's *Republic*, 210
  women's access to, 219-220, 223, 224
Egalitarian societies, 29
  Neolithic, 43
Ego formation, 45
Eleithyia, 159
Elohim, 186-187
Emancipation, definition, 237. *See also*
    Woman's emancipation
Enammatumma of Isin, 68
Endogamy, taboos on, 24
Engels, Frederick, 49, 50
  analysis of hetaerism, 123-124
  *Origin of the Family, Private Prop-
    erty and the State*, 21
  understanding of women's position in
    society and history, 21-23
Enkheduanna, 66-67
Enki (god), 152, 153, 185
Enkidu, 193
Enlil (god), 151, 152
Enmenanna, 67
Enslavement. *See also* Debt pledges
  processes for, 79-80
  techniques of, 78
  of war captives, 85. *See also* War
    captives
  of women
    by conquest, 70, 78-83, 86-87
    as opposed to men, 87-89, 260*n*
    significance, 78-80
Enuma Elish, 150, 153, 183
Epicene, 263*n*-264*n*
Epstein, Louis, 114, 118-119, 170, 175,
    177
Erishti-Aya, 73
Estan (sun-goddess), 157, 158
Eunuchism, 82
Eve, 188
  Adam's naming of, 277*n*
    symbolism of, 181
  Adam's re-naming of, 197
  conditions imposed on, after the Fall,
    197-198
  meaning of name, 185, 278*n*
Exchange of women, 25, 46-47, 53, 212-
    213
  and development of private property,
    49

matrimonial, in Jabesh-Gilead, 174-176
Exodus, the, 164

Fall, the, 185, 188, 201
  Biblical account of, 194, 196, 197
  Sumerian account of, 194
Family
  emergence of, Engels's description of, 22
  patriarchal, 89, 121-122, 216-217
    institutionalization of, 140
    as prefigure of archaic state, 209, 212
    in Semitic tribes, 163
Father, absolute rights over children, 89, 90, 106, 117, 121, 140, 202, 251*n*
Feigin, S. I., 95
Feminine characteristics, 27
Feminism
  definition of, 236
  woman's rights, 237
  women's emancipation, 237
Feminist consciousness, definition, 243
Feminist scholarship, 3
  double vision of, 11-12
Feminist thought, current state of, 232-233
Feminist world-view, 225, 229
Fertility, symbolization, shift from female to male, 9
Fertility cult, 146, 147
Fertility-goddess, 31, 196
  association with tree of life, 194-195
Finley, M. I., 85, 87
Fisher, Elizabeth, 46
Freedman, R. David, 184
Freedom, vs. perpetual unfreedom, 95
Freud, Sigmund, 19, 144
  account of mother-infant bonding, 39-40
  on anatomy as destiny, 52-53
  on male aggressiveness, 45-46
Fromm, Erich, 144, 199

Gaia (goddess), 149, 204
Garden of Eden, symbolism of, 184-185
Gelb, I. J., 81-83, 258*n*
Gender
  creation and establishment of, 212
  definition of, 10*n*, 238
  as metaphor of power relations, 211
  and social roles, 21, 214, 224

sociology of, 43-44
symbols and metaphors, 10-11
Western construct of, 10-11
Generativity, 180
Genesis, Book of, 161, 180
  accounts of slave women as concubines, 92
  assumption of paternity by males in, 185-186
  authorship, 161-162
  social conditions reflected in, 162-163
Genovese, Eugene, 241
Germanic tribes, of Roman Empire, enslavement of conquered women, 86
Gideon, 165
Gift exchange, 266*n. See also* Bride price; Dowry
Gilgamesh, 59
  epic of, 132-133, 144, 150, 193-194
Gilman, Charlotte Perkins, 26
Gimbutas, Marïja, 146
God
  gendered nature of, 178, 277*n*
  incorporating generativity, 180
Goddesses, 9
  at Çatal Hüyük, 33-34
  declassing of, 141
  power of, 141-144
  replacement by male gods, 9
Goddess figures, symbolic attributes, 148
Gods, male, in creation myths, 151-152
Goody, Jack, 108, 265*n*
Great Goddess, 158-159. *See also* Mother-Goddess
  cults of, 148
  transformation of, 159
Greece
  ancient, slavery in, 83-84
  historical scholarship in, 201-202
  subordination of women in, 202
Grimké, Sarah, 184
Gschnitzer, Fritz, 86-87
Gudea of Lagash, 110, 194

Hacilar, 56
Hagar, 171
Hammurabi, 101, 153, 154
  reign of, 261*n*
Harems, 71, 83, 133, 256*n*
Harimtu, 130-133, 137
Harris, Marvin, 251*n*
Harris, Rivkah, 266*n*

Hattusilis I, 155, 275n
Hattusilis III, 156
Hawwa, 185
Hebrew Covenant Code. *See* Covenant law
Hebrew law, on miscarriage, 120
Heiros gamos. See Sacred Marriage
Hekate-Artemis, 148
Hepat, 158
Hera, 159
Herder Wedding Song, 189
Herodotus, 129-130, 201
Hesiod
  misogyny of, 204
  Theogeny, 204
  Works and Days, 204
Hierodule, 125, 272n
History. *See also* Pre-history
  according to Bible, 161, 201
  androcentricity, 12-13, 15, 36
  beginning of, 57
  definition of, 4
  function of, 221
  and invention of writing, 57, 151, 200
  recording, women's role in, 13
  significance of, 221
  women's role in, 4-5, 37
History-making, male dominance in, 4-5
Hittite law, 101-102
  on miscarriage, 120
  sec. 17, 120, 270n
  sec. 18, 120, 270n
  sec. 77A, 120
  sec. 197, 114, 267n
  sec. 198, 114, 267n
Hittite society, 154-157
Homogamy, 108, 111
Honor, for men, as compared to women, 80
Hoplite, 202-203
Horowitz, Maryanne Cline, 207, 278n
Horticultural society, social relations in, 30, 49, 51
Huldah, 176, 275n
Human sacrifice, 60, 61
Hunting
  and warfare, relationship of, 251n
  women's participation in, 41, 251n
Hunting-gathering societies
  egalitarianism, 29
  in Paleolithic and Neolithic periods, 39

prehistoric, infant mortality in, 251n
  sex roles in, 17-18
  social relations in, 49
  women's subordination in, 30
Hypergamy, 94

Idolatry of women, coexistence with low status of women, 29
Igi-du-nu, 81, 258n
Ilbapiel of Eshnunna (king), 262n
The Iliad, 83-85
Illness, gods and goddesses of benefit in, 142-143
Immortality
  of generation, 197
  human concern with, 200
  knowledge of, 197
  man's quest for, in Epic of Gilgamesh, 194
Inanna (goddess), 66-67, 126, 148
Inca society, 58, 253n
  concubinage in, 93-94
Incest, laws against, in Mesopotamia, 116
Incest taboos, 24, 50, 53, 247n
Infancy, 42
  human, 38-39
  prolongation, in prehistoric eras, 41
Infanticide
  patriarchal father's power of, 89, 202, 251n
  in Sparta, 203
Infant mortality, in prehistoric societies, 251n
Inheritance
  diverging devolution system, 265n
  in Hebrew tribes, 169, 276n
  Mesopotamian laws pertaining to, 108-109, 265n
  primacy of rights of legitimate sons, 171
  rights, of temple servants, 128
Iroquois women, 30, 52, 249n
Irrigation, and rising elites, 55, 56
Isaac, 171, 187, 190
Ishmael, 171, 182
Ishtar (goddess), 66, 126, 129, 142-143, 148, 156, 187, 188, 192, 195, 272n
  association with taverns and prostitution, 131
  cult of, 131
  temple of, 142

Isis (goddess), 154, 159
Israel
  goddess figurines in, 147
  kingdom of, 166
Istanu (sun-god), 157, 158

Jabesh-Gilead
  Israelites' war against, 174
  matrimonial exchange of women in, 174-176
Jacob, 168, 171
Jael, 165
James, E. O., 146, 154
Jewish women, role and status of, 177-178
Joshua, 164
Judah, kingdom of, 166
Judges, Book of, story of Levite's concubine, 173
Judges, period of, 164-165
Jung, 144
Justus, Carol F., 157-158

Kelly, Joan, 11-12
Khaya-Sumu, 71
Ki (goddess), 149, 152
Kingship, rise of, in Mesopotamia, 66
Kinship groups
  in protohistorical period, 58
  and rising elites, 55
Kirum, 71-72, 75, 256n-257n
Kish, dynasty of, 59
Koschaker, Paul, 109-110, 114, 167, 266n
Kramer, Samuel Noah, 152-153
Kubab, 148
Kubaba (goddess), 59
Ku-Baba (queen), 59
Kulmashitum, 128, 137, 272n
Kunshimatum (queen), 69-71, 75

Lambert, W. G., 103
Langdon, Stephen, 185
Language
  sexism structured in, 232, 241
  and thought, 232
Law, as reflection of social conditions, 102, 171
Leacock, Eleanor, 30, 249n
Leah, 167, 170
Leisure time, and social relations, 51
Levirate, 118-119, 169, 170
Lévi-Strauss, Claude, 46-47, 49, 213

explanation of women's subordination, 24-25
Leviticus, 177
Lex talionis, 104, 119, 263n, 270n
Life cycles, effects on changing life roles, 20
Life span, human, in prehistoric society, 41, 251n
Literary criticism, feminist, 225
Literature, women's voice in, 225-226
Lot, 172, 173
Lugalanda, 62-63, 154, 254n
Lugalzaggisi, 65-66
Luther, Martin, interpretation of story of Lot, 172

Maekawa, K., 63
Malaya
  concubinage in, 93
  slavery in, 87-88
Male bonding, 45
Male dominance
  explanations for, 245n
  modern, 239
Mami (goddess), 149, 278n
Man, natural superiority of, 17
Man-the-hunter, theory of subordination of women, 17-18
Marduk (god), 127, 128, 151, 153, 157, 182
  temple of, high-priestess, 129
Mari (city), 74, 163, 276n
  society in, 68-69
Marriage, 181, 214
  in Ancient Greece, 202
  angel, 187
  arranged, 106-107
  ba'al, 168
  Babylonian, 109
  beena, 109, 167-168
  brother-sister, 155
  by contract, 112
  dynastic, 67-68
  and exchange of women, 47
  without joint residence, 109-110
  levirate, 269n
  matrilocal, 167
  Mesopotamian, 106-107
  monogamous, 22-24
  patriarchal, 109, 110, 168
  political, 71-72
  by purchase, 109-110, 112, 114, 266n
  Sumerian term for, 266n

Marriage contract, 107, 109, 112, 264n, 265n
Marriage settlement. *See* Dowry
Married women, autonomy of, 235
Marxist anthropology, 48
Marxist-Feminists, 21, 227
Maternalist theory, 26-29, 248n
Matriarchy, 21, 30, 36, 249n
  in Čatal Hüyük, theory of, 34
  definitions of, 31
  vision of, women's need for, 250n
Matrilineal succession, in Hittite society, 155-157
Matriliny, 29-31, 49, 53
  in Biblical text, 167-168, 276n
  in Čatal Hüyük, 34
Matrilocality, 29, 30, 47, 53
  in Čatal Hüyük, 34
McNeill, William H., 203
Mead, Margaret, *Male and Female*, 245n
Meillassoux, Claude, 49, 50, 51, 53, 99
Mellaart, James, 32-35
Men, gender-defined roles, 21, 214, 224
Mendelsohn, Isaac, 87, 272n
Menstruation
  as bar to women's participation in hunting, 251n
  as symbolic weapon, 45
Mesopotamia
  Ancient, civilization in, sources of evidence, 58
  dynasties of, 59
  establishment of patriarchy in, historical process of, 7-8
  urban revolution in, 55-75
Mesopotamian law, administration, 104
Metis, 205
Mexico, Central, urban revolution in, 58
Meyers, Carol, 275n
Middle Assyrian Laws, 101-102, 104, 140, 272n
  provisions on chastisement of wives, 117
  sec. 15, 114, 267n
  sec. 21, 120, 270n
  sec. 29, 264n
  sec. 30, 269n
  sec. 31, 269n
  sec. 33, 118, 269n
  sec. 40, 122, 134-140, 198
  sec. 46, 118, 269n
  sec. 50, 119, 270n
  sec. 51, 270n
  sec. 52, 270n
  sec. 53, 120, 270n
  sec. 55, 116, 117, 268n
  sec. 56, 117, 269n
  sec. 57, 117
  sec. 58, 117
  sec. 59, 117
Miles, John C., 89-90, 109, 110, 121, 128, 136, 261n, 266n, 268n
Militarism, development of, 56-57
  hypotheses for, 45
Military, exclusion of women from, and exclusion from elites, 254n
Millet, Kate, 227
Miriam, 275n
Miscarriage, Mesopotamian laws pertaining to, 119-120
Mishpahah, 168-169
Monotheism, 193, 197, 200-201
  development in Book of Genesis, 198
  Jewish, 163, 167
  origins, 152
  and shift from female metaphysical power to male, 9-10
Morgan, Lewis Henry, 21, 123
Moses, 163, 164, 188, 190, 191
Mot (god of death), 153-154
Mother
  obligations to, under law, 113
  power of
    in prehistoric societies, 40
    psychoanalytic concept of, 40
  upgrading of status in Hebrew law, 106, 171
Mother-child bond, 39-40
  social necessity of, 42
Mother-Goddess, 39-40, 125, 130, 152, 159, 180, 205
  changing position of, 154
  demotion of, 145
  and female power, 29
  figurines, 146-148
  worship, 146-147
Motherhood, under patriarchy, 44, 252n
Mother Right, 22
Mui Tsai, 88
Mutilation, of prisoners and slaves, 81-82
Mutterrecht. See Mother Right
Mylitta (goddess), 129, 159
Myth. *See also* Creation stories
  and social reality, 144-145

Nabu-naid, 129
Name-giving, 150-151
  power of, in Genesis, 181-182
  symbolism of, 182, 277*n*
Nammu (goddess), 149
Namu (goddess), 153
Naram-Shin the Great, 67
Nation-state, formation of, 66
Nature vs. culture, women's status re-
  lated to, 25
Neolithic Age, women's status in, 31
Nephilim, 187
Ningirsu (god), 62, 154
Ninhursag, 148, 152, 185
Ninlil, 152
Nin-shatapad, 68
Ninti (goddess), 185
Nintu (goddess), 149, 152
Noadiah, 275*n*
Noah, 188
Nun (goddess), 149
Nurturance, as feminine principle, 27
Nuzi (city), 163

O'Brien, Mary, 28, 46, 248*n*
The Odyssey, 97-98
Old Testament, role of women in, 176-
  177
Oppenheim, A. L., 103, 105, 148
Oppression
  definition, 235
  meanings of, 233, 234
Oppression of women, 233-234
  effect on symbol-systems, 222-223
  and slavery, 77
Oracles, 142
Ortner, Sherry, 25, 94
Osiris (god), 127, 152, 159
Otwell, John, 176
Ouranos, 204-205

Paternalism
  definition of, 240
  and slavery, 241-242
Paternalistic dominance, 217-218
  definition of, 235, 240
Patriarch, Biblical, 168
Patriarchal dominance, 231, 239
Patriarchal thought, stepping outside,
  228
Patriarchy
  in classical antiquity, 239
  creation of, 212-229

definition of, 238-240
establishment of, in Ancient Near
  East, 7-9
in European development, 239
as historical system, 6
history of, 37
modern, 239
Oriental, 239
origins of, hypotheses about, 46
sanctioned, in Book of Genesis, 197-
  198
transition to, 38-53
women's cooperation in, 6, 36
  means of securing, 217-218
Patriliny, 30, 49, 53
Patrilocality, 47, 50, 53, 175
Patterson, Orlando, 78-80, 258*n*, 259*n*-
  260*n*
Paul, L., 44-45
Pentateuch, 162, 167
  history of, 275*n*
Personality, gender-defined, development of, 43-44
Philosophy of history, 201
Plato, *The Republic*, 210
Poet, woman, first known, 67
Polis, 202
Polyandry, 63
Polygamy, 170
Population control, and control of female sexuality, 47
Power
  female, 31
    metaphysical, 9-10
    vs. status, 31, 249*n*
  of goddesses, 141-144
  male, 100
    to incorporate others, 104
    metaphysical, 9-10
  sharing, between sexes, 31
Pre-history, perceptions of, 15-16
Priestess, 111
  in ancient Mesopotamia, 66-67
  en, 126, 127
  entu, 126
  at Mari, 256*n*
  naditum, 72-73, 127, 262*n*, 271*n*,
    272*n*
  marriage, 113, 266*n*
  married, and provision of concu-
    bines for husbands, 93
  role in family economy, 266*n*
  nin-dingir, 126, 127

Priestess (*continued*)
  power of, 141
  Sal-zikrum, 264n
Priesthood, all-male, 178-179, 201
Private property, 8, 213
  development of, 49, 51-52
  and institutionalization of concubi-
    nage, 91
  linked to inception of patriarchy, 239
  and subordination of women, 21-23
Procreativity, 180, 186, 187
  control of, 8
  emanating from God, 187-189, 192
  of human beings, 197
  male, Aristotle's doctrine of, 205-208
  male assumption of power of, 205-
    206, 220
  males' role in, and theogeny, 185-186,
    192
  severed from creativity, in monothe-
    ism, 201
  symbolism of, mother's role omitted
    from, 192
  symbolization, in monotheism, 10
  women's, commodification, 8, 196,
    212-213
Promiscuity, 123
Property, in Biblical texts, 168-169
Prophetesses, Biblical, 176, 275n
Prostitutes
  attached to temple, 130
  male, 131
  professional, 272n
  and veiling law, 135-137
Prostitution, 23, 123, 272n. *See also*
    Concubinage; Concubines
  commercial, 130, 133-134
  historic development of, 124
  laws pertaining to, 138
  linguistic development, 131
  and slavery, 87, 133
  temple, 124-125, 130, 271n
Protohistorical period, 57
Psychology, patriarchal bias in, 19, 246n
Pu-abi (queen), 59-60
Puduhepa (queen), 156, 158
Pulleyblank, E. G., 94

Qadishtum, 128-129, 137, 272n
Queen
  role in selecting concubines, 70
  status of, in ancient Mesopotamia, 69-
    70

  in Sumerian society, 61-62
  with wives, 48

Race oppression, and sexual use of
    women, 88, 260n
Rachel, 167, 168, 170, 276n
Ramses II, 164
Rape, 46
  of child bride, 107
  in coercion of women, 87
  of conquered women, 78, 80, 81
  in Israelite society, 170
  literature on, 260n
  Mesopotamian laws about, 116-117,
    268n
  in *The Odyssey*, 98
  of virgin, Mesopotamian laws about,
    115-116
Rapp, Rayna, 55
Redman, Charles, 55-56
Reification of women, 47, 84, 99, 111,
    213-214
  and private property, 49-52
Religion, changes in, and changes in
    society, 144-145
Re-naming, symbolism of, 182
Revolutionary thought, 227-228
Rhea, 204-205
Rich, Adrienne, 28, 248n, 252n
Rim-Sin of Larsa (king), 262n
Rimush (king), 81
Rohrlich, Ruby, 34
Rosaldo, Michelle, 37, 250n, 252n
Rossi, Alice, 248n
Rubin, Gayle, 25, 238

Sacred Marriage, 126-127, 150, 271n
Sanday, Peggy Reeves, 145, 274n, 275n
Sarah, 170, 182
  exclusion from covenant, 190
Sarai. *See also* Sarah
  re-naming of, 190
Sargon II, 166
Sarna, Nahum M., 172
Saul, 165
Science, 202
Scribes, women as, 68
Sea-goddess, 149
Secretu, 130
Semenov, I. I., 258n
Semonides, 204
Serpent
  association with fertility-goddess, 196

in Epic of Gilgamesh, 194
Servants and masters, sexual relations of, 88, 260*n*
Sex, definition of, 10*n*, 238
Sex-gender system, definition of, 238
Sexism, definition of, 240-242
Sex relations
  as class antagonism, 24
  evolutionary theory of, in Engels's work, 23
Sex roles, 245*n*
  complementary, 18, 30, 246*n*
  egalitarian, 29-30, 35
  modern psychology's view of, 19
  and technological advances, 20
Sexual asymmetry, 16-17, 245*n*
Sexual division of labor, 17, 24
  Biblical account of, 185
  and development, 20, 247*n*
  earliest, 41-42
  Engels's description of, 21-22
  and male bonding, 45
  maternalists' views on, 26
  necessity for, in prehistoric societies, 40-41
  and origins of patriarchy, 52
  varieties of, 22, 247*n*
Sexual dominance
  as foundation of Aristotle's thought, 209-210
  as origin of class and race dominance, 209
  of women, and women's class oppression, 89
Sexuality
  female
    associated with weakness and evil, 201
    as civilizing influence, 132
    commodification of, 8, 212-213
    control, for population control, 47
    controlled by law, 102, 121, 216
    Engels's speculations on, 22-23
    males' control of, 8
    in Mesopotamian vs. Hebrew society, 171
    reification of, 50, 213-214
    severed from procreation, 196
    socially destructive potential, 247*n*
    state control of, 140
  sacrifice of, to goddess Ishtar, 192
Sexual knowledge, in the Fall, 196
Shagshag (queen), 64-65

Shamash (god), 127, 271*n*
Shamash-nuri, 93, 96
Shibatum, 71-72, 256*n*-257*n*
Shibtu (queen), 70, 74
Shin-kashid of Isin, 68
Shtetl, 249*n*
Shulshag (god), 62
Shu-Sin (king), 81
Sin (moon-god), 129
Singh, P., 34
Sippar, temple of, 127-128
Sky-god, 149, 152
Slavery, 9, 95-96, 213. *See also* Enslavement
  in ancient Greece, 83-85
  Aristotle's discussion of, 208-209
  development of, 48, 75
  in Greece, 202
  institutionalization of, 57, 75, 76, 99-100
  invention of, 77, 78
  in Israelite society, 169
  in Mesopotamia, 66
  origins of, 76, 175
  and paternalism, 241-242
  in Pharaonic Egypt, 86
  preconditions of, 76
  and prostitution, 87, 133
  sources of, 76
  stigma of, 99-100
  in U.S., 260*n*
Slaves
  culture, 222
  group consciousness of, 219
  marginalization of, 262*n*
  as outsiders, 77, 257*n*
  and veiling law, 135-137
  women, sexual use of, 87-88, 105, 260*n*, 263*n*
Smith, J. M. Powis, 102, 105
Snake. *See* Serpent
Snake-goddess, 148, 149
Sociobiology, 248*n*
  feminist criticism in, 248*n*
  views on gender, 19-20
Sodomy, 175
Solomon, King, 166
Solon of Athens, 204
Song of Songs, 176-177
Spartan society, 203
Speght, Rachel, 183
Speiser, E. A., 168, 172-173, 187
Sragon of Akkad, 66-67

Stanton, Elizabeth Cady, 26, 27, 28, 227
Storm-god, 157-158, 180
Strabo, 129
Struve, V. V., 255n
Subarean veil, 70, 256n
Subordination, definition of, 235
Subordination of women, 5-7, 100, 234-235, 245n
    biological-determinist theory of, 16-18, 23, 247n
    divine sanction for, in Genesis, 182
    incorporated into symbols and metaphors of Western civilization, 211
    sexual, institutionalization, 9
    traditionalist view, 16-17
    universality, 18, 25-26, 28, 35
        questioning, 16, 21
    women's cooperation in, 6, 36, 217-218
Sugitum, 128
Sumerian religion, 62
Sumerian society, in Early Dynastic period, 59
Sun-god, 149, 157-158
Suppiluliumas I, 156
Symbol-making, 199-211
    exclusion of women from, 200, 231
Symbol systems
    and class struggle, 222
    early, 57
    male hegemony over, 200, 219-220, 223, 231

Tammuz, 127
Taru (storm-god), 157
Tawananna, 155-156, 158
Technology, and changing life roles, 20
Telepinu, 155
Temple, Babylonian
    kings' taking over of, 154
    sexual activities in and around, 129, 131
    significance of, 125
Temple, Jewish, women's place in, 177-178
Temple servants, 130, 142
Temple-towns, development of, in Mesopotamia, 56-57
Teraphim, 168, 276n
Teshub (storm-god), 187
Tesup (storm-god), 158
Teubal, Savina J., 276n

Theogeny, changes in, and societal changes, 152-153
Theory formation, 223
Thought. *See* Abstract thought; Feminist thought; Patriarchal thought; Revolutionary thought
Thucydides, 201
    History of the Peloponnesian War, 85-86
Tiamat (goddess), 149, 153
Tizpatum, 72
Todd, Ian, 34
Tokens, 57
Tools, and human development, 39
Transvestites, in cult worship, 131
Tree of knowledge, 196, 279n-280n
Tree of life, 194-197, 279n-280n
    associated with fertility-goddess, 194-195
Tribes, in Canaan, 163-164, 167
Trible, Phyllis, 176, 184, 277n
Tuthaliya (king), 155-156
Tyumenev, A. I., 255n

Ugbabatum, 256n
Ungnad, Arthur, 280n
Ur
    excavations at, 59-62
    royal graves at, 254n
Uranos, 149
Urban revolution, 54-55
Ur III dynasty, 67
Urnammu of Ur, 195
Uruinimgina. *See* Urukagina of Lagash
Uruk
    fertility rites at, 126
    sculpted head from, 59
Urukagina of Lagash, 57, 62-63, 254n, 255n
    reforms of, 62-64

Veiling of women, 134-135, 256n
    enforcement of, 135-138
Venus, 159
Virgin-goddess, 149
Virginity, 186, 193. *See also* Chastity
    as financial asset of family, 94, 134, 140
    in Israelite society, 170
    and marriage, 114
Virgin Mary
    images of, 147
    power of, 143

Von Rad, Gerhard, 186, 277*n*
Votaress, 272*n*
Vulva, offering of, to goddess, 142, 143, 273*n*

Wara-ilisu, 70, 71, 256*n*
War captives. *See also* Enslavement
  fate of, in Roman Empire, 86
  female, fate of, in ancient Mesopotamia, 78-83, 86-87
  male
    blinding of, 81-82
    fate of, in ancient Mesopotamia, 78, 79, 81, 85, 87-89, 258*n*, 260*n*
Warfare, 245*n*
  and hunting, relationship of, 251*n*
  and patriarchy, 252*n*
  rise of, 45, 46
Warrior, 214
Warrior culture, emergence, 49
Webster, Paula, 250*nn*
Westermann, William, 85
Wibur, C. Martin, 95
Widow
  almattu, 269*n*
  inheritance rights
    in Biblical text, 276*n*
    in Israelite society, 170
  restrictions on remarriage of, in Mesopotamian law, 64
Widowhood
  Mesopotamian laws pertaining to, 269*n*
  women's dependency in, 117-118
Wife
  chastisement of, Mesopotamian laws about, 269*n*
  husband's obligations to, under law, 113
  under patriarchal dominance, 95-96
  second, 113, 128
  stand-in, 214
Wife-as-deputy, 74
Wilson, E. O., 19
Winks, Robin, 87
Wives
  class distinctions between, 112, 266*n*
  instrumental use of, 92
Woman, creation from Adam's rib, symbolism of, 183-184
Woman-centered, definition of, 228
Woman's culture, definition of, 242-243

Woman's emancipation, 281*n*
  definition of, 236-237
Woman's liberation, definition of, 237
Woman's peace movement, 248*n*
Woman's rights, definition of, 236-237
Women
  Babylonian, status of, 171
  commodification of, 8, 212-213
  deliberative faculty, Aristotle's discussion of, 208
  deviant, 225, 226
  elite, of Mari civilization, 68-74
  gender-defined status of, 213-214, 224
  group consciousness of, 218
    impediments to development of, 218-219
  historical situation of, 5
  in history, 4
    women's lack of knowledge of, 222, 226
  history of, dialectic of, 5
  inferiority of, 6, 16-17, 99
    Aristotle's doctrine of, 209, 210
    biological-deterministic explanation of, 16-18, 23, 247*n*
    scientific, Darwinian explanations of, 18-19
  Israelite, 169-171, 276*n*
  lower-class, sexual exploitation of, 214
  marginalization of, 77, 200, 232
    in Bible, 188, 198
  Mesopotamian, social conditions of, reflected in laws, 106
  "natural" experience of, devaluation of, 224
  Plato's view of, 210-211
  in precivilized society, skills of, 43, 251*n*
  in priestly role, 67-68. *See also* Priestesses
  in public affairs, in ancient Mesopotamia, 68
  relationship to political power, 156
  relationship to society and historical progress, 5-6
  respectable vs. not, 9, 135-137, 139, 215
  role in society, as subject to change over time, 38
  roles and functions of, in Mesopotamia, 64
  sense of self-worth, 242
  single, social status of, 215-216

Women (*continued*)
  special aptitude for reform and community service, theory of, 28, 248n
  theft of, 49
  treatment in Urukagina's edicts, 63-64
  as victims, 5, 234, 250n
Women-as-group, conceptualization of, 232
Women's development, 43-44
Women's health, 19th-c. views on, 18-19, 246n
Women's History, 221, 227, 229
  effect on students, 3
  interpretation of, 235-236
  scholarship of, 3
Women's Studies, 243

Woolley, Leonard, 59-61
World historic defeat of women, 21-23, 49, 50
Writing, invention of, 57, 151, 200

Yahweh, 180, 188
  gendered nature of, 18, 277n
  procreative role, 188
  transformation into Father-God and Lord, 185
Yahwism, 166
Yarimlim of Yamkhad (king), 262n
Yasmah-Addu of Mari (king), 69-70

Zeus, 204-205
Zimri-Lim of Mari (king), 70-72, 83, 195, 262n
  daughters of, 71-73